Applied Social Care

An Introduction for Students in Ireland

THIRD EDITION

Applied Social Care
An Introduction for Students in Ireland

THIRD EDITION

Edited by

KEVIN LALOR and PERRY SHARE

Gill Education
Hume Avenue
Park West
Dublin 12

www.gilleducation.ie

Gill Education is an imprint of M.H. Gill & Co.

978 07171 5623 8

Print origination by Carrigboy Typesetting Services

Index by Cliff Murphy

Figure 5.1 drawn by Derry Dillon
Figures 7.1, 7.2 and 7.3 drawn by Denise Lyons

The paper used in this book comes from the wood pulp of managed forests. For every tree felled, at least one tree is planted, thereby renewing natural resources.

A CIP catalogue record is available for this book from the British Library.

Contributors

Vicki Anderson is Lecturer in the Department of Humanities in the Institute of Technology Carlow, where she is the director of the BA in Applied Social Studies (Professional Social Care). She is currently the Vice President of the Irish Association of Social Care Educators (IASCE) and a committee member of Social Care Ireland.

John Byrne is a social care worker and Lecturer in Personal and Professional Development in Waterford Institute of Technology. He has over 20 years' experience of working in a wide range of social care services. He is also a practising humanistic/integrative psychotherapist and founder of the TRAV programme (Therapeutically Responding to Aggression and Violence).

Tamsin Cavaliero is Assistant Lecturer in the Department of Social Sciences in the Institute of Technology Sligo, with research interests in Traveller Culture, Intercultural Practice and Professional Practice. She produced the film *R.E.C.A.L.L*, a local history project, which documented relationships between the Travelling community and the settled community in Co. Sligo over the last 100 years. She is currently undertaking a PhD entitled 'Travellers, Culture and Identity'. Prior to taking up her lecturing post she worked with the Travelling community in Co. Sligo in a variety of posts in the Youth Work and Education sectors.

Grant Charles, PhD, is Associate Professor in the School of Social Work in the University of British Columbia in Vancouver, Canada. He is co-editor of the Canadian journal *Relational Child and Youth Care Practice*.

Áine de Róiste, PhD, is Senior Lecturer in Social Care in Cork Institute of Technology. She is the author (with Kevin Lalor and Maurice Devlin) of *Young People in Contemporary Ireland* (Gill & Macmillan, 2007) and (with Celesta McCann James and John McHugh) *Social Care Practice in Ireland: an integrated perspective* (Gill and Macmillan, 2009). With her CIT colleague Joan Dinneen, she undertook commissioned research for the Office of the Minister for Children and Youth Affairs on young people's recreation and leisure. She has worked in the field of early intervention and is a registered psychologist with the Psychological Society of Ireland.

Maurice Devlin, PhD, is Jean Monnet Professor and Director of the Centre for Youth Research and Development in the Department of Applied Social Studies in NUI Maynooth. He is a member of the National Youth Work Advisory Committee, joint chair of the North-South Education and Standards Committee for Youth Work, Irish correspondent for the European Knowledge Centre on Youth Policy and a member of the Pool of European Youth Researchers. He chairs the editorial board of *Youth Studies Ireland* and is a member of the editorial board of *European Perspectives*.

Judy Doyle is Lecturer in Principles of Professional Social Care Practice, Cross-Cultural Care and Management Practice in the School of Social Sciences and Law, Dublin Institute of Technology. She has worked in social care practice for 17 years, both as a residential care practitioner and as a manager in social care work. As a consultant to the social care sector, she has carried out independent investigations, service reviews and service evaluations and provides professional supervision to social care managers and practitioners. Areas of research include Travelling culture and care, black children in care, and inequality in the affective domain. She is a PhD candidate with the School of Social Justice, Equality Studies Centre, UCD.

Eileen Farrell is Assistant Lecturer in the Department of Humanities in the Institute of Technology Carlow. She lectures in the area of Sociology and Social policy. She is a qualified social care worker and has an MA in Social Work. Prior to taking up her lecturing post she worked as a Probation Officer for eight years and spent over six of these years working as a prison-based Probation Officer in Mountjoy (Men's), Midlands and Portlaoise Prisons.

Tom Farrelly, DEd, is Lecturer in Sociology and Research Methods on the Social Care, Youth and Community Work and Nursing programmes in the Institute of Technology Tralee and on a part-time basis in the School of Education in Trinity College Dublin, also in Research Methods. In the past he has worked as a job coach with intellectual disability services and as a community education organiser. His research and development interests currently include technology-enhanced learning and research methodology.

Karen Finnerty, D.Soc.Sci, is Director of the Open Training College and a Fellow of the Irish Institute of Training and Development. Within her role is responsibility for staff training and development in St Michael's House, Dublin, a disability service provider employing over 1,600 people. She is also leading a major service initiative on the voluntary implementation of the HIQA quality standards prior to the commencement of statutory inspection of disability services. Her areas of interest are the professionalisation of the social care role in disability services; service quality measurement and improvement; and adult education and life-long learning.

Eleanor Fitzmaurice, PhD, is Senior Lecturer in Principles and Practice of Social Care in Limerick Institute of Technology. She is a Fellow of the Irish Institute of Training and Development. She has extensive experience in developing and teaching undergraduate and postgraduate professional social care courses, and is a trainer and practitioner in professional supervision. In her early career, she worked for almost twenty years as a social worker in the field of intellectual disability.

Carmel Gallagher, PhD, is Lecturer in Sociology and Social Policy in the School of Social Sciences and Law, Dublin Institute of Technology. She has developed and taught on professional courses in social care and is currently Programme Director of the MA in Child, Family and Community Studies. Her research interest is in older people in Irish society. She is currently working on an EU-funded project 'Together Old and Young' (TOY) on older people and younger children learning together. She is author of *The Community Life of Older People in Ireland* (Peter Lang, 2008).

Thom Garfat, PhD, is President of TransformAction Consulting and Training. He is the co-founder and editor of *www.cyc-net.org* and senior editor of the Canadian journal *Relational Child and Youth Care Practice*.

Per-Axel (Pelle) Hallstedt, PhD, is Senior Lecturer in the Department of Social Work, Malmö University, Sweden. He lectures in Psychology and Social Work, as well as in the programme Pedagogic Social Work with the Elderly (Äldrepedagogprogrammet). His doctorate in pedagogy was gained for his study (with Mats Högström) 'The recontextualisation of social pedagogy: a study of three curricula in the Netherlands, Norway and Ireland' – a comparison of three social work/social pedagogical educational programmes.

Mats Högström, PhD, is Lecturer in the Department of Social Work, Malmö University, Sweden. His doctoral thesis from 2005, co-authored with Pelle Hallstedt, is a comparison of three social work/social pedagogical educational programmes in Ireland, Norway and the Netherlands. In recent years he has been interested in issues concerning older people and lectures mainly on the programme Pedagogic Social Work with the Elderly (Äldrepedagogprogrammet).

Frank Houghton, PhD, is an avid researcher with diverse interests. He is well-published in journals in the fields of geography, psychiatry, medicine and psychology. He holds a doctorate in health/medical geography, as well as a Masters in Population Health Evidence (MPHe). He also holds three other Masters degrees. He has six years' experience working as a Researcher in a Department of Public Health in Ireland, as well as one year's experience working as a Health Geographer in Public Health in New Zealand. He has health policy experience as Research Officer for the National Council on Ageing & Older People (NCAOP) and as Head of Research for Focus Ireland. He is Independent Chair of the Traveller Health Committee in the Mid-West region and a member of Limerick Food Partnership.

Sharon Houghton, PhD, is a clinical child psychologist employed as a Lecturer and Placement Co-ordinator on the Doctorate in Clinical Psychology in the University of Limerick. She has a Professional Doctorate in Clinical Psychology and a PhD in Psychology. She has worked in St Louise's child sexual abuse validation and therapy unit in Crumlin Children's Hospital and on CAMHS teams in both Ireland and New Zealand. She was formerly Acting Principal Clinical Psychologist and Manager of Children's Services with Brothers of Charity Services in Limerick. Her recent research has focused on mindfulness as an intervention in clinical settings for adolescents, and she has conducted an evaluation of mindfulness programmes for use in schools.

Kevin Lalor, PhD, is Head of School of Social Sciences and Law, Dublin Institute of Technology. He is the editor of the *Irish Journal of Applied Social Studies* and a member of the editorial boards of *Child Abuse and Neglect: The International Journal* and *Children, Youth and Environments*. In 2012 he was Principal Investigator for the DIT research team that conducted the data analysis for President Michael D. Higgins's youth consultation initiative 'Being Young and Irish'. He is editor (with Mary P. Corcoran) of *Reflections on Crisis: the role of the public intellectual* (Royal Irish Academy, 2012).

Denise Lyons is Lecturer in the Department of Humanities in the Institute of Technology Blanchardstown, with research interests in creative studies and personal development. She has worked as a social care practitioner in residential child care, and later as a consultant trainer. She qualified in art therapy in 2003, and is the editor of *Creative Studies for the Caring Professions* (Gill & Macmillan, 2010).

Celesta McCann James, PhD, is Head of Department of Humanities in the Institute of Technology Blanchardstown and former President of the Irish Association of Social Care Educators (IASCE). She co-authored *Social Care Practice in Ireland: an integrated Perspective* (Gill & Macmillan, 2009) with Áine de Róiste and John McHugh.

Patrick McGarty is Senior Lecturer in the Institute of Technology Tralee. He has extensive experience of the development of social care education programmes in Athlone, Blanchardstown and Tralee institutes of technology. He is a past President, and founder member, of the Irish Association of Social Care Educators (IASCE). A founder member of Social Care Ireland, he was Chairman of the HETAC National Standards Committee on Social Care. Research interests include the management of change and the development of leadership and teamwork in organisations.

Hannagh McGinley is a PhD candidate in the School of Education in the National University of Ireland, Galway. She is an Irish Research Council scholar and recipient of the Dr Mary L. Thornton Scholarship (2011). Additionally, she won an award from the Irish National Teachers' Organisation. She is a member of the Irish Traveller community with a background in post-primary school teaching and she has a decade of experience working in the field of community development on issues affecting Travellers.

John McHugh is Lecturer in Applied Social Studies and Programme Board Chair of the Masters in Therapeutic Child Care in Carlow College, St Patrick's. He is co-author (with Celesta McCann James and Áine de Róiste) of *Social Care Practice in Ireland: an integrated perspective* (Gill & Macmillan, 2009). He is a PhD candidate at the University of Limerick where his doctoral research is in the area of professional identity.

Danny Meenan is a social care manager with the Health Service Executive. He has worked as a social care practitioner and manager in residential child care for almost twenty-five years in the voluntary and statutory sectors. He was the course co-ordinator of the work-based BA in Applied Social Studies, a joint project between the HSE and the Institute of Technology Sligo, from 2004 to 2007 and lectured in management, professional practice, social administration, personal development planning and placement planning. He qualified in social work in Northern Ireland in 1994, and has a post-qualifying award in child care from Queen's University Belfast and an MBA in Health Services Management from University College Dublin.

Majella Mulkeen is Lecturer in the Department of Social Sciences, Institute of Technology Sligo, where she teaches Sociology and Equality Studies. She is co-author (with Margaret Gilmore) of the IASCE *Practice Placement Manual*; she is a member of the editorial board of *Youth Studies Ireland* and has published in the *Irish Journal of Applied Social Studies*. Her research interests include gender and residential care practice.

Riitta Nilsson, MSW, is Lecturer in Social Work in the Department of Social Work, Malmö University, Sweden. She lectures mainly in the programme Pedagogic Social Work with the Elderly (Äldrepedagogprogrammet). Her interest (in co-operation with her colleagues Mats Högström and Pelle Hallstedt) lies in developing elderpedagogy as a discipline and as a profession and she has been actively involved in developing the programme since its start in 2003.

Colm O'Doherty, PhD, is Lecturer in Applied Social Studies in the Institute of Technology Tralee. He is a qualified social worker and holds a doctorate from University College Dublin. He has researched and published in the areas of social policy, child protection, domestic violence, social work theory and practice, social care theory and practice, and family support. His first book, *A New Agenda for Family Support: providing services that create social capital,* was published in 2007 (Blackhall). He is the author (with Ashling Jackson) of *Community Development in Ireland: theory, policy and practice* (Gill & Macmillan, 2012).

Eileen O'Neill is an independent trainer and consultant with a particular interest in professional practice and development. She has researched and published in the field of professional supervision and her book *Professional Supervision: myths, culture and structure* was published by the Resident Managers' Association in 2004.

Jacqueline (Jackie) O'Toole is Lecturer in Social Research and Sociology in the Department of Social Sciences, Institute of Technology Sligo. Working within a feminist sociology paradigm, her research and teaching interests are in the areas of gender, social care, narrative inquiry, health and critical body studies. She is author of numerous reports and publications and has presented her work to national and international audiences.

Mairéad Seymour, PhD, is Senior Lecturer in the Department of Social Sciences, Dublin Institute of Technology. She researches and publishes in the areas of crime and social order, comparative youth crime, crime and homelessness, and alternatives to custody. She is author of *Youth Justice in Context: community, compliance and young people* (Routledge, 2012).

Perry Share, PhD, is Lecturer in Sociology and Head of Department of Social Sciences, Institute of Technology Sligo. He is the co-author of *Sociology of Ireland* (4th edn, Gill & Macmillan, 2012) and co-edited two volumes of the *Irish Sociological Chronicles* (Institute of Public Administration, 2008 and 2010). He is a founder member of the Irish Association of Social Care Educators (IASCE) and a Research Associate of the Irish Social Science Platform.

Acknowledgements

We are grateful for the continued enthusiasm of the individual chapter authors for this volume, which significantly lightened our editorial duties. Marion O'Brien and Catherine Gough at Gill & Macmillan provided guidance and support at all stages of the process. Jennifer Armstrong was our super thorough copy-editor. Finally, we thank our families for their continued patience and encouragement.

Kevin Lalor and Perry Share

Contents

Overview of the book

The chapters of this book fall into four sections. In Part I (Chapters 1 to 4) we attempt to sketch out the parameters of the field, drawing on experiences gained in Ireland, Europe and North America. It will become clear that social care practice, while having many common elements across contemporary developed societies, has different nuances and emphases that reflect varying political, ideological and social systems across the world. You are encouraged to view social care practice in this international context. It is always good to see what is happening elsewhere, in particular to draw on international best practice, but also to be aware of national traditions, histories and particularities. We discuss the issue of professionalism in social care, an important and pertinent theme that you will no doubt encounter at every stage of studying or working in this field.

Part II (Chapters 5 to 10) identifies some of the theoretical bases of social care practice. These include ideas drawn from psychology, sociology and social policy. There is an examination of the fundamental role of the 'self' in social care practice and of the key discourse of equality. The theory base of social care practice is evolving and has developed through the interplay of theory building, evidence gathering, policy development and polemical debate. We can expect to see the emergence in Ireland of an increasingly distinctive body of knowledge and thought in relation to social care practice that will be inextricably linked to the development of professionalism.

Part III (Chapters 11 to 16) focuses on key practice issues. These range from broadly based practices such as student placement, workplace supervision and multidisciplinary teamworking, to specific aspects of practice such as responding to challenging behaviour. We do not claim to address every aspect of the dynamic and expanding field of social care, but to provide some knowledge about, and insight into, the realities of social care practice, as well as linking that practice to theory.

Part IV (Chapters 17 to 25) examines social care practice with particular social and demographic groups such as young people, older people, homeless people, people with disabilities, Travellers and new immigrant communities. You will detect common themes such as respect for the people social care practitioners work with and the practitioner's close relationship with the worlds of others. You will also learn about the skills and approaches associated with working with people in specific social structures and circumstances. Social care practice is becoming a complex mosaic and this section tries to illuminate some of its components.

Part I

1

Understanding social care

Kevin Lalor and Perry Share

OVERVIEW

There is a good chance you are reading this because you are planning to be, or already are, a social care practitioner. Yet for many in Irish society, even those entering the field themselves, the meaning of the term 'social care' is not self-evident. A common question directed at social care students and professionals alike is, 'What do you do?' Misconceptions abound and in many cases practitioners are not accorded the recognition or status they deserve, partly as a consequence of a limited understanding of what the term means.

This chapter explores the notion of social care itself. Some definitions are examined, phrase by phrase, to see what is involved. A short history of social care in Ireland is provided, placing the current set of institutions and practices in a historical context. Aspects of social care practice are described, such as what qualities practitioners possess; what sort of work is involved; what practitioners do and where they do it; how much they get paid; and the difference between a social care practitioner and a social worker. It is hoped this opening chapter will answer some of the basic questions voiced by students, practitioners and others.

DEFINING SOCIAL CARE PRACTICE

It is difficult to define social care practice. Indeed, it has suited governments and some agencies not to have a standard definition as it helps keep salary and career structures vague. As of March 2013, full implementation of the Health and Social Care Professionals Act 2005, the legislative basis for defining social care practice, has yet to occur. A linked issue is the contested notion of social care as a profession. There is something of a chicken-and-egg situation here: it can be hard to define social care because of the lack of a clearly identifiable profession we can point to as 'practising social care'; this in turn makes it hard to pin down what social care practice might be.

We hope that by the time you have read this book, and certainly – if a student – by the time you qualify, you will have a clearer idea of what social care practice means. Inevitably, this will be complex: you will have become aware of social care's flexible nature; its contested position vis-à-vis other practices and occupations (such as nursing, social work, counselling, occupational therapy); and, above all, its dynamism. Social care is a rapidly changing and developing field, in Ireland as elsewhere. We hope that you pick up something of this energy from this book, from your studies, from your interpretation of the world around you and from your own practical experience.

A concise definition agreed over a decade ago by the Irish Association of Social Care Educators, the body that represents the educational institutions in the field, is that social care is:

> . . . a profession committed to the planning and delivery of quality care and other support services for individuals and groups with identified needs.

This definition is sketchy and could be applied to many helping professions. Nevertheless, it incorporates a number of key terms that help to mark out the 'professional territory' of social care practice. Let us deconstruct it:

'a profession'

Social care practice is not just an ordinary job. Nor is it done on a voluntary or amateur basis, which distinguishes it from the (equally valuable) care that is carried out informally in Irish society by family and community members. 'Professionalism' implies an occupation with some status that requires access to a specific body of skills and knowledge.

'planning and delivery'

Social care is not just about providing services, it is also about devising and planning them. This process requires various skills and types of understanding; for example, an ability to provide hands-on care and support to people, an ability to identify what people require, an ability to plan accordingly, preferably drawing on available evidence and policy guidance, and an ability to communicate directly with people in an authentic way.

'quality care and other support services'

Social care is about the provision of quality care, and also about providing other supports. For example, advocating on behalf of another, turning up in court to speak before a judge or knowing where best to refer a person who has a specific problem.

'individuals and groups'

Social care can be provided on a one-to-one basis, but it can also involve working with a small or large group or a community. It requires well-developed interpersonal communication skills and a good knowledge of group dynamics.

'with identified needs'

Social care practitioners in Ireland (as in many other countries) have traditionally worked with children, young people and people with disabilities, who are in the care of state or voluntary organisations. While caring for these groups remains an important task, social care practitioners now work with a broader range of people, of all ages, who have special 'needs' or vulnerabilities. There are people whose needs have been identified only recently, such as survivors of clerical sexual abuse or children with hyperactivity disorders. New sets of identified needs may emerge at any time. For example, due to recent immigration patterns, it is quite likely that there will be a need for ethnically appropriate care of older people in Ireland in the future. The dynamic nature of society helps to explain why social care is a constantly changing field of practice.

So, even a single sentence can constitute quite a complex definition!

A second definition (more a description) of social care work emerged from a 2011 consultation with practitioners, managers and educators. Members of the Irish Association of Social Care Workers (IASCW), Irish Association of Social Care Educators (IASCE) and Resident Managers' Association (now, Irish Association of Social Care Managers, IASCM) were asked by the Professional Regulation Unit of the then Department of Health and Children to suggest a definition that would capture the full range of activities involved in social care work. This definition would facilitate the translation of overseas qualifications for people coming to work in Ireland, especially from other parts of the European Union. The following description of social care work emerged:

> Social care workers plan and provide professional individual or group care to clients with personal and social needs. Client groups are varied and include children and adolescents in residential care; young people in detention schools; people with intellectual or physical disabilities; people who are homeless; people with alcohol/drug dependency; families in the community; or older people.
>
> Social care workers strive to support, protect, guide and advocate on behalf of clients. Social care work is based on interpersonal relationships which require empathy, strong communication skills, self awareness and an ability to use critical reflection. Teamwork and interdisciplinary work are also important in social care practice.
>
> The core principles underpinning social care work are similar to those of other helping professions, and they include respect for the dignity of clients; social justice; and empowerment of clients to achieve their full potential.
>
> Social care practice differs from social work practice in that it uses shared life-space opportunities to meet the physical, social and emotional needs of clients. Social care work uses strengths-based, needs-led approaches to mediate clients' presenting problems.

Social care workers are trained, inter alia, in life span development, parenting, attachment and loss, interpersonal communication and behaviour management. Their training equips them to optimise the personal and social development of those with whom they work. In Ireland, the recognised qualification is a 3-year Level 7 degree. In Europe, social care work is usually referred to as social pedagogy and social care workers as social pedagogues.

This description of social care work contains most of the elements of previous definitions and attempts to describe roles, values and formation of professionals in the field. Some key phrases are evident:

'Social care workers'

This term has been replaced in most educational and many professional settings by the term 'social care practitioner'. Neither is inherently superior to the other, but we have largely used the latter term in this book for reasons of consistency. It also helps to clearly distinguish social care practitioners from social workers.

'plan and provide'

This phrase emphasises the autonomous, independent nature of social care practitioners, who do more than simply implement the plans of other professionals.

'professional'

All definitions and descriptions of social care practice claim professional status and the associated benefits of pay, prestige and status. 'Professions' are socially constructed and particular groups must advocate for the social privileges that come with this status; it is not enough to simply claim it.

'personal and social needs'

Social care practice is manifestly a helping profession.

'Client groups are varied'

While the origins of social care practice in Ireland (as elsewhere) lie in residential child care and work with people with disabilities, the role has now expanded to include multiple settings and groups.

'support, protect, guide and advocate'

The term 'care' is considered in a more dynamic way today than it was in the past, to include ideas of advocacy, education and development.

'interpersonal relationships'
This is how social care practitioners work towards change: a central idea is that of the 'self' as the 'toolbox'.

'empathy, strong communication skills, self-awareness and an ability to use critical reflection'
Education and training alone are not sufficient. As with all the helping professions, particular personal attributes and dispositions are required.

'Teamwork and interdisciplinary work'
Social care practitioners should be capable of managing the dynamics of working in groups, including interdisciplinary teams.

'core principles . . . include respect for the dignity of clients; social justice; and empowerment of clients'
These core principles are shared with other helping/social professions but have typically not been articulated explicitly in previous descriptions of the role of social care practitioners.

'differs from social work . . . uses shared life-space opportunities'
In Ireland, social work is the older profession and has a considerably longer education and training history, based on the British model. Thus, it is not surprising that a description of social care work will emphasise how it differs from social work. In truth, the two professions are closely related and the distinction made in Ireland is less pronounced in other jurisdictions.

We have now discussed several elements that you could assemble to create your own definition of social care practice. Such descriptions will help you to understand what social care practice is, but the reality of social care practice does not always adhere tightly to any definition. Some ideals may not be attained; some are favoured in specific situations. There are political debates and disagreements over what social care practice should be. We suggest that you make use of these ideas to examine and think about examples of social care practice you encounter directly or through reading and research. Ask yourself: Which aspects are brought to the foreground? How could things be done differently? How could they be done better?

In the broader European context, social care practice is usually referred to as social pedagogy, and social care practitioners as social pedagogues. In the United States, Canada and South Africa, the term 'child and youth care' (abbreviated as

CYC) is commonly used, with the derivation child and youth care worker. These alternative models are explored in greater detail in the chapters that follow.

How does social care work differ from social work?

Students of social care work often ask how it differs from the profession of social work. In a sense, the answer is straightforward.

Social workers are typically employed by the health authorities (different branches of the health services or the Child and Family Support Agency) and are allocated 'cases' to manage. Legislation empowers the health authorities to take children into care and social workers are usually the officers used for this function. Section 4(1) of the Child Care Act 1991 states, 'where it appears to a health board that a child who resides or is found in its area requires care or protection that he is unlikely to receive unless he is taken into its care, it shall be the duty of the health board to take him into its care under this section'. Social workers may initiate and manage this process.

Social care practitioners typically work in a more immediate way with service users, sharing their daily living environment and interacting across a range of care, domestic, education and semi-therapeutic settings. They do not have a specific legal role, nor the power that comes with it. They are less likely to spend their working day in an office or behind a desk (although this is always a risk!) and are more likely to be found in a residential setting, at a youth club, in the street, at a community centre or with a family. The differences of work orientation between the two professions are outlined in Table 1.1.

Table 1.1. Social work and social care practice: orientations

Social work focuses more on:	Social care practice focuses more on:
• Social and community networks. • Social problems. • Organisations and policies. • Knowing about children and families. • A wide variety of societal groups and issues. • Problem-solving. • Gaining power and societal influence.	• Individual and interpersonal dynamics. • Human development. • People and relationships. • Living and working with children and families. • Specific needs of particular groups. • Helping and growth process. • Gaining self-awareness and personal growth.

Source: Anglin (2001: 2)

It is fair to say that, in Ireland, social care practice and social work have developed on parallel yet separate paths. Social care practice is a 'newer' professional area than social work. Its origins can be traced to various sources, but most specifically to the residential care of young people and the care of people with disabilities. It does not yet have a legal definition or regulation, although this will change with the establishment of a registration board for social care work, as provided for in the Health and Social Care Professionals Act 2005. Education of social care practitioners is carried out predominantly in the institute of technology sector, with elements in the further education and private sectors. It is largely confined to undergraduate programmes at Level 7 and Level 8 on the National Framework of Qualifications (NFQ), although with an increasing number of Masters (Level 9) and other postgraduate programmes. The number of entrants is not controlled by any overarching body and the number of students of social care practice has increased rapidly and substantially in the twenty-first century (Lalor, 2009).

The historical development of Irish social work has been comprehensively described by Skehill and others (Kearney and Skehill, 2005; Skehill, 1999, 2003). It is the story of an occupational group seeking to develop a coherent professional identity, shaped by contemporaneous processes in the United Kingdom and elsewhere. This process has resulted in a recognition by the Irish state that social workers have key, legally defined roles in relation to areas such as child protection and adoption, and also have a specific location in the health services and in the justice services, for example in probation work. Social work education is confined to the university sector, often at postgraduate level, and the number of places is strictly limited and controlled.

Professional convergence?

In practice, internationally, the distinction between social care work and social work is becoming increasingly blurred. The phrase 'social work' has different meanings in different countries and is as complex to define and describe as social care work. Sarah Banks, a leading British writer in the field of social work ethics, notes (2012: 1–2):

> Social work is . . . a difficult occupation to encapsulate. It is located within and profoundly affected by diverse cultural, economic and policy contexts in different countries of the world. Social work embraces work in a number of sectors (public, private, independent, voluntary); it takes place in a multiplicity of settings (residential homes, neighbourhood offices, community development projects); practitioners perform a range of tasks (caring, controlling, empowering, campaigning, assessing, managing); and the work has a variety of purposes (redistribution of resources to those in need, social control and rehabilitation of the deviant, prevention or reduction of social problems, and empowerment of oppressed individuals and groups).

Although social work practice is contested, and varies from country to country, the International Federation of Social Workers (IFSW) uses the following definition to seek to unite all social workers (ifsw.org):

> The social work profession promotes social change, problem solving in human relationships and the empowerment and liberation of people to enhance well-being. Utilising theories of human behaviour and social systems, social work intervenes at points where people interact with their environments. Principles of human rights and social justice are fundamental to social work.

What is interesting from our perspective is how broad this definition is, and how it could apply to social care practice, for example in:

- The assertion that the discipline is a profession.
- The emphasis on 'problem solving', providing services to people with needs.
- The use of theories of human behaviour and social systems to inform practice.
- The goal of empowerment and liberation of service users. This aspect of the professional's work is perhaps less explicitly stated in Irish definitions of social care work (notwithstanding references to advocacy), compared with social work, where the definition also contains a commitment to principles of human rights and social justice.

Using terms and concepts that we have seen in earlier definitions of social care practice, the School of Applied Social Studies, University College Cork (UCC, n.d.) defines social work as:

> ... a profession that is primarily concerned with supporting and helping people in a variety of situations and settings. It is also about working in solidarity with socially excluded people and groups in meeting the challenges that their social exclusion creates. Social workers work in a wide range of settings and with different groups of people. Social workers work with individuals, families, groups and communities. Their work can span a wide variety of roles including counselling, group work, lobbying, advocacy and political activism. Social workers often have to network with other professions such as gardaí, doctors, public health nurses, and schools, as well as service-user and advocacy networks. Ultimately, social work aims to support people to live more successfully within their local communities by helping them to find solutions to their problems.

Clearly, there are commonalities across the two professions. Indeed, some suggest that social care practitioners have 'picked up' work that used to be performed by social workers, before they were engulfed in such high volumes of child protection case work management. That said, there are considerable differences in the roles, in Ireland and elsewhere. Child protection guidelines, *Children First* (DoHC, 1999), acknowledge 'the need for multi-disciplinary and inter-professional responsibility, [but] clearly locate primary responsibility for child protection with community care social work teams' (Skehill, 2003: 146). This gives priority to the social work profession – even if such teams also contain social care practitioners. When *Children First* was updated in 2011 the social worker's central role in child protection and welfare was re-emphasised: 'all personnel involved in a case should consistently make efforts to remain in contact with the key worker (who is normally the HSE social worker)' (DCYA, 2011: 19) and 'reported concerns about child protection and welfare are normally followed up by a HSE social worker. . . . the HSE Social Work Manager may allocate this role to another professional or agency closely involved with the family' (2011: 30).

While there is much similarity in the nature of social work and social care practice, and quite a degree of convergence, we can see that the pathways into practice are quite different, as is the status of the profession in relation to the state. Social work has greater public influence and recognition and consequently is more open to public scrutiny and criticism. Social care practitioners are much greater in number, may potentially have a much greater impact on the day-to-day delivery of social services and are to be found in a much broader spectrum of activities but, despite this, have a much lower public or professional profile. Increasingly, both groups are to be found in multidisciplinary teams along with others such as nurses and psychologists. It will be interesting to see how the different yet overlapping occupational and professional identities develop in the future.

A BRIEF HISTORY OF SOCIAL CARE IN IRELAND

In order to understand social care, it is important to understand where it has come from. Any attempt to sketch out a history of social care practice in Ireland inevitably results in a strong emphasis on the institutional context. Modern social care practice was born out of 'serious deficiencies in the running of children's centres . . . and the recognition of the need for professionally trained staff' (Kennedy and Gallagher, 1997). In independent Ireland, social care was historically provided on behalf of the state by the Catholic and other churches (Fanning and Rush, 2006) and, until very recently, was largely unregulated or, perhaps more accurately, regulated in a very fragmentary way. For example, preschool regulations were introduced only in 1996, after decades of both public and private provision. In relation to the care of children, a piece of British legislation, the 1908 Children's Act, provided the legislative framework in Ireland for the greater part of the twentieth century. But by 1991, the social and political situation with regard to children 'at risk' had changed significantly, reflecting a greater consciousness of the centrality of the rights of the child (Buckley et al., 1997; Focus Ireland, 1996; O'Higgins, 1996).

The Child Care Act 1991 is in total contrast to the 1908 Act, which imposed negative duties to rescue children who had criminal offences committed against them or who were being cruelly treated. Specifically, the 1991 Act recognises the welfare of the child as the first and paramount consideration. The rights and duties of parents are important (and are endorsed in the Constitution), but due consideration must be given to the child's wishes. The Children Act 2001 governs the administration of juvenile justice and, as such, impacts on the work of social care professionals in children's detention schools (formerly industrial schools and reformatory schools). More recently, the Criminal Justice Act 2006 contains a number of provisions for juvenile justice (Lalor et al., 2007) and, in 2012, the passing of the Children referendum (thirty-first amendment to the Constitution) enhanced the legal position of children vis-à-vis the family.

Several influential reports have helped to shape the development of social care practice. Reflecting broader international trends, they aimed fundamentally to reorient the direction of social care provision away from care in large institutional settings and towards care in small-scale units and in the community. They also emphasised the rights of the 'cared for' and criticised many aspects of institutional practice. These reports have been extensively reviewed and described by a range of writers (Buckley et al., 1997; Ferguson and Kenny, 1995; Focus Ireland, 1996; Gilligan, 1991; O'Higgins, 1996; Skehill, 2005), so we will not outline them here. The most significant reports were arguably the Tuairim report (1966), Kennedy report (DoE, 1970), report of the Task Force on Child Care Services (1980) and *Report of the Kilkenny Incest Investigation* (McGuinness, 1993). There has also been a succession of influential reports in the disability sector, the most important of which has been *A Strategy for Equality* (Commission on the Status of People with Disabilities, 1996). In the education and training sector, the *Report of the Committee on Caring and Social Studies* (NCEA, 1992) laid out the basis for the range of educational programmes in social care practice. These documents all comment on aspects of social care provision and, amongst other things, have influenced the type of education and training that social care practitioners should receive and changed the skill sets of practitioners. There is now less emphasis on some 'practical' skills (such as homemaking and health care) and a greater emphasis on research, policy issues and academic knowledge. There has been, and still is, much debate about the virtues or otherwise of such a shift.

Social care practice has long been associated with residential child care. This emphasis has changed dramatically, especially with the decline of large institutions (such as children's homes) and the emergence of alternatives such as foster care, community-based projects and community child care. The field of social care has expanded greatly in recent years, in Ireland as elsewhere. It has been acknowledged that the types of skills and knowledge that social care practitioners exhibit can be constructively applied in other areas, such as in the care of people with disabilities, in working with older people and in responding to the needs of a broad range of people from drug users to victims of domestic violence to asylum seekers. Inevitably, this brings social care practitioners into contact with other professions, including medical professionals, social workers and An Garda Síochána. Social care practitioners' participation in multidisciplinary professional teams is now quite common, which presents challenges to how people work in these fields. For example, the introduction of models of social care practice to the care of older people will involve a challenge to the highly medicalised practices in this field, where nurses and other medical practitioners have been dominant. This will lead to debate and perhaps even conflict between professional groups.

Three social care representative bodies were mentioned above. The Resident Managers' Association (now the IASCM) was founded in 1930, the IASCW was established in 1972 and the IASCE in 1998. Historically, each of these three organisations had separate memberships, structures, conferences and publications. Recognising strength in numbers, they came together in 2011 to form Social Care Ireland, an umbrella or federation body for social care. It has established a joint annual conference, and the *Irish Journal of Applied Social Studies* (online in open access format since 2010) has been adopted as its professional journal. The goal is to create a single, vibrant professional body, with special interest groups for education, management and specialised areas of practice (for example, residential child care, intellectual disabilities, addiction work).

When the first edition of this book was published in 2005, it was the first integrated attempt by educators and practitioners in the social care field in Ireland to define and describe the practice of social care. Inasmuch as it has been widely adopted by educators, students and practitioners of social care, it has represented one small step in unifying the field of social care. A more extensive body of knowledge has subsequently emerged (for example, Charleton, 2007; Garavan, 2012; Hamilton, 2012; Jackson and O'Doherty, 2012; Lyons, 2010; McCann-James et al., 2009; O'Connor and Murphy, 2006; O'Neill, 2004; *Irish Journal of Applied Social Studies*).

WHAT PERSONAL QUALITIES DOES A SOCIAL CARE PRACTITIONER REQUIRE?

We can see that a social care practitioner must have a wide range of personal and intellectual attributes. 'Academic' qualities include: a broad knowledge base, an ability to work independently and as part of a team, research skills and a problem-solving approach. Much social care education and training aims to assist students in developing these skills. In addition, certain personal attributes tend to char-acterise practitioners, such as reliability and trustworthiness, altruism, maturity, empathy and compassion. Social care practitioners must be open-minded and prepared to examine, and perhaps even change, their attitudes towards others. It is open to debate whether these qualities can be taught or are somehow 'innate' in people who are attracted to social care practice as an occupation.

How a social care practitioner develops as a person and as a professional depends on:

- The quality of the practice environment.
- The quality of undergraduate education and training available and, after graduation, the quality and accessibility of continuing professional development (CPD) training.
- The quality and consistency of professional supervision.
- The philosophy of one's work peers about the work and about service users and their families.
- The ability to be self-reflective in one's work.
- The ability to take constructive criticism and turn it into 'best practice'.
- A determination to keep up to date in reading, in seeking out evidence-based solutions and in considering and evaluating new approaches to work.
- A willingness to be an advocate for the profession.

This list constitutes a comprehensive and demanding set of challenges for the social care practitioner.

WHAT QUALIFICATIONS DOES A SOCIAL CARE PRACTITIONER NEED?

In Ireland, the professional qualification for social care practice is a BA (Ordinary) Degree in Social Care Practice or Applied Social Studies. The recognised qualifications are detailed in Schedule 3 of the Health and Social Care Professionals Act 2005. The Act uses the old terms of 'diploma' and 'national diploma', even though these qualifications were reconfigured in 2001 as the BA (ordinary) degree (Level 7) by the National Qualifications Authority of Ireland. Most qualified practitioners go on to complete an honours degree (Level 8) in the field, and an increasing number progress to postgraduate qualifications.

Professional-level programmes in social care are now offered at all institutes of technology, with the exception of Dún Laoghaire, as well as at Carlow College, the Open Training College (based in Goatstown, Co. Dublin, and specialising in the field of intellectual disability) and NUI Galway (which commenced provision in 2008). Significant numbers of students are also enrolled on FETAC Level 5 social care/applied social studies programmes in colleges of further education (FE), such as Ballyfermot College of FE, Coláiste Dhúlaigh College of FE, Inchicore College of FE and Cavan Institute.

A course of study in social care typically includes subjects such as sociology, psychology, social policy, principles of professional practice, law, creative skills (art, drama, music, dance, recreation), communication and research methods. Many courses offer specialised modules in particular areas, such as community, youth or disability studies. A key element of studying to be a professional social care practitioner is involvement in a number of supervised professional practice placements of several months' duration. Some students already working in the field ('in-service' or 'work-based-learning') may undertake their placements at work, closely supervised.

The question of a potential 'oversupply' of social care graduates is sometime raised, but difficult to assess. There is no national system to monitor the education of social care practitioners. Colleges survey graduates regarding employment and further education experiences and, although response rates to such surveys are generally poor, they do provide some indication of graduates' success in securing relevant employment. A 2011 survey of social care graduates of Dublin Institute of Technology yielded a response rate of 83 per cent and showed that only 7 per cent were seeking employment. The remainder were in employment (66 per cent), not available for employment (24 per cent) or in further study/training (3 per cent). Of those in employment, 89 per cent were in the social care sector. These employment levels are more positive than might have been expected given the deep recession that Ireland has experienced in recent years. Overall, there is a strong argument for the ongoing monitoring of graduate output by individual colleges, by the IASCE and by the Higher Education Authority.

There have been some significant developments in social care education in recent years. In particular, two documents have been published that will do much to shape the nature and development of the profession. First, the Higher Education and Training Awards Council (now part of Quality and Qualifications Ireland) published national award standards for social care work (HETAC, 2010), which detail the learning outcomes and competencies expected of social care graduates from NFQ Levels 6 to 10 (higher certificate to doctoral level). These standards provide a national benchmark for education providers. They were produced by an expert panel of practitioners, managers and national and international academics, which represents the most comprehensive consultation with the sector regarding education and training standards to date.

Second, the Health and Social Care Professionals Council (CORU) has published *Criteria and Standards of Proficiency for Education and Training Programmes* (CORU, 2012). The Health and Social Care Professionals Act 2005 empowers CORU to approve and monitor education and training programmes for the various health and social care professions, including social care work and social work. Consequently, following the establishment of professional registration boards for each of the health and social care professions, CORU will have an oversight role in approving education and training programmes nationwide. As of March 2013, only the registration boards for social work and radiography have been established. The registration boards for dietitians, occupational therapists and speech and language therapists shall be established during 2013. No date has been set for the establishment of the registration board for social care work.

WHAT DO SOCIAL CARE PRACTITIONERS DO?

Anglin (1992) has observed that social care practitioners work in two main areas, with a very broad range of practices, as listed in Table 1.2.

Table 1.2. Key tasks of social care

Direct service to clients	Organisational activities
Individual intervention	Case management
Group intervention	Client contracting
In-home family intervention	Report writing and formal recording
Office-based family intervention	Court appearances/legal documentation
Assessment of child	Programme planning and development
Assessment of family	Use and interpretation of policy
Child management	Individual consultation with other
Child abuse interventions	professionals
Employment counselling or assistance	Participation in professional teams
Life skills training	Co-ordination of professional teams
Health management	Contracting for services
Education remediation	Supervision of staff, students or volunteers
Recreational leadership	Staff training and development
Arts and crafts leadership	Public relations/community education
Counselling on death and dying	Organisational analysis and development
Therapeutic play	Policy analysis and development
Parenting skill training	Financial analysis/budgeting
Sexuality counselling	
Marriage counselling	
Stress management	
Lifestyle modification	

Source: Anglin (1992)

Many of the chapters in this book expand on different types of work that social care practitioners carry out. If we were to prioritise, we might suggest that the main role of the practitioner is to work alongside service users to maximise their growth and development. The social care practitioner is also, crucially, an advocate for change.

WHERE DO SOCIAL CARE PRACTITIONERS WORK?

In Ireland, social care practitioners may be employed in:

- The state (statutory) sector; for example, the Departments of Children and Youth Affairs, of Education and Skills or of Justice and Equality.
- The non-governmental sector; for example, Barnardos, the Brothers of Charity, Enable Ireland or Focus Ireland. These organisations are fully or partially funded by government.
- Community-based organisations such as community development projects or Garda Youth Diversion Projects.
- The private sector, where there has been a recent increase in providers operating in the residential child care and foster care areas. Companies such as Positive Care Ireland and Fresh Start have grown to become considerable actors in the field.

In the early 2000s the Joint Committee on Social Care Professionals (JCSCP, 2002) enumerated some 2,904 social care practitioners who were working in community child care (71), in children's residential centres (1,214) and in intellectual disability services (1,619). Of these, just over 55 per cent held a professional qualification, with 14 per cent holding no qualifications at all. In 2011 CORU estimated that approximately 8,000 people will be eligible to register as 'social care workers' when the relevant registration board is established; this estimate is still considered accurate in 2013.

Social care practitioners make valuable contributions in emergent and developing areas such as community development, family support, Garda and community youth projects, women's refuges, county childcare committees, care of older people, and research and policy work. The breadth of chapters in this book reflects some of this diversity, but statistics for the numbers working in such areas are hard to quantify.

SOCIAL CARE PRACTICE: A CHALLENGING OCCUPATION

Social care work can be very challenging, emotionally and physically, and can mean working in some very difficult environments. It can also be uniquely rewarding. For example, the profile of children in residential care may often include multiple loss, rejection, deprivation, neglect and abuse. As a consequence, there can be a large gulf between desires, expectations and reality. The work of the social care practitioner calls for a unique mix of skills and personal attributes. Risk is now synonymous with child protection and welfare (Bessant, 2004). Attention is increasingly directed at what are variously termed 'high risk', 'high challenge' and 'at risk' children, with a child protection service concentrated on a small number of cases at the heavy end of the (perceived) spectrum of risk.

Unfortunately, it is not uncommon for social care practitioners to fail to receive formal supervision on a regular basis, to receive verbal and sometimes physical abuse from service users, to work in under-resourced areas, and to work unsocial hours. With increasing professionalisation and regulation of the field, there is a hope that many of these issues will be addressed in the future.

Salary scales

The late 1990s saw a period of considerable activity by social care practitioners and their trade union representatives for an improvement in salaries and career pathways. This led to a significant salary increase in 2001, by as much as 33 per cent for some grades. In 2009 the salary scales of social care workers were similar (albeit slightly higher) to those of nurses and primary teachers (Lalor and Share, 2009: 19), ranging from €33,000 to €46,000. Since then, all salaries in the public sector have seen significant decreases. In January 2011 the salary scale for new entrants was €29,993 to €39,875 (impact.ie). Further significant cuts to public sector pay have been foreshadowed.

CONCLUSION

Social care has been a growth area in Ireland. It is a demanding but rewarding occupation, as social care practitioners make a real difference in the lives of others. Formal social care had humble beginnings, located within a largely clerical or philanthropic context, but has now expanded to include the statutory, community and voluntary sectors. Social care practitioners are now educated to degree, and increasingly to postgraduate, level. Salaries and career structures have improved since the 1990s. A statutory registration system is being established that will ultimately oversee future professional development in the field. The management and reporting structures in social care practice are moving towards an acceptance of the social care practitioner as an independent, autonomous professional. Social care work remains a rewarding and fulfilling career and occupational choice.

2

What is social pedagogy? A new way of working with older people in Sweden

Mats Högström, Riitta Nilsson and Per-Axel Hallstedt with Perry Share

OVERVIEW

As highlighted in Chapter 1, it can be difficult to explain the concept of social care practice to people outside, or even within, the field. One reason for this is that it has yet, arguably, to develop a coherent and well-recognised theoretical or philosophical basis. It has developed from a combination of elements of social work, youth and community work, different models of therapy, moral frameworks, often religious ones, and very pragmatic notions of action and behaviour. As it develops, it is likely to continue to draw on these sources, but it will also draw on others – and one that may become more influential is the European tradition of social pedagogy.

Social pedagogy is a field of practice, thought and research that has developed in many countries of continental Europe over a period of more than a century. It is found in different forms from Norway and Russia to Portugal and Hungary, but receives varying levels of official recognition and respect. In Ireland, there is some familiarity with the social pedagogy of the Nordic countries, in particular Norway, Sweden and Denmark, due to many years of student and staff exchange between Ireland and those countries. More recently researchers, practitioners, government agencies and educators in parts of the United Kingdom have sought to introduce social pedagogy into that state. Given the heavy dependence of Ireland on models of theory and practice from Britain, it is likely that this will provide further stimulus to the development of social pedagogical approaches in Ireland. It might be argued that social care practice in Ireland already shares many features of the social pedagogical approach, as do elements of Irish practice in youth work, community development and community and adult education.

This chapter briefly outlines the nature of social pedagogy and some of the principles that underlie it. The bulk of the chapter comprises a case study of the application of social pedagogy in elder care in Sweden. The chapter concludes with some reflections on the implications of moving towards a stronger element of social pedagogy in Irish social care practice.

WHAT IS SOCIAL PEDAGOGY?

Speaking at an Irish symposium on social pedagogy in 2012, a Finnish expert in the field suggested that the concept is 'difficult to catch' because it is used in different ways and contexts; it has a multiplicity of theoretical self-conceptions; it is influenced by different philosophies and ideologies, political interests and professional aspirations; and it has diverse country-specific traditions (Hämäläinen, 2012). That said, there are some common elements and theories underpinning the approach. There is an expanding English-language literature in social pedagogy – some translations of Nordic texts, some originally written in English. Any student or practitioner wishing to explore the concept of social pedagogy will find these sources useful (Cameron and Moss, 2011; Kornbeck and Rosendal Jensen, 2011, 2012; Smith, 2012b; Storø, 2013; Stephens, 2013; thempra.org.uk).

Social pedagogy has long historical roots and geographical origins, but most immediately emerges from mid-nineteenth-century German ideas about education and society. Like many modern ways of thinking about society, it was a response to the forces of industrialisation and urbanisation in Europe and America. Thinkers in many fields (such as sociology, psychology and education) struggled with the apparent breakdown of local (often rural) communities and the rise of individualism. The concept of social pedagogy, as its name suggests, sought to combine ideas of education (of children, young people and adults) with a consciousness of the needs of community.

Social pedagogy combines philosophical concepts of the nature of humanity (and how people find their potential) with an understanding of social conditions and problems and with 'pedagogy', or instruction towards change and development (Smith, 2012b). It can be argued that social pedagogy moves beyond individualistic notions of education or social work that focus on the individual or the family unit – it purposely addresses human beings in the context of their community. It has much in common with certain types of youth work, community development practice and community and adult education.

In practice, social pedagogy means working with people in the context in which they live – their life world in a holistic sense. It may take place over an extended period, involve in-depth communication and perhaps living in the same space, and have an overt developmental purpose. It is not just about solving people's 'problems', although that may be part of the response. It usually means working with people to enhance their self-management skills and capacities.

Social pedagogy is most commonly used with children and young people and in this context has become of particular interest to policy makers and practitioners in Britain (Cameron and Moss, 2011) and Ireland (galteeclinic.ie). But, as emphasised by Böhnisch and Schröer (2011), it can be applied across the whole lifespan; indeed, social pedagogues do work across all age groups in Denmark and some other places.

Fristrup (2012) notes that ideas about old age are changing. Rather than being segregated, older people are now expected to participate in, and contribute to, society more extensively than before. This presents a challenge to traditional institutions that provide care for older people, which in Ireland, as in many other societies, tend towards a medical model of care that focuses on older people's deficits rather than their capacities (see Chapter 18). Social pedagogy has been identified by some as a new and better way of working to support Europe's ageing population.

The remainder of this chapter features a case study of the application of social pedagogy with older people in Sweden. While social pedagogy is an established means of working with children and young people in that country, it has not yet been applied on an extensive scale to working with older people. You will note the issues of communication, activity, self-actualisation and sociability that underpin the social pedagogical approach, as well as its basis in certain philosophical concepts and sources.

CASE STUDY

Introduction

In 2006 one of the social districts of the city of Malmö, Västra innerstaden, employed two 'elderpedagogues'. Elderpedagogues are social pedagogues who have been trained to work with older people, using the theories and techniques of social pedagogy as it has developed in Sweden and elsewhere.

Research among a sample of elderly people in Malmö had found that older people were mostly content with the care they received in residential care settings and through home help services, but a significant number complained about long and dreary days during which nothing much happens. This finding reinforced a growing awareness of the connection between health and social situation and that close relationships, physical activity and having something meaningful to do promote health and wellbeing for older people. These circumstances called for new measures, something different from the traditional care provided.

Social workers in a home help service identified a number of older people who were lonely and unhappy. To alleviate this situation, a project was launched in which two elderpedagogues, Lotta and Beata, were employed. Lotta and Beata began to visit the older people and succeeded in establishing good relationships with them. In one case, Beata offered to accompany Elsie, an 82-year-old woman, to the hairdresser's salon. This visit offered a mutual interest and potential topics of conversation. It was also the first time Elsie had been outside her home in a year. She had been afraid to leave her apartment due to a combination of depression and a fear of going out alone.

After a few more visits Beata thought Elsie was ready to meet new challenges. Beata and Lotta had started conversation groups at the neighbourhood day centre and so Beata suggested to Elsie that she visit the centre. They went there together and Elsie found it to be a friendly place with many other older women in similar situations. After making a couple of visits to the centre with Beata, Elsie began to go there unaccompanied.

Lotta and Beata aim to improve the situations of the older people they work with. Their educational aim is to put an end to loneliness and to persuade individuals to socialise with other people. They must consider carefully the best way to approach this process. For example, Beata had to reflect on the opportunities available to Elsie and how they should be presented to make them appealing to her. Embedded in this process is the eternal question of pedagogy: Are you allowed to influence the other? (Hallstedt and Högström, 2005; Nilsson, 2004, 2006). Is Beata a transmitter of certain values and norms (such as that it is 'normal' to meet and socialise with people)? To avoid coercion, Beata needed to engage with Elsie in a symmetrical relationship.

Communicative actions

We can draw on the concepts of communication developed by the German social theorist Jürgen Habermas (1984) and ask: Is the elderpedagogue in this situation bound to communicate to reach success (as a means to an end) or is there an opening for communication that seeks to reach mutual understanding? The second option is the right one for the pedagogue.

Take a common situation where an elderpedagogue is convinced that a specific activity would be good for an older person. This activity is something that the older person really could prosper from and is within cultural norms (otherwise it would not be possible to reach an agreement). Elderpedagogues must understand, however, that while they are in a position to persuade the older person to take part in the activity, the older person's views and arguments against the proposal are valid. So, when is it right to use persuasion in this kind of relationship? When can persuasion lead to a mutual understanding? One way of looking at this is to take the relationship between the two parties into consideration. Persuasion can be used only when there is an element of symmetry in the seemingly asymmetrical relationship. The element of symmetry, or equality, in the relationship makes it possible for the older person to oppose the elderpedagogue's proposition, and present alternative arguments.

The proposition is something that the elderpedagogue really wants to happen, not just something that should be done as a duty or part of the job. We can distinguish between the preferred in a personal sense and in a professional sense. There is a difference between personally feeling that something is right and knowing that it is right from a professional point of view. It is professional authenticity that matters in professional life. It is possible for the parties to meet in communicative dialogue within this professional framework. They are communicating for a successful outcome, but, crucially, this communication is based on the development of a mutual understanding between them.

Elsie found her place at the day centre and visited it often. She appreciated meeting and chatting with other older people. Now and then the elderpedagogues were leaders of their conversations. As professional pedagogues they had an aim for these conversations: small talk is important but sometimes deeper issues need to be raised and discussed. Conversations are a powerful tool in elderpedagogy, but the elderpedagogues have to be sensitive that they do not threaten the integrity of the older people.

Bildung

A central concept in social pedagogy is that of *bildung*. There is no direct translation of this German word, derived from the philosophical writing of Immanuel Kant, into either English or Swedish, but it relates to how the individual and the development of the individual's personality are linked to the outer world (Gustavsson, 2010). It is about developing individual skills for partaking in the community of everyday life and also for creating an inclusive way of living; another key element is 'the basic individual and social anchorage in the world, which makes the formation of identity possible (self-confidence, self-respect and self-esteem)' (Madsen, 2007: 265–6). *Bildung* is associated with learning and development: people, within a concrete and social praxis, develop competencies that will enable them to participate in other life contexts; individual human beings contribute to creating the conditions for integration and inclusion.

Gustavsson (2010: 20–1) interprets *bildung* as a tool for discussing and understanding the world we live in and notes that we are social creatures who 'become what we are in relation to others'. From meeting the 'other', the unknown, emerges the thought of '*bildung* as a journey, an excursion and a return'. Gustavsson refers to Hans-Georg Gadamer's idea of the essence of *bildung* being the encounter with the other, where we seek our own self and become at home in it, then return to ourselves. Kristian Lundberg (2011) reflects on this idea in his review of (Swedish American writer) Gösta Larsson's novel *Ships in the River*: 'You can read yourself home to yourself through a story . . . to become yourself by being somebody else for a moment.' Writing about pedagogical work with people in fragile or marginalised situations, Gustavsson (2010: 24) finds that 'this is the art of pedagogy, to find the right balance between the known and the unknown, or to, in dialogue, find the pre-understanding that opens up for a new understanding'.

Conversation and the coming into being – theoretical insights

German philosopher Paul Natorp (1854–1924) is considered one of the founders of social pedagogy; Martin Buber (1878–1965) is a Jewish philosopher best known for his philosophy of dialogue, in particular the difference between considering the other as 'It' and as 'You' – in the former, the other is treated as an object, and in the latter, there is mutual co-existence and dialogue. Both philosophers have written about an individual coming into being as an 'I' in a relationship with a

'You', where both are recognised by the other. In I–You relationships, we experience wholeness, continuity and meaning in our lives. In *bildung*, encounters with others are essential. In these encounters we communicate with each other.

Through language we are able to give a mutual response but also to create a distance from ourselves, which means that we can, as subjects, see ourselves as objects (Eriksson and Markström, 2000). This distance gives us the possibility to reflect on our experiences, and thus to be involved in the process of *bildung*; in meeting the other we meet ourselves. Conversations as communication can thus become a means for *bildung*. Here one might also refer to Jürgen Habermas's theory of communicative action (1984). In the life world, social integration happens through communicative action, where participants strive for mutual understanding in order to come to an agreement. Thus, solidarity, identity and meaning are created, and this is the foundation of human life.

We can also refer to the German philosopher Axel Honneth's concept of recognition. Social recognition is conveyed to the individual who is seen to act according to society's values. Older people should experience recognition as individuals. This presupposes that they themselves recognise the culture of the society, which has gone through considerable change during their lives, and that they can relate to that change whether they consider it positive or negative.

The concept of learning is also important. Danish educationist Knud Illeris (2007) defines learning as a process that creates long-term changes in the individual. According to Illeris, learning has three dimensions: cognitive, psychodynamic and societal. The societal dimension has two levels: interaction and culture.

Research study

Conversations are a powerful tool in supporting the *bildung* process. Older people often experience a diminishing social network and a lack of opportunities for conversation, which might have a negative impact on *bildung*. To investigate this idea, with the help of elderpedagogues in elder care, we selected a small sample comprising four older women aged from eighty-two to ninety-four years. They were all widows, living in the same neighbourhood and visiting the same venue for activities for older people. We had conversations with the women, focusing on their life and present situation in society. The conversations lasted between one and two hours.

The overall aim was to explore the potential of conversations in the *bildung* process. We were particularly interested to see whether combinations of the regular and the unexpected, the familiar and the unfamiliar, would appear in the conversations, and what impact that would have on *bildung*. The limits of conversation as a tool for *bildung* were considered, as well as the need for caution in light of the vulnerability of older people.

Our research seeks to contribute to the understanding of the options for the continued development of personality. Which conversations add to these options, and what hinders them? How could we adhere to the different needs of individual older people? In short, what is a 'good conversation' that contributes to the *bildung* process for the older individual, as far as learning is concerned?

Content of the conversations

The type of conversations that we had with the four research participants were very different from the everyday conversations that they described taking place at the day centre. Conversations at the day centre appear to be much shallower in content than those conducted during the research. The day centre conversations, often led by the elderpedagogues, are very much appreciated, but seemingly for the act of coming together rather than for the actual topics discussed. One respondent said she was merely listening to the others and concluded that she did not view the content to be of any interest to her. Another stated that it was very important for her to go to the meetings, to see people, but when asked what they talked about she answered, 'I don't know.' Such responses indicate that it does not really matter what is spoken about: to meet people is what matters.

As researchers, we came to the conversations with a few intended themes: daily life; what they talk about in the day centre; their life stories; what happens in the world today; people they meet; and how they feel about meeting people. The research participants are identified below as IP1 to IP4 to assist in recognising the different voices.

Lack of opportunities for conversation

'There are many days I don't talk with anybody.' (IP1) This was a typical comment from all four participants. 'I see almost nobody. I have no relatives, no children, nobody. I have one old acquaintance.' (IP4) Weekends are especially difficult to handle. They had all been married and their spouses had died two or three years earlier. With one exception, their children live far away and telephone conversations have replaced face-to-face conversations.

Contact at any cost

The participants talked about the day centre, which they like very much. They are fond of the elderpedagogues, but they do not always find it easy to take part in the scheduled conversations. Some incidents convey moments of strain. People with reduced hearing capacity have been criticised, another person has been accused of speaking too low, and a proposition to see a film brought to the meeting was met with disinterest. Still, nobody would refrain from going there. One respondent tells us of a woman who can neither see nor hear but who still shows up every week.

Life stories

Each participant told us a long and rich story about her schooldays, travels, work, marriage and views on contemporary life. All the women were professionals, with a long record of work. They seemed to be content with their experiences of working life. They were quite happy with their school years and described them vividly and with pride in their knowledge and skills. It was obvious that the women were pleased that someone was interested in hearing their life story, and one woman pointed out that there are often no opportunities for such meaningful conversations.

Encounters with other cultures, modern times

All participants were aware of what was going on in the world. They watch television, read newspapers, listen to the radio and reflect on the latest events. Talking about the situation in north Africa, one woman said, 'Well, it is horrible, it is, but it is difficult for us living so protected to understand. I listen to the radio a lot and there is much talk about Muslims and I don't know what to believe, because it is not always correct what they say on the radio or TV. But it is terrible for people to always live in a state of war.' (IP1) Another woman had a lot to say about unemployment and felt it was a disgrace that people had lost their jobs in the elder care service.

One of the women compared her daughter's way of life with what she herself had experienced, and expressed her pleasure with her daughter's free and open life. She recognised the cultural developments that had made this possible and reflected on the fundamental changes in the situation of women on many levels, not least their increased access to the field of education. Theoretically, in this dialogue, the researcher found a link between the particular and the universal, a pre-understanding that opened up a new understanding (Gustavsson, 2010).

Sensitivity

The participants enjoy the meetings and conversations at the day centre, in spite of describing them as lacking deeper meaning or sometimes even lacking topics on which to speak. One respondent was looking forward to the spring, when everyone can go out more and thus find new things to talk about. It is possible to just sit at the venue and listen to the others, or to speak with the person next to you. People's visits to the venue and the ordinary chit-chat they participate in there have an important function of giving variation in an otherwise rather monotonous everyday life.

One participant stated that the depth of conversation in the research interview was very different from the way the people speak with each other at the centre. We understand that both kinds of conversations are important. It is good to have someone's whole attention and to be able to reflect on life, loneliness and the diminishing strength of body and mind. If this kind of conversation is to be carried out at the day centre, however, care must be taken to prevent the conversation getting too personal or too revealing. Staff must also have a sense of whether each person has the psychological capacity to receive new information that could change their views on important matters, that is, to learn (Illeris, 2007).

Role of the elderpedagogues

'[They] are wonderful, they have raised my spirits and enhanced my life,' says one respondent (IP4), giving voice to the general feeling about the elderpedagogues.

At the day centre the elderpedagogues sit at the meetings together with the women, but sometimes they have other things to do, and then the conversations tend to be more superficial: 'we only talk rubbish' said one of the respondents (IP2), but with no derogatory tone at all. Although our participants did not specifically mention it, the elderpedagogues also make individual visits to the women's homes, which would provide an opportunity for deeper conversations.

In their training at Malmö University, elderpedagogues learn that elder pedagogy is about leading a pedagogic process, together with the older person, towards a goal. How does this relate to the *bildung* process?

In their work the elderpedagogues create a will in the older people to take part in the meetings, to go there and to continue to go there, and so they create an opportunity for inclusive meetings. Equally important is that the older people are encouraged to talk with each other. The *bildung* process is promoted by someone being interested in your life and thoughts. It makes you keep track of yourself and forms a basis for opening up your mind to new things. When you tell your life story to somebody, you are involved in a process that can lead to a better understanding of yourself.

Conversations that would not add to the *bildung* process include those that are brought to a halt because one or two of the participants find the topic too personal or disturbing. Nor does it benefit the process if the participants are there just for 'small talk' or if they show little interest in the proposed topic. It is vital that elderpedagogues reflect on what happens with the older people during their conversations and encourage a balance between chit-chat and deeper topics. Chit-chat is important as it provides a setting for deeper conversations.

It is for the elderpedagogues to bring elements to the conversation that could stimulate the *bildung* process and create the conditions where one could see oneself in others. The means for this include questions about events during the life course, modern times and phenomena in modern multicultural society. Conversations may centre on the people themselves or approach topics indirectly through discussion of characters in literature or the media.

What next?

We plan to examine the use of *bildung* as a concept for elderpedagogy in further empirical studies; for example, we want to test different topics and different ways of opening conversations and to test the ability of students to reflect on their actions during conversations. We see this as an important and interesting way to develop elderpedagogy and to explore one particular area in the field more deeply.

Reflection from an Irish perspective

This case study provides an insight into an alternative concept of care. It presents a different way of thinking about the care of older people – one that incorporates a social, rather than a medical, model of care (see also Chapter 18). Drawing on the concept of *bildung*, it sees this model as active and developmental, rather than passive and static. It is assumed that older people have a desire to interact in a range of ways with others, and to continue to be mentally challenged and to learn. It treats this potential for interaction with sensitivity: it is important to fully consider the motivations of all participants, the interaction – the conversations – must be based on an authentic mutual co-existence with the other person and not be patronising or manipulative. The case study also reveals something of the complex philosophical thinking that supports the concept of social pedagogy. This is perhaps where it differs most from social care practice as it has developed in Ireland. Outside of some consideration of ethics and values, the study of philosophy is rarely incorporated into the education or practice of social care in Ireland. With emerging debates about professionalisation, and contested notions of what care is, who should be doing it and how much we value it – it may well be that more philosophical discussions should be taking place.

3

The practice of child and youth care in North America

Grant Charles and Thom Garfat

OVERVIEW

Child and youth care (CYC) work in North America refers to social care practice that focuses primarily upon the wellbeing and treatment of children and young people and, increasingly, their families. It has existed for well over 150 years, although not always in the form recognisable today. Indeed, the term itself is relatively recent. This chapter provides an overview of CYC in North America. It defines and describes CYC; traces the historical roots of the discipline; provides an overview of education and training programmes and opportunities; and discusses current trends and challenges that affect North American practitioners.

The delivery systems in Canada and in the United States for child and family services, in which most CYC practitioners work, are quite often philosophically and instrumentally distinct from each other. This is a reflection of the value differences between the two countries as well as how services to children and families are conceptualised, organised and funded. As a result, the two countries have not experienced an equal development of CYC. Nevertheless, there is enough common ground to be able to provide an overview of CYC work across North America.

While there has been a great deal of debate as to whether CYC in North America is a 'profession', a 'discipline' or a 'field' (Beker, 2001; Burmeister, 1960; Jull, 2001; Krueger, 2002; Stuart, 2003), the terms will be used interchangeably for the purposes of this chapter.

HISTORICAL ROOTS

It is difficult to locate the exact origins of child and youth care (CYC) in North America, but there are four paths along which the historical roots can be traced. The first starts with the orphanages established in the 1700s in a number of communities and originally run by religious orders (Charles and Gabor, 2006). By the mid-1800s, as they expanded, they began to hire lay staff, although often remaining under the auspices of religious orders. The lay staff tended to work directly with the children in the institutions. Many of the children who entered these orphanages were not orphans in the true sense of the word; rather, their parents were unable to provide adequately for them due to poverty or illness. It was not unusual, for example, for men to be away from home for extended periods, working in the forests or fisheries or fighting in wars, and unable to provide adequate support for their families. In such cases, children were placed in orphanages, usually on a short-term basis, until the financial situation of the family improved or the absent parent returned to the family home.

CYC in North America can also trace its roots to the recreational and 'fresh air' movements that occurred during the big waves of immigration from the mid-1800s to the early 1900s. Millions of people migrated to North America, primarily (but not only) from European countries, during this time. Organisations such as the Young Men's Christian Association (YMCA), the Young Women's Christian Association (YWCA) and the Boys' and Girls' Clubs were founded, in part to provide services to young people who came from backgrounds of poverty, which was common in the greater immigrant population. While these organisations were not established to work exclusively with 'troubled' youth, they were among the first to do so in North America. They set up community-based recreational and social service programmes and residential youth homes as a means to help those young people who would nowadays be termed 'at risk' to become productive members of society. As with the orphanages, these services were generally set up with a Christian orientation, although 'Ys' (YMCAs and YWCAs) and Boys' and Girls' Clubs tended to be run by laypeople.

A third historical foundation of CYC was in the 'correction' movement, which included the industrial and training schools for juvenile delinquents, as well as the hospitals for the 'mentally or physically deficient' (Charles and Gabor, 2006). These facilities were usually, but not exclusively, run by state or provincial governments. Many of the programmes were set up as a part of, or in conjunction with, adult services, but by the early 1900s separate services for adults and children had been established. Although frequently serving children from urban centres, many of these facilities were located in rural communities or on the outskirts of cities so as to hide 'deficient' children from the eyes of society or to remove them from the corrupting influence of urban life. Even though North America was becoming increasingly urban during this period, rural life was still idealised.

A parallel movement occurred with the establishment of residential schools for Aboriginal youth in the second half of the nineteenth century (Charles and Gabor, 1990, 2006; Chrisjohn and Young, 1997; Fournier and Crey, 1997). These were run by Roman Catholic and Anglican religious personnel, although they may have been funded, as was the case in Canada, by the government. As with the orphanages, they tended to be managed by members of religious orders (such as the Oblates) but staffed by laypeople. Their purpose was to assimilate Aboriginal youth into mainstream society (Bombay et al., 2011; Charles and Gabor, 2006). While each of the previously mentioned services sought to assimilate children and youth into 'society', the residential schools were a deliberate attempt to destroy Aboriginal culture. They separated young people from their families, in essence creating cultural orphans. The aim was to replace traditional indigenous socialisation processes with what have become known as Eurocentric values and beliefs (Elias et al., 2012; Rogers et al., 2012). The role of CYC in these schools has left a negative legacy that is felt throughout Aboriginal communities today.

North American CYC was born in such orphanages, recreational programmes, correctional institutions and residential schools. It is not the only professional group to evolve from these services: recreational therapy, psychiatric nursing, rehabilitation services, correctional services and social work can also locate their origins in all or in part in these institutions. The roots of CYC were highly ethnocentric as these organisations reflected the values and beliefs of the Anglo-Saxon elites of North America. Others, whether Aboriginal, Irish, Italian or Asian, were considered inferior and in need of assistance to become contributing members of society. The poor, regardless of ethnic origin, were also seen to be in need of proper socialisation and corrective intervention (Charles and Gabor, 2006).

The organisations in which the 'original' CYC workers were employed reflected their times, which tended to be moralistic, exclusionary and, often, oppressive. That is not to say that some good work was not done. Indeed, many children owed their lives to the efforts of these original workers. But we cannot deny that assimilation, with all the associated negative consequences, was a goal and that the original workers were agents of these assimilation policies. With the exception of some of the programming by the 'Ys' and the Boys' and Girls' Clubs, the origins of CYC lie in residential programmes of one sort or another.

In the 1950s, with the emergence of the deinstitutionalisation movement, North America saw the beginning of the professionalisation of CYC. Beforehand, people in the institutions worked in positions that were not recognised as a distinct profession, discipline or field. Governments began to close the large institutions and replace them with specialised treatment facilities (Charles and Gabor, 2006). Many of these were administered by the same, albeit revamped, organisations that had run the old institutions, although there was a significant decrease in the number with formal religious affiliations. The large institutions did not disappear overnight; indeed, it was a thirty-year process, with closures peaking in the late 1960s and early 1970s. Some of the correctional and hospital facilities are still in existence, but often on a much smaller scale than they were in their 'glory days'.

The new treatment facilities were smaller, more focused and more likely to be located in urban areas. They tended to be managed by professional rather than lay staff. It was in these programmes that CYC first began to be acknowledged as a discipline with specialised skills and knowledge. This acknowledgment led to specific professional training. The first formal training programme in CYC in North America was established in 1957 at the Thistletown Hospital in Ontario (OACYC, n.d.).

DEFINITIONS AND DIFFERENCES

The definition of CYC has evolved as the field has changed. Ferguson (1993) suggests that, as a field, CYC had its beginnings in residential care. Early definitions made little distinction between CYC and residential work. Since then, the field has expanded to include school- and community-based care, infant development, child life in hospital settings, juvenile justice, rehabilitation and recreation. As such, the definition of CYC has broadened to take into account the skills and competencies needed to work in these areas (Krueger, 2002; Stuart et al., 2007). For example, the Child and Youth Care Association of British Columbia (CYCABC, 2012) uses the following definition:

> Child and youth care practitioners work with children, youth and families with complex needs. They can be found in a variety of settings such as group homes and residential treatment centers, hospitals and community mental health clinics, community-based outreach and school-based programs, parent education and family support programs, as well as in private practice and juvenile justice programs. Child and youth care workers specialize in the development and implementation of therapeutic programs and planned environments and the utilization of daily life events to facilitate change. At the core of all effective child and youth care practice is a focus on the therapeutic relationship; the application of theory and research about human growth and development to promote the optimal physical, psycho-social, spiritual, cognitive, and emotional development of young people towards a healthy and productive adulthood; and a focus on strengths and assets rather than pathology.

The problem with this definition, and many others used over the years, is that there is little in it that is different to that used by other professions who work with children. Social workers, psychologists and nurses who work with young people would also claim to 'focus on the therapeutic relationship; the application of theory and research about human growth and development to promote the optimal physical, psycho-social, spiritual, cognitive, and emotional development of young people towards a healthy and productive adulthood'. This overlap contributes to 'territorial' conflicts with other professions, who argue there is not enough distinction between CYC and themselves to warrant recognition of CYC as a separate profession. These conflicts not only impede the development of the profession but can also have negative repercussions for the young people served. Service suffers when the professions fight rather than collaborate with each other (Salhani and Charles, 2007).

There has been much debate over the past thirty years as to whether CYC is a profession or a discipline. Those who would argue that it is a profession, or at least a developing profession, make their case based on the uniqueness of the work performed with clients. Anglin (2001) believes that CYC is unique in that it focuses primarily on the growth and development of children; is concerned with the totality of a child's functioning; has a social competency base; is based upon, but not restricted to, day-to-day work with children; and involves the development of therapeutic relationships with children.

On the other hand, Gaughan and Gharabaghi (1999) argue that while the ability of CYC staff to work in the daily life of children distinguishes CYC workers from other professions such as psychology or social work, this in itself is not enough to make CYC a profession. They suggest that CYC lacks a disciplinary epistemology whereby the field produces its own unique knowledge. Rather, they argue, CYC 'knowledge' is borrowed from other disciplines. They also suggest that there is a lack of role distinction when CYC is compared with other professional disciplines. These points suggest that CYC does not have control over a specialised or specific knowledge base and therefore is not really a profession.

Overlap remains between CYC and other professions and disciplines. In some jurisdictions, such as the Canadian province of British Columbia, child protection work is conducted both by social workers and CYC workers. There can also be an overlap in hospital settings between CYC, social work, occupational therapy and rehabilitation. This adds to the confusion over whether CYC is a distinct profession or discipline. This debate has not been resolved and is likely to continue for years to come.

EDUCATION, TRAINING AND ACCREDITATION

It is interesting that the forty-year span in which many of the old institutions were closed or downsized saw a blossoming in the establishment and later expansion of formal higher education programmes in CYC. In Canada, the provinces of Ontario and Quebec were leaders in this area, with the establishment of two-year (later expanded in Ontario to three years) specialised educational programmes at the community college level (similar to Irish higher certificates and ordinary degrees). The first formal training programme in North America was established in Ontario in 1957. Similar diploma-level programmes were set up in a number of states and provinces although, even fifty-five years later, there are many jurisdictions that do not have college-level training programmes. Despite a number of openings in recent years, university-level programmes in CYC are still rare in North America and educational opportunities beyond the undergraduate level are almost non-existent.

There are approximately twenty degree-granting CYC programmes evenly divided between the two countries although it should be noted that the United States has ten times the population of Canada. Not all are 'pure' CYC programmes. In Canada, the programmes are either distinct CYC or child study programmes. In the United States, they are almost exclusively youth development programmes. The 'study' programmes tend to place less emphasis on practice than do the CYC degrees. There are few graduate programmes available to students. The School of

Child and Youth Care at the University of Victoria in British Columbia offers a graduate and doctoral programme in CYC and Clemson University in South Carolina has a graduate programme in youth development leadership.

Overall, Canada has focused primarily on formal post-secondary education of practitioners and the United States has given more attention to on-the-job staff training. Canada is more developed in terms of formal CYC education programmes with, proportionately, more diploma and degree programmes than the US. This means there are significantly fewer post-secondary-trained CYC practitioners in the US than there are in Canada. This is not likely to change in the near future. The way the US has dealt with this shortage has been to offer continuing education training opportunities for staff. For example, Casa Pacifica, a youth-serving organisation in California, provides training opportunities across the country to CYC workers who have work experience but no formal education. There are a number of similar organisations in the US.

The majority of CYC staff members across North America are untrained. Anglin (2002), in a study of residential programmes for young people in British Columbia, notes that a significant number of staff do not have specialised tertiary-level training in CYC. Others may come from post-secondary programmes that may or may not be related to CYC, while some have little or no education past high school. Stuart and Sanders (2008), in the most recent available system-wide review of staff qualifications in Ontario, found that approximately 50 per cent of CYC workers in mental health services, 40 per cent in child protection services and 30 per cent in private residential services have CYC diplomas or degrees. This is the case even though Ontario has a long history of providing post-secondary CYC education opportunities and is in the jurisdiction with the highest number of post-secondary CYC education programmes. Other provinces and states have far fewer trained CYC workers.

Also to be noted is an unfortunate recent trend whereby agencies, unable to attract sufficient numbers of men to work in their programmes, have shown a tendency to lower their formal hiring criteria so as to attract men to the field. This situation has come about as a result of the limited number of men in educational programmes in the 'helping disciplines'. A concurrent problem with regard to the education and training of CYC workers is the limited funds available to agencies to provide professional development for current staff. While some funds are always available, they tend to be spent on mandatory or legislated training, such as violence management, with the result that few agencies can provide training that would enhance the workers' abilities to provide effective services to young people and their families. The end result is that, with the exception of agencies able or willing to hire graduates, many programmes stagnate at their current level of service.

An encouraging sign in Canada is the establishment of an accreditation process for CYC diploma and degree programmes. The Child and Youth Care Educational Accreditation Board of Canada (CYCEA) was legally incorporated in 2011 to enhance the quality of CYC training. It grew out of a task force on child and youth care education accreditation and the Canadian Council of Child and Youth Care Association's work on professional regulation. CYCEA will describe educational standards and develop the process by which programmes become accredited.

CERTIFICATION AND REGISTRATION

To address the disparity in staff qualifications, some jurisdictions have begun to develop a certification process for CYC workers. The most successful has been the province of Alberta, which has provided a certification process for government workers since 1979 and for all other CYC workers since 1985 (Berube, 1984; Phelan, 1988). British Columbia developed a certification plan well over a decade ago, but it has yet to be implemented (Stuart, 2001). Texas, Ohio and Wisconsin also have certification programmes.

Certification programmes tend to be replacement programmes rather than supplementary programmes to formal education. For example, while it recognises formal education, the Alberta certification process has a 'grandfather clause' for workers who do not have formal qualifications (CYCAA, 2000; Stuart, 2001). This 'grandfather clause' permits such workers to apply for exemption based upon work experience. In other words, the certificate programmes are most often developed as a way to ensure a minimal training standard for frontline staff. They have not been developed as a means of professional registration, as would be the case in some other disciplines in the caring fields. This ability to regulate educational expectations, entry qualifications and the use of the name of the profession is a central consideration in North America in determining whether a profession is 'truly a profession', both legally and in the eyes of other professions.

In 1992 CYC leaders came together to create the International Leadership Coalition for Professional Child and Youth Care Workers (ILCFPCYCW). A code of ethics, addressing such areas as responsibility for self, clients, employers and society, was developed as a common guide for workers in their interactions with clients (Krueger, 2002). The North American Certification Project was initiated by ILCFPCYCW in conjunction with the two national associations to develop common certification standards for Canada and the US. This led to the coming together of a group of CYC practitioners and academics under the auspices of the Association for Child and Youth Care Practice (ACYCP), which in turn led to the establishment of the Child and Youth Care Certification Board (CYCCB), which has designed a framework for credentialing child and youth care workers (ACYCP, 2007; Curry et al., 2010). Participants must pass an exam and submit a work experience portfolio before they can be certified. CYC workers in twenty-three states and provinces had achieved certification through this process by 2012.

PROFESSIONAL ASSOCIATIONS, EVENTS AND PUBLICATIONS

While the first CYC state or provincial association was established in Ontario in 1959 (MacKenna, 1994), there has never been a time when all of the provinces and states have had active associations. At the peak, in the 1980s, fewer than half of the US states had CYC associations (Krueger, 2002). Nevertheless, CYC workers in North America are represented by national organisations. In the United States, the ACYCP provides national leadership. In Canada, the same function is carried out by the Council of Canadian Child and Youth Care Associations. These separate organisations co-operate on matters of common interest: they jointly sponsor an international CYC conference that is offered on alternating sites between the two countries and they have also co-operated in the development of standards for certification.

Neither association has a high national profile, unlike their counterparts in professions such as social work, nursing, psychology or medicine. For example, the CYC associations tend to have a much lower profile in terms of government lobbying, which is partly due to a comparative lack of funds, but also related to the low profile of the profession in the minds of the general public. Few people in either country are aware that CYC is a separate professional grouping under the general umbrella of the caring professions. This situation is partly an outcome of the failure of the associations to formulate a strategy that will raise CYC's profile.

This is not the only difficulty facing the two national associations. A disturbing trend has been a significant decrease in membership levels in many state and provincial organisations, corresponding with the disappearance or weakening of some of the CYC associations themselves. Unlike other professional or discipline-specific bodies, many CYC associations depend on a small group of dedicated people for their survival or at least effective functioning. As these people move on, the associations often go into a period of stagnation or, in some cases, disappear altogether. The result is a constant ebb and flow of associations, which makes effective long-term planning and lobbying difficult, if not impossible.

Several other groups have been founded to contribute to the development of the profession in North America. Two CYC organisations worth mentioning are the Academy of Professional Child and Youth Care and the North American Consortium of Child and Youth Care Education Programmes (Krueger, 2002; Ricks et al., 1991). The former consists of selected leaders in the profession, and the latter represents educators from college and university CYC programmes. Both have been active in promoting issues relevant to the field. Of the two, the latter remains the most active and influential: it holds regular meetings to discuss common issues related to education and training.

Conferences

Although the roots of CYC go back many years, the Valley Forge Conference in Pennsylvania, first held in 1975, was one of the first forums for CYC practitioners to come together to discuss common issues. The first national CYC conference in Canada was organised at the University of Victoria, British Columbia, in 1981; and the first international conference was held in Vancouver, British Columbia, in 1985. Although there has been a decrease in the number of provincial and state conferences in recent years, the attendance at the Canadian national and the international conferences continues to be strong. The first CYC World Congress was held in St John's, Newfoundland, in 2013.

Journals and associated writings

Four major journals promote CYC in North America. The journal *Relational Child and Youth Care Practice* (formerly the *Journal of Child and Youth Care*) is a Canadian publication currently published from Ryerson University in Toronto. *The Child and Youth Care Forum* and the *Journal of Child and Youth Care Work* are both published in the US. Although the subscription base for these journals is relatively small, they tend to be highly influential in the field. CYC-Net is a web-based journal, published monthly. It is published in South Africa, but many of its contributors and readers are based in North America and it has a significant impact on Canadian and American workers. In the year to October 2012 there were over 1,500,000 distinct visits – just under 4,000 a day – to CYC-Net, with a strong representation from Canada and the US (cyc-net.org).

Many of the individual CYC associations also publish newsletters that contribute to their local memberships. A number of new books on practice in CYC (Garfat and Charles, 2012; Gharabaghi, 2012; Gharabaghi and Stuart, 2013) have built upon the foundation work of recent decades (Charles and Gabor, 1988; Fewster, 1990; Krueger, 1998).

CHALLENGES

CYC practitioners in North America face many challenges, including the lack of a recognised professional identity, with a corresponding lack of respect from other allied professions. It is not that the other professions are deliberately disrespectful towards CYC, rather they are unaware of its specific role. The same tends to apply for governments across the spectrum of services. Few acknowledge that CYC is anything but a job description, even in programmes that they run directly. CYC is not recognised as a profession in the legislation under which most of the caring professions are governed, although the provinces of Ontario and Alberta have made tentative steps to address this issue. This is a lengthy process that may take until the 2020s to actualise, if it happens at all. Governments have a fiscal vested interest in it not happening as legally recognised professionals command higher rates of pay. There has also been resistance from other professions, such as social work, who see it as an intrusion into 'their territory'. While this stance does not create a new problem for CYC practitioners, it does reinforce an existing one. The caring fields tend to be poorly paid in North America, and CYC is one of the poorest of the poor. This creates a high turnover in workers, as people are forced to look for other means of making a living.

The lack of recognition is reflected in the low membership figures of professional CYC associations: the vast majority of CYC workers do not belong to a provincial or state association. In turn, the low numbers of members mean that the associations have to survive on minimal budgets, which significantly handicaps their ability to lobby governments for official recognition. This lack of recognition also means that, unlike most other professions in the caring fields, CYC cannot demand mandatory registration, which would provide money to assist in the lobbying efforts. Mandatory registration would go a long way to ultimately solving the whole issue of whether or not CYC is a profession.

In many ways, CYC is a young person's profession. Many people, regardless of where their heart lies, leave CYC for other professions that have higher profiles and more status and pay. It is not unusual for social workers, teachers and psychologists to have begun their careers in CYC before moving on to their new profession. It is often these very people who have either contributed in some way to the leadership of the profession or who would have been likely to have taken a leadership role in the future, in other words the very people the profession cannot afford to lose. CYC is seen as a stepping-stone profession where one can acquire excellent skills and knowledge that can then be used to be successful in other fields. This is beneficial to the individual worker but hurts the long-term development of CYC.

Besides the high turnover of staff, there is also a lack of men working in CYC. Male staff members are both hard to recruit and hard to retain, especially when the economy is healthy. This is a problem in many of the caring fields, but is particularly acute in CYC. The vast majority of students in college and university programmes are female, which means that those men who are hired tend to be the least qualified in terms of education and training. These difficulties are compounded by the fear that many men have of residents making false allegations of abuse. In North America, as in many jurisdictions, allegations of abuse have come from past residents of some of the institutions. Some are founded and some unfounded. There have been situations where government investigations of abuse have been inappropriately conducted, with the result that innocent staff members were branded as abusers (Vedan-Jones et al., 2008). This has created an atmosphere of fear that contributes to the turnover of male staff.

Workers leave CYC because of what they believe to be poor work conditions. An increasing problem, especially in residential programmes, is the belief that there has been an increase in the amount of violent behaviour exhibited by young people. Whether this is actually the case is under debate, but the belief that it is true is widely held (Gharabaghi, 2012; Sadeler and Gharabaghi, 2007). This belief may be a self-fulfilling prophecy where staff in fear of violence create an atmosphere that is tense and sometimes dangerous. This situation contributes to staff turnover, especially in smaller programmes or in remote or rural areas where there may not be access to the same level of support that may be found in larger programmes.

If current working environments are more dangerous, this may not necessarily be related to an increase in the numbers of violent young people – it may be a reflection of the numerous cutbacks that have occurred in recent years in many states and provinces. Cutbacks have caused the closure or downsizing of programmes, with the result that many young people are referred to services that are not equipped to meet their needs. The situation is compounded by cuts in staffing levels and training budgets, which contribute to people leaving CYC as it becomes increasingly difficult to do their job. As people leave, so does their collective wisdom. The result is a vicious circle that contributes to a downgrading of the quality of programmes. As experienced people leave, the knowledge of how to work with troubled youth also leaves, causing interventions to focus more on behaviour than on relationships and creating situations that are about control rather than change, with a greater consequent likelihood of violent rather than growth responses from young people. Unfortunately, the pace of cutting children's services appears to have accelerated since the beginning of the current global financial crisis (Charles et al., 2012). Governments have been either freezing or actively cutting the budgets of child services. The impact on the field has been significant, as people are being asked to do ever more with less.

Cutbacks are also affecting hiring practices. Lack of funds is forcing many programmes to hire inexperienced or untrained staff in order to meet budget quotas. Even though CYC is not a high-paying field, experienced and higher-educated staff are paid more. The issue is compounded by a decrease in staff training and development budgets, often the first to be cut in times of restraint (Charles et al., 2012). This is bad enough when staff members are experienced and well trained, but potentially deadly when dealing with poorly trained or inexperienced staff. Children died in care in Canada because staff had apparently not been properly trained in the appropriate use of physical restraints (restoringdignity.org/orphan2). The misuse of restraints is a problematic issue that is receiving much attention (OPACYO, 2010).

Another issue influencing the direction of services, and therefore people, in CYC is the increased demand by governments and funding agencies for proof that money being spent on children's services is having an impact (Stuart et al., 2007). The need for programme and intervention accountability is primarily being met by the development of service standards. Organisations such as the Child Welfare League of America and the Alberta Association of Services for Children and Families have long had standards of service that are used by many of the organisations that hire CYC staff. What is new is that funders expect agencies and facilities to become accredited even though there is no uniform accreditation process in North America: bodies are local, national or continental. The funders often dictate which body an individual organisation accesses. The aim of accreditation is to improve service delivery, but, at a time of staff cuts, the effort required for an organisation to become accredited often takes away from the work being done with clients. Few jurisdictions provide funding for agencies to go through what can be a lengthy and time-consuming process. Thus, the desire to increase standards often results in a lessening of service quality.

Related to the development of standards is the corresponding development of outcome measures, again with the goal of service improvement. This long-needed initiative requires that interventions be performed on a planned and measured basis, rather than in the intuitive manner in which many interactions occur. As can be expected, there is some resistance by CYC workers (and other professions) to the development of outcome measures (Charles et al., 2003). Although many support this initiative, not everyone wants to have their work examined or analysed. Similar resistance is evident among some towards service standards and accreditation. But it is unlikely that governments and other funding bodies will back away from their demands in these areas. Accountability will be a strong force in children's services, and in CYC, for the foreseeable future (Charles and White, 2008).

It must be recognised that one of the leading challenges to CYC is the development of a common definition of the field itself in a way that articulates the purpose, role and value of CYC. While writings within the field, as noted, have increased significantly in the past thirty years, there is still a general misunderstanding of what it means to practise CYC. Various models drawn from the behavioural sciences, for example, compete for position with those founded with a more phenomenological orientation. This can lead to confusion as to what is meant by a CYC approach. The lack of an agreed definition creates confusion in other professions (some of which still think of CYC as a simple supplement to their own work) and limits the ability of the field to promote itself. Added to this is the current debate, at least in Canada, regarding the societal mandate of CYC, which is seen by some as oppressive and supportive of the limited discourse of capitalism. Although not a widely held view, this 'radical CYC practice' philosophy is gaining some traction in academic circles (Skott-Myhre, 2004; Skott-Myhre and Skott-Myhre, 2007). Whether it receives a wider acceptance in the practice field remains to be seen.

CONCLUSION

The key challenge that faces CYC in North America is that of change. At the core of this process is the debate about the professional status of CYC, but this is in some ways a false issue. What ultimately matters is whether the mandate of

CYC is being met. Its current mandate is to promote the healthy growth of children and youth and to help them to become contributing members of society. This is not to say that the work to promote CYC as a profession is a wasted effort. Anything that contributes to the growth of CYC as a viable force in the caring fields will contribute to the wellbeing of children. Such initiatives help CYC workers to deal with the changes demanded and are clearly influenced by the massive change occurring in children's services and in North American society as a whole. Perhaps it is fitting that a profession that has at its core the responsibility to promote change in young people is in itself inextricably involved in the process of change.

4

Social care practice, professionalism and post-professionalism

Perry Share

OVERVIEW

'Professions . . . are all conspiracies against the laity.'
(George Bernard Shaw, preface to *The Doctor's Dilemma*, 1906)

This chapter addresses the question of professionalisation and social care practice. What does it mean to be a professional? Is social care practice a profession? Does it matter? And, if so, to whom? The concept is not as simple or straightforward as it might first appear. This chapter explores the concept of professionalism, pointing, in particular, to how sociologists have interrogated it. They have drawn attention to power as a key aspect of the creation and maintenance of professional groups. To say you are a professional gives you power in society, but you also need access to power to be able to make this claim.

Professions are not timeless – each one has a history – and this is no less the case for social care practice. Analysis of the 'professional development project' (the complex process by which those in this occupation, and other interested stakeholders, have sought its recognition as a profession) highlights the importance of language and 'discourse'. This chapter looks at the key terms and arguments needed to convince society that social care practitioners merit the label of 'professional'.

The chapter also considers how social care practice is being influenced by growing demands for 'accountability' from an increasingly managerial state. This situation might lead to new ways of thinking about being a professional that are centred on responding to the demands of employers and regulators. These different threads come together in the concept of 'professionality', which has implications for social care practitioners.

There is more than one way of being professional. A typology of 'professionalisms' for social care is outlined, not as a way to divide up the existing workforce, but rather as a set of suggested strategies that aspiring social care practitioners may, individually or collectively, adopt. The chapter questions the very usefulness of the term 'professional', and puts forward the possibility that we are entering a 'post-professional' era. If this is the case, what are the implications for those now entering, or already within, this occupational field?

SOCIOLOGY OF THE PROFESSIONS

Fundamental to an assessment of professionalism and social care practice is a critical analysis of the term 'profession'. Professionalisation is a process whereby an occupational group can claim special status and power for itself. We recognise that certain occupational groups, in particular doctors, lawyers and priests, have traditionally enjoyed high levels of respect and status in society and also considerable power, both over their own lives and over the lives of others. Their status is generally reflected in significant levels of influence and, often, income and wealth. But how can we critically understand this process? How do certain activities, individuals or occupations come to be associated with the label of 'profession'? How does this change over time, and why is it that professionals tend to be highly favoured in our society?

Sociologists have long been interested in the professions. An early analyst of the phenomenon, pioneer sociologist Émile Durkheim (1858–1917), saw the development of professionalism as a way that the personal power and status of certain individuals and groups could be balanced against the needs of society. Professionalism was a trade-off: certain individuals could enjoy the status of being a professional, but they agreed to be bound by certain ethical principles and a measure of accountability to society (Aldridge and Evetts, 2003: 548).

The sociologist Max Weber (1864–1920) argued for a more critical approach. He saw professionalisation as a means by which those with power and status could limit the ability of others to access them. Professionalism is thus a form of 'social closure'. Those who enjoy privileged membership of a professional group can make it very difficult for others to join them, for example through establishing long and expensive courses of study, limiting the numbers admitted, discriminating against certain categories of people (such as women or members of particular religious groups) or creating difficult and complex bodies of knowledge that people must master (such as having to learn Latin or complex mathematics). This model of professionalism reflects the Western experience of the traditional 'learned professions' of religious ministry, medicine and law.

The American writer Eliot Freidson (1923–2005) was the dominant socio-logical analyst of the professions for over forty years. His primary work, *Profession of Medicine* (1970), was followed by further discussions of the topic (1990, 1994, 2001) that responded to criticisms of his initial analysis and amended his theoretical and empirical approach. Freidson sought to make the concept of profession a central one in sociology and his work has been highly influential.

Another major contributor to the field (especially concerning the medical profession) is British sociologist Robert Dingwall, who has published a collection spanning over three decades of his writings on professions (Dingwall, 2008) and who continues to work on the topic. Anyone wishing to explore the sociology of professionalism should start with the work of the above writers.

More recently the sociology of the professions has sought to reflect the contemporary world of work, typified by managerial control, the importance of 'knowledge work', more precarious careers, financial pressure and increasing calls for accountability to external players such as corporate structures, the public and the state (Evetts, 2012). Some writers have discussed a fundamental change in the nature of professions, and even suggest that we are entering a 'post-professional' age (Burns, 2007).

TRAIT APPROACH

There have been many attempts to provide a checklist of the qualities or attributes that turn an ordinary occupation into a profession and the people who engage in it into 'professionals'. For example, Scottish residential care expert Margaret Lindsay (2002) bases her definition of the term on a series of interviews with members of the 'general public'. They came up with a set of defining characteristics of professionalism, which are listed in Table 4.1.

Table 4.1. Defining features of a 'professional'

Feature	What it means	Questions for social care
Learning	Professionals have specific expert skills and knowledge, and knowhow; training is long and demanding and it requires hard work to build up the expertise required	What specific knowledge and skills do social care practitioners have?
Attitude	Professionals have a calling or a vocation; there is a moral dimension and a sense of duty to others; this requires an active role in society	Do social care practitioners exhibit a vocation? Do they act in society to further their profession?
Responsibility and autonomy	Professionals have responsibility for what they do and are personally accountable for their work; they have a high degree of autonomy and have to exercise judgment	Are social care practitioners autonomous? Are they accountable to society as a whole?
Public image	Professionals are highly regarded and trusted by the public; they command trust, respect, even awe	Are social care practitioners held in high regard by others in society? Do they enjoy status and respect?

Source: Lindsay (2002: 76–7)

This approach to the analysis of the professions is referred to as the trait approach and it focuses on the attributes, or traits, of the profession itself. Williams and Lalor (2001: 77) present one such list, broadly reflective of the literature within this approach. Thus, they say, a profession displays:

- Ownership of a recognised body of knowledge exclusive to that profession, with development of new knowledge through research.
- Self-government through a body that sets and monitors its own standards of practice.
- Control of training and recruitment.
- Monopoly of practice in its own field of work, with registration by the state.
- Conformity to moral and disciplinary codes of behaviour.
- Autonomy of practice and greater individual accountability.
- A public ideology of service to a client group.

Criteria similar to these have been widely used by many other writers to assess and judge the extent to which an occupation can be said to be a profession. They are useful in pointing to some of the strategies that occupational groups have undertaken, but many contemporary writers argue that the trait approach is no longer adequate for understanding professionalism. Nevertheless, it remains an influential way of thinking about professions. It also continues to be adhered to as a strategic map by many occupational groups that seek enhanced power, influence and status through the attainment of 'professional' status (Burns, 2007; Brock, 2013).

Contemporary analyses, in arguing against this checklist-type approach, stress the importance of seeing professionalisation as a dynamic and complex process or even as a form of social 'game'. Professionalisation must be viewed as a result of interaction between groups in society (Craig, 2006: 15–16). Whether or not nurses can call themselves professional, for example, is not just about what nurses themselves do, but is an outcome of their interaction, as an occupational group, with other groups such as medical doctors, legislators, patients, the media and hospital managers. If Irish social care practitioners are to attain professional status, it will be as much a result of their interaction with senior civil servants, social workers, health service line managers, CORU (the registration board) and – crucially – the broader 'lay' public (Dingwall, 2008: 11) as it will be due to the content of social care practice itself.

CONSTRUCTING PROFESSIONALISM

What might this more dynamic analysis of professionalisation look like? Initially, it must focus on the strategic activities that an occupational group can engage in to increase its social standing and power (Evans, 2008). Such strategies may involve claims by a group to possess particular types or levels of commitment and skills or knowhow. Freidson (1990: 3) suggests that professionalism has two key meanings. First, it 'represents a more than ordinary commitment to performing a particular kind of activity' – the notion of 'vocation' voiced by Margaret Lindsay's interviewees. Second, it refers to 'the productive labor by which one makes a living, a full-time occupation that entails the use of some sort of specialized skill'

– Lindsay's 'learning'. Only when these two attributes are combined, suggests Freidson, do we find a distinctive 'profession'. To apply this analysis, a person might be very skilled at hairdressing, but we do not think of this occupation as a 'vocation'. Similarly, a person might be a very dedicated carer, but we may not define them as 'professional' unless they have a particular type and level of training and education.

Freidson makes the further important point that in the contemporary world a particular profession cannot be thought of outside of the specific and distinctive institutions of society. This argument has been further developed by researchers who focus on the organisational and institutional basis of contemporary professionalism. Thus, one cannot be an intensive-care nurse without the institution of the modern hospital; or a lawyer without the system of legislation, courts, tribunals and so on. By extension, it can be argued that it is impossible to be a professional social care practitioner unless you are connected in some way (perhaps as an employee or as a consultant) to an institution that provides social care services. We can see that, from Friedson's perspective, any occupational group that claims professional status must be able to: (1) demonstrate access to a specialised area of skills or knowhow; (2) link into an institutional basis in society; and (3) appeal to some higher level concept of altruism, service or 'vocation'. Clearly, this is quite a challenge.

Another distinctive aspect of 'professional' occupations is that, compared with most others, workers have a high level of control over the terms, conditions and goals of the work they do (Freidson, 1990: 14):

> The occupational group determines whom it recruits, how they shall be trained, and what tasks they shall perform. It has a monopoly in the labor market over a specific set of tasks, an exclusive jurisdiction. Furthermore, members of the occupation have the exclusive right to evaluate the way their tasks are performed and the adequacy of the goods or services their work produces. Neither lay executives in work organizations nor individual consumers have authority over the performance and evaluation of professional work.

For Freidson, it is this level of control and autonomy in relation to work that distinguishes professionals from other types of occupations. In practice, most professionals now work in and for organisations – from legal partnerships to global managed care corporations – and this shapes the nature of their everyday practice (Evetts, 2010). The notion that they are free from external control is now less tenable, although they may continue to have considerable freedom of action within an organisation. This institutional dimension helps us to link the analysis of professions with the broader study of work.

Another important commentary that relates to issues of professional power comes from feminist writers who have stressed the gendered aspect of profession-alisation. The profession of medicine, for example, was at least partially founded on a process of replacing 'folk' knowledge about healing, largely maintained and used by women, with 'professional' knowledge that was exclusively the property of men. Thus, the female occupation of midwife has come to be dominated by the male-centred practices of obstetrics and gynaecology (Ehrenreich and English, 2010). The issue of gender is particularly important when looking at care-related professions, which have long tended to be dominated by women; it is also important to understand how caring professions (and occupational groups that are not thought of as professions) are shaped by intersecting relationships of gender, class and ethnicity (Duffy, 2011).

Overall, Freidson (1990: 9) sees professionalism as a positive force in contemporary society, particularly inasmuch as it provides a 'third way' or logic between government regulation on the one hand and the unfettered free market on the other. A crucial dimension that professionalism supports, according to Freidson, is a strong element of trust. Neither the free market nor a system of bureaucratic control, he suggests, can produce the unique relationship of trust that exists between professionals and their clients. Yet, recent decades have seen these trust relations coming under threat, as a number of professional areas have been riven by scandals of abuse, incompetence and dishonesty. Examples in Ireland include the problems in relation to the blood transfusion service (O'Carroll, 1998), the so-called Neary case involving Our Lady of Lourdes Hospital, Drogheda (Inglis, 2008) and numerous cases of child sexual abuse within the religious and teaching professions (Commission to Inquire into Child Abuse [Ryan report], 2009). A key element of the maintenance of professional status is about repairing such trust relationships; any 'new' profession will have to actively build trust from a more sceptical public.

We can see, then, that any occupational group aiming to pursue a 'professionalisation project' faces a complex task. As well as defining a specific field of knowledge and gaining a high level of autonomy and control, it must also link to key institutional sites of power in society. In addition, it must develop and sustain more ephemeral and intangible sets of relationships and values related to vocational commitment and trust with clients or users as well as the broader public. This is where language – or discourse – becomes crucial.

DISCOURSES OF PROFESSIONALISM

Discourse refers to talk and written text, and the contexts that produce and control these. In relation to the analysis of professionalism, discourse could range from interviews with professionals, to media presentations, to training manuals or educational programmes. In the organisational setting, it might be job descriptions, codes of ethics or the records of disciplinary hearings. Aldridge and Evetts (2003) suggest that professionalism has become a way that both workers and their managers talk about work practices – a process that can have benefits, and drawbacks, for each. They argue that, above all, 'professional' has entered the English language as a generic term that represents something good (2003: 555):

The discourse of professionalism is now used as a marketing slogan in advertising to appeal to customers, in recruitment campaigns and company mission statements, in organizational aims and objectives to motivate employees, and has entered the managerial literature and been embodied in training manuals.

As Freidson (1990: 2) had earlier pointed out, 'professional' is 'an ambiguous [term], used more often symbolically and globally than precisely and concretely'. As a term, it is highly desirable – it makes workers feel better about what they do – but employers and managers may also use it to exercise control over employees' behaviour. For example, professional workers can be encouraged to work harder and longer. They may be told that, as 'professionals', they should stay at work until a job is finished instead of knocking off at five o'clock, or they can be expected to bring work home at the weekends or during holiday periods. There is evidence that an increasing number of jobs entail this sort of open-ended commitment ('always on'), especially in the services sector (Gregg, 2011: 46).

Following the work of French writer Michel Foucault (1926–84), Aldridge and Evetts (2003: 556) argue that professionalism today has much to do with self-discipline and self-management. The successful employee is one who self-consciously fits into an occupational hierarchy, where 'the community of fellow workers and the hierarchy of positions in organisations and other workplaces (such as peers, superiors and juniors) constantly reiterate and reinforce this sense of self and position as well as appropriate behaviours and work decisions and choices'.

Much of 'being a professional' is to become accepted, by one's peers and the broader public, as working within a distinctive occupational community and having and expressing a professional self-identity (Costello, 2005). There is much talk now of the professional 'role' and even of 'professionality' (Evans, 2008). This suggests that issues of personal and professional identity are becoming increasingly linked in contemporary society, and the role of the 'managed self' is an important theme in the recent sociology of work (Southwood, 2011). Increasingly one is expected to subsume one's personal identity into one's work, which has important implications for professionals' self-management, but also for their wellbeing. As Craig (2006: 21) notes, 'when professionals identify so intimately with their work, it can be almost impossible to "switch off" when it is time to go home'. The result can be high levels of work-related stress and potential burnout: a phenomenon well known to those in the social professions (Maslach, 2003) and increasingly spreading to other occupations (Gregg, 2011).

The discourse of professionalisation is sometimes deliberately used to effect change in organisations and occupations. This is often linked to new forms of organisation; to legislation and regulation; to a greater emphasis on formal education and accreditation; and to new forms of technology, such as computerisation. To be professional is to be open to change, even to welcome it, and above all to be flexible. Change can be a difficult and conflictual process: 'an occupational identity crisis may follow, emerging as discontent particularly on the part of older and more experienced groups of workers' (Aldridge and Evetts, 2003: 556). This may become a major issue in the professionalisation of social care practice in Ireland and elsewhere, as newer, degree-qualified practitioners work with, or compete with, less formally qualified but more experienced workers. It is also an issue as job boundaries become blurred and occupational identities less secure. In all these examples, professionalisation is constituted through language – in how people use the term. But this use of language is always social: it involves negotiation and a struggle for power between different groups. The concept of profession can be deployed towards particular strategic ends. When a group embarks on such a strategy, it is involved in a 'professional development project'.

THE PROFESSIONAL DEVELOPMENT PROJECT IN SOCIAL CARE PRACTICE

Hallstedt and Högström (2005: 18) suggest that all occupations in the field of welfare 'are fighting for the right to call themselves professions'. In effect, they are aiming to emulate the more 'established' and prestigious professions, especially those in the medical field.

In the Irish context, Farrelly and O'Doherty (2005: 81) refer to the 'slow and tortuous process' of the professional development project in social care. In the early 1990s sociologist Pat O'Connor (1992) suggested that, in Ireland, the prospects for professionalisation in what was then called 'child care' were not high. Not long after, Crimmens (1998: 314) referred to the training of social care workers in Ireland as a 'professional qualification'. By the end of the 1990s Gallagher and O'Toole (1999: 78) identified the issue of professionalisation as 'central to the development of social care work' but argued that development of a 'coherent professional identity' was stymied by a lack of internal unity, fragmentation across qualification levels, diverse client and administrative settings, a changing role and exclusion from key policy-making structures in the bureaucratic professional hierarchy of state welfare services (1999: 83). In 2001 Williams and Lalor saw that 'the profession [of residential child care] is presently at a young stage in its development' (2001: 73), but by 2005 Farrelly and O'Doherty concluded that 'the promise of official and public definition and acceptance of social care work has [now] become a reality' (2005: 81). Does this mean that the professional development project in Irish social care has been finalised? And if so, who has been responsible for pursuing it?

Hallstedt and Högström (2005: 18) argue that the three main sets of actors in the professionalisation project are practitioners, academic institutions and the state. It is worth examining how these different sectors have engaged in the process in Ireland, where, arguably, the emergence of a professional discourse has not been the result of extensive organisational activity within the occupation itself. The representative body for social care practitioners, the Irish Association of Social Care Workers (IASCW), has historically tended to be fragmented, unrepresentative and relatively ineffective as an organisation (Byrne, 2005) and has not been able to sustain a push towards professional status. The social care managers' organisation, formerly the Resident Managers' Association (RMA) and now the Irish Association of Social Care Managers (IASCM), has been better organised and more reflective of its membership base. Through its conferences, publications and involvement in state-sponsored consultative groups, it has had a greater impact on the professionalisation process. In the educational field, the representative body, the Irish Association of Social Care Educators (IASCE), has been active since 1998. IASCE members have carried out research on topics related to professional development, facilitated discussion on the issue at conferences and supported the production of the first textbook in the field – this one. Its journal, *Irish Journal of Applied Social Studies*, has carried a number of articles related to the academic and professional development of social care practice. Development has also occurred in social care practice curricula and in 2010 IASCE worked with the Higher Education and Training Awards Council, now part of Quality and Qualifications Ireland (QQI), to develop awards standards for social care work (HETAC, 2010).

In 2010 the three representative bodies came together to form Social Care Ireland (SCI), a body that seeks to represent and develop the whole of the social care sector. SCI has been active in the organisation of conferences; in working with the Health and Social Care Professionals Council (CORU) on the issue of registration; in making submissions to government; and in linking practitioners, students and educators. It has yet to achieve any discernible public profile; for example, it had minimal public impact during the Children referendum of 2012, even though the issues under discussion related directly to the work of social care practitioners.

Arguably the most influential occupational groupings have been the major trade unions that represent social care practitioners (IMPACT and SIPTU, which have been successful in significantly enhancing the salaries and conditions of their members) and major employers (such as the health service and some in the non-governmental sector, which have established minimum standards of qualification, at degree level, for practitioners in some employment sectors).

The state remains the strongest influence on the social care professionalisation project in Ireland. In November 2005 the most significant piece of legislation to date in relation to the professionalisation of social care practice, the Health and Social Care Professionals Act 2005, was signed into law. The background to this legislation, and its possible implications, are explored in detail in Farrelly and O'Doherty (2005). Nevertheless, at the time of writing in 2013, the statutory registration of social care practitioners is still some distance away.

The professionalisation project in social care practice in Ireland has been relatively weak. Those in the occupation have not coherently pursued professionalisation and it has largely been left to employers and unions to shape the occupational landscape. The education sector has been influential to a limited degree, but has only recently been included in major institutional discussions and decision-making processes. The main impetus has come from the central state, in the form of proposed registration, but this is proving to be a very slow process. In light of these factors, it could be said that the professionalisation project in social care has been less than successful, although it remains the case that social care practitioners in Ireland are better educated, are more generously paid and have superior career structures when compared with those in many other Western countries.

KEY ISSUES

The remainder of this chapter examines some key issues in relation to the professionalisation project in more detail. These include the problem of defining 'social care practice'; the content of such practice; the relationship between the professionalisation project and broader issues of institutional change; and the counter-discourses that express themselves as resistances to professionalism. The chapter closes with a suggested typology of ways that social care professionalism may be developing and considers the possibility that we are entering a 'post-professional' era.

The challenge of definition

Social care work has been defined in the British (Banks, 2004) and European (Lorenz, 1994) contexts as one of the 'social professions'. In the Irish context, it has become an increasingly complex field to define, as discussed in the first chapter of this book. From a clear point of departure in the provision of care in defined institutional contexts (reformatories and industrial schools, and large centres for people with disabilities), social care practice in Ireland has evolved into a loosely linked set of practices that spans youth work, residential care, community child care, project work, educational work, community development and aspects of therapeutic practice. This apparent lack of homogeneity may well pose a barrier to an emergent profession of social care practice.

As Farrelly and O'Doherty (2005: 84) point out, there is a blurring of boundaries, as 'traditional points of demarcation are less credible as a result of the changing circumstances surrounding the education, training and deployment of qualified social work and social care practitioners'. Petrie et al. (2005: 2) note, in the English context, that 'borders and relations between different types of services are changing, workforce issues are to the fore, and there is a desire to find new approaches'. There is a convergence between social work, social care practice and youth and community work, but at the same time a fragmentation of roles as new job titles and occupational identities are created (such as various types of project and community-based work). Interprofessional and interagency work may be on the increase (Pollard et al., 2005) but, at the same time, the nature of the individual 'professions' involved is less clear.

In the European context (particularly in Scandinavia, Germany and the Netherlands), the term 'social pedagogy' points to a certain set of traditions, practices and professions (Kornbeck and Rosendal Jensen, 2011, 2012; see also Chapter 2 of this book). Social pedagogy is itself a somewhat amœbic term, having 'joint contents with many other occupational groups such as educational workers, social care workers, youth workers, child welfare nurses, welfare nurses, and animators' (Hallstedt and Högström, 2005: 29). The history of the term varies in different societies, and the divisions between social pedagogy/care practice and social work, and the relations between them, vary in different countries. These divisions may be breaking down, as suggested by Van Ewijk (2008: 10): 'the time of defending territories and insecure professionals appears to be over and replaced by a more positive attitude towards . . . a common identity of social professionals'.

As discussed in Chapter 3, in North America the field is commonly referred to as child and youth care (CYC) and focuses on the welfare of children and young people – other professional groupings direct their efforts at people with disabilities or other client categories. The basis of CYC can be found in a multiplicity of locations: in religious-run orphanages, in the 'fresh air' movements of the nineteenth century, in the state correctional facilities for deviant and criminalised youth and in residential centres for indigenous young people, especially in Canada. Since the 1950s CYC has seen the emergence of professionalising strategies. The CYC approach tends to be individualistic, therapeutic and case-based. As with social care practice in Ireland, CYC has extended from its residential base into community-based activities and strategies.

In Ireland, Farrelly and O'Doherty (2005: 84) suggest that 'the necessary expansion of education and training routes . . . has in turn generated a professional social care project concerned with determining the combination of theories, practices, methods, organisations, responsibilities and other features that characterise . . . social care work'. This refers to the internal activities that are helping to coalesce the discursive constructions of social care practice (production of textbooks such as this one; founding of Social Care Ireland). But there has been little external discussion; for example, there has been no forum where the relationship between social care practice and social work can even be named, let alone debated. This situation may change now that the two fields are co-located under the umbrella of CORU and subject to similar regulatory processes.

Social care practice in Ireland developed as a range of activities that people carried out within and for institutions, such as residential centres, the health service and voluntary bodies. With professionalisation has come a breaking of the nexus with specific organisations. The professional care practitioner can now potentially be a 'free agent', who can offer a portfolio of experience and who can lay claim to a certain range of competencies. The content of social care practice then becomes a much bigger issue. It is no longer a question of 'Who do you work for?' but 'What do you do?' and, perhaps more importantly, 'What can you do?' and 'What are you willing to do?'

Ultimately, a feature of care work is that it is replete with uncertainty, ambiguity and unresolved (and perhaps irresolvable) tensions. Schön (1991a) argues that this is a feature of all professional practice: it eludes the attempts of technocratic rationality to 'pin it down'; he says (1991a: 19):

> . . . professionals have been disturbed to find that they cannot account for the processes they have come to see as central to professional competence. It is difficult for them to describe and teach what might be meant by making sense of uncertainty, performing artistically, setting problems, and choosing among competing professional paradigms.

This raises challenges when the arena of professional practice encounters the powerful discourses of managerialism and performativity.

Performativity and institutional reform

The 'content' of social care practice is just one of the complex factors that shape the professionalism discourse. Such practice takes place in a range of institutional contexts. The social professions in general are very much determined by the activities and structures of the contemporary welfare state; indeed, the 'social professions' are an important link between civil society and the state.

'Traditional' notions of professionalism are increasingly open to challenge. Part of this is due to the increased climate of 'risk' that pervades aspects of contemporary society. Dent and Whitehead (2002: 1) suggest that part of the social pressure that is helping to shape professionalism is a 'loss of faith, trust and sense of order, an increased perception of risk'. This may particularly be the case in Ireland, as suggested earlier, with a succession of high-profile 'failures' of professionalism in, for example, the religious, political, medical, planning, judicial and business arenas.

The state is neither a monolith nor a static entity. In recent times there have been major shifts in how contemporary states conduct their business. A powerful discourse has emerged, derived at least in part from the globalised business sector, that refers to concepts such as the 'new accountability', 'joined-up thinking' and 'modern management' (Banks, 2007; Dewe et al., 2006). The ideologies of 'efficiency' and 'accountability' have been reinforced in Ireland and across the world by the impact of the global economic and fiscal crisis.

In Ireland, the penetration of business and managerialist discourse has been explicitly expressed through the Strategic Management Initiative (SMI) of the Irish government, and more recently through the Public Service Reform Plan. These initiatives have been translated into the activities of a wide range of state departments (such as the Department of Children and Youth Affairs) and agencies (such as the Social Services Inspectorate). Farrelly and O'Doherty (2005: 87) suggest that 'managerialist practices and thinking' are impacting in a negative way on social work practice in Ireland. In recent years overt managerialist and technocratic approaches have been expressed through monitoring bodies such as HIQA (Health Information and Quality Authority) and the Centre for Effective Services (effectiveservices.org).

Such state initiatives, found in all developed economies, impinge on and help to shape definitions of 'professionalism'. The effects are contradictory, as Banks (2004: 34–5) points out:

> On the one hand these moves towards standardising practice can be seen as advancing the professional project insofar as they have resulted in clear definitions of the purpose and nature of the work of the occupations . . . regulation of entry and standards of conduct. This could be seen to advance the credibility, status and public trust in the occupational groups. On the other hand the standards and controls have been initiated by the state, and although practitioners have had a role in their development, their room for manoeuvre has been somewhat limited.

For Dent and Whitehead (2002: 1), accountability is now all-pervasive: 'the professional has no escape from being managed nor, indeed, from managing others'. The consequence is a 'culture of performativity', where the rewards go to those who can demonstrate that they can perform in relation to a range of discourses: flexibility, reflexivity, teamwork, lifelong learning, market orientation, managerialism and entrepreneurialism. Such attributes are often couched in the language of 'competencies' (the ability to do something well using necessary skills and knowledge) that can often be quite narrowly and instrumentally expressed (Miller, 2008), but can also be constructed in more holistic and imaginative ways (CoRe, 2011). Professionals must be prepared to be subjected to performance measurement and competitive assessment according to various modes of calculation – often administered by their peers. The successful professional must be able to live and perform within these discourses.

Some practitioners see a conflict between managerialism and professional autonomy, expressed in terms of 'deprofessionalisation', where it is felt that the decision-making function is being taken away from those involved at the coalface in favour of managers who may not be practitioners (Clark, 2005). Here, the processes of regulation and managerial control serve to remove professional discretion from practitioners, replacing it with adherence to more abstract rules and procedures defined by external bodies. At best, this may be expressed as working in accordance with evidence-based practice; at worst, deprofessionalisation may require practitioners to act in ways they would not want or that may not be in the best interests of those they work with. There is considerable debate as to whether deprofessionalisation has taken place in the social professions. While it is clear that they may be increasingly subject to regulation, especially by the state, it can also be argued that this is at least partly a consequence of the greatly increased power of social professionals, including social care practitioners, to determine others' lives. In other words, if social care practice is closely regulated, this is indicative of the greater power of social care practitioners, not a sign of their weakness.

It is perhaps more likely that we are seeing the emergence of strategies of 'soft bureaucracy' and 'soft coercion' (Sheaff et al., 2003), whereby professional groupings are dominated through 'sophisticated management strategies' that operate on the basis that 'experts' accept limitations on their autonomy. 'Soft coercion' is often based on responses to perceived threats to an organisation from the state, competitors or the legal system. It involves 'technically legitimated rules of professional practice which regulate the individual professional's work' and, ideally, 'control is exercised by a supervisory stratum from within the ranks of the profession itself' (Sheaff et al., 2003: 421). One such strategy may be the move towards 'evidence-based practice', discussed in Chapter 9.

The powerful discourses of accountability and efficiency give rise, of course, to discourses of resistance. There are tensions here. Part of the notion of 'social profession' expresses a relationship, indeed perhaps an obligation, to 'society' – a relationship of accountability. After all, many social professionals are quite literally described as 'public servants'. Yet for many, the demands of employers seem to be taking precedence over the welfare, needs and respect of service users. Agency values, translated into detailed procedures, can come to dominate the work at the expense of professional values relating to respect for service users, confidentiality and so on, and the scope for professional judgment based on expertise and professional values seems to be seriously constrained by the new accountability requirements and external control (Gradener and Spiers, 2006).

Banks (2004: 140) points out that there is 'an identifiable strand of reluctance towards moves to professionalise' in the social professions, as this can involve the creation of increased distance between practitioners and their clients. This point connects back to the issues of asymmetry of power mentioned earlier. As Banks suggests, 'professional culture' can be a way that distinguishes 'us' from 'them', marking out 'our way of doing things' (based on our values, language and methods of working) from 'their way of doing things'. This conflict may run counter to more egalitarian and inclusive occupational discourses, such as anti-oppressive practice and 'person-centred care'.

The new professionals?

Based on the discussion in this chapter, I propose a fivefold typology of professionalising strategies that may be adopted by social care practitioners. It is not suggested that any single professional care practitioner falls easily into one category or another – rather, these strategies or styles may be adopted by or may be reflected in the actions and attitudes of those who define themselves as professionals.

- The *manager/practitioner* buys into the 'new accountability' and the 'audit culture'. Relates closely to state and organisational projects for change, restructuring and reform. Endorses concepts of accountability, self-management, competition and performativity. May also favour 'evidence-based practice'.
- The *traditional professional* tends to be modelled on the established professions, in particular medicine and social work. Focuses on content of knowledge, especially in terms of academic material. Endorses technical rationality in Schön's (1991a) sense; endorses the boundaries that surround, contain and 'protect' the professional group; is collegial and group focused. Is anti-managerial and sees accountability as an unwarranted intrusion into personal and professional autonomy.
- The *reflexive professional* is person- and client-centred rather than group-focused. Sees the 'self' and work on selves as the basis of professional work. Has a therapeutic and individualistic bias. Favours flexibility and indeterminacy. Is opposed to rigid structures, externally mandated competencies or checklists.
- The *democratic professional* is community-focused and consultative, 'works with collectivities, is participatory and acknowledges a primary responsibility to users' (Banks, 2004: 44). Leadbetter (2006) refers to the professional who works within 'postindustrial public services, which are more collaborative, networked and distributed'.
- The *entrepreneurial professional* is opportunistic, network-focused, project-focused. Is non-organisational but can use organisation as a resource. Is individualistic and eclectic. Is a strategic, flexible, portfolio worker.

Further research in the field of social care practice is required to establish the extent to which this categorisation is justified in the Irish context, and whether it helps us to better understand the self-definitions of care practitioners.

POST-PROFESSIONALISM?

New Zealand sociologist Edgar Burns (2007) argues that the focus on professions per se is outdated. Rather, he suggests, it is important to shift the focus away from the attributes and fortunes of specific occupational groups towards a broader analysis of occupations in the context of broader theoretical ways to understand contemporary society. This he calls 'post-professionalism'. It is an approach that echoes many of the themes discussed in this chapter: a focus on discourses of professionalism; an analysis of professionalising projects; a recognition of the increasing interpenetration of organisations and professions; and attention to what he terms 'professional normativity', which would involve a discussion of why we think professions themselves are a 'good thing', and what is 'good' about them.

As the number of potential 'professions' increases exponentially, and as the field becomes increasingly complex, it is no doubt worth reflecting on how useful the concept of 'professional' is in today's occupational and organisational landscape. It may be past its use-by date.

CONCLUSION

The issue of professionalisation has been around in Irish social care for a long time. It has begun to interest government, which is, however slowly, beginning to pay more strategic attention to the range of social care occupations and settings. The trade unions that represent many social care practitioners have used the concept in order to improve the pay and conditions of their members. Employers use the term in recruitment advertisements.

It is crucial to the future of social care in Ireland that practitioners themselves engage seriously with the concept of professionalism and begin to discuss what it might, or should, mean. Are social care practitioners seeking to become another type of social worker, nurse or some other favoured 'professional' group, or are there other models that can provide a more liberating and, perhaps, empowering form of professionalism? How might this be achieved? Or should practitioners dispense with the term altogether? And if they did, what might replace it? The social care practitioners of the future will be the ones to help determine the future of social care.

Part II

5

Psychological theories of child development

Áine de Róiste

OVERVIEW

Developmental psychological theories offer the social care professional a rich repository of different perspectives from which to consider and support human development. This chapter examines three main sets of theories: theories of cognitive and language development (Piaget, Vygotsky); learning theory (Skinner, Bandura); and theories of socio-emotional development (Maslow, Erikson, Bowlby). In the closing section, Bronfenbrenner's ecological theory will be introduced as a model that enables the integration of psychological, sociological and other theories to help us understand human development and behaviour from a holistic, multidisciplinary standpoint.

THEORIES OF COGNITIVE AND LANGUAGE DEVELOPMENT

Cognitive development refers to the advance in thought processes across child-hood, while the specific process through which children come to understand and express language is described as language development. These processes are described in the theories outlined below.

Piaget's constructivist theory

Jean Piaget's (1896–1980) theory of cognitive development is a 'domain-general' theory in that advances in one area of cognitive ability are associated with progress in other cognitive abilities. This contrasts with 'domain-specific' theories (for example, Fodor, 1992), where development is seen to vary across different cognitive abilities and areas of the brain.

For Piaget (1959), cognitive development is a series of stages, each with distinct qualitative differences in thinking. This development is underpinned by genetic maturation and thus is more rooted in 'nature' than 'nurture'. Piaget was a 'constructivist', seeing children as actively 'constructing' their own development. Mental schema (representations, sets of perceptions, ideas and/or actions that go together) initially develop through sensorimotor activity (thought being seen to develop from action) and are the building blocks of cognitive development. The processes of assimilation (taking material into the relevant mental schema in the mind from the environment) and accommodation (an alteration or difference made to mental schema to fit in the new information acquired via assimilation) contribute to the further development of these mental schema and are central to the advance of all cognitive abilities.

Across the stages, thinking becomes more logical and abstract with the achievement of key milestones, including object permanence, conservation, decentring, diminished egocentrism, increased symbolic representation and meta-cognitive understanding (these milestones will be explained below). Research into object and spatial categorisation (how we categorise objects and spatial relations such as above/below and in/out) supports this developmental trend towards increasing abstraction (Quinn and Eimas, 1997).

Piaget's stages of cognitive development are:

1. Sensorimotor stage (birth–2 years)

This stage is divided into six sub-stages:

a. Reflexive stage (0–2 months): simple reflex activity such as grasping, sucking.
b. Primary circular reactions (2–4 months): reflexive behaviours occur in stereotyped repetition, for example, opening and closing fingers repetitively.
c. Secondary circular reactions (4–8 months): repetition of interesting change actions; for example, kicking feet to move a mobile.
d. Co-ordination of secondary reactions (8–12 months): responses become co-ordinated into more complex sequences with intention. Achieves object permanence (realising things exist even when no longer visible).
e. Tertiary circular reactions (12–18 months): discovery of new ways to achieve the same consequence; for example, pulling a cloth to get a toy on it.
f. Invention of new means through mental combination (18–24 months): greater symbolic thought by symbolising action sequences before real actions are shown. Responses now arise to symbols, such as a parent putting on a coat (symbolising the parent's imminent departure).

2. Pre-operational stage (2–7 years)

Language (verbal representation) is now used to represent objects (thinking about an object without the object being present). However, understanding is still not 'firm', as the appearance or perceptions of objects (how they look) dominate a child's judgment of them. This is apparent in how children classify objects; for example, a child grouping together all the green blocks regardless of shape or all the square blocks regardless of colour. The child grasps some logical concepts but still does not 'decentre', focusing attention on one aspect of an object while ignoring others (centration). Children are still not able to see situations from the perspectives of others. Play becomes more symbolic and imaginative rather than being just simple motor play.

3. Concrete operational stage (7–11 years)

The child now thinks in a logical, concrete way but is still concerned with the manipulation of objects as opposed to ideas. Thinking shows conservation (realisation that objects remain the same even when they are changed about or made to look different) and classification (the child can classify objects and can order them in series along a single dimension such as size). Thinking is less egocentric than before, with the child showing a greater capacity to see the world as others do and to empathise. In play, there is more evidence of co-operation and the understanding of games with rules.

4. Formal operational stage (11+ years)

In this stage, thinking is more flexible and creative, with irony and sarcasm now shown. Scientific thought incorporating the systematic testing of hypotheses and logical thought about abstract propositions are in evidence. Thinking becomes more abstract and greater ability to reason is shown, with greater attention to the hypothetical and to the future. A child is now less likely to immediately accept one answer to any given question as true and is more likely to see other possible answers (Glaser, 1984). Symbolically, the child can think in terms of proportions, abstract processes and propositional logic and can do algebraic manipulation. Metacognitive understanding (reflection on one's own thinking) is shown in terms of greater self-awareness and self-reflection.

Piaget's theory has made a momentous contribution to our understanding of the development of children's thinking. It has provided a frame of reference, a body of concepts and a series of research experiments with which to examine intellectual development. At a practical level, Piaget's theory has influenced teaching, emphasising 'discovery learning' and a child's 'readiness to learn' in class planning.

Criticism of Piaget's theory has been levied at its narrow focus on reasoning and logic and lack of attention to other facets of thinking, such as creativity and intuition, which may develop at different rates (indicative of domain-specific theories of cognitive development). Still others oppose the principle of the stage-based progression in cognition and criticise Piaget's theory for neglecting the role of individual differences (thinking styles, IQ) between children, as well as social (instruction), cultural (social values, the mass media) and contextual factors (Goswami, 2001; Kuhn et al., 1988; Vygotsky, 1978). For example, propositional logic (based on propositions – true or false statements), indicative of formal operations thinking, is lacking in cultures with no formal schooling, implying that some features of this stage are not universal but depend upon culture (Case and Okamoto, 1996; Suizzo, 2000).

The methodology of Piaget's research has also been criticised in that most of his research was based solely on observations of his own children and his research experiments were not easily understood by children. More 'meaningful', 'real-life' versions of his experiments have found children to show cognitive abilities much earlier than Piaget's research indicated (Keating, 2004).

Vygotsky's social-constructivist theory

Lev Vygotsky's (1896–1934) theory emphasises social interaction and cultural tools, as opposed to Piaget's emphasis on the child's independent constructive actions. According to Vygotsky (1978: 57), 'Every function in the child's cultural development appears twice: first, on the social level, and later, on the individual level; first, between people (interpsychological) and then inside the child (intrapsychological) . . . All the higher functions originate as actual relationships between individuals.'

The key role of social interaction in Vygotsky's theory can be seen in his concept of the 'zone of proximal development' (ZPD), a level of development attained when children engage in social behaviour. Full development of the ZPD depends on social interaction, as the range of skills developed with adult/peer guidance surpasses what can be attained alone. Instruction, guidance and encouragement are features of the ZPD: children who cannot solve a jigsaw puzzle on their own, master it following interaction with a parent, sibling or peer. For Vygotsky, more experienced others are crucial to cognitive development. They show a child what to do, discuss activities and 'make sense' of what is going on. They also create 'cognitive conflict', challenging children to progress in their thinking (Tolmie et al., 2005). Bruner's (1993) concept of 'scaffolding', where structured support is provided to help a child resolve a problem in how they think about or approach a task, relates to this. Vygotsky's emphasis on the value of collaboration is found in 'peer tutoring' and group-based activities in the classroom (Littleton et al., 2004).

In contrast to Piaget, Vygotsky saw 'culture' as a powerful influence on development. Through social interaction, children internalise or 'take in' cultural tools (language, social rules, writing and number systems, computers) and use them in their thinking. Cultural developments, such as information technology, lead to changes in how people relate to the world. Thus, to comprehend the development of children in different cultures, we need to understand development in its cultural context. We should not expect all children to be computer literate or good swimmers by a certain age, but see development in all abilities, including these, as anchored in a child's cultural context.

Language development

Piaget and Vygotsky also differed on the topic of language development. For Piaget (1959), language developed as a consequence of symbolic development, an inner constructed capacity dependent upon maturation and based on genetics. Vygotsky (1978), in contrast, saw language as being developed primarily through meaningful social interaction. This development is assisted by 'motherese' (also now called 'parentese'), which is those features of talk that caregivers adopt when talking to an infant (such as higher vocal pitch, simpler speech content) and attention strategies (such as gestures).

Much debate exists over whether language development is genetically or environmentally determined. Chomsky (1968), Pinker (1994) and others argue for the innateness of language, based, first of all, on the universality of language (language being found in all human groups across different environments), and second, on the fact that children can produce language they have never heard before, meaning that they could not have imitated or learned it. In the words of Pinker (1994: 32), 'children actually reinvent language, generation after generation – not because they are taught to, not because they are generally smart, not because it's useful to them, but because they just can't help it'.

Research on brain structure and function shows that language is genetically based in the left temporal lobe. Neuropsychological studies of brain damage do, however, show that other regions of the brain can support language development, implying that environmental factors can lead to alterations in brain and language functioning (Neville et al., 1998). This finding suggests that the brain's ability to process language is more anchored in general brain structure and shaped by the environment than being genetically pre-wired in a specific brain region. Theories of first and second language acquisition are explored in Mhic Mhathúna (2012).

Milestones of language development

The first three years of life are particularly important for language development, as this is a period when the brain is developing and maturing. A language-stimulating environment at this time is one that is rich with sounds, sights and plenty of exposure to speech.

The newborn communicates by vocalising and crying for food, comfort and companionship. Soon after birth newborns show a preference for the human voice over other sounds and recognise the sound of the maternal heartbeat, and by four weeks they prefer their mother's voice to other female voices (DeCasper and Fifer, 1980; Mehler and Dupoux, 1994). This suggests that humans are born prepared for communication and language. As they grow, infants sort out the speech sounds (phonemes) that compose words and by six months they recognise the basic sounds of their native language. Infants also quickly develop a preference for language familiar to them, probably based on the prosody of the language (intonation, stress, rhythm). Head turning, looking/not looking and sucking are some of the behaviours used by researchers as indicators of infant preference, as they are controlled by infants from birth. For example, infants will adapt their sucking on a 'dummy' to hear their 'preferred' language, that is, the language they are familiar with (Christophe and Morton, 1998).

As the jaw, lips, tongue and vocal tract mature, an infant is able to make controlled vocalisations (Harris, 2004). Word comprehension begins at about seven months, with the child's own name, family members' names (including 'mummy' and 'daddy') and names of familiar objects (such as 'bottle' and 'teddy') being amongst the first words to be understood (Harris et al., 1995). By twelve months most children say a few simple words, with girls being typically ahead of boys, possibly because they are spoken to more but the evidence is not conclusive (Fenson et al., 1994). Children are probably unaware of the meaning of their first words, but soon learn these from the responses of others. Bruner stressed that children associate words with people, objects and steps of a routine, so words acquire a social meaning. There is a strong correspondence between what a parent says and what is happening with gaze direction, head turning and pointing used by adults as 'cues' to refer to something being spoken about (Harris et al., 1983).

Table 5.1 provides an approximate guideline to the typical milestones of language development. Caution needs to be exercised, however, in applying these to children, as many factors are known to influence language development. Poor health, sensory problems, birth order and communication patterns in the home all influence the language milestones exhibited by any child.

Table 5.1. Language milestones

Birth to 6 months
- Vocalises sounds of pleasure and displeasure (giggles/fusses).
- Makes noise when talked to.
- Sounds begin to be used communicatively.
- Watches a face when it speaks.

6–11 months
- Babbles (ba, ma, da) with syllables (canonical babbling).
- Understands no-no.
- Tries to communicate by actions/gestures.
- Reduplicated babbling (8 months).

- Tries to repeat sounds spoken to him/her.
- Variegated babbling (ba-da, da-de).

12–17 months
- Points to objects, pictures, people.
- Says two to three words to label a person/object.
- Follows simple directions given with gestures.
- Answers simple questions non-verbally.

18–23 months
- Points to simple body parts, e.g. nose.
- Says eight to ten words.

- Asks for common foods by name.
- Makes animal sounds, e.g. moo.
- Pronounces most vowels and begins to combine words.
- Understands simple verbs, e.g. 'eat', 'sleep'.

2–3 years
- Knows about fifty words.
- Knows pronouns, e.g. 'you', 'me', her, 'him'.
- Knows adjectives, e.g. 'happy', 'sad', 'big'.
- Answers simple questions.
- Begins to use plurals, e.g. 'shoes', and verbs in past tense ('ed').
- Speaks in two- or three-word phrases.

3–4 years
- Identifies primary colours.
- Uses verbs ending in 'ing'.
- Can describe use of simple objects, e.g. 'ball', 'fork'.
- Expresses ideas and feelings.

- Enjoys rhyme and language absurdities.
- Uses consonants in sentences.

4–5 years
- Says about 200–300 different words.
- Understands spatial concepts, e.g. 'behind'.
- Answers why questions.
- Understands complex questions.
- Uses irregular past tense verbs, e.g. 'ran', 'fell'.
- Describes how to do activities, e.g. painting.

5–6 years
- Engages in conversation.
- Sentences can be eight or more words.
- Understands time sequences (what happened first, next).
- Uses imagination to create stories.
- Describes objects.
- Names opposites and days of the week.

LEARNING THEORY

Learning theory arises from the school of psychology called behaviourism, which emphasises the study of what is observable in people: behaviour. Behavioural psychologists identified different ways in which people (and animals) learn, which are the core of learning theory.

Classical conditioning

Classical conditioning is where learning arises through association. Ivan Pavlov (1849–1936) identified classical conditioning from his experimental work with salivating dogs. Pavlov (1927) found that dogs automatically salivated to food and he called this an 'unconditioned response' reflecting an 'unconditional reflex'. The unconditional stimulus (food) automatically elicits an unconditional response (salivation); the term 'unconditional' is used as the response to the stimulus happens naturally. Pavlov then looked at what happens if something is associated with the presentation of food. Pavlov rang a bell (a neutral stimulus) just before presenting an unconditional stimulus (UCS), such as food, that unconditionally evoked a response (salivation). After a number of times, the neutral stimulus, termed the conditioned stimulus (CS), came to evoke the same response (salivation) on its own without the UCS. Thus, the dog came to associate the bell's ring with food, reacting in the same way (salivating), after repeated exposure to the bell and food combination, to the bell on its own as to the food. The dog had learned to salivate in response to the bell. Pavlov called this a 'conditioned response'. When the CS (bell) is presented without the UCS (food) following it, the dog learns over time that the bell is no longer associated with food and stops displaying the conditioned response (salivation). Pavlov referred to this as 'extinction', the conditioned response having become 'extinguished' (see Figure 5.1).

Figure 5.1. Classical conditioning

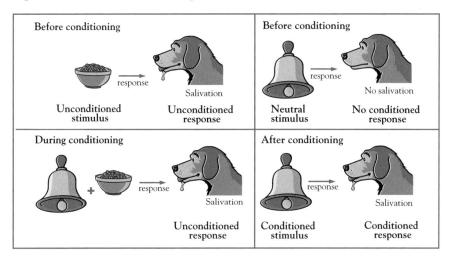

These observations were then extended to explain how humans learn, even including the learning of fears and phobias. The learning theorist J.B. Watson (1878–1958) conducted an infamous study with an eleven-month-old boy called 'Little Albert'. Watson found that the child came to fear objects through their association with something unpleasant (Watson and Rayner, 1920). In this study, a rat that previously did not induce fear in Albert was shown to Albert in conjunction with a loud banging noise, and after a number of pairings the rat alone induced fear in Albert. This experiment showed that emotional responses could be conditioned, or learned.

Operant conditioning

Another type of learning is operant conditioning, where an association is formed between a behaviour and a consequence. B.F. Skinner (1904–90) coined the term 'operant conditioning' as a type of learning in which behaviour is influenced by its consequences. Consequences have to be immediate or clearly linked to the behaviour for the learning to occur. Anything that increases a behaviour is a 'reinforcer', while anything that decreases it is a 'punisher'. Four possible consequences follow on from any behaviour (Skinner, 1953):

- Something good can start or be presented, resulting in an increase in the behaviour (positive reinforcement).
- Something good can end or be taken away, resulting in a drop in or reduction of the behaviour (negative punishment).
- Something bad can start or be presented, resulting in a drop in or decrease in the behaviour (positive punishment).
- Something bad can end or be taken away, resulting in an increase in the behaviour (negative reinforcement).

In positive reinforcement, a behaviour is strengthened by the consequence of experiencing something positive. For example, if a child receives a sweet as reward for doing a household job, the child's behaviour of doing household work is increased. Another example is providing positive reinforcement (rewards) once certain behavioural goals (not showing inappropriate behaviour) are achieved, such as a trip to the cinema once x number of inappropriate behaviours are not shown in a set time period.

In negative reinforcement, or 'avoidance learning', a particular behaviour is strengthened by the consequence of stopping or avoiding a negative condition. For example, someone driving a car too fast and receiving a speeding fine learns not to drive so fast in order to stop this negative consequence from happening again. Negative reinforcement increases a behaviour by ending or removing something bad or aversive. Someone is rewarded by feeling better, increasing the likelihood that they will repeat the behaviour that was occurring when the 'bad event' ended or was avoided.

When something bad is removed or avoided, relief is often felt, so another way to think of negative reinforcement is that you are providing relief, which makes it an example of positive reinforcement – thus positive and negative reinforcement can be confused. This behaviour highlights 'internal reinforcers', which are difficult to identify and assess, but play a role in learning. These may often lead to a behaviour becoming 'self-reinforcing' in that the unobservable, internal consequence of the behaviour positively or negatively reinforces that behaviour; for example, stress or boredom relief gained from screaming can reinforce the behaviour of screaming. Guilt, on the other hand, is an internal punisher, reducing the likelihood of the behaviour that elicited the guilt occurring again.

In punishment, a behaviour is reduced by the consequence of experiencing something negative. Negative punishment reduces a behaviour by removing something good, whereas positive punishment is something that is presented that reduces a behaviour. When used correctly, punishment is one of the most effective ways to end unwanted behaviours, but it does not teach what behaviour is appropriate (Baum, 2005).

Shaping is another contribution from learning theory seen in social care practice. Shaping (also known as successive approximation) is where a behaviour is encouraged by rewarding incremental improvements in that behaviour. For this to happen, the target behaviour is broken down into small steps that are rewarded as they become progressively closer to the target behavioural goal. This is often used in behavioural charts or reward systems and in teaching particular skills (Baum, 2005).

Observational learning

Another type of learning is where a person learns through observation: by seeing something done and seeing the consequences of that action. This has been called 'observational learning' or 'modelling'. Through observation, a person learns not only what to do, but also what actions produce positive or negative consequences and what distinguishes situations requiring different behaviours. The psychologist Albert Bandura (b. 1925) drew attention to the significance of observational learning (1965) and stressed that it has four steps (1977):

1. *Attention:* paying attention to a model's behaviour.
2. *Retention:* remembering the model's behaviour.
3. *Reproduction:* the physical ability to reproduce the behaviour.
4. *Motivation:* the desire to reproduce the behaviour, which is strongly based on what we expect to arise from doing the behaviour.

Bandura's seminal 'Bobo doll' experiments (Bandura et al., 1961; Bandura, 1965) showed the role of observational learning in aggression. Children who were exposed to a model acting aggressively towards a 'Bobo doll' were more likely to act aggressively towards the doll afterwards. When children viewed the aggressive behaviour being rewarded, ignored or punished, those children who saw the model being punished were less likely to display aggressive behaviour than the other children. These experiments stimulated much research into the impact of seeing violence. Some research suggests that viewing media violence increases the likelihood of aggression while also reducing human concern about the suffering of others and their sensitivity to the violence itself (Fraser et al., 2012; Huesmann and Taylor, 2006).

The significance of observational learning for understanding learning and the importance of modelling good behaviour in social care practice cannot be over-emphasised. Observational learning can also be used in peer tutoring as a way for some service users to show others what to do. This then means that it is not always the professional, but sometimes the service users themselves, who become the 'teachers', which is empowering. An example of the use of learning principles, including observational learning, is the Irish 'Parents Plus' parenting programme, which uses video modelling and other principles from learning theory (Quinn et al., 2007).

One of the primary limitations of learning theory is that it neglects the role of consciousness (expectations and interpretations) in learning. Cognitive behavioural therapy (CBT) explores the role of a person's thinking in various conditions such as depression and eating disorders, applying learning principles to their amelioration (Carr and McNulty, 2006a, 2006b).

Another development in the field of learning theory is 'relational frame theory', which takes a behavioural analysis approach to explaining language and cognitive development in terms of relational frames, networks and rules (Barnes-Holmes et al., 2004; Hayes et al., 2001). This theory focuses on how humans learn language through interactions with the environment and show relational responding, reflecting new generalisations of learned behaviour.

Applied behaviour analysis

Applied behaviour analysis (ABA) is the application of learning theory to establish a structured environment to enable children to communicate, learn and behave better. It is used in particular with children with autism spectrum disorders, conduct disorder and attention deficit hyperactivity disorder (ADHD) (Duffy and Healy, 2011; Snyder et al., 2006). In ABA, the child and instructor are observed and functional assessments of behaviours (what the child is trying to achieve or communicate in the behaviour) are undertaken to help understand the child's behaviour. Intensive individualised programmes are developed, focusing on literacy, problem solving, self-management and the teaching of individual behavioural repertoires (Cooper et al., 2007). In Ireland, a number of schools for children with autism spectrum disorders run a CABAS (combined applied behavioural analysis) programme.

THEORIES OF SOCIO-EMOTIONAL DEVELOPMENT

Socio-emotional development refers to how children develop in how they relate to others and express, understand and regulate their emotions. Many theorists emphasise the critical role that others play in children's growing ability to relate to others and to themselves and their own feelings. Consequently, social and emotional development are often considered in combination by theorists. The theories described below highlight the integral role played by other people in socio-emotional development.

Maslow's hierarchy of needs

Abraham Maslow's (1908–70) theory of motivation from a developmental pers-pective emphasises personal growth, with a person intentionally growing towards 'self-actualisation' or personal fulfilment. He proposed a hierarchy of needs (see Figure 5.2), with individuals motivated to progress from basic to higher needs.

Figure 5.2. Maslow's hierarchy of needs

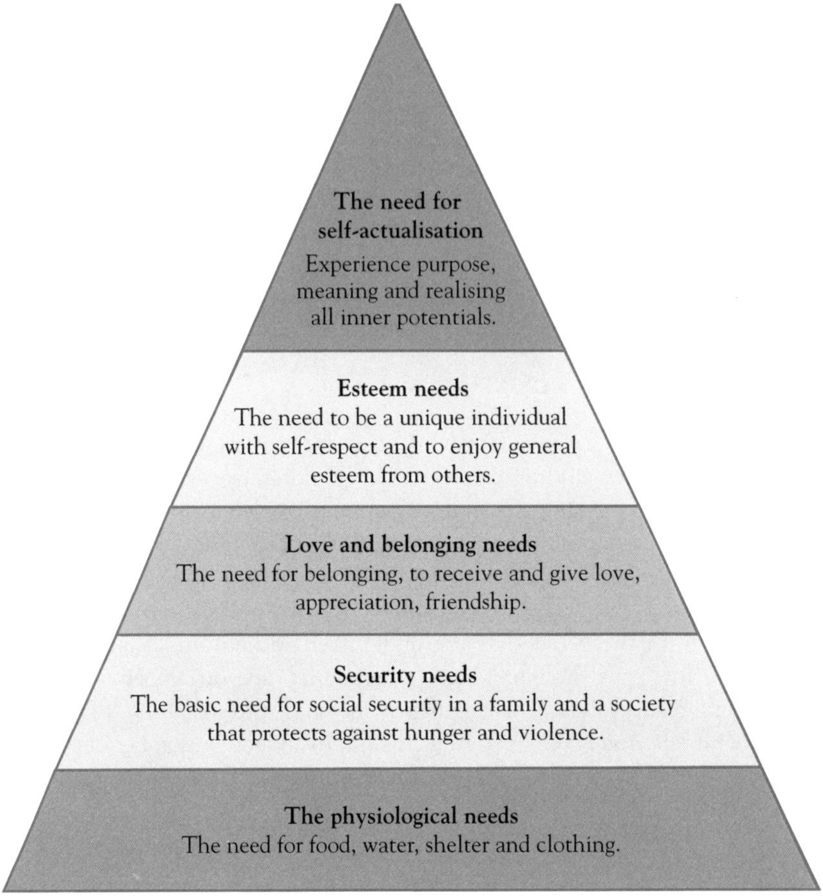

The need for
self-actualisation
Experience purpose,
meaning and realising
all inner potentials.

Esteem needs
The need to be a unique individual
with self-respect and to enjoy general
esteem from others.

Love and belonging needs
The need for belonging, to receive and give love,
appreciation, friendship.

Security needs
The basic need for social security in a family and a society
that protects against hunger and violence.

The physiological needs
The need for food, water, shelter and clothing.

Source: Maslow (1970)

According to Maslow (1970), the lower needs in the hierarchy are the most fundamental, so a person needs to address these before moving on to higher needs. Through research involving the biographical analysis of people who Maslow felt were self-actualisers, including Abraham Lincoln as well as people who were not famous, Maslow identified qualities characteristic of self-actualisers. These include humility and respect, creativity, self-acceptance (being as you are rather than being pretentious or artificial), acceptance of others (taking people as they are, not wanting to change them), differentiating what is fake from what is real, and comfort with autonomy while also enjoying deep personal relations with a few close people (rather than more shallow relationships with many). Self-actualisers also tend to have more 'peak experiences' (where a person feels euphoric, intensely happy and part of the infinite and the eternal) than the average person.

Maslow's theory is not without criticism. There is little evidence to support the hierarchy. Some theorists contend that esteem needs occur before love needs, in keeping with Erikson's theory (see below) that people progress through identification to intimacy with a need to form a strong sense of self and identity prior to being able to form a loving relationship (Goebel and Brown, 1981). Many people show qualities of self-actualisation yet have more primary needs unmet. For example, many famous musicians, artists and scientists, such as Beethoven, Rembrandt and Galileo, lived in poverty without their basic needs being met. Others reach fulfilment but then turn their back on their ability, thereby apparently putting a stop to their self-actualisation. Much criticism has also been made of how Maslow developed his theory. He selected a small number of people whom he identified as self-actualising, using his reading and interviews to determine what self-actualisation was, all of which is very poor scientific practice as it is open to bias and lacks reliability and generalisability.

For social care practice, this theory highlights the importance of addressing lower needs, such as reducing physical discomfort, tiredness or hunger, first, before trying to work on higher needs. Safety and security needs can be met by making people feel safe, having routines, protection from danger (perceived or actual) and by building up a relationship of trust. The concept of a 'secure base' from attachment theory is related to this – having a trusted person one can go to enhances a child's sense of safety and nurtures independence. Love and belonging needs can be enhanced by developing social skills, a social network and a sense of belonging to, for example, a group, place or organisation, and by supporting a child's relationships. Problems from past relationships also need to be addressed, such as a fear of abandonment or intimacy.

Esteem needs can be addressed by acknowledging a child's qualities and helping that child to identify and develop self-competencies. This might take the form of displaying a child's creative work of art or going to a concert or match in which they are participating. Respect can be shown by allowing children to make choices and by facilitating their involvement in the making of decisions that pertain to them. This approach is applied in 'person-centred planning' in care work.

Irish research by Timonen and O'Dwyer (2009) used Maslow's framework to gauge the met and unmet needs of a sample of adults in institutional care. They found that 'higher' and 'lower' needs are closely intertwined and mutually reinforcing and recommended that they should be accorded equal emphasis by care professionals.

Erikson's psychosocial theory

Erik Erikson (1902–94) was a neo-Freudian who developed a theory of psycho-social stages in personality development. Each stage is focused on a particular issue ('crisis') to be resolved and has a basic virtue or strength and a secondary virtue attained by a helpful balance between the extremes in each stage.

Erikson's (1970, 1980) stages of personality development are:

1. Trust versus mistrust (0–18 months)

The infant forms a loving, trusting relationship with the caregiver or deals with feelings of mistrust. The task is to develop trust without completely eliminating the capacity for mistrust. Through parental responses, the child learns to trust their own body and biological urges. Trust is lost and mistrust arises with abuse or neglect, while a false sense of trust arises if an infant is overprotected or overindulged, with no feelings of surprise and a lack of ordinary reality. With a proper balance between trust and mistrust, the child develops the virtue and inner strength of hope; the belief that things, even if not going well, will work out well in the end; and a trust in life, the self and others. If an infant is too trusting, the maladaptive tendency of 'sensory maladjustment' arises, whereby they become overly trusting, gullible and naïve. Excessive mistrust results in withdrawal, characterised by fear, depression and paranoia.

2. Autonomy versus shame/doubt (18 months–3 years)

The child focuses on developing physical skills (walking, grasping and rectal and sphincter control) but may feel shame and doubt. Autonomy refers to self-reliance and self-confidence, whereas shame and doubt refer to the emotions that undermine independence and self-confidence. Parental responses and encouragement of a child's growing independence enable a child to become autonomous. Parental behaviour that is too discouraging or pushy leads a child to doubt their own abilities and feel shame about their efforts at independence. If a child is given too little freedom or helped to do what they should do for themselves, they will feel that they are not good for much. A little shame and doubt are useful, as otherwise 'impulsiveness' occurs, that is, excessive wilfulness and recklessness. Too much shame and doubt leads to 'compulsiveness', where a child obsesses about everything for fear of making a mistake. A good balance between autonomy and shame/doubt leads to the virtue of 'willpower', including self-efficacy, or what has been called a 'can do' attitude.

3. Initiative versus guilt (3–6 years)

In becoming more assertive, the child takes more initiative, but this may lead to guilt. Initiative refers to feeling purposeful and the capability to devise actions with a self-belief that it is fine to do so, even if there is a risk of failure or being seen as stupid. Guilt, on the other hand, refers to feeling that it is wrong or inappropriate to initiate something oneself. Being encouraged to take a risk or chance and to engage in experimentation or adventure supports the development of initiative, as does curiosity and imaginative activities.

Guilt arises when children are given out to, told that they are a disappointment or know that their actions are disapproved of. A good balance is thus
needed between encouraging children to try things out while simultaneously
protecting them from danger. If there is too much initiative and too little guilt,
'ruthlessness' arises, where a child becomes exploitative and uncaring. Too
much guilt and too little initiative results in 'inhibition' – a lack of adventurous-
ness. A good balance leads to the psychosocial strength of purpose, where a
child is willing to take action and achieve meaningful goals.

4. Industry versus inferiority (6–12 years)

In dealing with learning new skills, the child risks feelings of inferiority and
failure. By 'industry', Erikson meant the development of competence, a sense
of self-efficacy in abilities, integral to the school experience. This refers to the
ability to do, to be productive, to apply oneself and to feel valued for one's
actions, skills or abilities. Children must learn that there is pleasure not only in
devising actions, but also in carrying these out, working by rules and towards
goals.

They must learn the feeling of success, in school or elsewhere. Experiences
of accomplishment lead a child to resolve this stage. If children experience
nothing but failure, with no development of their own capabilities, they
experience feelings of inferiority with low self-worth. Racism and sexism also
contribute to this, since if a child believes success is related to who you are
rather than to how hard you try, then why try?

According to Erikson, too much industry results in 'narrow virtuosity',
whereby children, such as child prodigies, spend all their energy and time on
one ability, associated with obsession. On the opposite side, too much inferiority leads to 'inertia', apathy and low self-worth. A good balance between
industry and inferiority, where a child develops and applies their abilities but
has enough inferiority to feel humble, leads to the virtue of competency.

5. Identity versus role confusion (12–18 years)

In trying to forge an identity, a young person must reconcile individuality with
a desire to belong to a peer group. This stage coincides with the Freudian
genital stage (puberty) and is the stage that Erikson wrote most about, as he
had a particular interest in identity formation. Identity refers to a sense of self
or individuality: how one sees oneself in relation to the world and to others in
it. In adolescence, young people strive to be part of a peer group, to 'belong',
yet at the same time seek to be individuals, distinctive in their own way.

Role confusion (an absence of identity and uncertainty about one's place in
society and the world) occurs when someone does not have a distinctive sense
of who they are and of their beliefs, opinions, values and individuality. If a
person has 'too much identity', they will be too self-important and narrow

minded, unable to recognise the perspectives of others, which is indicative of 'fanaticism'. A fanatic believes that their way is the only way. Too much role confusion leads to 'repudiation' – a person denies their need for an identity, cutting themself off and becoming 'lost' in a group that provides a ready identity. The virtue of fidelity (integrity to yourself) is achieved if this stage is successfully negotiated.

6. Intimacy versus isolation (19–40 years)

The person tries to become closer to others but may feel isolated. The focus is the forging of close relationships with family and a marital or sexual partner. Intimacy involves the ability to be close to others, as a lover, friend and so forth. To be intimate involves the reception and expression of love and the honesty and capacity to commit with others for mutual satisfaction. Conversely, isolation means feeling excluded from the life experiences of mutually loving relationships with feelings of loneliness.

Too much intimacy results in 'promiscuity', being sexually needy and becoming intimate too freely without any emotional involvement. Too much isolation results in 'exclusion', self-containment and the tendency to distance oneself and withdraw from love, friendship and community. 'Fear of commitment' is an example of immaturity in this stage.

Successful negotiation of this stage results in the virtue of love and being able to set aside differences and conflicts through 'mutuality of devotion'. It includes not only the love in a good marriage, but the love between friends and the love of one's neighbours.

7. Generativity versus stagnation (40–65 years)

The adult strives to give something to future generations but may become self-absorbed. Generativity refers to being productive, in work and other areas, as well as the unconditional giving of parental love for a child and contributing to future generations. It is a concern for the next generation and future generations and thus is less 'selfish' than the love present in the intimacy of the previous stage.

It is giving without the expectation of reciprocation. While raising children is one way of being productive, other ways include social activism, teaching, writing, invention, the arts and sciences – anything, in fact, that satisfies the 'need to be needed'. Stagnation is where intimacy turns inward in the form of self-interest and self-absorption, representing feelings of selfishness, self-indulgence and a lack of interest in future generations and the wider world.

Too much generativity results in 'overextension', where people are so extreme that they become too involved in something and leave no time for themselves, which ultimately undermines their generativity or contribution to the world, such as someone who takes on so many causes that they cannot effectively contribute to any particular one. Too much stagnation, on the other hand, results in 'rejectivity', characterised by cynicism. Successful negotiation of this stage results in the virtue of 'caring'.

8. Ego integrity versus despair (65+ years)

This refers to the development of a sense of oneself as one 'is', feeling fulfilment or, on the other hand, feeling a sense of despair about oneself and one's life. In this last stage, the task is to develop integrity and feelings of contentment with oneself and the world, with a minimal amount of despair and regret. Integrity means coming to terms with your life, and thereby coming to terms with the end of life. If one is able to look back and accept the course of events, the choices made and the life as one lived it, then death is not feared.

Most people in late adulthood experience a detachment from society through retirement or reduced participation, which can be associated with feelings of uselessness. Poor health and illness may compound such feelings, along with bereavement for the loss of spouse, friends and family, which understandably contributes to despair. Despair also includes regrets and wishing to be able to turn back the clock and have a second chance. In response to despair, some people become preoccupied with the past, when life was better, while others become preoccupied with regrets.

Successful negotiation of this stage leads to the virtue of wisdom, a generosity of spirit characterised by a non-judgmental acceptance, tolerance and calmness of mind. Assuming too much integrity results in 'presumption', characterised by conceit and pomposity, which is superficial and blocks the attainment of true insight and acceptance. Too much despair blocks acceptance and integrity, resulting in 'disdain', a lack of fulfilment and a contempt of life (one's own or anyone else's).

Maladaptive tendencies and malignancies represent extremes in response to the 'crisis' of each stage, reflected in behavioural traits manifested to various degrees, as opposed to being clinical problems.

Erikson's research relied heavily on biographical case studies that lack scientific credibility. Critics suggest that his theory fails to accommodate individual change in, for example, identity across the lifespan. Nevertheless, it is widely applied in the social care sector in a variety of ways, such as in personal development groups, therapeutic work and even supervisory relationships (Ruch, 2005). Along with other socio-emotional theories, these theories are also drawn upon in experiential group work and personal and professional development modules in social care degree programmes.

Attachment theory

John Bowlby's (1907–90) attachment theory is based on ethological and psycho-analytic ideas and emphasises the immense role of primary attachment relationships upon psychological development and social relationships across the lifespan. It identifies infants as relation seeking and emphasises the influence of relationships on personality, social development and psychopathology.

According to Bowlby (1952), attachment is a biologically based 'behavioural system' and is a need as fundamental as the need for food and water. It is visible in proximity-seeking and separation-protest behaviour. Attachment formation develops from six months to three years and is not dependent upon physical care, but rather develops through interaction with the primary caregiver(s), typically the parents. Warmth, responsiveness, sensitivity and consistency are critical features of parenting that enhance attachment formation.

Comforting interactions that involve relaxation after raised arousal, such as comforting a crying infant (arousal–relaxation cycle), and pleasurable inter-actions, such as face-to-face games and cuddling (positive interaction cycle), also contribute to attachment formation (Bowlby, 1969, 1978; Holmes, 1993). These all assist children in learning to regulate their own emotions and in appreciating the emotional states of others.

A person's social and emotional development are anchored in their early attachment relationships because experiences of responses from significant others are the foundations of a child's 'model' of relationships and how the 'self' and relationship behaviour are thought and felt about (Lewis et al., 2000). How a child expresses and interprets relationships is shaped by their early attachments. For example, whether the relationship is experienced as positive, involving trust and love, or negative, involving the fear of rejection or abandonment. This inner organisation of attitudes, feelings and expectations about the self, others and relationships was called an 'internal working model' (IWM) by Bowlby (1973). More recent theoretical developments on this involve 'scripts' (typical action sequences and expectations associated with various events, activities and places) (Fivush, 2006; Waters and Waters, 2006).

According to Bowlby, an insecure primary attachment is characterised by a lack of trust, consistency and sensitivity, so the child comes to view others as hostile and untrustworthy and to see the self as inadequate and unworthy. Consequently, the child is likely to show poor social skills and to be distrustful. In contrast, a child with a secure attachment is more likely to be optimistic, positive and trusting in relationships, with good social skills (Lewis et al., 2000).

Interestingly, the national research study on children in Ireland, *Growing Up in Ireland*, looked at parent–child relationships in terms of some attachment-related aspects (such as separation anxiety) in their infant study (Williams et al., 2010). The research found high levels of attachment in respect of both mothers and fathers, with little variation according to socio-demographic characteristics. Lower family income was associated with a slightly higher proportion of mothers who reported that their child showed more features indicative of separation anxiety upon being left at child care. Any significant disruption in an attachment leads to feelings of grief and loss.

Rutter (1981) argued that Bowlby had confused maternal privation (children who had never received maternal care) with deprivation (children who had experienced a relationship with their mother but who had then lost it) and neglected attachment distortion (where the relationship is altered, for example through separation or divorce). While cases of maternal privation tend to show more problems, the consequences are more difficult to predict for cases of maternal deprivation and attachment distortion, as care from substitute others may ameliorate the effects (Howes and Hamilton, 1992). Thus, Bowlby may have overstated the case that it is not any and every separation from the primary caregiver that is harmful, but rather only certain types of separation and how they are handled (Rutter, 1995).

Mary Ainsworth and colleagues (1978) developed 'the Strange Situation', an observational procedure of mother–child and stranger–child interaction, classifying one-year-old children into different types of 'attachment strategies'. The procedure involves a series of episodes: mother and child are together; the child is left alone by the mother; a stranger enters and approaches the child; the mother returns and is reunited with her child. Attachment classification is based primarily on the child's observed proximity and responses to the mother during the reunion episodes.

The 'secure' attachment strategy is the most prevalent form. These children show a distinct preference for their attachment figure over strangers and trust their attachment figure's availability and responsiveness. The securely attached children also show better emotional expression and regulation, fewer behavioural problems and better social skills than their insecure counterparts (Ainsworth et al., 1978; Kochanska, 2001).

The second type of attachment strategy is 'insecure ambivalent-resistant', characteristic of 'chaotic parenting'. These children and their attachment figures tend to have a fractious relationship, tinged with anger and resentment. They are unable to predict the response to their attachment behaviours and so experience anxiety about their own safety and comfort. They show poor emotional regulation and tend to seek out, yet simultaneously resist, their attachment figures, which is indicative of emotional ambivalence (Graham, 2006b; Kochanska, 2001).

The third type is the 'insecure-avoidant' attachment strategy, characteristic of cold, rejecting parenting. These children are emotionally self-contained, with little emotional expression, and aggressively independent. They have learned to suppress their emotions and see intimacy as threatening.

The fourth type is 'insecure-disorganised' attachment strategy, where children show marked and pervasive fear in the presence of their attachment figure. It is fright but without a solution for the fright and these children often display a 'freezing' response. These children are at high risk for behavioural problems and this attachment strategy is characteristic of maltreatment and unpredictable early care (Ainsworth et al., 1978; Dozier et al., 2001; Main, 1995).

Caution must be exercised in the interpretation of these types, as every child is unique with a distinctive relationship context. These attachment types should thus be considered as a light to illuminate behaviour rather than as rigid fact. 'The Strange Situation' is also problematic, as it is culturally biased with questionable validity. Rather than labelling someone as (in)secure, it may be more appropriate to apply the label to the particular relationship (McMahan-True et al., 2001; Rutter, 1995). Children have different relationships with each parent and vice versa (Dunn, 1993) and adverse environments that predispose to insecurity usually include risk factors for later psychopathology. Thus, it may be these factors, as opposed to an insecure attachment per se, that underpin later problems (Dunn, 1993; Rutter, 1995).

In reviewing attachment theory, it is important to note that many of Bowlby's original ideas were reformulated by him and others. Rather than emphasising one primary attachment figure, contemporary attachment research sees children as having a hierarchy of attachment figures or an 'attachment network' of whom the mother is usually (but not necessarily) the most important (Holmes, 1993). After the mother may follow (in varying orders of importance) the father, grandparents, siblings, care minders and possibly pets or transitional objects. In the absence of the most preferred, the child will turn to the next most preferred. Children may also have different types of attachment relationship with different people (Kosonen, 1996).

Attachment theory has many important implications for social care practice, some of which were outlined in more detail in the first edition of this book (de Róiste, 2005). Attachment theory emphasises: the significance of early relationships for psychological development and for understanding why children (and adults) behave as they do in relating to others; the importance of supporting a child's sense of continuity in belonging to a family to which they feel attached and identify with; the role of grief and loss in how children respond to attachment disruption; and the significance of considering attachment history in therapeutic work with children who have any problematic attachment histories.

Graham (2006a, 2006b) outlines how a social care professional might work with children showing different attachment strategies in the family context. For a child with an avoidant strategy, this work focuses on building up a sense of safety and comfort, whereas for a child displaying an ambivalent-resistant strategy, it involves supporting the attachment figure to respond in reliable, consistent ways. With the child showing a disorganised strategy, professional work should focus on modelling parenting practices and helping the attachment figure(s) to control their own emotions when with their child.

Other psychological theories that relate to socio-emotional development and social care practice include Klein's object relations theory and the theories of Freud and Winnicott (Dennehy, 2006).

ECOLOGICAL THEORY

Bronfenbrenner's (1979) ecological model (see Figure 5.3) – or in its more recent inception, Bronfenbrenner and Evans's (2000) 'bioecological' model – provides a systemic framework in which to consider various psychological and sociological theories in respect of human behaviour and social events. From a developmental contextual perspective, child development is placed in a multi-layered socio-cultural context, with development seen as the culmination of many direct (genetic) and indirect influences (including culture) mediated through various 'layers' or systemic levels in the child's ecology. Children both act 'in' and 'on' their world and are influenced by: the timeframe in which they live (chrono-system); general cultural and social structures, such as economic conditions and cultural values (macrosystem); contextual factors influencing the child via others, such as the local neighbourhood (exosystem); and immediate relationships, such as parent–child and child–peer (microsystems), as well as the relations between these, such as how a relationship with a parent affects a child's relationship with a sibling (mesosystems).

Figure 5.3. Bronfenbrenner's ecological model

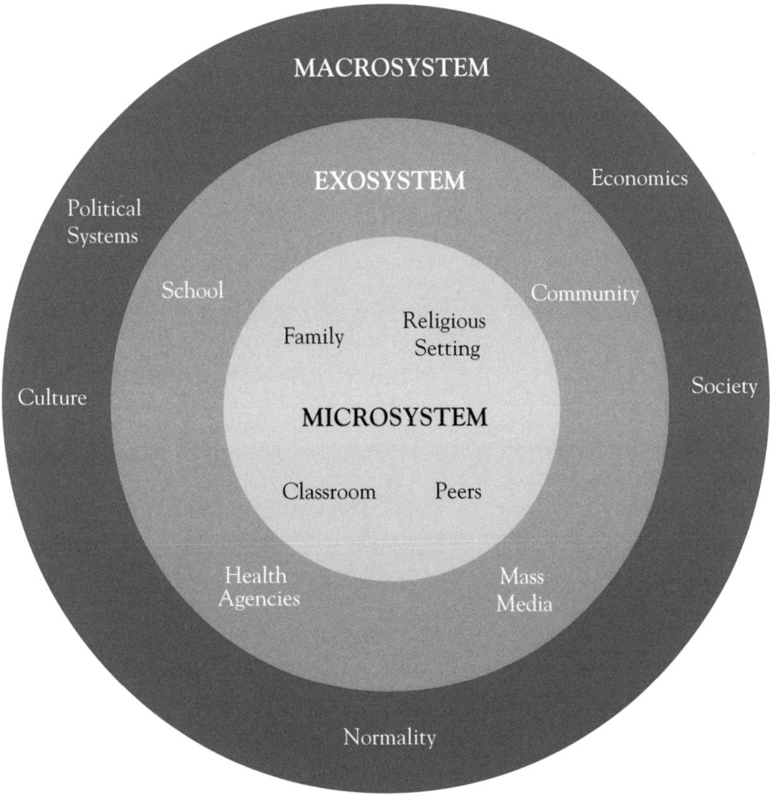

Source: Bronfenbrenner (1979)

Bronfenbrenner's model recognises that contextual variables may combine additively or multiplicatively to explain individual differences in child development, vulnerabilities and resilience. It helps in designing interventions with children, whether at a one-to-one level (microsystem) or at the broader systemic levels of the community and culture. It also ensures that attention is paid to what makes childhood a unique as well as a shared experience for each individual. Sociologically, it is useful as it facilitates links to be made between social institutions, structures, changes and events and childhood experience. Useful readings on this in an Irish context are Greene (1994) on 'Growing up Irish' and Smith (2012a) on sociological perspectives on childhood. Bronfenbrenner's model is used as a conceptual framework for the *Growing Up in Ireland* study and by the Irish Centre for Autism and Neurodevelopmental Research at NUI Galway (nuigalway.ie/ican).

CONCLUSION

This chapter has introduced some of the most widely used psychological theories that inform and guide social care practice. In conjunction with theories from other disciplines, these theories provide a reservoir of knowledge to understand behaviour, guide interventions and evaluate practice.

6

Equality: a challenge to social care

Majella Mulkeen

OVERVIEW

This chapter seeks to engage social care students and practitioners in an exploration of equality and inequality in Ireland. The space occupied by social care practitioners offers a unique opportunity to challenge inequalities, which is particularly important with the demise of the Celtic Tiger, the disappearance of the equality agenda from the public arena and the dominance in public discussion of economistic thinking.

This chapter outlines the case for a more equal society and shows how campaigns and groups have challenged inequality and how the government has responded to these challenges. It introduces the link between equality and care: because care work is not often considered as an equality issue. It offers a critique of current definitions of social care in order to explore models of practice that are more committed to challenging inequality and working towards a more equal society.

RECENT DEVELOPMENTS

Just a few years ago discrimination was a matter of public debate in Ireland, and had been since the passing of the first Employment Equality Act in 1998 and Equal Status Act in 2000. There were regular rulings from the Equality Tribunal on discrimination and the Equality Authority commented on and mounted challenges to discriminatory practices in the public and private sectors. Media coverage was not always positive but the issues of equality and discrimination were visible. Irish equality legislation and case law were impressive by European standards and the role of the Equality Authority in fostering a more inclusive and open dialogue about diversity in Irish society was widely recognised.

Although there was vociferous resistance to this agenda from significant parties in the media and powerful interest groups, equality-focused institutions provided a supportive backdrop to the work of the Equality Authority. The Combat Poverty Agency (CPA) identified and analysed the causes of poverty and provided a framework for addressing the issue, as well as an important independent critique of the record of successive governments. The National Consultative Committee on Racism and Interculturalism (NCCRI) spearheaded anti-racism work and had a key role in implementing the government's National Action Plan against Racism, as well as monitoring and responding to racist incidents. The Irish Human Rights Commission (IHRC) protected human rights by promoting awareness, providing education and training and recommending to government how human rights standards should be reflected in Irish legislation, policy and practice.

Then in 2008 and 2009 these organisations were either shut down completely or had their work severely compromised. Among the first government cuts at the start of the economic recession were those to the Equality Authority and the IHRC, whose budgets were reduced by 43 per cent and 23 per cent respectively. The NCCRI was closed at the end of 2008, the CPA in 2009, and in 2011 it was proposed to merge the Equality Authority and the IHRC. These moves were a significant blow to voices of dissent in Irish society. The official commitment to equality, diversity, human rights and ending poverty has been thoroughly undermined.

According to Crowley (2010: 112–14), among the factors that contributed to the demise of these agencies is a counter-cultural role that stood witness to inequality and discrimination in the midst of a wealthy society. Crowley also identified the resistance of the statutory sector to the equality agenda. In 2007 69 per cent of Equality Authority case files under the Equal Status Acts related to allegations of discrimination by people availing of public services and 49 per cent of case files under the Employment Equality Act related to allegations of discrimination by employees of public sector bodies. For Crowley, the hierarchical culture of the statutory sector did not sit easily with advocacy from its employees or the exercise of non-discrimination rights by those seeking access to public services.

Cutting funding to organisations that cause embarrassment or challenge the status quo, and enforcing contracts that prevent organisations or individuals from speaking out, is on the increase (Frazer, 2010). For example, the Charities Act 2009 does not allow an organisation that aims to advocate in relation to human rights to be registered as a charity. There is a consistent effort to suppress the voices of those who advocate on behalf of the marginalised. It is hard not to interpret the silencing of the equality organisations as part of a wider effort at political control. As with all efforts at political control there is resistance. Campaign and grassroots groups, such as Is Féidir Linn, Claiming Our Future and TASC, demonstrate the real desire for change in civil society.

EQUALITY AND SOCIAL CARE

By virtue of their role and the social groups with whom they engage, social care practitioners witness the impact of inequality on people's everyday lived experience. But it cannot be taken for granted that social care as a profession has a commitment to promoting equality. Evidence of the experiences of people with intellectual disability (Ryan, 1999), children placed in industrial and reformatory schools (Raftery and O'Sullivan, 1999), families living in poverty (McKay, 2007), people with mental illness (Crowley, 2003) and Travellers (Kenny and McNeela, 2006) demonstrates that high levels of inequality persist. Furthermore, social professionals charged with responsibility for the delivery of services can amplify the exclusion and oppression of the people they are there to 'serve'. Their power to act as gatekeepers, influencing the life chances of those they are engaged with, as well as the potential of the social professions to act as a site of resistance and empowerment, have been articulated by a number of writers (Adams et al., 2002; Duyvendak et al., 2006; Garfat, 1998; Knorth et al., 2002; Lindsay, 2002; Thompson, 2012).

DEFINING EQUALITY

What does equality mean, who is entitled to be treated equally and what goods or opportunities in life should be equally distributed? While many attest to a belief in equality, differences arise about how to define it, who should be equal to whom and in what circumstances. The concept is hotly contested. Many believe that inequality is natural and good for society. In 2005 then Minister for Justice, Equality and Law Reform, Michael McDowell, argued that inequality is necessary in a capitalist society (specifically Ireland) as it provides an essential incentive to work harder and achieve (Wilson, 2005). Of course, the strongest advocates of this perspective rarely experience the brunt of inequality themselves.

Douglas Jay (1962: 5) asked:

> Why should I have more right to happiness than you? . . . If we believe that all human beings have an equal right to happiness and a civilised life, then . . . we should seek to establish a society in which these rights are embodied. The ultimate ground for condemning inequality is that it is unjust, not that it causes resentment or envy.

This belief remains evocative today. Equality is a traditional idea: it has been a guiding principle behind political, economic and social reform in European and other countries for over two centuries. Political ideologies such as liberalism and socialism have placed equality at their core, even if they interpret the concept quite differently. Revolutions and wars of independence have been fought to banish centuries of privilege and inequality. Democratic systems of government are often couched in terms of 'equality for all'. For example, the Irish Constitution states in Article 40.1: 'All citizens shall, as human persons, be held equal before the law', and the Universal Declaration of Human Rights (1948) states: 'All human beings are born free and equal in dignity and rights' (Article 1).

Basic equality is the cornerstone of all egalitarian thinking: that at a very basic level all human beings have equal worth and importance and so equally deserve concern and respect (Baker et al., 2009). As concepts such as 'worth', 'respect' and 'concern' can be widely interpreted, definitions of basic equality usually include a list of minimum standards, as expressed in documents such as the Universal Declaration of Human Rights. They include, for example, prohibitions against cruel and degrading treatment, protection against violence and at least some commitment to providing for people's most basic needs such as food and shelter (Crowley, 2006: 2–3).

Liberal and radical definitions of equality

When discussion about equality moves beyond such basic definitions, different views emerge about who should be equal to whom, and what should be equalised. Two different perspectives are examined below: one is concerned with equality between *individuals* and claims that everyone should have equal *opportunities* in life and the other is concerned with equality between *social groups* and claims that everyone should have roughly similar or equal *outcomes* in their lives. The first is called the liberal, or equality of opportunity, perspective; and the second is the radical, or equality of outcomes, perspective.

Liberal equality

The liberal understanding forms the basis of how equality in Irish society is usually defined and has much popular support. It is primarily concerned with equality between individuals. As individuals differ in their aptitudes, interests and abilities, liberal egalitarians assume that inequalities between people are unavoidable and inevitable. Equality strategies in any society should aim to manage these inequalities in a fair manner. This is accomplished in two ways: by strengthening the minimum everyone is entitled to in a society and by providing fair and equal opportunity to access valued social goods, such as jobs and services. In practical terms, the government (or state) in a society provides a social welfare system that seeks to protect people from extremes of poverty when they can no longer work or are ill. It may also provide a minimum of education, health care and housing supports to citizens. This provision is often referred to as a 'safety net' and a state that provides this minimum is called a welfare state. Currently, many welfare states are effectively being dismantled by governments who want people to be responsible for themselves alone, with no state support.

The second tenet of liberal equality is that opportunities to compete in an unequal world should be governed by the principle of equal opportunity. This is the view that advancement in life is gained through individual effort. For example, success in the Leaving Certificate is attributed to the hard work and 'ability' of the individual and failure is associated with inadequate preparation or less ability. Ability is considered to be innate (one is born with certain amounts of it) and no reference is made to the social context of learning such as the supports and opportunities available to enable individuals to strengthen their 'innate' abilities (access to the Internet, books at home, money for grinds and so on).

This individualistic approach neglects disparities between social groups in their access to valued social goods such as education, health and employment. For example, access to such services is more difficult for people with impairments as they experience barriers and unfair treatment, which impact on the efforts of individuals to achieve, no matter how talented they may be. Even when barriers are removed, individuals may need a lot of support. In this way, equality of opportunity is limited in its ability to address deeply entrenched experiences of discrimination and inequality.

A third tenet of the liberal egalitarian perspective is respect for difference. Individuals and groups are different in their customs and beliefs and tolerance of such differences (as long as they respect basic rights) is embedded in freedom of conscience and opinion. Liberal equality holds that the basic arrangements of our society should be impartial among different beliefs, cultural customs, sexual orientation and so on (Baker et al., 2009). We should not exclude, harass or persecute people because of their perceived differences. For example, Irish society no longer makes it a crime to be a gay man, nor does it tolerate sacking women who are single parents, or agree with burning the houses of people who practise different religious beliefs. All of these practices were common in Ireland, some until quite recently. A liberal perspective has made tolerance of difference more acceptable and people are treated less harshly when they are perceived as different.

The dominance of liberal perspectives in Western democracies has contributed to strategies to prohibit discrimination and remove formal barriers to access for social groups that have historically been denied opportunities. For example, women were not allowed to register as students in Trinity College, Dublin until 1904, but even then restrictions on their access and movements remained until the 1960s. The 'marriage ban', which meant that women working in the Irish public sector had to resign on marriage, was not abolished until 1973. The criminal status of homosexuality was removed from the Irish statute book only in 1993, on foot of a ruling from the European Court of Human Rights. These changes are significant achievements. Prohibitions on discrimination and the legal requirement to implement equality of opportunity have contributed to greater equality in Irish society. Nevertheless, significant inequalities persist in Ireland, and globally, and liberal definitions of equality have failed to make significant inroads in this regard.

Radical equality

The notion of equality of outcomes is a more radical perspective and challenges the inevitably of inequality. It points to the fact that inequalities are generated by social structures that have been amenable to change in the past and can be shaped in an egalitarian manner in the future. For example, during the first half of the twentieth century in Ireland, many women who gave birth to a child outside marriage were sent to Magdalene laundries and their children placed for adoption. Children with intellectual disabilities were sent to institutions where they remained for the rest of their lives, with little attention given to their education or personal development. These approaches are unthinkable today as such inequality in the treatment of women and children is no longer acceptable.

The radical perspective on equality has outcomes rather than opportunities as its focus. It claims that provision of equal opportunities must lead to roughly equal outcomes for individuals in different social groups. From a radical perspective, persistent and significantly unequal outcomes for some social groups when compared with others suggests that certain groups are privileged and others disadvantaged. Irish society, for example, accommodates the able-bodied but not those with mobility or hearing or learning impairments. Individuals whose opportunities are shaped by the disabling nature of such social structures are likely to experience exclusion from the benefits accruing to income, education, employment and so on. This suggests that opportunities cannot be equally provided unless the distribution of power and privilege is examined. Central to a radical perspective is an emphasis on how social structures serve to privilege some groups and disadvantage others, emphasising the influence of social factors on people's choices and actions, rather than treating individuals as solely responsible for their successes and failures (Baker et al., 2009).

Strategies for equality within this perspective focus on a world where people's overall resources are much more equal than they are now, so that their prospects for a good life are roughly similar. This perspective seeks to massively reduce the current scale of inequalities. This does not mean a demand for sameness or mathematical equality, but for a society where the enormous inequalities between social groups are altered to ensure all people have genuine opportunities to develop their talents and abilities, regardless of gender, family background, ability levels, ethnicity and so on. It would involve a dramatic change in the distribution of income and wealth and in access to public services (Baker et al., 2009).

This perspective accepts that people differ in their talents and motivations and should be rewarded accordingly, but suggests that the privileges that accrue to some social groups are at the expense of other groups and cannot adequately be explained by the different talents and abilities of individuals. Thus, while there are many talented and able women in the paid labour force, privileges accrue to many men at the expense of women. This disparity cannot be overcome by the efforts of individuals alone. Instead we must examine how the social structure of masculinity operates to privilege men in work settings and how the social structure of femininity makes it more difficult for individual women to experience equality, despite their individual efforts. This is not a new idea; Tawney (1952: 57) put it succinctly:

> To criticise inequality and to desire equality is not, as is sometimes suggested, to cherish the romantic illusion that men are equal in character and intelligence. It is to hold that while natural endowments may differ profoundly, it is the mark of a civilised society, to aim at eliminating such inequalities as has their source, not in individual differences, but in its own organisation.

The third way that the equality of outcome approach contrasts with the liberal approach is in its approach to difference. It is critical of the liberal view that tolerating difference is sufficient. 'Tolerance' is viewed as problematic, as it sits easily with ignorance and contempt and can be viewed by the dominant group as a badge of superiority (Phillips, 1999). A radical perspective demands that difference and diversity be accommodated and celebrated rather than just tolerated. This does not mean it is wrong to criticise beliefs we disagree with. Since all cultures include oppressive traditions, none are above criticism, and this includes the dominant culture in any society (Baker et al., 2009).

In comparing the two perspectives on equality, I have focused on who should be equal to whom (equality between individuals or equality between social groups); how each perspective views society (unavoidably unequal or open to change); how resources should be distributed (the alleviation of poverty or a dramatic reduction in inequalities between social groups); how difference is viewed (tolerance or accommodation and celebration); and how equality is conceived (equality of opportunity or equality of outcome). In many respects, equality of outcome is a logical extension of the liberal perspective – it builds on its achievements but also seeks to address its shortcomings. In the following section I invite you to think about equality in terms of 'difference' and how it is linked to traditional understandings of equality as being concerned with the distribution of income and wealth.

EQUALITY AND 'DIFFERENCE'

Phillips (1999: 20) states that 'for much of the twentieth century inequality was associated with the distribution of income and wealth . . . equality was conceived as a substantially economic affair'. The rise of the feminist and anti-racist movements modified this significantly and in more recent years the relationships between equality and difference have moved centre stage in Western societies. This points to the complex nature of equality. Those who believe in a more equal society seek to have resources distributed more equally among social groups and individuals. Those with least access to a fair share of income and wealth are among those social groups viewed as 'different'. They share the experience of exclusion: people with disabilities; women; Travellers; black and ethnic minorities; people who are gay, lesbian or bisexual; the very young; and older people. For many, poverty exacerbates their exclusion (Combat Poverty Authority and Equality Authority, 2003).

Phillips (1999: 25) states that 'the notion that we make people equal by ignoring or suppressing their differences easily turns into a statement of inequality . . . the resulting emphasis on equality through difference is probably the most distinctive feature of contemporary thinking on democracy'. Calls for the recognition of difference have informed, for example, the provision of maternity leave for women and reasonable accommodation of people with disabilities. Recent Irish campaigns seek to establish legal recognition for same-sex marriages and an end to the discrimination experienced by same-sex and cohabiting couples in matters of tax and inheritance. The decision of An Garda Síochána to ban the wearing of turbans by Sikh members of the force while on duty (Honohan and Rougier, 2012: 84) and the legal requirement on employers and service providers to reasonably accommodate people with disabilities signify different opinions on how diversity should or should not be accommodated.

Parekh (2002: 240) notes:

> Equality involves equal freedom or opportunity to be different, and treating human beings equally requires us to take account both of their similarities and their differences. When the latter are not relevant equality entails uniform or identical treatment, when they are, it requires differential treatment ... Essentially equality involves full recognition of legitimate and relevant differences.

This way of thinking about 'equal treatment' is useful in highlighting the wide range of inequalities experienced by diverse groups in Irish society. It highlights how factors such as gender, disability, ethnicity and/or sexual orientation can undermine equal citizenship. While our society remains a highly unequal one, it is the duty of those committed to changing this situation to envisage a new alternative in the sense of a picture of a better society. This means identifying sites where resistance can be mobilised and concrete actions taken to generate equality (Baker et al., 2009; O'Connor, 2006).

MORE EQUAL SOCIETIES DO BETTER

Research by Wilkinson and Pickett (2009) maps levels of inequality among rich countries and demonstrates the impact of rising inequality. Per capita GDP is much less significant for general wellbeing than the size of the gap between the richest and poorest 20 per cent of the population (the basic measure of inequality the authors use). Among rich countries, the more unequal ones do worse according to almost every quality of life indicator. Whether the test is life expectancy, infant mortality, obesity levels, crime rates, literacy scores, even the amount of rubbish that gets recycled, the more equal the society the better the performance invariably is.

The research shows that the best predictor of how countries will rank is not the differences in wealth between them but the differences in wealth within them. Significantly, this pattern holds inside the United States as well, where states with high levels of income inequality also tend to have the greatest social problems (Runciman, 2009). The research shows that, almost always, Japan and the Scandinavian countries are at the favourable 'low' end of the inequality scale and the United Kingdom, US and Portugal are at the unfavourable 'high' end, with Canada, Australasia and continental European countries in between.

Crucially this has nothing to do with total wealth or even the average per-capita income (Hanley, 2009). European research also demonstrates that higher levels of inequality result in a lower level of economic prosperity, lower level of education and poor institutions that have more corruption, more political instability and are less democratic (Juul, 2011).

EQUALITY AND INEQUALITY: THE ROLE OF THE STATE

The dominant understanding of inequality in a society will shape action to address it and the extent to which equality can be realised. After the Second World War many Western societies began to address the persistence of economic inequality. This led to the development of welfare states that aimed to ensure a more egalitarian distribution of resources and there was a marked decline in socio-economic inequality up to the late 1970s. Inequality of household incomes fell in countries such as the US, France, Sweden, UK, Germany and Japan (Kirby, 2001: 5). Equality was the pervasive value of many such societies in this era. Then, from the late 1970s, an emphasis on market-led approaches to economic development and the slimming down of government – widely termed neo-liberalism – resulted in policy approaches characterised by targeting resources on the poorest and on programmes to integrate marginalised groups into the paid labour market. A poverty reduction approach gradually replaced socio-economic equality as the main distributional goal of public policy (Kirby, 2006).

Sen (1992, cited in Kirby, 2001: 9) identifies 'two implicit programmes' that inform discussions about how the state provides for its citizens: one based on the social welfare model and the other on social justice. The former is concerned with poverty reduction and selectively targets resources on the poorest sections of society. The latter is concerned with how to reduce inequalities in society as a whole and focuses on the universal provision of high-quality public services. This latter programme has its fullest expression in the development of social democratic welfare states such as Sweden, which 'pursue an equality of the highest standard, not an equality of minimal needs' and where 'services and benefits are at levels commensurate with even the most discriminating tastes of the new middle classes' and 'workers have full participation in the quality of rights enjoyed by the better off' (Esping-Andersen, 1990).

INEQUALITY IN IRELAND

Ireland is a country with a serious problem of socio-economic inequality. It had declining levels of consistent poverty alongside growing inequality during the boom times, but now has rising levels of consistent poverty and even greater levels of inequality. The Irish percentage of gross domestic product (GDP) spent on social protection (18 per cent) continues to compare badly with not only high spenders such as France (31 per cent) and Sweden (31 per cent), but also the

EU-15 average of 28 per cent, the UK (26 per cent), Greece (24 per cent) and Portugal (25 per cent) (Eurostat, 2009).

Between 1973 and 1994 the gap between the incomes of poorer and richer households in Ireland was narrowing. The decrease in inequality was slow and modest, but the trend was nonetheless positive. Then, as the boom took off, that trend halted. Inequality was maintained at relatively high levels over the boom years (O'Toole, 2008). In 2010 the average income of those in the highest income quintile was 5.5 times that of those in the lowest income quintile. This ratio had been 4.3 one year earlier, signifying an increasing level of inequality in income distribution (CSO, 2013b). The deprivation rate (those experiencing two or more types of enforced deprivation) was almost 23 per cent compared with just over 17 per cent in 2009. The deprivation rate for those at risk of poverty was 39.4 per cent in 2010 representing no statistically significant change from the 2009 figure, but the rate for those not at risk of poverty was 19.3 per cent, a significant increase from the 13.7 per cent rate a year earlier. Since 2007 the deprivation rate among this group has more than doubled (CSO, 2013a). Enforced deprivation refers to the inability to afford basic identified goods or services, such as two pairs of strong shoes, a warm waterproof overcoat, heat to keep the home adequately warm or furniture to replace worn-out items.

Ireland continues to lag behind not only other wealthy European Union states but also poorer states in its spending on social provision such as 'benefits for sickness and disability, old age, survivors of deceased persons, family and children, unemployment, housing and other forms of social benefit' (Eurostat, 2009).

Since 2009 Irish society has seen a catastrophic change in the economic and social climate, with spiralling national debt and unemployment rates at 15 per cent (late 2012); sharply increasing levels of inequality; and an austerity programme that has seen cuts in public services and increasing numbers of people living in consistent poverty. The 2012 update for the government's national reform programme (DoT, 2012) notes that from 2008 to 2010, those in consistent poverty rose from 186,000 to 277,000, an increase of almost 50 per cent, which was a result of 'almost a trebling of the unemployment rate from 4.5% in 2007 to 13.6% in 2010' and 'the fiscal consolidation on social welfare adult and universal child payment rates'.

The Organisation for Economic Co-operation and Development (OECD) and the United Nations (UN) have long pointed out that Ireland is among the developed world's more unequal societies. The UN (2007b) has ranked Ireland eighteenth out of nineteen OECD countries in the Human Poverty Index. Evidence from TASC demonstrates that when the basic tax and welfare changes from budget 2011 are examined for employees and for people reliant on state transfers, households on different income levels were affected in a significantly unequal way. Austerity measures in recent budgets have had a disproportionately negative impact on the living standards of people on lower incomes. Likewise, the available evidence shows women to be more badly affected by that budget than men (TASC, 2011).

Bell and Blanchflower (2009) show how unemployment leaves people stressed and unhappy. The psychological imprint of joblessness leads to loss of self-esteem, fatalism and loss of control over daily life, and is associated with a physical impact to health, heart disease and poor diet. While the social and personal cost of unemployment is shared very unevenly across communities, unemployment also causes an increase in general unhappiness and insecurity.

The evidence suggests that greater equality in the distribution of resources is important, given the level of personal and social stress and insecurity, the impact on general prosperity and on economic inequality in Irish society. Certain social groups have higher poverty rates than the rest of the population and experience higher levels of discrimination in their efforts to access employment and services. For many individuals in such groups, poverty, economic inequality and discrimination are inextricably linked. The positions of women, black and minority ethnic groups, lone parents, people with disabilities and children are bound up with economic indicators.

The response of civil society

The challenge to address poverty and exclusion in Irish society was met by agencies and campaigning groups emerging during the 1990s with unprecedented vigour. The women's movement, the disability movement, anti-racism movements and children's rights campaigns highlighted issues of poverty, unemployment, low pay and lack of participation as critical in achieving greater equality. They exerted a powerful influence on the direction of government policy.

Organisations such as the Irish National Organisation of the Unemployed; National Women's Council of Ireland; Forum of People with Disabilities; Pavee Point, the Irish Traveller Movement; and Age Action Ireland have worked for many years to provide innovative responses to need and to campaign for material improvements and greater equality for specific social groups. Such work was supported by the Irish state, a pioneer internationally in establishing agencies such as the CPA, NCCRI, the Equality Authority and the IHRC – all devoted to addressing major challenges in Irish society (Kirby, 2006: 112). Even if such pioneering has now been abandoned, it is in this intersection of sometimes contradictory and different emphases in government policy and commitments that a space emerges for action to promote equality by exposing contradictions and developing alliances for positive change. The state is a site of oppressive practices, but also contains sites of resistance where strategies to build a more egalitarian society can co-exist with policies that perpetuate inequality.

Three significant policy documents from the 1990s/early 2000s enabled the advancement of an equality agenda for significant segments of the population. A key strategy for organisations and groups campaigning for equality during this period was the targeting of resources to the constituent group and the enactment of anti-discrimination legislation:

- The Commission on the Status of People with Disabilities was set up in 1993 with the active involvement and support of a representative group of disability bodies and state agencies. It published its seminal report, A *Strategy for Equality*, in 1996.
- The Task Force on the Travelling Community's report set out the policy agenda in relation to Travellers (Government of Ireland, 1995).
- The Fourth World Conference on Women took place in Beijing in 1996 and Ireland signed up to a Platform for Action and set up a Gender Equality Monitoring Committee to monitor the implementation and recommendations of the Second Commission on the Status of Women (Government of Ireland, 1993). The Gender Equality Monitoring Committee produced its first progress report in 2002 (Government of Ireland, 2002).

Patterns of inequality

Discrimination and inequality follow clear patterns: economic, political, cultural and affective. Economic inequality arises from the unequal division of a society's resources between different social groups and ultimately between individuals. It takes the form of inequalities of income and wealth as well as of other income-related resources such as education, health and housing. Economic inequalities shape social class formations, where privileged classes have more resources, greater power, better working conditions and better access to education (Baker et al., 2009).

The comparative lack of political representation from many marginalised groups in Ireland signals the existence of significant political inequality. Such groups and individuals have minimal representation in local or national institutions charged with making or implementing decisions that impact on their lives. As then Minister for Finance Brian Cowen said in 2004, 'for many years the disability programme was at the end of the queue for resources. It did not benefit from the type of professional lobbying and support which acute hospitals and primary care programmes got from traditionally strong organised interests' (cited in Crowley, 2006: 121). The same could be said for many other groups.

At the level of cultural representation, there are inequalities in how 'difference' is understood and accommodated in Irish society. The status and respect accorded to different groups in a society are often manifest in the language used in the media or education to describe those constructed as 'different', whether on gender, disability, class, income, sexual orientation or ethnic grounds.

At the level of affective relations, it is a critical element of human existence that people have access to relations of love, care and solidarity. Individuals and groups who experience hostility, isolation and a removal of opportunities for caring relationships are subjected to inequality, as are those who carry a disproportionate burden of care work.

Social care practitioners witness these patterns of inequality in their daily work with individuals and families who struggle against poverty and discrimination. The face of inequality is familiar to them in their work in family resource centres; neighbourhood youth projects; with people with intellectual impairments living independently, in group homes or attending day centres; with people with physical disabilities struggling to establish or maintain independence; with children and young people looked after away from their family; with migrant workers; or with women as lone parents struggling to access support in their care roles. The question for social care practitioners is how they can promote a more egalitarian society in these settings. Clarifying what a more equal society might look like is a critical first step in a transformative approach.

WHAT WOULD A MORE EQUAL IRISH SOCIETY LOOK LIKE?

A more equal society is likely to be shaped by pursuing a radical perspective of equality with an emphasis on equality of outcomes. There is a need to promote a more egalitarian sharing of economic resources in Irish society, particularly in light of the links established earlier between group membership, inequality and poverty, and a variety of serious social problems and income inequalities. There is an appetite in civil society for greater income equality: TASC (2010: 1) research found that 91 per cent of people want the government to take active steps to reduce the gap between high and low earners; 16 per cent favour raising the minimum wage; 29 per cent support a maximum wage; and 49 per cent favour a combination of the two approaches. In addition, 35 per cent would be willing to pay higher taxes to fund improved public services.

As spending on social protection decreases, there is an increasing challenge for civil society to highlight this situation and lobby for change (Kirby, 2006). Social care practitioners have a particularly important role here, as they work with groups with the least access to economic resources. Access to power to influence decisions that impact on one's life and 'having a say' are critical to a sense of belonging, particularly if one is a member of a group routinely excluded from such decisions.

Empowerment of the currently disadvantaged is a prerequisite for, rather than a consequence of, more equitable social policies (Phillips, 1999: 31). Until people become active participants in the policy process, the policies adopted cannot be expected to reflect their needs. There is a rich opportunity for social care practitioners in all arenas of professional practice to ensure that service-user participation is not tokenistic, but committed to sharing power and knowledge so as to better address needs as defined by those who experience them. Developments in self-advocacy among people with intellectual disabilities offer a positive example, where many social care practitioners have taken the initiative. A culture of respect and recognition is necessary so that the diverse individuals and social groups in Irish society can live without the burden of contempt and enmity (Baker et al., 2009).

THE ROLE OF THE SOCIAL CARE PROFESSIONAL

Given that social care professionals work at the intersection between marginalised and subordinated groups and the state, there is significant potential to challenge exclusion and to build a more equality-focused practice. A commonly used definition of social care from the Joint Committee on Social Care Professionals (JCSCP, 2002: 13) is:

> … the professional provision of care, protection, support, welfare and advocacy for vulnerable or dependent clients, individually or in groups. This is achieved through the planning and evaluation of individualised and group programmes of care, based on needs, identified where possible in consultation with the clients and delivered through day-to-day shared life experiences.

This definition points to varied roles and places them in the context of 'established best practice and an in-depth knowledge of lifespan development' (JCSCP, 2002: 13). But the focus on 'vulnerable or dependent clients' neglects any analysis of the context in which people become and/or remain dependent or vulnerable. Nor does this definition identify the role that social divisions play in the maintenance of dependency and vulnerability. Clearly, factors such as gender, social class, ethnicity, disability, sexual orientation and age shape inequalities and the resultant dependencies (Baker et al., 2009).

The definition does not say what constitutes 'established best practice'. While an elucidation of the skills and knowledge required is outside the scope of a definition, explicit acknowledgment of the impact of social inequality on the lives of those receiving social care services is missing, as is a professional commitment to effect change in such situations. While the provision of care, protection, support and welfare may be necessary roles for a social care professional, they are all deeply contested concepts. O'Connor (2008: 102–4) argues that the 'popular practice' of social care is 'paternalistic and protective', albeit embellished with new principles such as choice and empowerment.

The inclusion of an advocacy role holds the best chance of developing an empowerment approach in social care work (Leadbetter, 2002). O'Doherty (2006) highlights that all service users engaged with social care practice are members of groups that are marginalised in Irish society. Practice needs to take into account the enormous power differences between people; but this can be lost when the focus is on supporting individual problem-solving capacities. In O'Doherty's view, although the day-to-day needs of clients are vitally important, if practice is limited to these, it is addressing only the symptoms, rather than the more deep-rooted challenges that require other interventions and strategies. Practice that focuses on the individual and the everyday may neglect the centrality of the state response as a critical determinant of the quality and type of social care practice possible in any specific setting.

An understanding of the structural nature of inequality and its impact on the lives of individuals is essential to enable social care professionals to develop the skills and commitment to bring about greater equality in life chances for those they work with. O'Connor (2006: 102–3) accurately identifies the broad focus of social care education, which can be stimulating and enriching for learners but, if pursued without a clear social care project, is a significant stumbling block for the profession. Social care practice is relatively new; it has a wide remit and a multiplicity of clients. Without integration it may resemble a large 'V', with activity going in opposite directions. In these sentiments are the seeds of a debate about the nature of social care practice – heretofore socially conservative – to which educational and professional associations can contribute (Mulkeen, 2012b).

CONCLUSION

This chapter has sought to engage social care students and practitioners with questions of equality and of how they can develop emancipatory practice. It has addressed contested definitions of equality and the sometimes contradictory role of the state in challenging and generating inequality in Irish society. A model for understanding patterns of inequality has been outlined alongside a vision for a more equal society. Finally, social care practitioners are challenged to contribute to the creation of such a society. I believe it is time to revisit how we define our work as social care practitioners. It is time to make a renewed commitment to egalitarian change, where the potential for oppression is replaced with empowerment and social care moves towards the development of a transformative project for itself.

7

Learn about your 'self' before you work with others

Denise Lyons

OVERVIEW

This chapter aims to encourage readers to have an open mind about engaging in a process of self-awareness during their social care education and practice. Here, the term 'self-awareness' relates to the process of looking at yourself with the hope of learning something that might benefit you as a person, and also help you as a practitioner. You may question the value of such reflection or worry about what might happen if you begin to look more closely. Based on my experience as a social care practitioner and lecturer, I believe that avoidance is not an option. Working with vulnerable people is both personally and professionally challenging, and the experience will affect you as a person and as a practitioner. So it makes sense to begin your training by getting to know who you are, and what attitudes, values and beliefs you hold, before you begin to learn how to work with others.

This chapter presents a working definition of the 'self', and a rationale for why you should engage in the challenging process of becoming more self-aware. Central to your ability to develop as a competent practitioner is this knowledge of self and of how your upbringing, experiences, values and beliefs affect your ability to work with vulnerable people. Self-awareness teaches us more about ourselves, which also impacts on the relationships we have with others, which is core to social care practice.

DEFINING THE SELF

> There is virtually no agreement on the characteristic features of selves, depending on whom you believe, selves may be concrete or abstract, material or immaterial, permanent or ephemeral, naturally occurring or human constructions, essentially subjective or publically observable, the same or not the same as people ... The Self is one of those. (Olson, 1999: 49)

Figure 7.1. Reflecting on your self

Based on the multitude of texts available with 'self' in the title, this topic has interested philosophers and psychologists for centuries. An academic discussion of the term 'self' emerged during the Enlightenment (1650–1700), especially in the work of Descartes, Leibnitz, Locke, Hume and Berkeley (Taylor, 2002). This wave of philosophical thinking inspired psychological and sociological discussions and research towards defining the 'self'. Table 7.1 illustrates a selection of key terms and definitions of the self.

Table 7.1. Selection of views of 'self'

Dates	Name	Discipline	Contribution to understanding of the self
1596–1650	René Descartes	Philosophy	'I think therefore I am' – Descartes argued that the self relates to the thoughts we have about who we are
1632–1704	John Locke	Philosophy	Self is 'Knowing', which is formed from all our experiences 'Person' is the self with the ability to think, reason and reflect
1711–76	David Hume	Philosophy	The self is not a thing, but a series of experiences
1724–1804	Immanuel Kant	Philosophy	When we reflect we look at the self from a different perspective, but it is still the one self
1808–73	John Stuart Mill	Philosophy	When we think about self we use 'memory', therefore the self we talk about is the memory of self

Dates	Name	Discipline	Contribution to understanding of the self
1858–1952	John Dewey	Philosophy and psychology	Conduct and consequences are part of the self, and the choices we make reveal the present self and influence the future self
1890–1961	William James	Philosophy and psychology	The terms 'self as known' and 'Self as Knower' refer to the beliefs we have about our self, and what we reflect upon when we use the terms self-awareness and self-reflection Theory evolved to include four parts of the self: 1. Body – a container for the self 2. Social self – receiving recognition from friends and family 3. Spiritual self – the reflective self that involves our thoughts 4. Pure ego – an element of what we learn about through reflection
1864–1929	Charles Cooley	Sociology	'The looking glass self' The pronouns 'I' and 'me' represent how we imagine that we are viewed and judged by others
1863–1931	George Herbert Mead	Sociology and philosophy	Theory of self related to others introduced notion of social self The self develops through our interaction with others
1902–94	Erik Erikson	Neo-Freudian psychotherapy	Looked at the development of self/identity, addressing question of 'Who am I?' Introduced eight life stages (see Chapter 5): 1. Trust versus mistrust (first year of life) 2. Autonomy versus shame and doubt (infancy) 3. Initiative versus guilt (early childhood) 4. Industry versus inferiority (middle childhood) 5. Identity versus role confusion (adolescence) 6. Intimacy versus isolation (young adulthood) 7. Generativity versus stagnation (prime of life) 8. Ego integrity versus despair (old age)

Dates	Name	Discipline	Contribution to understanding of the self
1902–87	Carl Rogers	Psychology	'The aware self needs maintenance' Self is awareness of characteristics of 'I' and 'me', abilities, values and relationships with others and the environment
1908–70	Abraham Maslow	Psychology	Self as subject (Self as 'Knower') – this refers to the beliefs we have about our 'self', and what we reflect upon when we use the terms 'self-awareness' and 'self-reflection' (see Chapter 5)
1927–	Rom Harré	Psychology and philosophy	A person portrays roles, but those roles are not the person but are part of a 'cluster' of theories and perceptions that are held by those we encounter in certain social settings Our self-esteem is two senses of self: personal and social The self-concept is related to strengths and weaknesses, and self-understanding is knowing our strengths, weaknesses, abilities, values and beliefs in different situations (Harré, 1998)

Sources: Hattie (1992), Lyons (2007), Leary and Tangney (2012)

Leary and Tangney (2012) argue that the multiplicity of sources and worldviews on the 'self' has generated confusion. At the risk of being overly simplistic, they state that the majority of definitions of the self refer to 'three basic psychological processes; attention, cognition, and regulation' (2012: 7). When people think about themselves, they are focusing attention on the self, and during this process they have the opportunity to reflect and possibly change thinking, behaviour and attitude.

The selection of thoughts on the self presented in Table 7.1 reflects a varied but limited perspective, as every discipline has a view on what defines the self. With the aim of offering some definition of the self, this chapter presents a specific worldview, reflecting my understanding of self and self-awareness, which is based on the theorists presented in Table 7.1. The following definition of self-awareness has provided a useful base for discussion on the self in the personal and professional development module that I teach to social care students, and may also make sense to you:

Self-awareness is the deliberate cognitive process of reflecting on the thoughts, attitudes and beliefs we have, and on why we might think that way, and on our actions in private and social situations. It is also about reflecting on what we think about ourselves as a person, in all the different roles we play, on how we are perceived by others, and how this imagined perception makes us feel. People are emergent, and are continually adapting based on new experiences, and self-awareness can influence changes in how people feel, think and behave.

WHY LEARN ABOUT THE SELF IN SOCIAL CARE?

Patricia Kennefick, former lecturer in personal development at the Cork Institute of Technology, defined the self as 'the principal tool of the social care worker' (2006: 213). When I think about 'tools for work', I imagine the plumber arriving to fix the sink, and then having to leave the task unfinished because he or she needs to get a specific part or tool to complete the job. Social care practitioners arrive on the job empty handed, and must rely on past experiences, knowledge obtained from college and collaboration with colleagues to meet the specific needs of the people in their care, there and then. Thus, the tool for social care practitioners is the total person, and everything that has influenced or shaped them to become the person they are. In any job, tools are only useful if you know how they work, and social care practitioners are not practising to their full potential if they do not know who they are.

Figure 7.2. The social care practitioner's toolbox

In 1998 I completed the Diploma in Social Care (now the BA (Ordinary) Degree in Social Care) and began to work full time in residential child care. During my social care education, and when I began to practise social care, I did not understand the importance of knowing my 'self'. My attitude changed when I began to study for a Postgraduate Diploma in Art Therapy and was required to attend weekly personal therapy and group therapy sessions for the three years of study. Interestingly, these intensive sessions brought up as many professional as personal issues for me, including:

• When I feel physically threatened by someone in work, how might this feeling change the way I work with the young person?
• What feelings do I have for the parents of children who did not call or show up as arranged; and when I met these parents, did my feelings show?
• How do I allow my ongoing personal/life issues to impact on my relationships with the people in my care?
• What aspects of my personality can help me in work, and do I use my self enough in practice?
• How do I deal with the emotions that are evoked through my work?
• How do I show the young people I work with that they are loved, or am I allowed to love them?
• Do I really know my self and how am I likely to react in different situations?
• How can I provide comfort with a hug without being afraid to touch someone?
• Do I abuse the power I have over the young people in my care?
• Am I assertive enough with my colleagues?
• Do I effectively communicate how I feel with my colleagues and the people in my care?

I was encouraged during the group therapy sessions to talk about the issues that came up for me, which was a very challenging but useful experience.

Should social care education provide the space for all students to reflect authentically on the issues, thoughts and fears that affect them, before they go out to work in social care? Social care is different from many other professions in that when things go wrong, practitioners cannot blame the tools, because they are the total package. Practitioners have to make the most informed decision they can at the time, and then work with the consequences of that decision. The student or practitioner, by the very nature of the work, is likely to encounter experiences that challenge their values, views and potential prejudices. Social care practice is about making decisions for and on behalf of others, and decisions are based on values, views and beliefs. If practitioners are unaware of their own issues, they will continue to work without regard to people's feelings, deeming that they know exactly what the other is feeling. In addition, they will ignore the effects that the other person's feelings, behaviour and experiences are having on themselves (Burnard, 1992). According to Thompson (2002: 4), 'in order to become attuned to other people's feelings, we need to be in touch with our own feelings, and aware of how situations are affecting us emotionally'.

Social care work becomes more complex because it is generally performed by teams, influenced by their collective values, attitudes and beliefs. Working within a team of different people with varying norms can be the most challenging part of social care. In an ideal world, all the members of the team will feel supported, their opinions will be valued and respected, they will speak freely and they will understand that people will constructively criticise their work in a way that feels safe and helps them learn. Ten years of teaching personal development to work-based and full-time students indicates that this does not always reflect the real experience of social care. Students frequently describe feeling personally as well as professionally judged by the team, and claim they do not feel safe enough to talk openly. Students also express a fear of being viewed as the 'bad worker' because they do not live up to the expectations of individual team members.

Figure 7.3. Am I the bad worker?

Social care is a unique profession in that the skills required vary depending on the aims of the specific service, and the individual needs of those using the service. Fear of not being a competent worker is experienced by both the qualified professional and the practising unqualified worker. In most professions the graduate will leave college with a proficiency in the core competencies of the practice. Social care practice is less definable, especially as the profession has evolved from residential child care specifically, to a generic profession of caring for a variety of people within very different services.

The European Centre for the Development of Vocational Training (Cedefop, 2010) researched the generic competencies of frontline social care staff in services for the elderly, homeless people and people with disabilities. Although 'social care worker' is not a term generally used to define similar professions in Europe, it was used in this report to define frontline professionals who work with the 'most vulnerable and disadvantaged groups' (2010: 3). The study was performed in five European countries: Germany, Poland, Portugal, Sweden and the United Kingdom. Six generic competencies were identified.

The methodology consisted of focus groups comprising service users, social care workers, managers and service providers. The focus groups indicated that personality characteristics of 'assertiveness, empathy, patience', followed by the ability to form a relationship based on trust and mutual respect, are the two key competencies. The remaining competencies related to empowerment and brokerage skills, understanding diversity, teamwork and leadership. The majority of these terms have also been identified as the core competencies of social care practice in an Irish context (see Chapter 11).

It may be useful to examine which competencies are specific to some settings, and which may be generic or core to all. As a profession, if social care practitioners do not know definitively what the required skills, knowledge and attitudes are for each setting, then it is understandable that practitioners may fear they are not living up to the expectations of varying services.

A key concern raised by students returning from placement is a feeling that they should appear all-knowing and that asking questions, or seeking support, may demonstrate a lack of confidence, or an inability to practise social care. Social care students may be concerned about:

- Forming and maintaining relationships appropriately and professionally.
- Adhering to the policies and working practices of the agency.
- Upholding the cleaning standards of colleagues, without really knowing what the expectations are.
- Handling challenging encounters appropriately.
- Communicating well, both verbally and on record, and spelling everything correctly.
- Being a consistent team member and supporting the democratic decisions made by the team, even if they personally disagree.
- Being on the floor (performing direct care tasks) at the right time, or doing office work without appearing to hide from a crisis on the floor.

The fear of being a 'bad worker' does not disappear after graduation, as success in college is not viewed as an indication of ability to do the job. Therefore, the social care graduate is reliant on the feedback of work colleagues for reassurance. To eliminate this fear, regardless of training and experience, practitioners need to recognise that they have the right to make a mistake and to acknowledge this mistake publicly, without fear of the internal or external judge. It requires the self-awareness to know that acknowledging weakness or mistakes is not a sign that you are a 'bad worker', but is characteristic of a reflective practitioner and someone who accepts that there is an opportunity for self-learning in every experience.

SELF TRAINING IN IRISH SOCIAL CARE EDUCATION

Training of the self was an intricate part of the social care course that began in 1971 as a Diploma in Residential Child Care from the Kilkenny School of Social Education. The school was established in the grounds of Bishop Birch's residence in Kilkenny. This course was unique in that the focus was on the development of the individual, and also on the social interactions of students with each other and within their practical and theoretical learning environments. The programme included a residential component during which students spent time living with each other. This experience formed the basis for weekly group discussions, where students explored their personal journey through the training. The course ran until 1981, educating many of the practice leaders of social care. During an interview in August 2012 Pat Brennan, founder of the programme, shared his thoughts on the importance of self training within social care education:

> Where possible it would be most conducive to the process of self-actualisation, if the central subjects of this course were centred on the concept and construct of the self, rather than the lectures/tutorials being focused on the subjects as subjects. It is not really necessary for the students to have a polished knowledge of say 'sociology' as if they were to be sociologists or teachers of sociology. Ideally then, only those parts of each subject that increase knowledge, awareness and insight with regard to the development and growth of the process of 'maturing', and what might damage or hinder this process, should be the focus. So in that scenario, the vulnerable other to be cared for, and the vulnerable person of and in the student, is the total focus of the learning process.

Social care education took a different direction with the introduction of the Diploma in Child Care in Dublin Institute of Technology in 1974, followed quickly by the National Diploma in Child Care at Waterford Regional Technical College. By 1990 child care education was provided by colleges in Dublin, Waterford, Athlone, Cork, Galway and Sligo and had evolved into a generic social care programme aiming to meet the training needs of workers within the caring professions. Ultimately, social care degrees came to be offered in sixteen Irish educational institutions and to enrol thousands of students every year.

In 2007 the Irish Association of Social Care Educators (IASCE) formed a Working Group on Social Care Education Standards. The report of the working group was informed by programme documents from Cork Institute of Technology and Dublin Institute of Technology, the *Practice Placement Manual* (IASCE, 2009) and the *Final Report of the Joint Committee on Social Care Professionals* (JCSCP, 2002). This report in turn informed the deliberations of an expert group established by the Higher Education and Training Awards Council (HETAC), which published the national *Social Care Work Awards Standards* in 2010.

The HETAC standards were presented as a guide for programme development and accreditation, and thus frame the knowledge, skills and competencies of current social care education. For 'competence insight', students are required to 'develop knowledge of self (including one's personal attitudes)' and 'recognise the influence of well-being and background on personal practice' (HETAC, 2010: 7). The document does not highlight the importance of self-awareness and personal development for social care training, which may mean that the area is not prioritised for students and may become lost within the curriculum, especially as student numbers continue to rise.

In 1971 the Kilkenny course had twenty students; since then student numbers on social care courses have been rising, with an average class size of fifty to sixty students, increasing to 120 in many cases or even above 200 (Courtney, 2012). The main requirement needed for social care education is the human resource of adequate contact time between the lecturer and student, and most importantly the appropriate size of the student cohort during the practical or experiential classes. Learning about the self requires time, and it also requires a small group experience where the student can open up and ask the difficult questions within a 'safe' learning environment. It is my concern that opportunities to learn about the self may not be offered in social care programmes in the future as they will be viewed as too expensive to provide, especially with more restricted budgets.

THE IMPACT OF REGISTRATION ON SOCIAL CARE EDUCATION

The development of the self has received a renewed focus with the forthcoming registration of social care workers. The Health and Social Care Professionals Act 2005 provides a legal framework for the statutory registration of twelve helping professions: clinical biochemists, physiotherapists, dietitians, psychologists, medical scientists, radiographers, occupational therapists, social care workers, orthoptists, social workers, podiatrists and speech and language therapists. This will involve the Health and Social Care Professionals Council (CORU). According to the 2005 Act, Part 2, Section 7, the main objective of CORU is 'to protect the public by promoting high standards of professional conduct and professional education, training and competence among registrants of the designated professions'.

Clarke (2003: 1) notes that, in light of the forthcoming professionalisation of social care, there are increased challenges for educators to direct the training towards achieving 'fitness for practice'. CORU has the authority under the 2005 Act, Part 5, Section 48(1)(b), to 'refuse to approve the programme if not so satisfied'. All colleges providing social care training will be required to sufficiently meet the educational standards devised by CORU in order to continue.

CORU has designed a framework, in consultation with all twelve professions, that categorises the main standards of proficiency for educators in six domains. Two of these make reference to the development of the self: Domain 2 (interpersonal and professional relationships) and Domain 4 (personal and professional development). Training of self is recognised by CORU as integral to the training of a 'fit and proper' social care practitioner.

CONCLUSION

Social care education requires a combination of knowledge, practice and self, thus enabling graduates to understand the importance of reflecting on the self for their practice. Social care is a complex and personally challenging profession and, despite over forty years of education in Ireland, we do not have a definitive understanding of the core competencies of practice within specific services based on empirical evidence. This situation means that graduates often feel unskilled when they begin to work in a new area, experiencing concerns over how their practice will be viewed by others. Self-awareness is essential for social care education because practitioners need to know who they are, and how values, attitudes and beliefs influence their work. In a time of reduced resources, and increasing student numbers, there is a fear that real opportunities for self-awareness may be missed if they are not deemed a priority by educators.

8

Gender, sexuality and social care

Jacqueline O'Toole

OVERVIEW

This chapter provides an overview of gender issues as they pertain to social care. It maps debates on gender and social care that are becoming central in the academic literature and in social care practice.

Gender is open to discussion from any number of vantage points. This chapter takes a feminist sociological approach that sees gender inequality as an underlying feature of contemporary global societies (Connell, 2005). I argue that gender continues to be one of the primary ways for organising social relations in society (Ridgeway, 2009; Share et al., 2012). Gender inequality tends to be reproduced through the interaction of institutionalised assumptions about gender differences and the everyday practices found in social care organisations. Social care practitioners can play a crucial role in the reproduction of gender inequalities but also, importantly, in the challenge to gender-based oppressions (Hanlon, 2009).

This chapter examines a number of gender issues that have implications for the contexts, meanings and practices of social care in Ireland. Three important themes will be addressed: the concept of gender; gender processes in social care; and the concept of sexuality particularly as it pertains to social care practice.

CHANGING LANDSCAPE

Since the publication of the first edition of this book in 2005, Gallagher and O'Toole's (1999: 70) call for a greater understanding of the contexts in which 'social care' is performed and the multiple meanings that exist amongst practitioners, educators, policy makers and employers is being realised. A body of published research in social care and the related field of early childhood studies has emerged. In addition, the social, economic and policy context in which care work is performed has significantly altered the social care landscape. Therefore, an account of the social organisation of care practice in Ireland is evolving (Lyon and Glucksman, 2008).

The dominant discourse of social care practice in Ireland suggests it involves a broad spectrum of specialised and professionalised interventions designed to alleviate and support the challenges that some people encounter in their everyday lives. These may result from poverty and disadvantage, from neglect and abuse, from marginalisation and oppression, to name but some. Hanlon (2009) and O'Connor (2008) comment that in and of itself this approach to social care work, whilst important, may result in an individualistic approach to care work that ignores the wider social, cultural, economic and political conditions in which poverty, disadvantage, neglect, abuse, marginalisation and oppression occur.

What this means is that it is not enough to embed an individualistic, therapeutic and 'professionalised' framework in the teaching and delivery of social care practice. Rather, in the light of increasing evidence of social inequalities of race, age, education, ethnicity, gender, sexuality and disability, social care practice must embrace a radical agenda that emphasises the structural context in which social problems are produced and reproduced (O'Connor, 2006: 89). Practitioners and social care client groups possess an economic, political and social existence in addition to having day-to-day needs. Gender is one aspect of the socio-structural context of social care.

WHAT IS GENDER?

Table 8.1. Traditional notions of a polarised gender identity

Female/feminine	Male/masculine
Submissive	Dominant
Dependent	Independent
Unintelligent/incapable	Intelligent/competent
Emotional	Rational
Receptive	Assertive
Intuitive	Analytical
Weak	Strong
Timid	Brave
Content	Ambitious
Passive	Active
Co-operative	Competitive
Sensitive	Insensitive
Sex object	Sexually aggressive
Attractive because of physical appearance	Attractive because of achievement

Source: Macionis and Plummer (2012: 394)

Sociologists have conceptualised the relationships between women and men through a distinction between sex and gender. Sex is seen as a biological category that refers to the different physical and biological features that women and men possess, including genitals, chromosomal structures, reproductive systems and secondary sexual characteristics such as the distribution of body hair and breast development (Macionis and Plummer, 2012). Sex is rooted in nature and gives rise to two categories: female and male.

Gender is viewed as a social category that refers to the socially constructed and variable notions of femininity and masculinity (Oakley, 1972). It is concerned with the socially ascribed characteristics associated with being female and male and with dominant ideas about what women and men should be like. At any time in any society, there may be much variation in understandings and expectations associated with the biological categories of female and male and the social categories of femininity and masculinity. Table 8.1 captures some historical notions of these understandings in Western societies, including Ireland.

While there have been many recent changes vis-à-vis feminine and masculine traits and the blurring of gender identities, Table 8.1 illustrates the idea that in many societies there exists a hierarchal gender order. In other words, this list is just one of specific characteristics: those listed for males are often seen as positive; those for females, negative. A gender order refers to how societies shape notions of femininity and masculinity into power relationships (Connell, 1987). When we discuss groups, such as may be found in a residential care home, a day care centre or a crèche, we can investigate the workings of a gender regime, which is the gender order as it works through in smaller settings.

The simplistic distinction between sex (nature) and gender (culture) has begun to be challenged. Cross-cultural evidence suggests that simple binary oppositions of female/male and femininity/masculinity may not capture the complexities of gender in people's lives. Indeed, the divisions that are drawn in Table 8.1 are also social constructions. The process of gender attribution, whereby we assign ideas about gender to females and males, is itself a social process that varies from one social setting to another: witness drag and transsexualism, for example. Each involves a transgression of historically given boundaries and notions of female/male and femininity/masculinity.

A final consideration when conceptualising gender concerns the acquisition of gendered identities. Various sociological theories suggest that some form of socialisation is a key part of this process. From an early age girls and boys are exposed to their society's understandings of gender: indeed, the process of learning about gender roles and identity begins even at birth. Clear messages about gender differences emanate from parents, caregivers, the media, peers, the education system and culture. The socialisation thesis, while interesting, is limited. A passive conception of the person is invoked, where the child is viewed as a sponge waiting to be 'filled up' by society and culture. There is a deterministic slant to socialisation that ignores the capacity of individuals to change, resist and alter dominant meanings in society. In addition, there is a sense in which gender identity becomes the central feature of a person's identity. Thus, although women may be differentiated according to social class, ethnicity and sexual preference, in socialisation theory, the fact that they are women appears to be the overwhelming constituent of their identity. Black, lesbian and post-modernist feminists have all questioned the validity of this assumption. Other identity indicators, such as social class, ethnicity and sexual preference, heavily influence the experience of being a woman or a man and mediate femininity and masculinity.

How do perceived gender differences lead to gender inequality?

Since the late 1960s gender has appeared as an organising concept in sociology and elsewhere. Inspired by the women's rights and civil rights movements, academics and activists started to examine how almost all societies appear to be organised in ways that benefit men more than women. It seemed to many social observers that women's and men's lives were radically different in various ways. For example, in relation to quality of life; experience of poverty; social status; access to income, education and employment; and participation in politics and economic life.

Women were perceived as second-class citizens whose main focus in life was on the reproductive sphere, through maintaining and rearing a family, while men were viewed as more important citizens as they concerned themselves with life in the public sphere of politics, culture and economics. Further, relations between women and men were conducted within these types of divisions. In Ireland, various movements and organisations, including the Irish women's rights movement, began actively to challenge these assumptions and the realities of everyday life and sought, at both a policy and an interpersonal level, to overhaul what they saw as an unequal society that disproportionately benefited men (Connolly, 2002). A key question that surfaced was: Why did these unequal relations between women and men exist?

Many people see gender inequality as socially constructed (made in society) and as linked to an understanding of power. In the 1970s feminists focused attention on the patriarchal nature of Western societies and on gender stratification to help explain continued unequal relations between women and men (Walby, 1990). Patriarchy is conceptualised as the systematic patterning of society in ways that men dominate, exploit and oppress women (Walby, 1990; O'Connor, 1998: 7). In an Irish context, O'Connor (1998) enunciates an understanding of patriarchy as a system made up of six key structures of social relations that enable men to dominate women: paid work, the family and household, culture, sexuality, male violence and state violence.

There are difficulties with the notion of patriarchy. It can be presented as a descriptive and universal category rather than one that is explanatory and historically specific. It suggests that all societies have always been patriarchal in nature and organisation. It tells us very little about the variation in gender relations that exists within and between societies or about the subjective experiences of women and men as they seek to challenge the existence of structures that dominate them in their everyday lives. While some degree of patriarchy is universal, Macionis and Plummer (2012) suggest that there is significant variation in the relative power and privilege of males and females around the world. Notwithstanding these conceptual difficulties, Share et al. (2012: 181) state that 'it is certainly the case that all societies are differentiated by gender and have been dominated in various ways by men'.

Thus, it may be a fallacy to ignore the important contribution that the concept of patriarchy offers as a descriptive and partial explanatory concept (Moane, 1999). Indeed, both Walby (1990) and O'Connor (1998) articulate accounts of British and Irish society respectively that clearly demonstrate the many ways in which each society is organised at an overall level to benefit men. Of course, every individual man may not benefit from this system, and not all women experience exploitation within such social arrangements.

To develop a more sophisticated understanding of gender differences and inequality, we can usefully turn to the work of Australian sociologist R.W. Connell (1987, 2001, 2005). Connell is concerned with the perpetuation of patriarchal social relations in the everyday lives of women and men and argues that although gender is typically thought of as a property of individuals, it is necessary to move beyond this and conceptualise it as a property of institutions (Connell, 1987: 139–41). According to Connell, gender is a fundamental feature of capitalist societies that are run mainly by, and to the benefit of, men. Every society has a gender order comprising attendant hierarchies. This is made up of a historically specific division of labour; a structure of desire; and a structure of power, authority and control. Processes and practices of patriarchal control exist at each of these levels.

A variety of masculinities (some dominant and some not) and femininities are generated within the gender order. One such form of masculinity is hegemonic masculinity, which involves active subordination of women and other men such as gay men. Connell (1987) argues that only a minority of men practise this type of masculinity, but most men gain an advantage from the subordination of women in terms of honour, prestige and the right to command: this is termed the 'patriarchal dividend'. The form of masculinity associated with this is complicit masculinity. Connell suggests that although the majority of men may not actively seek to dominate women, it is in their wider interests that traditional gendered ways of 'doing things' remain constant. Other forms of masculinity include marginalised (black men, working-class men), subordinated (gay men) and resistant (pro-feminist men) masculinities.

Some men view certain changes in society as an attack on their patriarchal privilege. Many other men in Irish and other Western societies are challenging and changing notions of hegemonic and complicit masculinity. This suggests that the concept of gender needs to be contextualised within a complex and sophisticated understanding of patriarchal social relations as they exist in particular societies at particular times.

GENDER PROCESSES AND SOCIAL CARE

Gender is implicated in all social processes. Social care work is a gendered sphere. Hanlon (2009) argues that there is a dearth of critical socio-structural focus in social care in Ireland. This situation has, by and large, resulted in the lack of a theoretical and applied analysis of gender (see O'Connor, 1992, and Gallagher and O'Toole, 1999, for initial attempts at such an analysis). If gender is included, it tends to act as a synonym for either 'women' (usually) or 'men', instead of addressing the social relations between them. But to explore aspects of the gender-related issues in social care, we first need to understand the 'language of care'. What exactly does 'care' mean?

Care is difficult to define and has been strongly contested as a concept. Unpacking the meaning of care (Fink, 2004) suggests that there are inconsistencies in how the term is understood, with variables including who undertakes the care, who receives it, the relationship between the two, and the social domain within which the caring takes place (Orme, 2001: 92). One of the difficulties when teasing out the meaning of care relates to the distinctions routinely drawn between paid and unpaid care work (Gallagher and O'Toole, 1999: 78), between formal and informal care work (Lynch and McLaughlin, 1995; Feder Kittay, 1999) and between the public and private spheres. Moss and Cameron (2004: 224) suggest that the distinctiveness of social care is that it can transcend these dualisms and has enormous scope to reach across the life course, encompassing work with children, young people and adults of all ages (see also Krojer, 2001). Lyon and Glucksman (2008) suggest that the distinction between paid and unpaid is not coterminous with that of formal and informal. There is no one-to-one pairing of paid with formal, or of unpaid with informal, evidencing yet again the need to understand contemporary transformations of (care) work across the full range of socio-economic sectors of activity.

In Ireland, at social policy and state levels, paid care work has come to refer to the provision of facilities and carrying out of tasks for those unable to do so for themselves. Carers are those paid to do this task (Orme, 2001: 93). Although Bubeck (1995: 127) defines care as both an activity and an emotional state, emotions may not necessarily be involved, nor indeed encouraged, in the context of formal care work (Ungerson, 1997). Some of the debates on professionalism maintain that a critical and emotional distance is necessary for social care as a profession. This is an interesting argument as what may actually occur is the careful management of emotions in the performance of the work. More research is needed in this area in Ireland.

An understanding of care must recognise those who receive care and the definitions they hold of the activities, tasks and relationships that unfold in the caring sphere. It is mostly women who provide and receive care in the informal sector (Gerstel and Gallagher, 2001; Hanlon, 2012; Herd and Meyer, 2002; Pease, 2011). This situation is largely a result of constructions of femininity that see caring as an innate female quality. It has repercussions for the formal/paid/public sector, as assumptions exist that it is only 'natural' that women will enter the caring field. In the caring marketplace, different values are placed on similar skills according to who is using them, the criteria frequently being the gender and power of the worker.

Women and men as social care practitioners

Social care practice can, in some ways, be seen as a non-traditional occupation for men. It is considered a 'caring' profession and, while some aspects of the work involve control and surveillance, the emphasis on care positions it as a feminised profession (Christie, 1998, 2001). Orme (2001: 14) believes that the connections between social care and gender are evident in that practitioners in this sphere work, in the first instance, within gender-constructed social relationships. She suggests that the combination of social relations and power makes the concept of gender useful when analysing social care. Further, understandings and constructions of femininity and masculinity explicitly and implicitly permeate the provision of care. Lyon and Glucksman (2008) believe that all forms of care work are predominantly undertaken by women. Despite a slight increase in the proportion of men employed in care, the high proportion of women in paid employment in care work remains entrenched, making formal, paid care work more gendered than unpaid informal care.

An emerging debate in social care concerns the small proportion of men amongst those entering the profession. It is interesting to note that an exploration of the meaning of both masculinity and femininity in caring contexts is at an early stage here. Debates range from the number of men working in the field to the role of men in social care and to the necessity of attracting more men into care. This requires ongoing research in an Irish context. Interesting work elsewhere suggests that a structural analysis of gender and attendant links with the notion of power provides a framework in which to analyse the roles women and men enact in the social care arena, both as carers and service users (Cavanagh and Cree, 1996; Dominelli, 1997; Hanmer and Statham, 1999; Hearn, 1999; Adams et al., 2002).

Women dominate the membership of full-time programmes in social care practice courses in Ireland. The consequences are manifold, an important one being that stakeholders are beginning to debate some of the issues, including 'making care work attractive to men', men as carers, and the possible outcomes of care provision, service use and receipt. Pease (2011: 406) ponders whether the presence of men in the profession of social work (an allied profession to social care practice) challenges discriminatory processes and occupational segregations. He argues that men certainly need to take more responsibility for caring roles, a view endorsed by Hanlon (2012) in an Irish context. But Pease (2011) cautions that many of the rationales for encouraging more men to enter the social care professions, such as the role model thesis, are unlikely to support alternative masculinities that will challenge gender inequalities.

As social care practice involves the sharing of life-space, and encompasses management, therapeutic and personal care tasks (Graham, 1995), gender social relations are paramount. Anecdotal evidence from the profession indicates that women and men perform quite different roles when providing and using care and, further, that such roles are rooted in a particular construction of essentialised femininity and masculinity (Orme, 2002). In relation to men, Dominelli (1997: 111–12) argues that 'feminists have been crucial in raising the problematic nature of masculinity for both men and women and have revealed how men are limited in expressing the full range of their emotions and organisational skills because certain characteristics have been defined as "feminine" and out of bounds to them'.

Research indicates that when men enter non-traditional occupations such as care work, masculinity may turn out to be a boon for them, as qualities associated with men become more highly regarded than those associated with women, even in predominantly female jobs (Cree, 2001: 153). Cree (2001) also observes that there are other advantages for men in non-traditional occupations, such as greater access to promotion, achieving more attention because of their small numbers and being rewarded for an ability to express feelings and emotions which, it would seem, are taken for granted in women. Men have been shown to be overrepresented in both managerial and higher status jobs in the social services generally (Pease, 2011). More research is required in an Irish context to interrogate masculinity and the potential impact of male privileging in the social care environment.

What it means to be a male in social care is an important question. But a gendered analysis demands that this question be critically linked to a number of other questions, including an interrogation of femininity, such as:

- What does it mean to be a woman in social care?
- How are gendered social relations enacted in the social care arena?
- What discourses of femininity and masculinity exist in the training of social care practitioners and in the social care work environment? What is the impact of these discourses on individual and collective social practices?
- How can men begin to address their positions in social care in a way that takes account of their privileged positioning as men in wider society? For instance, how is it that men, although considerably fewer in number than women in the education and training of social care practitioners, dominate the management positions in the educational institutions?
- Why is social care seen as a conventional career decision for women?

There is little published material in Ireland that explores the gendered social relations that infuse social care. Recent work by Hanlon (2007b, 2009, 2012) and Mulkeen (2012a) addresses this dearth through examining gender and related processes as they are understood and manifest in social care. A main goal of social care work is to empower those who use services to reach their full potential as human beings. As reflective practitioners, social care practitioners must be aware of how their practices are underpinned by and connected to gender and power. To ensure non-oppressive practice, the generation of knowledge about gender and power, both in society and in social care, is necessary. Moreover, interactions and interventions between practitioners and users of a service must also be understood in the context of social class, sexuality, race and ethnicity, and attendant power relations.

SEXUALITY

Sexuality, like gender, is a social construction. There is no one 'true' sexuality or way of expressing desires; rather, there exists a variety of sexualities in all societies. Sexuality is thus 'a diverse field of experience and behaviour that is brought together at certain times through a common body of language or discourse' (Share et al., 2012: 195).

At different times in the history of societies, different meanings and practices emerge that guide our understanding and expression of sexuality. For instance, in many Western societies, expressions of homosexual and lesbian sexuality have been negated and denied as they do not fit into dominant meanings of sexuality that emphasise heterosexuality as the norm.

Inglis (1998a, 1998b) suggests that there are powerful discourses moulding sexuality in Irish society. Discourse refers to the dominant ideas and understandings about a topic that define how people experience and behave in their everyday lives. These become established as a knowledge or way of looking at the world. There may be a number of different and competing discourses at play at any one time: hegemonic and resistant masculinity, for instance. Discourses are linked to discipline. This means that individuals tend to be positioned in particular ways according to discourses and may be forced to behave in particular ways through self-imposed or externally imposed discipline. Importantly, within any discourse, there is always the potential to resist the demands placed on individual experience and behaviour.

According to Inglis (1998b), some of the more powerful discourses that mould sexuality in Irish society are generated in the family, the education system, medicine, popular culture, religion and the legal and political systems. Inglis argues (1998a) that, from the nineteenth century until the 1960s, the social construction of sexuality was immersed in discourses of sexuality promulgated by the Catholic church, through the words and actions of bishops and priests. Sexuality was not so much hidden or repressed as talked about and enacted in a different sort of way from today. In particular, sexuality was viewed as a powerful force that needed to be regulated within the institution of marriage. The discourses linked sexuality to notions of sin, control, danger, guilt, suspicion, celibacy, purity, innocence, virginity, humility, piety and regulation that emphasised Catholic moral and social teaching (Inglis, 1998b).

The Catholic church imposed a strict discipline of sexual morality, through which both men and women were encouraged to feel ashamed of their bodies. This imposition may have been experienced differently by women and by men. Condron (1989) and Inglis (1998b: 178–200) state that women were expected to embody Catholic morality by being virtuous, chaste and virginal (Hilliard, 2003). If women contravened the conventions, strict sanctions were imposed.

O'Connor (1998) suggests that historically women's sexuality was constructed around notions of reputation, marriage, childbirth/rearing and family. Since the foundation of the Irish state, women have grown up within a discourse of sexuality that specifies the woman as mother, as carer, as wife. O'Connor asserts that female sexuality continues to possess the following attributes: active heterosexuality, difficulties with contraception, an emphasis on the complex notion of 'love', experiences of sexual harassment, the stigmatising of abortion, powerful and contradictory messages around body image, sex being viewed as a consumer product and pressures against saying 'no'.

Dominant understandings of male sexuality were constructed around the notions of the uncontrollable and insatiable nature of sexual expression for men. Historically, in Ireland, male sexual expression was deemed powerful and a man's right to express himself sexually was, within reason, inalienable. Up until 1990, for instance, a man, upon marriage, had the right to demand sex from his wife, even if she resisted. In 1990 legislation was passed to criminalise rape within marriage and effectively remove the notion of wife/woman as male property. It must be noted that the experiences of many men in Irish society did not and do not conform to these dominant discourses.

Great change has taken place since the 1980s with regard to sexual attitudes and practices. Sexuality has become public in Irish society: a new way of speaking by a variety of commentators has emerged to directly challenge and contest Catholic discourses of sexuality (Hug, 1999). Diversity, pleasures, preferences and choices have become the concepts that underpin the deployment of sexuality in contemporary Ireland (Layte et al., 2006). Freely available contraception, cohabitation, decriminalisation of male homosexuality, equalisation of age of consent between lesbians, gay men and heterosexuals, and the public celebration of sex in and outside marriage have all been part of the new discourses of sexuality.

Sexuality is 'out there' and 'in here': in the media, the school playground, the nightclub – in the minds and bodies of Irish people. Inglis (1998a) believes that we now require an analysis of Irish sexuality that describes and analyses how sexuality was and is seen, understood and embodied by participants in Irish social life. There are still substantial gaps in knowledge about sexual attitudes and behaviour in Ireland (see Layte et al., 2006, for the first attempt at a systematic sociological analysis of sexuality in Ireland). Much has changed in terms of sexual expression, including greater acceptance of the multifarious ways in which people live their sexual lives. But sexuality must be understood as linked to particular understandings of femininity and masculinity in society and to gender social relations and power.

Sexuality and social care

We have seen that it is important to reach a better understanding of gender social relations in the social care environment. It is also important to explore the links between gender, power and sexuality in social care environments. One issue that is being spoken about in the literature on masculinities concerns sexuality. Thus, one of the professional problems that men face in social care relates to assumptions being made about their perceived sexuality status (Pease, 2011). As care generally and social care work specifically has historically been constructed as a feminised occupation, men have reported being questioned about their (hetero)sexuality if they choose to enter the profession. This raises important questions. Could these assumptions have consequences for the types of work and care that men do in social care settings? Are men constrained by such assumptions? Does this act as a barrier to men entering the profession? Why is hegemonic masculinity challenged by men as carers?

As social care work is constituted by the sharing of life-space, expressions of sexuality permeate the everyday interactions of social care practitioners and service users in a variety of ways that include touch, looking, physical stance, clothes and language. In the social care setting, this can have major consequences for the level and type of interactions, concerns with and about behaviour, planning and controlling activities, developing care plans, specifying interventions, and general day-to-day living.

Sexuality has been talked about in a variety of ways in social care. The topic has been addressed in the development of 'good' models of practice in the disability sector and within children's and youth centres. Organisations are developing in-house programmes and policies with regard to people with learning difficulties and sexuality. Topics inherent in such programmes and policies include self-advocacy in terms of sexual expression, protection of vulnerable people against sexual exploitation, age-appropriate sexual behaviour, development of relevant sex-education programmes and responsibility in sexual behaviour. Such programmes may become particularly relevant in an Irish context with the many recent revelations of sexual abuse in institutional care. Many such programmes and policies operate within a discourse of sexuality that has placed issues of regulation and control at the forefront. The increasing emphasis in wider society on liberal attitudes to sexuality suggests that issues of self-advocacy and the role of appointed advocates are central to the debates on sexuality, especially as service users demand greater control over their sexual selves.

Managing sexuality and sex in human relationships is difficult. Humans have developed complex ways to manage and deal with their feelings in all kinds of relationships (Cree, 2001). Since the mid-1990s protection has become a key element of the practice in Ireland of social care work and allied social professions. The numerous accounts of sexual abuse have left social care practitioners and service users with a legacy so powerful it now guides the types of physical and intimate interactions that occur.

It is necessary to develop good practice models that protect all actors in these kinds of social relationships. The issues are complex. On the one hand, the protection of service users and practitioners is paramount. On the other, a crying child, missing its parents, sometimes needs the security and intimacy of human touch. The fear attached to expressions of affection between practitioner and service user must be unpacked to uncover what this fear is about and where it comes from. Sex and sexuality are sometimes viewed as sensitive areas, too difficult to discuss with service users. Yet, as many social care practitioners act *in loco parentis*, it will be necessary at some stage to deal with such issues.

As in all social relationships, it is imperative that social care practitioners develop an awareness of their own sexuality. Increasing awareness will help social care practitioners to acknowledge their feelings and desires and how these affect their professional relationships. Social care practitioners must understand and acknowledge their sexuality in order to work effectively and safely with others.

An important dimension of any discussion on sexuality is language. How people speak about sexuality and sex and the terms they use impact on social behaviour. Language usage is connected to power and the ability of certain people to speak for and about others. For instance, terms such as 'slag' and 'slut' may have particular consequences for women's feelings and actions in their everyday lives (Lees, 1993; O'Toole, 1998). Words such as 'sissy', 'cunt', 'faggot' and 'queer' are currently employed as terms of abuse, which, if used in the social care context (or in any social context), contribute to oppressive practices. Words for sexual behaviour and genitals carry considerable power. Social care practitioners must examine their own use of language and the use of language in the social care context to avoid perpetuating oppressive behaviours.

A final issue to consider with regard to sexuality and social care is the link between sexual preference, particularly homosexuality, and anti-oppressive practice. Share et al. (2012) suggest that one of the more rapidly changing discussions around sexuality in Ireland relates to the experiences of lesbians and gay men. In 1993 sexual relations between men were decriminalised. Women had never been covered by the Victorian legislation that had criminalised sexual relations between men. Although equality legislation has been enacted to protect gay people, amongst others, this has not necessarily meant that the everyday lives of gay people in Ireland are left untouched by anti-gay feeling and outright discrimination.

O'Carroll and Collins (1995) and O'Brien (2003) document aspects of the many and varied lives of gay people in Ireland, including their experiences of coming out, relationships, discrimination, national identity and sense of self. Despite significant changes in Irish society with regard to sexuality, there is still considerable work to be done to achieve an egalitarian existence for gay people. However, much has changed in recent years. Civil partnership was introduced for gay men and lesbians in 2010, with the first such ceremonies taking place in 2011. Organisations such as Marriage Equality are pushing to extend the legislation further to include full marriage and related rights for gay people. BelongTo, a gay youth organisation, has won international plaudits and national recognition for its support and advocacy work on behalf of young gay people.

Within care work, cognisance must be taken of the issues that affect gay men and lesbians as practitioners and client service groups. It is only in recent years that learning about homosexuality has been removed from 'abnormal' psychology modules. Labelling anything 'abnormal' is questionable in the context of the need to explore the value of anti-oppressive practice. It is useful if social care practitioners develop an increased awareness of their own sexuality and attitudes to sexuality. Anti-oppressive practice – part of social care work training and practice in many countries, including Britain – demands that the lives of gay people be both protected and celebrated within the social care environment (Thompson, 2012; DoHC, 2007). Social care training in Ireland makes limited use of anti-oppressive practice in its training and education programmes (Hanlon, 2009). Modules on equality are part of some social care programmes. Anti-oppressive practices refer to the need to challenge not only attitudes and practices towards gay people but also other ways in which people are discriminated against, including ethnicity, race, gender, social class, age, disability, education, marital status, family status and religion.

CONCLUSION

This chapter has introduced an array of gender processes that are central to an understanding of social care practice in Ireland. Gender is a complex concept, the meaning of which must be contextualised within an understanding of social relations in wider society. Forms of femininity and masculinity vary within and between societies. Their constructions within care practice may provide an insight into how gender is understood in society generally. Social care would benefit from a socio-structural focus to interrogate the relational categories of both femininity and masculinity as they are enacted by relevant social actors in the various social care arenas.

9

Evidence-based practice in social care

Tom Farrelly

OVERVIEW

It would be nice if all of the data which sociologists require could be enumerated because then we could run them through IBM machines and draw charts as the economists do. However, not everything that can be counted counts, and not everything that counts can be counted.

(Cameron, 1963)

If you have asked, or have been asked, 'How did you do that?' or 'Why did you do it that way?', you have engaged in research. We often think of research as a ponderous calling pursued by serious-minded people removed from the hustle and bustle of 'real life'. Research is considered a remote activity, particularly by those at the coalface of practice. Yet many practitioners are engaged in the research process, even if they do not realise it. Every time you read a study, report, journal article or review document, you are consuming research. If there were no readers, there would be no research, which makes you an invaluable link in the research chain. However, as well as being consumers of research, practitioners can and should strive to be producers of research.

This chapter introduces the concept of evidence-based practice and discusses how it might be used in social care practice or other similar social professions. As a current or future professional practitioner, you are encouraged to develop a 'research-minded' approach to your practice. At the same time you need to be mindful of the need to adopt a critical and inquisitorial approach to research or, more importantly, evidence. In adopting this inquisitorial approach we need to ask ourselves what constitutes best evidence and how we choose one source of evidence over another (Sheppard, 2004). This chapter offers an introductory-level framework that can be used to help in the analysis of evidence. It encourages you to become an active participant in the research process, but also advises you to adopt a cautionary approach in your use of evidence and how it guides your practice.

WHAT IS EVIDENCE-BASED PRACTICE?

Evidence-based practice has become a byword for better, more appropriate and efficient practice. In essence, an evidence-based approach asks that practitioners use the best available evidence to guide and inform their practice. There is nothing particularly new about the idea that policy and practice should be informed by the best available evidence. Evidence-based practice (EBP) was first introduced in medicine and allied health professions. More recently it has been advocated in social work as an alternative to 'authority-based practice' or practice based solely on the expertise and experience of practitioners (Edmond et al., 2006). Gibbs and Gambrill (2002: 452) define EBP as 'the conscientious, explicit, and judicious use of current best evidence in making decisions about the care of clients'. EBP represents a move away from opinion, past practice and precedent and towards a decision-making framework that relies on greater use of research and evidence. The basic principles underlying the EBP movement are that there is a hierarchy of evidence and that modern information systems can make the evidence available to practitioners at the point of care.

Why an evidence-based approach to practice?

The Department of Health and Children's (DoHC) policy document *Working for Children and Families: Exploring Good Practice* outlines seven management principles that should underpin child and family services, including the need for practitioners and their managers to 'ensure that their practice and its supervision are grounded in the most up-to-date knowledge' (2004: 15). More recently, the Health Information and Quality Authority's (HIQA) *National Standards for the Protection and Welfare of Children* state that standards need to be person-centred and 'based on evidence and best international practice' (2012: iii). Furthermore, the standards place an onus on staff to 'engage in continuing professional development and keep up to date with evidence-based practice in their area of practice' (2012b: 44). Similarly, the *National Quality Standards Framework for Youth Work* (OMYCA, 2010) also calls for practice to be evidence-based.

Gaffney and Harmon (2007: 8), in an overview of the proceedings of a National Economic and Social Forum (NESF) conference on evidence-based policy making, note that while it is not the role of the research community to design policy, it does have a role to 'assist in the design of policy, evaluation of its effectiveness, and, perhaps challenging the policymaker . . . based on the available evidence'.

Williams (2000) argues that the benefits of an evidence-based approach for social care work are:

1. More effective social care interventions.
2. Improved resource efficiency.

3. Improved analytical practice.
4. Raising the status of social care professionals.
5. Improved public confidence in social care.

Given that social care services have come under increasing public scrutiny in recent times, particularly in the wake of high-profile abuse scandals, it can be appreciated that anything that increases public confidence in social care provision is to be welcomed. Marsh and Fisher (2005: 3–4) make some convincing arguments for the adoption of an evidence-based approach to practice and these are summarised in Table 9.1.

Table 9.1. Arguments for the adoption of evidence-based practice

Reason	Argument
Impact on the immediate life chances of service users	In extreme cases, for example child protection decisions may influence life or death situations, practitioners should be as informed as possible
Impact on the long-term life chances of service users	As decisions made may affect, for example, educational outcomes or mental health, practitioners should be as informed as possible
Challenge to fundamental assumptions about social care	Evidence may produce a shift in the way practitioners, service users, the public and other allied professions see social care work
Provide safeguards to service users	There are substantial areas of social care where professionals have strong powers or where the courts may make decisions regarding major aspects of people's lives – having the best available evidence is an important way of controlling this power
Encourage and facilitate a more informed public	An informed public can engage better with relevant debates about services, and it is right that citizens have access to the best evidence
Inform service user and carer communities, and individuals	Direct involvement in services and engagement with the development of services requires access to the best evidence

Source: adapted from Marsh and Fisher (2005: 3–4)

Few would argue that social care interventions should not be as effective as possible. Few would disagree with the view that the use and application of new or existing interventions should be informed by evidence. While the arguments for the adoption of an evidence-based approach may be convincing, it should be noted that finding and using research, particularly of high relevance and good quality, is not always easy.

ISSUES IN ADOPTING AN EVIDENCE-BASED APPROACH TO SOCIAL CARE PRACTICE

Stevens et al. (2007) have reviewed the research priorities of practitioners working with children in social care in the United Kingdom. They highlight a number of important issues with regard to the expansion of the use of EBP. They found that social care practitioners make limited use of research findings in practice. The barriers to using research include lack of time, lack of research skills and research resources and, in many organisations, an underdeveloped culture of research use. Another problem highlighted was the range of target groups in social care: practitioners work with a wide range of clients, thus making it more difficult to adopt a unified approach to research.

Similarly, Rosen (2003: 199) identifies five factors that impede the implementation of EBP:

1. Characteristics of the knowledge to be used.
2. Characteristics of the practice situation and setting.
3. Attributes of the medium through which the knowledge is communicated.
4. Characteristics of the practitioner.
5. The socio-cultural context in which utilisation takes place.

While all of these factors certainly impact on the extent to which EBP is employed, there is little doubt that the characteristics of the practice situation and setting are a crucial factor. The characteristics of the setting create the context in which EBP is seen (or not) as an integral element in the working life of the practitioner. Adopting an EBP approach takes time; time to source and read research and time to implement new ideas and practices. If EBP is seen as having a low priority in a setting, then the necessary time may not be allocated.

In an Irish setting, O'Connor and Pettigrew's (2009: 1018) study of speech and language therapists found the most significant barrier to the implementation of EBP was a 'lack of time to read research' at 71.9 per cent, followed by 'methodological inadequacies' at 62.5 per cent and 'insufficient time to implement new ideas' at 59.4 per cent. If social care professionals are to be accorded greater professional recognition and standing, then the incorporation of EBP as an integral activity of practice needs to adopted, and that includes the allocation of sufficient time.

What constitutes evidence?

Using research in social care requires the integration of different types of knowledge. Pawson et al. (2003) have usefully produced a system for the classification of the sources of social care knowledge (see Table 9.2).

Table 9.2. Sources of social care knowledge

Type	Source
Organisational knowledge	Gained from organising social care, through governance and regulation activities
Practitioner knowledge	Gained from doing social care, which tends to be tacit, personal and context-specific
User knowledge	Gained from experience of and reflection on using social care services, which again is often tacit
Research knowledge	Gathered systematically within a planned strategy, which is mostly explicit and provided in reports, evaluations and so forth
Policy community knowledge	Gained from the wider policy context and residing in the civil service, ministries, think tanks and agencies

Source: Pawson et al. (2003: 22)

This system of categorisation should not be taken to imply that all sources of knowledge are equally regarded. Knowledge derived from positivist research generally appears to be held in the highest esteem. Not all research is regarded equally; health care, for example, has a well-established 'hierarchy of evidence'. At the top of this hierarchy are randomised controlled experiments and systematic reviews; conversely, studies employing observation are regarded as having less rigour and credibility (Davies and Nutley, 1999). This dichotomy in sources of evidence is frequently characterised by the conceptual shorthand of quantitative and qualitative for different approaches to research.

Qualitative research is a generic term for a range of different methodologies (Flick et al., 2004). While these vary in their object of investigation and methodological focus, they share a number of defining characteristics. For Bryman (2012: 380), the qualitative approach 'tends to be concerned with words rather than numbers . . . [where] the stress is on the understanding of the social world through an examination of the interpretation of that world by its participants'. It rejects the practices and understandings of the natural scientific model that is positivism and emphasises how individuals interpret and construct reality. From this perspective, the social world is not the same as the natural world: human beings can react differently in similar situations. Research methods or tools associated with this approach include observation, diaries and interviews.

Quantitative research is, as its name suggests, 'a research strategy that emphasizes quantification in the collection and analysis of data . . . in which the accent is placed on testing theories' (Bryman, 2012: 35–6). It reflects the practices and norms of the scientific or positivist model with its understanding that social reality is an external, objective and measurable reality (Sarantakos, 2005). This type of research is characterised by the tight control of the variables under investigation, protocols for measurement and intervention and the use of statistical testing to establish levels of confidence in the results (Houser, 2008). Research methodologies associated with this approach often include quasi- and natural experiments and surveys and sophisticated statistical analysis.

As previously noted, the two research approaches are not necessarily regarded as being of equal value. For example, with its presumed adherence to superior procedural rigour and validity, it is argued that quantitative studies 'produce some of the strongest evidence for the benefits of an intervention' (Houser, 2008: 38). Conversely, qualitative research is sometimes accused of being too impressionistic and subjective and it may be difficult to generalise findings (Bryman, 2012).

Some advocate that this either/or dichotomy should be treated with a degree of caution and scepticism. Layder (1993) claims that this debate is no longer useful; going so far as to suggest that it is a false distinction with no real merit. Punch (1998) argues that being at loggerheads about which approach is better misses the point, which should be about choosing the most appropriate method to answer the particular research question posed. Regardless of the research approach used, the knowledge produced by empirical studies is frequently regarded as superior to the knowledge produced by users and practitioners; an issue that we shall return to later in the chapter.

How do I critique evidence?

There is sometimes a tendency to overestimate the quality of a piece of research, particularly if the reader is less than familiar with the topic in question or inexperienced in evaluating research. Just because a study has been published does not necessarily mean it is good-quality research. The informed practitioner is someone who not only knows what the research says about the topic, but is also able to judge the quality and the relevance of the research (Sheppard, 2004). Becoming an evidence-based practitioner requires adopting a critical stance to research. Being critical does not mean *criticising* by simply pointing out the limitations of the study (Burns and Grove, 1997). Rather, it is about *critiquing* a piece of research through a methodical appraisal of the strengths and weaknesses of a study in order to determine its credibility (Coughlan et al., 2007). The key word in this instance is methodical: we need to adopt a step-by-step process that will enable us to make an informed judgment about the quality of the evidence offered. The framework outlined in Table 9.3 uses the questions a journalist might ask in order to understand a story: who, what, why, when and where? No framework can be considered exhaustive and this one is no exception. Nonetheless, it provides the novice researcher with a useful way to begin the process of evaluating empirical evidence.

Table 9.3. Critiquing research – an introductory framework

Who	Who are the authors? Are they practitioners and/or academics? What qualifications and experience do they have? Are they noted in their field of expertise?
	Who commissioned the study? Could there be an issue of funding bias (whoever pays the piper may call the tune)?
	Who was the target population of the study? Are they so dissimilar to the group that you work with that lessons may be difficult to apply?
	Who is the study aimed at? Is it meant for general readership, academics, policy makers and/or practitioners?
Where	Where is the study published? Is it a peer-reviewed journal? Is it a government report? Peer-reviewed journals generally adopt a more rigorous approach and consequently the study may have greater integrity and reliability
	Where was the study conducted? If the location is very different from your own, can the findings be applied? For example, if the study in question focuses on interventions in a residential setting, and you work in a community setting, are the findings applicable?
Why	Why was the study undertaken? Is it part of a postgraduate programme? Was it undertaken to evaluate an intervention or initiative?
	Why did the author(s) adopt one research method in preference to another? Is the methodology justified and consistent with the overall research approach, whether qualitative or quantitative? Do the methods chosen add to the general credibility and reliability of the study? Was it carried out in an appropriate manner?
When	When was the study carried out? How recent is the publication? Has the context changed much over time?
What	What operational definitions were employed? For example, if the study is about investigating poverty, what definition of poverty is being employed?
	What ethical safeguards were put in place? Were participants fully informed about their rights, such as confidentiality, anonymity and being able to withdraw at any time?
	What was the timeframe? Was it a longitudinal or a cross-sectional study? A cross-sectional study simply provides a once-off 'snapshot' of a phenomenon or event, which can be useful but it is understandably limited
	What is the research question? Is this question clearly stated? Qualitative studies are interested in understanding, rather than testing, thus they will simply have a question, whereas quantitative studies employ testable hypotheses and set out to either prove or disprove them
	What size was the sample and how was it selected? Quantitative studies generally require a sample size of at least thirty in order to be considered statistically significant, and the method of sample selection is also very important: probability or randomly selected samples are considered to be more appropriate. Qualitative studies are less concerned with probability and minimum sizes, rather they are concerned with providing a greater depth and richer understanding of the topic
	What is the strength of the link between the evidence and the conclusions and recommendations? Has the author(s) made a logical and believable argument?

Where can I find critiqued research?

As you become more adept at evaluating research, you may wish to enhance your range of research sources. Sifting through a series of research documents can be very time consuming. What the hard-pressed student or practitioner needs is a clearing-house for research. Luckily, there is such an organisation: the Campbell Collaboration. This resource is based on a well-established facility, the Cochrane Collaboration, which contains systematic reviews of research in the biomedical arena. A systematic review is an extensive and rigorous literature review that focuses on a single question with the aim of identifying, appraising and summarising existing research studies in order to derive guidelines that can inform practice (Houser, 2008). From the perspective of students or practitioners, a systematic review can take much of the drudgery and guesswork out of finding and evaluating a wide range of studies.

The Campbell Collaboration has adopted the protocols developed by its older sister organisation: it maintains a large group of members, reviewers and contributors who undertake systematic reviews in the areas of crime and justice, social welfare and education. The Cochrane Collaboration, with its medical focus, may be of less use to social care practitioners, but can provide useful material on topics such as mental health and health promotion.

Table 9.4. Useful websites for social care research

Organisation	Website
Health Research Board	www.hrb.ie
Institute for Research and Innovation in Social Services	www.iriss.org.uk
Social Care Institute for Excellence	www.scie.org.uk
The Health Well (All-Ireland evidence-based practice forum)	www.thehealthwell.info
Centre for Effective Services	www.effectiveservices.org
The Children's Research Network for Ireland and Northern Ireland	www.childrensresearchnetwork.org

If you have access to some form of institutional online library facilities you may well have access to a number of databases such as EBSCO and CINAHL. Without an institutional linkage, access to such databases is often not an option for many practitioners. Nonetheless, it is still possible to access pertinent and reliable evidence. For example, a number of charitable and voluntary agencies, supranational organisations (such as the Organisation for Economic Co-operation and Development and the European Union) and government departments provide a range of publications in the form of statistical returns, reports and policy papers, the majority of which are available on the Internet. A wide array of reputable organisations have websites through which quality research can be sourced without cost and recourse to an institutional online library. Given the huge number of possible resources, it is impossible to even begin to scratch the surface. Therefore, and with respect and apologies to the many organisations that I have omitted, Table 9.4 should simply be viewed as a starting point.

The socialstudies.ie website is another particularly useful starting point. It maintains a select database of hundreds of annotated web links to a very wide range of sources, organisations and documents that focus on areas of interest to the social professions, with a particular, if not exclusive, Irish focus.

Another recent phenomenon that has provided a source of reference for countless students throughout the world is the world's leading online encyclopaedia, Wikipedia. As with all sources of evidence, it is important to exercise caution and judgment when using Wikipedia. The problem with judging the trustworthiness of information 'on the World Wide Web is becoming increasingly acute as new tools such as wikis and blogs simplify and democratise publications' (Dondio et al., 2006: 362). On Wikipedia, topics are edited by the users, allowing any user to contribute information on a topic, but the site also relies on other users to correct errors found on the site. While a number of stories have highlighted the vulnerability of Wikipedia to hoaxes (Parfitt, 2006), there have also been studies that argue that Wikipedia is generally reliable. As a source of information to help clarify or introduce a topic, Wikipedia can be useful. However, as a source of definitive evidence upon which to base practice, the best advice is the Latin phrase *caveat emptor* (let the buyer beware).

Whichever source is used, it is vital that clear search terms are used. Gossett and Weinman (2007: 147) provide a helpful step-by-step guide to using electronic sources for locating evidence:

> *Step 1:* Convert client needs into answerable questions. Questions that lend themselves to searching for the best evidence must be specific enough to generate an answer in an electronic search.
>
> *Step 2:* Locate the best external evidence to answer the question. This step requires access to bibliographic databases such as the Cochrane Collaboration or Campbell Collaboration. In addition to database access, the skills to effectively navigate the various sources are important.
>
> *Step 3:* Critically evaluate the evidence. The framework in Table 9.3 can be employed as a useful starting tool.

When critically evaluating the evidence, Gibbs (2003) recommends the use of a rating form, such as the Quality of Study Rating Form, which can be located in his book *Evidence-based Practice for the Helping Professions* or its companion website: evidence.brookscole.com.

It is important to note that despite the huge advantages that the Internet presents to the student, researcher and practitioner, other media continue to be of great importance. Traditional sources of evidence such as books, theses, print journals and conference proceedings can inform practice. Regardless of the source of evidence, a systematic and critical approach should be employed (Tremblay and Downey, 2004).

PRACTITIONERS AS RESEARCHERS

Social care is a practice-based discipline, so there remains a potential difficulty in reconciling empirical scientific knowledge with that derived from experience and practice. As noted above, the former has taken precedence over the latter (Brechin and Siddell, 2000), reflecting what Schön (1991a) has termed 'technical rationality'. The philosopher Gilbert Ryle (1963) suggests that prepositional or 'knowing that' knowledge 'precedes and informs "knowing how" – that we must first learn the theory before applying it to practice' (cited in Rolfe et al., 2001: 6). If this is the case, then it can be appreciated how scientific theories or the 'knowing that' knowledge came to be seen as having pre-eminence over experiential 'knowing how'.

While Garfat (2009: 62) does not dismiss the contribution that an EBP approach can make, he encourages researchers and policy makers to work in harness with practitioners, warning them:

> . . . you had best be prepared for the fact that we are sceptical, so unless you have proof that involves the voices of youth, families and practitioners, you are in for a tough battle. And we, who are experienced . . . are watching you. If you are willing to work together then maybe together we can do a better job. But if you are here simply to tell us what to do, go someplace else.

The former director of research at the Joseph Rowntree Foundation, Janet Lewis (2001), offers a balanced view of the knowledge base for social care:

knowledge = evidence + practice wisdom + service user and carer experiences and wishes

As you can see from this formula, there is no hierarchy; knowledge is derived from the equal combination of all three components: evidence (empirical research), the practice wisdom or practitioner knowledge and the users' and carers' experiences and wishes. This formula maintains that practitioners as well as researchers can be the producers of knowledge and evidence. From this perspective, it can be argued that as well as using knowledge to become evidence-based practitioners, practitioners can produce knowledge and so inform others in their practice.

Engaging in research is widely accepted as being one of the defining characteristics of a profession. For Tripodi (1974), many of the processes and skills used in professional practice transfer easily and support the tasks required to undertake research. For example, in social care work, practitioners are required to make an initial assessment, while the researcher is required to formulate a question. The practitioner then designs an implementation plan, and the researcher designs a strategy that will enable the collection of the data, and so on. In essence, research and practice are about applying a methodical approach to solving a problem. You may already have begun the process of becoming a research-minded practitioner without necessarily being aware of it.

So, where does one begin? Table 9.5 provides some suggested entry points for beginning research. Research can involve a large team with plenty of resources focusing on a large number of people. It can also be a lone researcher focusing on one or two people. Just because the focus of a piece of research may be small, or it may have little widespread applicability, does not mean that undertaking that study is not worthwhile.

Table 9.5. Entry points for research

Research aim	Possible scenario
A problem in practice – an idea to test	A number of social care practitioners have reported that the effectiveness of therapeutic crisis intervention (TCI) with children in residential care for longer than two years appears to markedly drop, why might this be so?
A gap in the available data	The child protection team has produced local guidelines to help indicate whether an injury to a child might be non-accidental; however, there appears to be no such guidelines to draw upon for the elder care team. Surely such guidelines must exist. Could guidelines be sourced and presented to the team?
Service evaluation	Your family support unit has introduced summer camps as a pilot project. Anecdotal evidence seems to indicate success but you need to evaluate the effectiveness if you are to seek continued funding

Source: adapted from the Research Mindedness Virtual Learning Resource (resmind.swap. ac.uk)

A CAUTIONARY NOTE

Evidence-based practice has become a byword for better, more appropriate and efficient practice. In essence an evidence-based approach asks that practitioners use the best available evidence to guide and inform their practice. But we need to ask ourselves what constitutes best evidence and how we choose between one source of evidence and another (Sheppard, 2004).

While there are apparent benefits to the adoption of EBP, it should be noted that there have been a number of concerns raised. Principally, these concerns centre on the appropriateness and validity of the scientific or positivist approach to the generation of evidence, and the genuineness of the motives behind the adoption of an evidence-based approach.

In terms of questioning the appropriateness and validity of an overly positivist approach to EBP, Garfat (2009: 59) articulates these fears very well, stating:

> I worry that we are once again bowing our heads in the face of the scientific evidence, humbling ourselves as we prepare to worship at a new shrine and rejecting what we have learned to be true – that being troubled is not a medical condition; that no child is an experiment; . . . no amount of generalised mass test results can speak to who this child, at this time, in this context, really is.

In terms of the suitability of adopting such an overtly positivist approach to the generation of evidence, Plath (2006: 57) argues that 'the association of evidence-based practice with a scientific or positivist paradigm can produce tension for social workers who recognise the importance of reflective, interpretive and humanist responses to the personal and social conditions encountered in practice'. This tension can result in the marginalisation of the esoteric and aesthetic elements of care work, such as intuition, empathy and reflection. These elements cannot easily be reduced to quantifiable, measurable constructs and hence do not lend themselves easily to positivistic reductionism.

The genuineness of the motives behind EBP adoption can also raise some interesting and noteworthy concerns. As highlighted, one of the arguments for introducing an EBP approach is that it should bring improved resource efficiencies. One needs to acknowledge that the adoption of an EBP approach may have more to do with implementing efficiencies than with introducing the most effective practice. Remember, effective and efficient are not necessarily the same outcome. The pursuit of greater efficiencies can only be carried so far; agencies do need adequate resources. Adoption of an EBP approach to practice requires an honest appraisal of a number of issues, not least an agency's ability to implement new regimes or ways of operating. Fundamental issues such as staff workload, physical resources and staff qualifications need to be considered. However attractive it may be to adopt a more evidence-based approach to practice, the mundane resource issues also need to be attended to. As Blome and Steib (2004: 612) argue, 'EBP will not overcome structural issues like caseload size.'

CONCLUSION

A formalised evidence-based approach to social care practice remains largely underdeveloped. Nonetheless, it should be acknowledged that many practitioners are engaged in practice that is informed and reflective. There is much research available that focuses on the topics of interest to social care practitioners, such as childhood, addiction, intellectual disability and so on. The amount of this research that constitutes 'quality evidence' remains debatable. Social services are by their very nature fluid and dynamic, and practitioners need to be mindful of the potential to adopt a dogmatic approach. Sheppard (2004: 23) argues that practitioners should be 'looking at information that can help provide *guidance* and *better-informed judgements* but not certainty' (italics in original). Perhaps, given the nature of the debate and the nature of the work that the social professions are engaged in, the term 'research-informed practice' might be more applicable than 'evidence-based practice'.

10

Therapeutic social care practice

John Byrne

OVERVIEW

This chapter explores the link between social care and counselling. It explains the concepts of therapeutic work and mental health care, before highlighting the therapeutic role of social care practitioners as part of the broader mental health service. Social care workers are encouraged to identify the theory that informs the therapeutic element of their practice and to use the opportunity of statutory registration to formalise the counselling function of therapeutic social care.

INTRODUCTION

In 2013 CORU, the body responsible for the implementation of the Health and Social Care Professionals Act 2005, is expected to complete the process of formal statutory registration of social care practitioners. Once complete, practitioners will be required to register in order to practise. In order to register, they will have to meet certain criteria as stipulated by the social care work registration board. The task of social care will be identified and in order to have their courses validated by the registration board, education providers will have to meet a strict set of criteria regarding course content.

It seems reasonable to assume that the registration board's definition of social care will be similar to the existing definitions, such as the one put forward in the report of the Joint Committee on Social Care Professionals (JCSCP, 2002: 2), which states that social care is 'the professional provision of care, protection, support, welfare and advocacy to vulnerable or dependent clients, individually or in groups'.

While this definition is quite specific, there is a need for clarity in relation to some of the tasks it identifies. O'Doherty (2006: 25) seems to interpret the protection, welfare and advocacy role of social care as 'championing social justice' in the pursuit of equality for the less well off or disadvantaged in society. According to Lyons (2010), the care and support role involves the provision of physical and psychological supports to clients. The questions for the registration board are: When does championing social justice become community development (a similar but different profession)? And when does psychological support become counselling? There are no black and white answers to these questions as people services often overlap in their purpose and function and it can be difficult to ascertain where one profession ends and another begins (Moss, 2008). On the question of where social care meets counselling, the overlap seems to be in the provision of therapeutic care.

WHAT IS THERAPEUTIC CARE?

The term 'therapy' is derived from the Greek word *therapeia* meaning healing (Nelson-Jones, 2009); so to provide therapeutic care is to provide care to someone for the purpose of promoting healing. In social care, the term 'therapeutic' is borrowed from counselling/psychotherapy, where it relates to work that promotes psychological (rather than physical) healing. In 2008, 8 per cent of social care practitioners identified themselves as providing therapeutic care to their clients (Byrne, 2008).

In recent years there has been a growing association between therapeutic care and social care (Kennefick, 2006). While there are no Irish undergraduate courses that provide qualifications in specialist therapeutic social care, social care degrees will generally have a practice-based component that teaches basic counselling skills (Kennefick, 2006). Educators are quick to point out that even though we may teach counselling skills and use the term 'therapeutic' in relation to practice, social care practitioners are not counsellors. Lalor and Share (2009: 11) provide a good example of this guarded and somewhat confusing association by stating that social care places 'an emphasis on therapeutic work, but not in the context of more formal counselling'. They quote Anglin (1992), who identifies a practice of social care as providing 'counselling' on issues such as employment, death and dying, sexuality and marriage.

In Britain, Moss (2008) says that counselling skills are the building blocks of all communication in the people services. He places counselling skills on a continuum from hard to soft. At the harder end, counsellors provide 'in-depth psychological interviewing', while at the softer end, they provide 'active listening', which is the depth of skill that is the 'common denominator of all people work' (2008: 73).

Therapeutic social care

When clients access a service for the purpose of receiving professional social care, there is usually some sort of issue that is posing a barrier to their quality of life. The role of the social care practitioner is to provide the context in which the issue can be explored and addressed so that the client has the same life opportunities as everyone else. This is the pursuit of equality and social justice referred to by O'Doherty (2006). Depending on the client, the work may require anything from minimal intervention to the provision of intensive full-time residential care.

Social care clients present with a range of issues. They may be homeless, in state care or have been in prison. They may have any one of a range of physical, intellectual or sensory difficulties or disabilities. They may have various addictions or be victims or perpetrators of abuse, neglect or maltreatment. In working with these clients, social care practitioners provide care in the form of both physical and psychological support (Lyons, 2010). Physical support may involve the provision of food, shelter, housing or literacy skills/training, and psychological support involves helping the client to identify, understand and come to terms with (insofar as is possible) the reasons they are in the service in the first place.

Not every social care client wants or needs a deep level of psychological support. Some clients may drop into day care facilities once for advice or guidance on a particular issue and may never return. Others may present in extreme crisis and require intensive supports to enable them to cope with daily life. Social care practitioners do not tend to engage in 'deep psychological interviewing', but they do provide clients with a safe, informal and confidential space where they can give healing attention to issues that are of concern to them in their lives. This 'healing/holding' space is where social care is therapeutic and where it meets and becomes a form of quasi-counselling.

MENTAL HEALTH AND THERAPEUTIC CARE

Life is difficult; every day we are all presented with a series of challenges and choices. Our ability to cope with these challenges is a reflection of our mental health (Corry and Tubridy, 2001). In life, as with physical health, most people will experience periods of positive and negative mental health. When experiencing negative mental health, the majority of people find their own way of dealing with it. For those who seek professional help, therapeutic responses fall into two broad categories: medical and psychological.

The medical response has its roots in psychiatry, the mental health specialism of general medicine. In psychiatry, symptoms are assessed in accordance with criteria set out in the diagnostic manual, the DSM-IV (APA, 2000), and the patient is diagnosed and treated accordingly. Treatment may involve chemical (drug-based) responses, counselling/psychotherapy or a combination of the two.

Psychological responses to mental health involve counselling and/or therapy. Counselling is where two parties meet, each party usually (but not always) consisting of one person. The counsellor facilitates a process of therapeutic change by enabling the client, through talking, to find solutions to, or find better ways of coping with, the challenges of life. The concept of therapy is much broader. Therapy also facilitates a healing process, but there are over 400 types internationally, from approaches that use drama, dance and art to those that focus on breathing and energy flow in the body (Corsini and Wedding, 2008).

In social care, therapeutic work occurs in the context of both the traditional two-person counselling style, and through the therapeutic use of creative studies such as drama, art, music, dance and leisure/recreation. The benefit of creative studies in therapeutic work is that traditional counselling is only of benefit to someone who can talk and who has the emotional and intellectual capacity to engage in the counselling process. Creative therapies, however, can be used with a far wider variety of clients and are particularly useful in social care work (Lyons, 2010). For the purposes of this chapter, the term 'therapy' refers to psychotherapy, a form of in-depth talking counselling.

In integrative counselling theory, people's actions are influenced by four different, but related, processes that are going on within them all the time. These are our thoughts, our feelings and our spiritual and bodily processes (Palmer and Woolfe, 2000). The therapeutic aim of counselling/psychotherapy is to enable clients to raise awareness of, and achieve balance between, each of these processes so they can have a better understanding of their actions. The thinking is that when we understand our actions, we can learn to regulate each process a little bit better. We can then maximise the likelihood of being able to cope with life and therefore achieve and sustain a more positive mental state.

Clients who attend community-based counselling are generally living independently and are quite well able to control and regulate themselves. They can cope with life from day to day, but may require assistance on a particular mental health issue such as psychiatric illness, relationships, anger management or addiction.

Clients accessing social care services often present with a range of mental health issues. Their lives may be in a greater degree of crisis or instability than an average counselling client, and they may be less well able to cope from day to day. Examples can be seen with social care service users who are in active addiction and some clients in residential child care who present with chaotic, assaultive or destructive behaviours. In contrast to counselling, social care clients do not always choose to be part of a service and they may actively resist any kind of help or support. In these cases, even if the client does not want, or is not committed to, a process of therapeutic change, the work of social care is to maintain a confident but gentle, compassionate, supportive presence and to try to ensure that the client's actions are not making their life situation any more difficult than it already is.

Viewed from this perspective, there are more similarities than there are differences between counselling and social care. This is the rationale for the various personal development and counselling skills modules that are taught throughout social care education (Kennefick, 2006).

Practice example 10.1 illustrates what can happen when a staff member in the caring services does not possess the counselling skills required to manage volatile or difficult clients.

Practice example 10.1

Michael is a 22-year-old staff member working in a residential children's home. He holds an arts degree in history and psychology but has no qualifications in social care. Joe is a 13-year-old resident who has been diagnosed with attention deficit hyperactivity disorder (ADHD) and conduct disorder. He is currently taking prescribed anti-psychotic medication and sleeping tablets as he has ongoing difficulties settling at bedtime. While on shift, Michael noticed a strong smell coming from Joe's bedroom and on closer examination discovered a substantial amount of what appeared to be human faeces behind some furniture. Michael felt shocked and was almost physically sick. He proceeded to the living room where Joe was watching TV with the other residents and asked Joe why there was a 'pile of shit' behind his wardrobe. Becky (a 14-year-old female resident) called Joe a 'dirty scumbag', and Joe became infuriated. He attacked Michael, breaking his nose and two of his teeth.

Practice example 10.1 highlights the craft of care, the sharp edge of practice that requires a high level of confidence, skill, intuition, compassion and knowledge on the part of the practitioner. We can see that Michael's actions initiated a sequence of events that had a negative outcome for all concerned. If he had been aware of basic counselling skills and the potential impact of his actions on Joe, he would have known to handle the situation differently and there would most likely have been a very different outcome. It also raises questions about whether Michael and his colleagues should be trained to provide a deeper level of on-site psychological support and about whether Joe should be referred to a specialist counselling service. Either way, if there is to be any therapeutic work done with Joe on the issues raised, the first challenge for Michael and his colleagues is to establish a therapeutic alliance.

THERAPEUTIC ALLIANCES

A therapeutic alliance is essentially a psychological contract between client and practitioner (Dryden, 1988). It is more than a relationship, it is a commitment from both parties to engage in a process of change. For social care practitioners, establishing a therapeutic alliance can be the single biggest challenge in their work, particularly if clients do not want to be involved with the social care service.

In some cases the presence of a genuine alliance will require acute intuition on the part of the practitioner, since a service user may deceive and manipulate the relationship in order to get his needs met. This intuition is called a 'felt sense' (Mearns and Thorne, 2007) and is a finely tuned awareness that is essential in therapeutic social care work.

> ## Practice example 10.2
>
> Mary is a third-year social care student in a hostel for homeless men. She began her placement fearful and anxious but quickly settled in, describing the residents as 'ordinary people who had very hard lives'. One evening on shift a 30-year-old client who was addicted to heroin told Mary how he became homeless. Mary seized the opportunity for some therapeutic work and tried to remember all of her counselling skills from college. She was flattered that the client had 'opened up' to her and was deeply moved by his story of growing up in care and the trauma and abuse he suffered. When the client said he needed €5 for the bus fare to visit his children the following day, Mary did not hesitate to give it to him. The following day Mary is informed that the client has not visited his children for over a year and that he regularly tries to extort money from new staff to buy heroin. Mary feels cheated, foolish and angry.

In Practice example 10.2 there is no way of knowing whether Mary had a real connection with the client or whether she was just being manipulated. The challenge for Mary is not to let her emotional response block her from re-engaging with that client. Manipulation is what addicts do, and while it is not all right, it is part of the illness and it is the worker's job to be aware of that as a possible dynamic in the relationship.

THE INTERVENTION PROCESS

Assuming an alliance has been formed between the social care practitioner and the client, and the issue requiring attention has been identified and agreed upon, both parties can decide on the most appropriate response or intervention. An intervention is any conscious action that has the purpose of working towards meeting the identified need of the client. Sutton (2001: 169) describes the formal intervention process as having four stages:

1. *Assess:* need is identified in consultation with the client.
2. *Plan:* negotiate and agree a shared plan to meet the identified need.
3. *Implement:* put the plan into action, keep records and review progress.
4. *Review/evaluate:* determine the extent to which the objectives have been achieved. This stage becomes part of the assessment for the next intervention cycle.

This process is the same whether the aim of the intervention is to provide physical or psychological support. When providing psychological support, interventions may be divided into three categories for the purpose of discussion. They are subliminal, inactive and active.

Subliminal interventions

A subliminal intervention involves setting the context for more structured work. It can be put in place without requiring the client to be present and involves managing the environment so that, when the client arrives, it is most likely to produce the context for therapeutic change. Lanyado (2003) describes children as being like tender young seedlings. She says that in residential therapeutic work with children, 'the emotional and physical environment can facilitate or prohibit growth. In the same way that a seedling needs good soil, water, warmth, light and nurturance to survive, a child needs an environment that is conducive to emotional and physical development in order to grow' (2003: 66).

In social care, examples of subliminal interventions are clean, warm, informal, uncluttered spaces, clean windows, adequate and well-maintained furnishings, no graffiti, comfortable and relaxing sleep spaces and well-maintained outdoor spaces. This is an important and often overlooked aspect of therapeutic work, but the environment can either promote healing and positive change or create its own anxiety.

Practice example 10.3

I once worked in a homeless hostel in a flats complex in a disadvantaged area of Dublin. Each morning when I got into the lift I would be struck by the smell of urine and the occasional dirty syringe or pool of vomit on the floor. Between the unpleasant smells and the scorch marks and graffiti that adorned the walls, my mood was almost always negatively impacted by the experience of travelling in that lift. I often wondered what it must be like to live there and have that experience several times a day.

Inactive interventions

Similar to subliminal interventions, inactive interventions include non-verbal communication such as the practitioner's appearance, clothes, tone of voice, facial expressions and proximity to the client. Clients will judge practitioners based on how they look and act (Thompson, 2002), so the way they present will influence whether the client is calm and relaxed or anxious and stressed and it will also set the tone for the relationship. Social care practitioners must manage themselves so that the image they present is compassionate and supportive and neither too formal nor too informal.

Active interventions

When providing physical support an active intervention is a planned action that works towards a particular goal. An example would be developing and implementing a literacy or independent-living programme with a client. When providing psychological support, active interventions refer to everything the practitioner says to the client. All comments are conscious and are influenced by counselling theory. The type of comments/interventions made by a practitioner will vary hugely depending on what theory or therapeutic modality informs their work. There are very many counselling theories but they can mostly be divided into three main schools of counselling thought: the psychodynamic school, the cognitive/behavioural school and the humanistic school (Nelson-Jones, 2009). Each school evolved from its corresponding school of psychological thought.

The psychodynamic school

When people think of psychotherapy, they sometimes think of a client lying on a couch with the therapist sitting behind him writing on a notepad. This image has its origin in psychoanalysis, the original form of psychodynamic psychotherapy (Corsini and Wedding, 2008). Psychodynamic or psychoanalytic therapy was developed by Sigmund Freud (1856–1939) at the turn of the twentieth century (Nelson-Jones, 2009). By the mid-1800s therapeutic work with prison populations and patients in psychiatric hospitals in France and central Europe had found that talking to patients and treating them with dignity and respect could produce positive mental health outcomes. Freud, an Austrian psychiatrist, was interested in this and developed his theories on talking therapy while working with patients who presented with hysteria and anxiety disorders. Initially his work involved encouraging patients through hypnosis to explore early life experiences. He found the catharsis that was achieved was therapeutically useful and he crystallised his ideas with the development of psychoanalysis in the late 1880s.

In psychoanalysis, the therapist plays an expert role, facilitating clients to explore their unconscious mind through the use of various techniques such as dream analysis and free association (Nelson-Jones, 2009). The thinking is that adult mental health difficulties are a result of a constant dynamic (hence the name psychodynamic) struggle between our conscious and unconscious selves. The therapeutic aim is to help the client to bring the unconscious into the conscious, thereby reducing the struggle and achieving a calmer more positive mental state. Much of Freud's original work focused on the issues of sex and aggression with one of his better-known theories emerging as a result of self-analysis. Freud identified the 'Oedipus complex' when he became aware of his own childhood passion for his mother and jealousy of his father.

Transference is also a key concept in psychodynamic psychotherapy. Freud believed that early childhood relationships form the basis of later personality development. Transference is a phenomenon where a client sees the therapist not as who he or she really is, but as who the therapist represents to the client. Counter-transference is the transferential response that the therapist makes back to the client (Maroda, 2004). Some classical psychodynamic therapists suggest that the therapeutic encounter is a constant exchange of transference and counter-transference between therapist and client.

Freud suggested that human consciousness has three levels: the id, the ego and the superego (O'Brien, 2011). In psychodynamic theory every action is a result of a constant struggle between these three levels of consciousness. The id is a pleasure-seeking unconscious subjective reality that contains primal impulses. The ego restrains the id by interfacing between it and the outside world. The ego is influenced by rationality and social norms and will either facilitate the id in the pursuit of socially acceptable pleasure or suppress unacceptable impulses with the use of defence mechanisms such as repression. Freud used the analogy that if the id were a horse, the ego would be the rider. The superego is the moral part of the ego and is influenced by how we were parented and our social and cultural values.

There is no doubt that Freud was the founding father of modern psychology and everything we know about psychology and counselling/psychotherapy has evolved either as a development of, or in contrast to, what he thought. Within psychodynamic theory there are various branches or schools of thought, including ego psychology, interpersonal theory and self psychology (Corsini and Wedding, 2008), but if a client was to access a psychodynamic psychotherapist today the dominant theoretical influence would most likely be Adlerian or Jungian therapy.

Possibly the most influential psychodynamic theorists within therapeutic social care are Donald Winnicott and John Bowlby. Winnicott's work with therapeutic communities in Britain is the primary influence for contemporary theorists in this area such as Adrian Ward (Ward et al., 2003). There probably is no social care practitioner in Ireland whose practice has not been influenced by John Bowlby's attachment theory (see, for example, Fahlberg, 1994).

The cognitive/behavioural school

The term 'cognitive/behavioural school' refers to a category of therapeutic approaches that incorporate both behaviourist and cognitive theories. Behaviourism evolved from the lack of scientific evidence to substantiate the psychodynamic theory. It has its origins in Ivan Pavlov's and B.F. Skinner's theories of classical and operant conditioning, although contemporary behaviour therapy is far more scientific and complex. Traditionally there are three main approaches to behaviour therapy: applied behaviour analysis, neo-behaviouristic meditational stimulus-response model and the social cognitive theory (Corsini and Wedding, 2008). While all behaviour therapy focuses on interpretation of experience (rather than on experience itself), the main difference between the three is the extent to which they believe that cognitive (thought) process influences behaviour. At one end of the continuum, applied behaviour analysis gives little significance to thought process and relies almost exclusively on Skinner's principles of operant conditioning, while at the other end, social cognitive theory is heavily influenced by cognitive therapies.

Cognitive therapy was developed by an American psychiatrist called Arron T. Beck in the early 1960s (Nelson-Jones, 2009). Beck was a medical doctor with an interest in neurology and, on completion of his internship, he trained as a psychoanalyst. In his therapy work Beck noticed that clients' thought processes were influencing their emotional responses to him as a therapist. He was a little surprised to find that his analytical assessment of his client's process was (on occasion) simply wrong, so he changed his style of work to ask clients what their spontaneous thought process was during the session. He found that clients would often have irrational thoughts that would lead to misperceptions, which in turn would lead to feelings of anxiety. Beck believed the best way to deal with the anxiety was to catch the irrational thought and change it, creating a domino effect that would alleviate the subsequent anxiety. Where the client's thoughts were not irrational, the therapeutic process involved exploring the issues that caused concern with a view to finding a better way to cope with it.

Beck believed in the value of psychoanalysis and said that it had much to offer the understanding of human neuroses but he did not like the psychoanalytic establishment of the time. In traditional psychoanalysis clients may attend therapy several times a week for several years but Beck discovered that, with his new approach, clients could attend for ten or fifteen sessions and essentially be healed, or at least no longer feel a need for therapy. He also stopped placing his clients on a couch and moved to face-to-face seated dialogue.

As therapeutic approaches expand and evolve, they begin to overlap (Corsini and Wedding, 2008). In this regard Beck also gives credit to the work of Albert Ellis, who founded rational emotive behaviour therapy (Dryden and Neenan, 2004; Corsini and Wedding, 2008) and Carl Rogers, who developed person-centred therapy (McMillan, 2004; Mearns and Cooper, 2007).

From a social care perspective, an awareness of cognitive/behavioural interventions is essential, particularly for anyone going to work in the intellectual disability sector. Applied behaviour analysis (ABA) is one of the most common approaches to working with children with autism in Ireland (Maurice et al., 1996). In residential child care, therapeutic programmes are also often heavily influenced by behaviourist theory.

The humanistic school

The humanistic school of psychology was developed in the 1950s by Carl Rogers and Abraham Maslow. The school was described as the 'third force' in psychology and developed in contrast to both the psychodynamic and behavioural schools. Humanists found the psychoanalytic school too analytical and the scientific approach of behaviourists too rigid and reductionist (O'Brien, 2011).

The fundamental principle of humanistic theory is that everybody is essentially good and that we all have a natural predisposition to grow to our full potential or to 'self-actualise'. There is an emphasis in the humanistic school on personal responsibility and the human capacity to influence one's own future. Maslow is probably most famous for his theory of human motivation, which claims that people have five basic needs that manifest in the following order: physical, safety, belonging, esteem and actualisation. He said that in order to progress to actualisation, all the previous needs must be at least partially met (O'Brien, 2011).

The therapeutic application of this principle was developed by Rogers (1951) in what he called client-centred therapy. Several humanistic therapies have evolved subsequently, such as psychosynthesis and gestalt therapy. In all humanistic therapies, the emphasis is on the 'here and now' rather than on past life experiences. That is not to say that the past is not important, but only insofar as it helps us to understand the present. Ultimately, clients are encouraged to take control and exercise choice over the decisions they make in their own lives. A key principle here is called the 'locus of evaluation' (Mearns and Thorne, 2007), or the extent to which we do things in life to please other people. While cognitive/behavioural approaches also emphasise the importance of the 'here and now', humanistic therapies are more inclined to emphasise the client's emotional rather than intellectual process. They may incorporate body-oriented therapies that explore how emotional experience manifests in physiological symptoms.

Rogers (1951) acknowledged the possibility of transference as a feature in psychotherapy but did not see it as a significant issue. He also saw clients as the experts on themselves and the therapist's role as one of a facilitator of a process where the client raised this self-awareness. In humanistic therapy the therapist pays particular attention to the dynamic in the relationship between the two parties. Relationships are central to humanistic (and most other) therapies. Rogers suggested that in order for a therapeutic relationship to be helpful it needed to have three key components or what he called 'core conditions':

- *Genuineness:* Rogers believed that the therapeutic relationship is based on trust and trust is built between client and therapist; when the therapist's words are consistent or congruent with his or her actions, the therapist is being genuine. According to Rogers, when a therapist is incongruent, the client will sense it and the relationship (and subsequent work) will be hampered.
- *Empathic understanding:* the ability to see the client's world from the client's perspective (insofar as is possible) while remaining detached enough to remember that it is the client's world and not your own. Rogers said that when clients feel empathically understood they feel heard, and this is therapeutically helpful.
- *Unconditional positive regard (UPR):* this is possibly the most difficult of the humanistic principles to truly integrate into one's professional personality. UPR is about recognising that people are separate from behaviour and that behaviour is simply an expression of need. While people may do things that are not socially acceptable, that does not make them bad people, it just means

that they made a bad choice and that given the right opportunity they could make a better or at least a different choice next time. The principle of UPR is that all human beings deserve to be treated with dignity and respect, irrespective of who they are or what they have done.

While the three schools of counselling thought may have differences in emphasis, they all aim to help the client to find ways to alleviate the distress that is being caused by a presenting issue. Research by Professor Alan Carr (2007) for the Irish Council for Psychotherapy states that one in four people experience a mental health difficulty and that psychotherapy has a success rate of between 65 and 72 per cent on a range of mental health disorders.

In Irish social care practice, some agencies and colleges identify the school of thought that influences their therapeutic approach. Examples include the MA in Therapeutic Child-Care in Carlow College (St Patrick's) and the various children's homes that affiliate themselves with the Charterhouse Group of Psychodynamic Therapeutic Communities in Britain. At undergraduate level it is probably fair to say that the therapeutic element of social care education is best described as integrative (drawing from two or more theoretical modalities), with its foundation or dominant modality being the humanistic Rogerian approach. Post-qualification, it is also common for social care practitioners in residential child care to train in a four-day programme of therapeutic crisis intervention (TCI). The programme is accredited by Cornell University in New York and, while it does not affiliate itself to any particular therapeutic modality, the content would suggest that the approach is predominantly cognitive/behavioural.

When practitioners identify themselves as providing therapeutic care it is important that they are clear about the approach that informs their practice. The reason is that where several practitioners are working with the same client, the active interventions will be different depending on the theory influencing each individual practitioner. Mixed approaches could lead to inconsistency in service provision and unhelpful or confusing outcomes for the client. According to Corsini and Wedding (2008), the one thing that all the main theorists in counselling and psychotherapy have in common is that they are inseparable from their approach. Who they are as therapists is who they are as people. In order to be effective as a therapeutic social care practitioner you should probably believe in, and be committed to, the approach that informs practice in your place of employment.

CONCLUSION

Social care practice is complex and multifaceted. It requires staff to draw on a wide range of knowledge and skills so that they can assume any one of several different roles with, or on behalf of, their clients. At one end of the continuum, social care practitioners are political activists and agents for social change

(O'Doherty, 2006), while at the other they are mental health workers providing physical and psychological supports to a wide range of people in various levels of distress.

In the provision of psychological support, social care practitioners provide a sort of quasi-counselling service that has yet to be fully defined either in practice or education but has come to be known as therapeutic social care. There is little doubt that counselling skills are required for therapeutic social care, but it is not yet clear where the boundary of professional competence lies between it and formal counselling. There is an argument to say that social care practitioners are best placed (as in Practice example 10.1) to provide a deep level of psychological support to clients, but that would require significant changes to both social care practice and education. The establishment of CORU provides the ideal opportunity to clarify this issue and readers are encouraged to participate in this process by joining and actively participating in their professional representative associations.

Part III

11

The social care practice placement: a college perspective

Judy Doyle and Kevin Lalor

OVERVIEW

The aim of this chapter is to examine the supervision, management and operation of social care students' practice placements and to outline the roles of the student, placement practice teacher and college tutor. It considers the purpose of the practice placement and key events before, during and after the placement. The latest national guidelines for social care practice placements are examined: the Irish Association of Social Care Educators' *Social Care Student Practice Placement Policies* (IASCE, 2011) and the Higher Education and Training Awards Council's *Social Care Work Awards Standards* (HETAC, 2010).

This chapter is illustrated by the placement experiences of two social care students from Dublin Institute of Technology, which provide valuable insights into the challenges and complexities of social care practice placements.

ABOUT PRACTICE PLACEMENTS

Placements are an integral and mandatory component of all professional social care programmes. Social care students may be placed in various statutory and non-statutory settings that care for vulnerable people of all age groups, such as residential care homes, special schools, high-support care, community work, homeless agencies, drug treatment centres, disability services and care of the elderly services.

On placement, students experience the world of work, with its ups and downs. They see the impact of dedicated staff in difficult situations. They encounter the teamwork that goes on behind the scenes in meetings and networking with other professionals and they learn to understand how interdisciplinary work is applied in social care environments. They get to know how organisations work and relate to each other. Hence, the student placement should offer a secure and supportive environment for learning and imparting knowledge.

Placements can be a daunting prospect. For some students, it will be their first experience of the world of work; for more, it will be their first exposure to a client group of which they have various misconceptions, apprehensions and stereotypes. They will almost certainly find the work physically tiring; and it may trigger a host of unexpected emotional responses. We examine these issues in further detail below.

The practice placement is an aspect of social care education that must be carefully managed. Although fortunately rare, negative placement experiences can lead to profound student discouragement, even to the extent of leaving the social care area altogether. The possibility of negative issues arising must be considered before, during and after the practice placement to maximise the number of students who find their placement to be a positive, rewarding and successful experience.

Placement requirements

A working group comprising representatives of practice, management and academia from Ireland and overseas came together in 2010 to produce the Higher Education and Training Awards Council's *Social Care Work Awards Standards* (HETAC, 2010). These standards focus on three dimensions: knowledge, skill and competence. They mandate social care programmes to include a minimum of 800 practice hours on placement in a recognised social care organisation (in practice, some colleges require up to 1,200 hours). Where these standards and minimum placement hour requirements are not met, the term 'social care' may not be used in the programme award title.

The following minimum requirements must be observed (HETAC, 2010):

- The expected cumulative volume of all assessed (social care work) practice placement is normally 800 hours or more.
- While working in practice placement, learners should be closely supervised (and provided with formative feedback on their work) by an experienced, qualified social care worker (or another appropriate professional) with over-sight of the student's work by a qualified social care professional.
- Recognising that practice placement supervisors require certain pedagogical skills, including supervisory and practice education skills, appropriate training should be made available for them.
- Provision of practice placement is a partnership between higher education institutions and service providers and is a key part of the education and training process. Clear learning outcomes need to be agreed between them.
- Assessment (formative and summative) is required to determine the individual's learning outcomes from practice placements.

The Irish Association of Social Care Educators' *Social Care Student Practice Placement Policies* (IASCE, 2011: 1) states that it is the institute's or college's responsibility 'to ensure it can support the numbers of social care students that are recruited by providing adequate resources to support the professional practice dimension of the programme. This includes allocation of appropriately qualified staff for placement preparation, co-ordination, visiting and reviewing.'

IASCE (2011) has adopted a practice placement policy based on best international practice. It refers to: provision of pre-placement preparation; mandatory attendance at professional practice modules; a portfolio of evidence of skills and knowledge acquisition; evidence of fitness to practise in social care; and successful completion of all placement assessment forms. Agencies that facilitate student placements are encouraged to ensure that, insofar as is practicable, practice teachers/supervisors are qualified social care practitioners and have completed the IASCE supervisor training programme. Agencies should demonstrate a willingness to facilitate active learning by meeting the student prior to placement, organising induction training and proactively engaging students in the day-to-day work of social care practitioners. Supervision meetings should occur on a weekly basis and offer constructive feedback on the student's progress, difficulties, risks and challenges. While supervision is a supportive forum for students, they and their practice teachers are obliged to be transparent and forthcoming about any risks or fitness to practise issues that may arise during the placement experience. Should serious issues arise, the college may be consulted to recommend a course of action to resolve such difficulties.

Key players

The student, college tutor and the placement practice teacher are central to the student's placement experience and form a triad in practical and academic communication. The practice teacher or supervisor is generally an experienced, qualified social care practitioner who has undertaken to supervise the student's work practice in the particular agency. The college tutor is generally a member of the lecturing staff who monitors the student's progress with regard to course requirements. Finally, and most importantly, the student is registered on a programme of study and is committed to becoming an effective social care practitioner.

This tripartite relationship (see Figure 11.1) is central to the 'learning by doing' model adopted by social care courses. The practice placement is the

Figure 11.1. Tripartite relationship between student, practice teacher and tutor

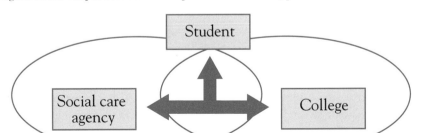

interface between theoretical knowledge and practical experience of hands-on work. Individual thresholds of stress, strengths and weaknesses are explored and tested at the coalface of social care practice. Coping mechanisms are enhanced and developed.

THE PURPOSES OF THE PRACTICE PLACEMENT

The purposes of practice placement are to expose the student to the practical world of social care work in a controlled manner; to facilitate the acquisition of practice skills and knowledge; and to link theory to practice.

Placements are designed to encourage the development of a professional social care practitioner who can work therapeutically with clients, solve problems, make decisions effectively and efficiently, implement and evaluate the effectiveness of treatment programmes, understand a client's value system, respond appropriately to collective and individual needs, and keep records and case files. Such practitioners are: aware of the needs and rights of various client groups, skilled in forming relationships, constructive teamworkers, respectful of confidentiality, reliable, responsible, intuitive, observant, and sensitive in communication with vulnerable people.

KEY EVENTS BEFORE THE PRACTICE PLACEMENT

Supervision by college tutors begins on a student's first day in college. It should involve induction training for first-year students along with individual and class tutorials, development of relationships with lecturers and monitoring of pastoral and academic wellbeing. Students are requested to read and familiarise themselves with IASCE and college student placement handbooks, where common standards on student placements are documented. A number of important factors for tutors to consider before a student is allocated a social care placement are noted below.

Quality of fit

An early consideration for the college tutor is the compatibility of the student's abilities with the requirements of the agency. While a majority of students will adjust well to most working environments, there are exceptions. Occasionally a placement will be terminated because of gross unsuitability. This may be a result of the particular demands of an agency or the personality of a given student. It is vital, therefore, that student placement 'fit' is given serious thought. Tutor familiarity with the demands and expectations of agencies is essential. A college tutor will strive to build up knowledge of care agencies that can provide high-quality supervision of students. In some circumstances, a student might present certain traits that are particularly demanding of supervisors. For example, a student may have encountered difficulties in practice placements in the past or shown resistance to instruction. Some supervisors pride themselves on being able to provide a positive learning experience for students who have previously had unhappy experiences.

The student's preferences must also be considered. Ideally a student should experience a range of social care agencies and client groups to gain an overview of the diversity of social care work situations. Students should have the opportunity to express preferences for particular client groups. Occasionally a student will have overwhelming apprehensions about a particular client group, often as a result of circumstances in their own background. Such fears must be respected, and students should not be placed in a position where they are fearful on work placement. Of course, confronting mild apprehensions is an important aspect of active placement and is usually resolved satisfactorily. Indeed, there is a strong sense of empowerment in overcoming initial apprehensions and learning to be comfortable, and work effectively, with a particular client group.

Garda vetting

Following lobbying by IASCE, individual colleges and other relevant associations, Garda vetting of all social care students became operational in 2007. Vetting is processed through a designated person in each institute of technology or college who liaises with the Garda authorities. The Garda Central Vetting Unit conducts the search of Garda records and returns the findings to the college's designated officer (often the admissions officer).

In the vast majority of cases, the vetting shows no recorded conviction against the student. In the small number of cases where a student is shown to have a criminal conviction, it is then the decision of the college authorities to determine whether the nature of the conviction makes the student unsuitable to register or re-register on a social care programme. Such judgments will be made according to a policy document in operation in each college. Many colleges use a template developed in University College Cork and approved by the Irish University Association.

It is important that all applicants to social care programmes who have a criminal conviction declare this to the appropriate college authorities before undergoing Garda vetting. Failure to disclose a conviction (even an apparently minor conviction unrelated to working with social care clients) is considered by college authorities to be a serious deception. Of course, having a criminal conviction does not make a person automatically unsuited to social care work. As noted above, college authorities will judge whether an individual should be allowed to register on a course of study. In turn, managers in practice placement agencies will determine whether they will accept the student on placement.

Pre-placement visit

Placement supervisors will be concerned that the student is mature, committed, amenable to instruction and reasonably comfortable with the client group. In order to determine this, a pre-placement visit should be arranged. In addition to allowing the supervisor to screen students, this visit also plays an important role in allowing the student to determine whether a proposed placement is workable. Students should arrange this pre-placement visit themselves so that they can begin to take control of, and responsibility for, the placement. It should be impressed upon students that it is their placement and their responsibility to ensure that it is as rich and rewarding an experience as possible.

Students should bring a CV to this meeting so that supervisors can keep on file a record of the student's relevant previous experience. Supervisors will often seek written and verbal character references for the student. This requirement is in line with standards of best practice set down by the Social Services Inspectorate and the Registration and Inspection Service for residential care homes that operates under the Health Information and Quality Authority (HIQA).

Pre-placement seminar

When students have been matched with suitable agencies, it is useful to hold a seminar to discuss the roles and expectations of practice teachers, students and tutors alike. Such a seminar is an opportunity to consider a range of important issues.

Professionalism

The minimum standards of behaviour expected of students on placement must be made clear, such as professional boundaries, ethical obligations, punctuality, reliability and confidentiality. The practice placement may be the student's first experience of the world of work and they may need clear guidelines. For example:

* *Punctuality and attendance*: the student's working week should be that of the social care staff in that agency.
* *Dress code*: the majority of agencies take a relaxed, informal stance on the issue of dress code. Practice teachers will require a level of professionalism in terms of dress code as they do not always approve of typical student attire.
* *Smoking*: this is not acceptable in the presence of many client groups and should never occur in the presence of children.

Students should adopt a kind, empathic approach to clients and ensure that organisational rules are consistently applied. Students must appreciate the importance of treating clients with respect. In residential care, the student is working in a home-from-home environment; this is a privileged position and students must be aware of their obligations in this regard.

Recognising limits

The desire to 'make a difference' is a natural and commendable aspiration of many social care students. Such an aspiration can sometimes be the product of an insufficient grasp of the complexities of the cases they are likely to encounter. A more realistic understanding of the nature of social care work will decrease the likelihood of disillusionment and disappointment in not achieving the elusive 'breakthrough' after a matter of weeks. The emotional aspect of care work should be recognised. Students come from a variety of backgrounds and will vary in their maturity and ability to deal with upsetting cases. It helps to acknowledge that social care practitioners work with vulnerable people. Strategies for dealing with upsetting incidents at work include having outside interests, such as sports and hobbies, informal support through discussion with others in the field and the formal support of tutors and supervisors.

Befriending clients

Another natural tendency for students is to strive to be popular. Of course, the primary goal of social care practitioners is to be effective in their interaction with their clients rather than to be liked. A common pitfall is that a student may become so friendly with clients that the separateness necessary to function professionally is lost. A common example is where a student becomes drawn into 'slagging' and overt criticism of staff, thus undermining their own position as a student on placement. Students should practice the principle of controlled emotional involvement at all times.

Altruism

Does altruism really exist? The pre-placement seminar is a useful opportunity to question our motives for becoming involved in social care work. Jungian psychologists suggest that there is a strong link between the impulse to help people and the need for power. As Hawkins and Shohet (2007: 8) explain, 'The role of helper carries with it certain expectations. Sometimes clinging to our role makes it difficult to see the strengths in our clients, the vulnerability in ourselves as helpers, and our interdependence.'

Evaluation and assessment

Ultimately, a judgment will be made as to the student's performance. The college's specific procedures for such an evaluation must be made clear to students.

Sometimes students fail a placement or the placement breaks down. The alternative arrangements that may or may not be made in these circumstances should be made clear in advance.

Student's pre-placement checklist

- Be professional in your dealings with agencies. Remember, you are an ambassador for your college and your course.
- Be aware of the legal framework, national standards and guidelines on child protection and welfare that govern social care practice.
- Recognise your limitations.
- Mind your own feelings and emotions.
- Do not befriend clients.
- Be aware of your duty of care.
- Be aware that Garda clearance is required.
- Be open to advice and constructive criticism. Remember, your performance will be formally assessed.
- Familiarise yourself with the agency's policies and procedures.
- Familiarise yourself with the agency's statement of purpose and function.

KEY EVENTS DURING THE PRACTICE PLACEMENT

Once the placement begins, the day-to-day management of the placement shifts to the student and practice teacher, although the college tutor retains an important role. Let us consider the roles of each part of this triad.

Supervisor/practice teacher

Practice teachers who agree to monitor and assess a student's practical learning have undertaken to provide an appropriate induction programme. At a minimum, this should involve introducing the student to staff and clients; familiarising the student with the aims and objectives, work practices and roles of different personnel; guiding the student through the physical layout of the agency; and clarifying the agency's rules and ethos. The supervisor should:

- Establish mutually agreed goals and learning objectives towards which the student will work during the placement. These goals should be formalised in a written document that can be reviewed periodically and should be linked with the college placement assessment form.
- Develop a relationship of trust and confidence with the student.
- Encourage the student to identify specific learning needs and target related goals.

- Set aside time for an agreed regular meeting with the student to give feedback on progress and discuss issues arising out of the placement.
- Facilitate the student in applied academic projects, portfolios, assignments or interventions.
- Make an end-of-placement report. Students should be involved in this process and be aware of the content of the report. The report should be signed by both the student and the practice teacher.

Student–practice teacher meetings should be predictable. They should be held at a set time each week. Some agencies claim to be habitually 'tearing busy' or 'in a crisis' and find difficulty in providing students with adequate supervision. The suitability of such an agency for further student placement should be carefully considered. Writing of social care staff supervision, Skinner (1994: 76) highlights the important link between supervision, good practice and integration of learning in residential care:

> ... staff should receive supervision from their line manager, covering both their day to day work and their professional development. Such supervision is not a luxury; it is a prerequisite for good practice and sound management. Regular individual supervision is always difficult to achieve with the constraints of a staff rota, and is extremely vulnerable to any kind of crisis large or small. But it is the means by which staff can integrate learning and experience.

Weekly student–practice teacher meetings should be held in order to facilitate feedback to the student and to provide an opportunity for students to discuss their learning. Students and supervisors should keep a written record of the salient points discussed at such meetings and future learning needs should be identified. The IASCE *Practice Placement Manual* (2009: 15) states:

> It is important that supervision is part of the training experience of the potential caring professional. As well as learning the 'what' and how' of the social care profession, the student must develop self-awareness and an ability to explore new practice challenges in a safe way. It is a central role of the supervisor to facilitate this process.

Student–practice teacher interaction should be an exercise in constructive criticism. It is not a forum for 'showing off' or 'nagging'. Nor should students perceive comments as 'put-downs' or an affront to their ability. Rather, it should be an opportunity for the student to benefit from the guidance of an experienced professional. Students and practice teachers should be open, honest and straightforward in their dealings with each other. It is only in this way that emerging difficulties can be identified and managed. In the words of the IASCE *Practice Placement Manual* (2009: 11), students must 'work through' rather than 'get through' the placement.

Student

Students have two primary roles while on practice placement, First, they must strive to make the placement as rich a learning experience as possible – to seek and heed guidance and instruction, where necessary, and to bring a positive attitude to dealings with colleagues, clients and families. Second, they must monitor the quality of the placement. For various reasons, the student–practice teacher relationship may become unsatisfactory. Students may feel that they are not being given adequate opportunities, or they may find that a practice teacher is no longer available due to, for example, holidays, illness or maternity leave. It is primarily the student's responsibility to communicate such developments to the college tutor so that a solution can be arranged.

Students are also ambassadors for their college. While each student should be taken on his or her own merits, the reality is that agencies will build an impression of a particular college and its courses based on its previous experiences with that college's students.

The ultimate goal for the student is to become a competent and skilled practitioner who has knowledge breadth and depth and who understands how to transfer this knowledge to social care practice in a skilled and professional manner.

Tutor

During the placement, the college tutor will continue to monitor the student's placement experience. This may be by way of small group discussions around relevant issues or through one-to-one tutorials. Tutors must be alert to issues that might require their intervention and be available to students to deal promptly with any such issues. A further function of tutors is to arrange placement visits where the student, practice teacher and tutor will meet formally to discuss the student's placement experience and decide on future targets and placement objectives. The visit will be arranged between the practice teacher and tutor, and the practice teacher should ensure that the student is informed about, and adequately prepared for, the visit.

CASE STUDIES

Justin's experiences

My social care placement experiences have been very positive and valuable. In my view, it has been the most important part of the course, as without it the academic knowledge acquired would not have had a clear applied link to practice. Being able to use what has been learned in lectures while also observing the practical skills needed to work in social care is what makes the practice placement so important.

My first practice placement was in the learning disabilities sector and, while I was not given a huge amount of responsibility, I did learn a lot about myself. It gave me the confidence that I could actually do this type of work, and also that I enjoyed it and it was something I wished to continue in. It is only through reflection that I also realise that I used classroom learning subconsciously during this placement.

Staff support was essential to this practical learning. While there are invariably some staff members who you may not see eye to eye with, having the support of most of the team can make or break a student's experience and confidence on placement.

How the staff and supervisor deal with certain situations is also crucial. Someone who will not let a student be in a situation they cannot handle, but who will allow some situations to develop to facilitate the student's learning is a supervisor who offers valuable and insightful opportunities to a student. This was exactly the type of supervisor that I experienced in youth and community work. The project workload was often hectic, but my supervisor was brilliant, making sure to fit my academic work in with the placement plan we had set out at the start. The supervisor trusted me and gave me appropriate responsibilities, and explained why she was getting me to do certain tasks and the importance of such tasks.

During our supervision meetings she set out what I was doing well and not so well, and explained how I could improve in certain areas of practice. One of her supervision techniques that impressed me was if I was making mistakes, she would let them run their course, as long as it was not putting anyone in danger physically, psychologically or emotionally. When this happened it made me realise the importance of shift planning and the need to be astutely aware of what is occurring in my work environment. Everyone makes mistakes, but not everyone will be fortunate enough to have a supervisor who will let certain mistakes happen and then teach you what you should or should not have done. This learning has remained with me and will influence my future practice.

As most students on social care courses are female, my placement agencies and clients were surprised to meet a male social care student. The lack of males in some agencies can affect the quality of care, for instance on outings. Not having a male carer for toilets and changing rooms can cause difficulties and embarrassment. As a male social care student, I may have been slightly more cautious in some circumstances. Clients put me in some awkward situations, but this was not a problem due to having strong staff to support me. Whether this is because I am a male or purely because I was a new member of staff and the clients wanted to test the boundaries, I'm not sure, but I was made to feel uncomfortable due to being a male. Social care needs to attract more males, and if it is done correctly, with appropriate safety measures in place, the benefits of having a gender-balanced social care team will enhance the level of care and provide appropriate role models for vulnerable people.

My placements have augmented my strengths and made me aware of my weaknesses. This is due to the support of supervision and the type of experience one can only get from working in a social care agency. I feel I will be a more capable and confident social care practitioner when I leave college because of my academic learning applied to experiences in practice placements.

Danielle's experiences

My first placement was in a special needs school for children with mild to profound learning disabilities. When I applied to do the BA social care course, I was unaware that I would be doing a placement in this area, so I had no idea what to expect and I was very anxious. On the first day of my placement, I sat in the hallway watching the children coming into school. Most of the children were in wheelchairs, some could not speak and others had very little body movement. I met with the school principal, who described the range of disabilities that the children have and the effect on their lives. The principal also explained how the school operates and gave me a copy of the mission statement before bringing me to meet the class where I would work during my placement.

Initially I was unsure of my role in this area of learning disabilities, as I did not have the specialised training of a special needs teacher. I felt useless, as I could not help with feeding or lifting the children, but as I observed the care practices it did not take long for me to adjust to the routines. The disability sector is very hands-on and although I could not do certain aspects of the work, I could spend quality time listening and doing art and drama activities with the children.

By the end of my placement I did not want to leave. Because the children had disabilities they were more vulnerable, and leaving them was stressful. The children loved to be cared for and to get hugs; and spending time with them and seeing their faces light up gave me great job satisfaction. Working in the disability sector has given me greater self-awareness. It has changed my perspective on my life and shown me how easily I can take things for granted, for example walking and talking. Furthermore, seeing how much these children love their lives and how resilient they are is a very humbling experience.

My third-year placement was with adolescents aged between twelve and sixteen who lived in residential care. I met my supervisor in the residential home prior to starting my placement. At this meeting, my supervisor provided me with information on their service provision, my role on placement and the specifics of work in a residential care setting. Meeting my supervisor before starting my placement gave me great confidence. I also received induction and external training during the first week in the residential home, which helped me feel like part of the team. My supervisor met me every second week and talked through my placement experiences. I felt supported, as supervision was carried out professionally.

I had prepared myself for children who would be challenging to care for because they had experienced many difficulties in their lives. However, I met young people who liked to laugh and play and who needed affection. They did have times when they were stressed and challenging, but because I had seen their vulnerable side, it made it much easier to understand and support them. Studying challenging behaviour, principles of professional practice, psychology, communications and child protection gave me direction during placement. Learning about working in the life-space of others helped me to assist the young people to feel self-worth by reflecting good times from their day.

'Principles of professional practice' had taught me self-awareness, to be professional and not to become too emotionally involved, and to keep my perspective on the heartbreaking life stories of the young people to myself. I learned that while I cannot change their past lives, I can make the time that I am with them memorable for good reasons, therefore on placement I began to understand what empathy really means.

In the disabilities sector, the social care practitioner's role is very hands-on as the young people need physical and emotional care and depend on you for day-to-day routines. In residential care, the young people are more independent and even though you are needed to cook and clean with them, your role is more observational and involves active listening. You need to be an emotional rock that will be strong and will not break, because at times they may break down or act up. Psychology plays an important part in both the disability sector and in residential child care, as you must be aware of the young people's psychological development in order to monitor how they are coping and to determine how much help they need.

At the end of each placement, the practice teacher completes an assessment form detailing how well you did during your placement. It emphasises the strengths and weaknesses that you brought to the placement. During the year, your college tutor visits you on placement, which can be daunting, as you might be very good in the classroom but it is very different when you work in the field. Placement is a time to put theory into practice. You are still learning and you can be unsure at times, so it is essential to have guidance and support from an effective supervisor. Seeing how valuable supervision was during my placement in residential care made me realise how much supervision was lacking in my previous placement.

Discussion

Justin and Danielle offer helpful insights on the placement experience in social care work from the student's perspective. Their accounts demonstrate the diversity of placement types and their different individual experiences as a male or female worker. It is interesting to note the influences that each placement had on them as students in their self-awareness development, and on their life perspectives and appreciation of their quality of life. The significant learning curve provided in the learning-by-doing model on practice placement clearly incorporates the social care practitioner's required core competencies (see Table 11.1).

Table 11.1. Social care practice: core competencies

COMMUNICATION	
• Empathy	• Care plans
• Observation	• Aftercare plans
• Culture awareness	• Reunification
• Behaviour triggers	• Role of family
• Empowering	• Action plans
• Active listening	
• Love and care	**INTERVENTION**
• Questioning	• Immediate needs
• Clarifying	• Long-term needs
• Validating	• Attachment issues
• Summarising	• Self-harm/abuse
• Evaluating	• Health care
• Monitoring	• Identity
• Report writing	• Cultural context
• Sensitivity to literacy	• Education
• Teamwork	• Confidence building
• Links to other professionals	• Self-esteem issues
• Networking with family and significant others	• Positive identity
	• Social skills
	• Life skills
	• Aftercare
ASSESSMENT	• Independent living skills
• Needs of service users	• Impulse control
• Cultural norms	• Anger management
• Relationships	
• Family dynamics	**SELF-AWARENESS**
• Sensory deprivation	• Self-management
• Prioritising essential needs	• Professional judgment
• Identifying long-term needs	• Stress management
• Risk analysis	• Objectivity
• Monitoring work climate	• Empathy
	• Calm in crisis
PLANNING	• Reflective judgment
• Situation analysis	• Appropriate power
• Strategic plans	• Emotional control
• Objective setting	• Externalising abuse/stressors
• Prioritising goals	• Identification of coping strategies
• Key work management	• Collusion avoidance
• Time management	• Ongoing up-skilling
• Policy knowledge	• Consistency
• Procedures and laws	

The importance of the practice teacher's delivery of supervision to a student is crucial on several levels of learning and in understanding the application of theory to practice. Justin and Danielle refer to the significance of formal, structured, consistent supervision and to the empowering role that the practice teacher plays in developing young practitioners' confidence in their ability to understand professional boundaries. Induction to placement and agency-based training are noted as informative tools that help to abate student anxiety. Danielle notes her experience of weak supervision in the disability sector, while Justin highlights the male perspective and the learning challenges that his practice teacher posed for him in allowing certain situations to develop.

KEY EVENTS AFTER THE PRACTICE PLACEMENT

The evaluation of a student's performance as 'satisfactory' normally concludes the practice placement. A student assessment form will be completed by the practice teacher/supervisor, in the presence of the student, and should be countersigned by the student. Generally speaking, placements are assessed on a pass/fail, rather than on a graded basis. Each student should be assessed at their own level – that is, a mark of 'satisfactory' does not indicate that their performance was that of a 'satisfactory' care practitioner, but that it was that of a 'satisfactory' student of social care work at a particular stage of development.

The student evaluation is primarily the role of the practice teacher/supervisor, but it is the college tutor who will present this result for ratification to the college examination board. Thus, the tutor must be satisfied that it is a fair assessment of the student's performance. Two further tasks remain for the college tutor. The first is to elicit feedback from students on the quality of supervision that they received on placement and the overall quality of the learning experienced (this may be done individually or at a collective placement review workshop). This information helps to ensure that the agencies in which students are placed offer high-quality supervision and learning experiences. The second task is to co-ordinate a practice teachers' meeting, which generally involves inviting practice teachers to attend a seminar where feedback on the management of student placements can be discussed. It is a useful opportunity to invite a guest speaker to talk about a topic related to supervision in social care.

End result

The staff team in an effective practice placement agency will collectively support and be inclusive of the student on placement, while the practice teacher will support the student in this steep learning curve. This is a dual process that should result in the student blossoming in the following areas:

- Self-knowledge and open accountability
- Proficiency in client advocacy
- Critical incident analysis
- Interpersonal skills
- Clarity of role, role expectation and task acquisition
- Reduced anxiety with awareness of potential stressors
- Aspiring to standards of excellence in their duty of care towards others

- Team player awareness
- Moral and ethical awareness of the use of power with vulnerable people
- Ability to handle fear
- Awareness of professional obligations in role-modelling; respectful behaviour to service users and colleagues
- Awareness of the unpredictable nature of the work and the need to look towards positive solutions based on consultation and participation
- Being child-centred, with an awareness of the relevant legislation, child protection and welfare guidelines and the UN Conventions on Human Rights and on the Rights of the Child
- Promoting equality by opposing oppression, discrimination and racism and by acknowledging ethnicity.

In conclusion, one of the most important attributes that students of social care can have is a sense of humour. While social care work can find practitioners working with some of the most vulnerable people in society, where sadness and poverty abound, there will also be good times with positive outcomes. Such good humour can prove invaluable and has often been used appropriately to ease tense situations.

When working with crisis, it can be easy to be wise in hindsight. Sometimes there is a sense that all the experience or learning in the world will not prepare us adequately for certain work-related circumstances. One can look back and feel a sense of achievement when, finally, a child happily returns home or is doing well in foster care, or an adolescent is successful in her exams, or Mum succeeds in giving up alcohol. Truly, such rewards are the essence of social care work.

ACKNOWLEDGMENTS

We would like to acknowledge the significant and insightful contributions of Danielle McKenna and Justin McCarthy, DIT social care graduates, to this chapter. Danielle and Justin have openly described their placement experiences; this valuable information will serve to enlighten academic tutors and practice teachers in their support to social care students.

12

Using professional supervision in social care

Eileen O'Neill

OVERVIEW

Professional supervision is an integral part of effective practice for many social care practitioners, but for others it can remain an irregular and confused experience. This chapter focuses on how to use supervision to ensure it is a positive resource that benefits staff at all stages of their career and contributes to the ongoing development of the organisation. Such supervision facilitates practice that is accountable and relevant to the needs of those who use the services at times of need.

Attention is paid in this chapter to what professional supervision is and why we need it. The chapter introduces the three functions of supervision and the dual-focus approach. It outlines how professional supervision can be used as a student, as a staff member and as a supervisor.

BACKGROUND

To ensure that supervision is used as a positive resource, it is necessary to understand fully its purpose and functions, and to accept that both supervisor and supervisee share responsibility with the organisation for its effectiveness.

As far back as 1950 Bruno Bettelheim identified the need for supervisory support for staff working in residential child care settings. Fifty years later the *National Standards for Children's Residential Centres* (DoHC, 2001a) in Ireland echoed this view by identifying that:

- All staff members receive regular and formal supervision, the details of which must be recorded. (2.13)
- There is an effective link between supervision and the implementation of individual placement plans. (2.14)

The inclusion of these criteria as standards has led to supervision becoming a reality for those working in residential child care services, although how participants experience supervision varies considerably. Those working in community-based services or those employed in the disability sector do not have such a mandated requirement for supervision, although, in recognition of best practice, some such organisations ensure that supervision is available.

In recent times a number of factors have contributed to highlighting expectations and improving practice around supervision. The Health Information and Quality Authority (HIQA) has made a significant contribution and continues to include attention to supervision in its inspections of residential child care settings. Section 2 of HIQA's (2009: 5.13) national quality standards for people with disabilities states, 'All staff receive regular supervision appropriate to their role'. Section 5 of the child protection and welfare standards (2012a: 5.3) highlights that 'all staff are supported and receive supervision in their work to protect children and to promote their welfare'. It adds that 'supervision and support are provided to staff so they are clear regarding accountability and reporting lines and the appropriate child protection and welfare procedures to be followed'. Furthermore, it requires that 'Written records are kept of each supervision given to staff. The record is signed by the supervisor and the individual at the end of each Supervision . . . and is available for inspection.'

Coupled with the above developments is a parallel increase in the attention paid to the role and practice of professional supervision in third-level colleges for students of social care practice, among others. This has led to students and newly qualified graduates entering the workplace with a more informed and realistic expectation of the place regular supervision plays in effective practice.

WHY DO WE NEED PROFESSIONAL SUPERVISION?

Society in general has become more demanding of service provision, with an increased expectation of quality and standards. Legislation has placed a higher requirement for accountability in all areas of working and public life. Key statutes in the area include the Safety, Health and Welfare at Work Act 2005, Freedom of Information Act 1997 and Protection for Persons Reporting Child Abuse Act 1998. Recent scandals in political life, in the business world and in professional services have also highlighted the need for a recognised framework for accountable practice and for the ongoing development of practitioners in a supportive environment. Professional supervision, when provided and used effectively, contributes to this.

The reasons why we need professional supervision may be summarised as:

- *Professional task:* the professional dimension to a discipline requires recognition, structure and monitoring. Supervision is part of accepted practice in a number of disciplines such as psychology, occupational therapy and social work as well as social care.
- *Inquiry reports:* inquiries into service deficits and abuse have identified the absence of regular, formal supervision for a range of staff in the health sector

(Laming, 2003; Leavy and Kahan, 1991; McGuinness, 1993). The recommendations of these reports strongly advocate the availability and use of regular, structured supervision, particularly for those working in the areas of child care and protection. Evidence of learning from the gaps and mistakes of the past must be integrated into responsible practice.

* *Accountability:* practitioners must be accountable for what they do and for how they do it. Employers need to have established structures that facilitate this process.
* *Workers are a vital resource:* investment in the human resources of services can aid staff retention and is recognised as beneficial for effective and improved delivery of services. Research (Sinclair and Gibbs, 1998) suggests that supervision is important for staff morale. This is crucial at a time when fewer people are expected to do more and when many experienced practitioners have left the workplace and have not always been replaced. Those who remain must be facilitated and supported to develop in a competently confident manner. People are more likely to stay in a job where they feel valued and good about what they do.
* *Continuing professional development (CPD):* now more than ever, practitioners see CPD as a necessary component at all stages of their career. Qualification is an entry requirement and ongoing development of skills and self-awareness is necessary in order to become a truly competent practitioner.
* *Duty of care and recognition of demanding work:* supports and structures to enable staff to work in demanding and potentially stressful working environments are recognised and accepted as necessary.

WHAT IS PROFESSIONAL SUPERVISION?

Professional supervision is a partnership process of ongoing reflection and feedback between a named supervisor and supervisee(s) to ensure and enhance effective practice and to support practitioners in carrying out their roles and responsibilities. It offers a structured opportunity to discuss work, to reflect on practice and progress and to plan for future development.

As supervision is a partnership, both participants have responsibilities. When entering any partnership it is necessary for both parties to be aware of what is expected of them and of what they can reasonably expect from the other. The partnership of supervision requires that there are clearly identified expectations and responsibilities on both sides. Examples of responsibilities shared by both supervisor and supervisee at supervision meetings include: preparing for supervision, contributing to a relevant agenda, starting on time, using the allocated time fully, providing honest two-way feedback and communication, and ensuring that there are no interruptions and that postponement is rare.

Describing supervision as a process indicates that the functions of supervision need to permeate beyond the supervision meeting and become integrated into practice. This process of supervision is evident when the supervisee leaves supervision with something to think about as well as identified objectives for their practice. Experiencing supervision as a process is more likely to contribute to the ongoing development of the participants and, potentially, of the service.

Reflection and feedback are recognised as key components in all supervision. Reflective practice is regarded as a means to develop self-aware professionals who possess the maturity and insight to learn from their experiences – the positive experiences as well as those that require improvement. Participating in supervision provides the opportunity for reflection on the detail of day-to-day practice as well as on any significant events that may have occurred. Reflecting on practice with another can lead to greater objectivity through exploration and feedback. Feedback in supervision is a two-way process: both supervisor and supervisee share responsibility for its effective use.

The core process of supervision takes place in regular, planned, structured time, between a named supervisor and supervisee(s). This time provides an opportunity to ensure the standard of service and care to those who use the services, and facilitates the practitioner's development in a supportive manner. Some circumstances may require additional supervision, perhaps in response to a particular change or difficulty. It is important that responsive supervision is available at such times.

While supervision in social care generally takes place on a one-to-one basis, it is useful if attention is also paid to the supervision of the team as a whole. Service delivery depends on the manner in which the team functions, and teams can benefit greatly from the opportunity to reflect in a structured way on their practice, with a view to identifying the strengths of the team and the areas that need further development.

Some people are confused about the role of supervision. One reason for this has been the many and varied ways in which supervision has been experienced by practitioners. For some, supervision has been experienced solely as a response to a concern or crisis and has thereby become associated with problems only. This limited view of supervision has contributed to negative interpretations and uses of what can be a positive and proactive resource. Other practitioners have found supervision to be nothing more than 'checklisting' to make sure that they have carried out certain tasks. This form of supervision often leaves supervisees feeling that they are back at school, having their homework corrected – not a very empowering experience for adults with responsible workloads!

Supervision will be used effectively only if its functions are identified and understood from the beginning of one's career and if supervisor, supervisee and organisations share common and realistic expectations regarding its implementation. It is necessary to know what supervision is not as well as what it is.

Supervision *is not* a casual activity that takes place over a cup of coffee, an occasional chat, an optional extra, a counselling session, an appraisal, a grievance session, a telling-off, something that happens only when there is a problem or something that happens only when there is nothing else to do.

Supervision *is* a regular opportunity to:

- Reflect on the daily work – the process as well as the content.
- Discuss any particular responsibilities of the supervisee.
- Monitor and ensure the quality of practice.
- Identify and further develop understanding and skills.
- Seek and receive support and feedback.
- Consider the impact of the work.
- Keep up to date with agency changes and requirements.
- Be constructively challenged.
- Identify areas for further professional development and implement a professional development plan.

Three functions of professional supervision

Traditionally three functions of professional supervision have been identified. Inskipp and Proctor (1993) used the terms 'normative', 'formative' and 'restorative' to describe these functions; these can be reframed as accountability, support and learning/development functions:

- *Accountability* for effective practice and service delivery. It is important that practitioners are accountable and are held accountable for their work.
- *Support* for individual staff members to carry out their work in a demanding work environment.
- *Learning* and ongoing development and self-awareness of the participants.

Locating these functions in a triangle (Figure 12.1) highlights the clear expectation that supervision must balance attention to all three areas to be at its most effective. These interrelated and overlapping functions are apparent over time in good-quality supervision. Ensuring attention to this is the responsibility of the supervisor, but they must also be understood by the supervisee who is required to be open to all three functions.

Figure 12.1. Balance of the functions in supervision

Accountability

Support   Learning

Source: based on Kadushin (1976)

Each of these three functions needs to be present in a balanced way over time if supervision is to meet its objectives. The skilled supervisor is aware of this and has the ability to home in on a particular need while remaining focused on the overall functions. The overlap between the three functions is apparent in the majority of situations brought into supervision, but regular overemphasis on any one or two components will not lead to the best use of supervision.

If the main focus is on *accountability* to the exclusion of the other two functions, there is a risk of 'checklist' supervision becoming the norm. This will monitor the content of the practice of the individual to a certain extent, but fails to pay due attention to the wider picture. Some managers may overemphasise this function, as ensuring accountable practice of others is the remit of the manager, but the supervisor must be aware of the fit between accountability and the other functions if supervision is to be truly effective.

If *support* is the primary objective of supervision, there is a likelihood that it may become a crutch for the individual while they move from one difficulty to another. Recently appointed supervisors or those who supervise colleagues can overemphasise the support function at times, at the expense of the other two. Professional supervision must facilitate supervisees in a supportive manner to help them deal with the reality of their work in an often complex and challenging environment. It must also be about more than support if it is to ensure the ongoing development of accountable practice.

When *learning* is regularly the main objective in supervision, there is a risk of it being viewed as a teacher/pupil interaction. In such situations, the supervisor is expected to be the source of all knowledge and the supervisee the receiver of the information. This can eventually lead to the supervisee, although well informed, having limited opportunity to develop through self-reflection and responsibility. Ongoing and lifelong learning are recognised as necessary in today's workplace. Supervision provides a regular and structured opportunity to integrate the learning from everyday work experiences and to become more competent in the process.

DUAL-FOCUS APPROACH

In the past supervision frequently had a single focus for many practitioners. It either focused on their responsibilities, with particular attention paid to checking up on the work, or provided a forum to focus solely on themselves, with little, if any, attention paid to the details of the work. Neither of these approaches on their own leads to effective supervision. Rather, a combination of both promotes the best use of the supervision.

Maintaining a dual-focus approach (see Table 12.1) ensures an operational and a developmental focus. The *operational* aspect considers the work: the detail of practice, with attention to the particular responsibilities of the individual in the context of their job description. The *developmental* aspect considers the person who carries out the job: the person as a practitioner.

Table 12.1. Dual-focus approach to professional supervision

Operational focus is on the task of the job and the tasks of the work	Developmental focus is on the person who carries out the job
• The purpose and function of the service • The job description and responsibilities • Policies and procedures • The client group – assessing needs, direct care, forming and maintaining professional relationships, etc. • Care plans, key work, recording, report writing, behaviour management	• The skills and strengths of the supervisee and areas for further development • The impact of the work on the practitioner • Reflection on practice, ideas, experiences • Being a team member and teamworking • Being an advocate • Formulating, implementing and evaluating a professional development plan (PDP)

Source: O'Neill (2004)

The skilled supervisor makes the link between these dual aspects. This is what moves supervision from being a discussion 'about' something to talking 'through' the issue. Supervision that only facilitates talking 'about' something is not likely to lead to greater insight, clarity or understanding, which should be objectives of quality supervision. To achieve these, it is necessary for the supervisor to display the ability to explore with the supervisee what is being said, and to examine the implications for practice and for the practitioner's role. It is by this attention to exploring or 'unpicking' that the supervisor helps supervisees to make sense of the situation and of themselves within its context. This approach also helps to identify areas in which the practitioner is skilled and competent and to highlight areas where further development is needed.

Skilled supervisors do not rush to find solutions to every point raised, rather they slow the process down and, through exploring the issue in its context, assist supervisees to become aware of their options or the actions required. This more inclusive means of supervision is less likely to perpetuate dependency.

PROFESSIONAL SUPERVISION IN PRACTICE

Professional supervision is an effective resource at all stages of working life, from student practitioners to experienced professionals in senior positions. This part of the chapter introduces Maria at three different points in her career and considers her use of supervision at each stage.

Maria – using supervision as a student

Maria is a student on a social care course. She has enjoyed her studies, particularly the varied nature of the programme, with its mix of theoretical and practical subjects. She knew that practice placements are part of the course and looked forward to this new experience with a mixture of anticipation and apprehension.

Preparation for placement had taken place throughout the academic year, with lectures considering the purpose and function of placements and the roles of the college, the student and the workplace. Maria had visited the workplace, as required, in preparation for her placement. She had met the manager of the service and the staff member who was to be her direct supervisor for the twelve-week placement. She was aware that regular, structured supervision was a requirement of all placements, but, despite all she had been told in class about what this would entail, she was not sure what she thought about it.

This situation was not helped by the mixed messages she was getting about supervision from fellow students and friends:

- One person had experienced supervision as a friendly chat with her supervisor, with whom she worked daily. The supervisor was herself less than a year out of college. After the first few weeks, this chat began to be more casual and less focused on the work. The student found this enjoyable at a personal and social level, but not helpful in using the placement as the learning opportunity it was meant to be.
- Others had very limited contact with their supervisor, whom they met only for periodic, brief supervision meetings because of frequently cancelled appointments. The students felt that the meetings were rushed and merely went through the motions of what supervision should be – there was little investment by either party in making them work. In fact, the students felt they did not need to make any effort at all, as the supervisor did most of the talking anyway.
- Supervision was experienced differently again by others who worked with an experienced member of staff as their supervisor. Although working together most days provided the opportunity to discuss aspects of the work as they arose, they also met, uninterrupted, once a week to reflect on themselves and on the work and to plan for the coming week. These students felt they had been challenged to do better and therefore supervision was a worthwhile experience, although not always easy.

With all of this in mind, Maria was curious as to how she would experience supervision in her placement. She had been told that the agency had a clear supervision policy for staff as well as students, but she was also aware that policy and practice do not always match.

Remembering from her placement class that both supervisor and supervisee are together responsible for how supervision is experienced, Maria realised that she had a part to play in making sure that she got what she wanted and needed from it.

Jane, who was to be her supervisor for the next twelve weeks, met Maria on the first morning of her placement. Jane had been working in the centre for three years. She explained that she had set aside an hour later in the morning for them both to consider the details of how the placement would be structured. Maria was given a copy of the centre policy on student placements and on professional supervision, for consideration later. In the meantime Maria was shown around and introduced to members of staff and to three adolescent boys who were residing in the centre at the time. So began her placement.

From the beginning, there was an expectation that all those working in the service, regardless of their experience or position, would participate in regular structured supervision at least every four weeks. The policy and practice matched perfectly in this regard, as supervision was incorporated into the working day for all.

Maria was told in the first meeting with her supervisor that they would meet weekly unless one or other was sick or there was an immediate crisis; in the latter case, supervision would be rescheduled for later in the day. The purpose of these meetings, as outlined in the policy and identified by the supervisor, was to enhance the placement experience through regular reflection and feedback in order to ensure that Maria began to look behind what she was seeing and experiencing and develop her understanding and self-awareness in the process.

In the early weeks, and based on the experiences of her friends, Maria was somewhat sceptical about the proposed frequency and expectations regarding supervision. She also experienced a little apprehension, as she feared that supervision might turn into nothing more than a litany of her mistakes and transgressions.

Maria and her supervisor did, in fact, meet weekly throughout the twelve-week placement and also had two extra meetings to ensure that the support and direction she needed were available to her when a particular crisis occurred. Because supervision happened regularly and frequently, as planned, Maria quickly became comfortable with meeting her supervisor and discussing all aspects of her placement experience.

Her supervisor helped Maria to consider the range of things that were included on the agenda. Examples of these were:

- The policies of the particular service and how they impacted on direct practice.
- The needs of adolescents in general and how such needs can be met in a group care setting, while also taking into account the specific needs of each young person and the reasons for their admission to care, as well as care plans, key work and working with families.
- The value of undertaking ordinary, everyday tasks for and with young people.
- Identifying her own strengths and skills and the areas she needed to develop further for professional practice. Maria received regular, balanced feedback throughout her placement. Her supervisor spoke honestly to her, highlighting areas of concern or difficulty and how she could improve, while also affirming, with specific examples, Maria's strengths and skills.

There was a clear focus on integrating reflection on practice at all stages of her placement experience. This introduced Maria to the practice and process of reflective practice, which was to stand to her in her future career.

Maria – using supervision as a staff member

Having qualified eighteen months ago, Maria now works as a social care practitioner in a residential child care service, with young people aged twelve to sixteen years. She is one of a team of eight staff who work closely with teachers, psychologists and social workers to ensure wide-ranging services to the young people and their families.

Maria finds her work satisfying and challenging in equal measure. Working with young people who present with such acute needs and individual behaviours ensures that every day is different, with no likelihood of boredom. Although in her second year out of college, Maria finds that she is still constantly developing skills and gaining new insights.

When Maria arrived in the service, her induction highlighted that she, like all staff, would participate in structured supervision every four weeks. Again, this information brought up a mixed response in her. It reminded her of her previous experiences of supervision as a student and she wondered what her new supervisor would expect of her. She was somewhat apprehensive, as she could not imagine how she would use supervision once she became familiar with the work. In chatting to other staff, she discovered that some staff used supervision to discuss the key work they were involved in or to look at a report they had to prepare – this sounded straightforward enough; others used it, they said, as a 'sounding board' – this sounded rather vague to Maria, who could not fully imagine what that meant.

Molly, who worked as one of two social care leaders on the team, was Maria's supervisor from the outset. The first supervision meeting explored their previous experiences and ideas of supervision and examined its purpose and function within the service. They discussed the possible uses of supervision and examined the service policy regarding how the details would work between them. The meeting concluded with both of them signing a brief contract of commitment to the supervision process. Before they finished, Maria was asked to consider what she had taken from the meeting and realised that she was more relaxed and clearer about supervision.

The features of the supervision would be:

- They would meet once every four weeks for one hour – this was outlined in the policy and was in keeping with residential services generally.
- The meeting would be recorded on the agency recording form at the end of each meeting. They would both be involved in the recording, which they would sign. The form would be kept by the supervisor, and Maria could access it through her or through the line manager at any time.

- The agenda, to which they would both contribute, would be decided at the start of each meeting.
- Information shared between them would not be discussed with the rest of the team members. Both had a responsibility to highlight with their line manager any difficulties that might arise if they were unable to resolve them together.
- Although supervision received a high priority within the service, it was acknowledged that there might be some circumstances that might require postponement of an occasional meeting. In such an event, they shared responsibility for rescheduling the meeting as soon as possible.
- Supervision would be reviewed between them at least twice a year. This would give them both an opportunity to give and receive feedback on how each of them was experiencing supervision, what was working and what needed to improve.

Maria also felt that she had begun to get to know a little about her supervisor from some of the discussion they had shared. She was surprised to find herself looking forward to the supervision to come, her apprehension considerably lessened.

In the early days of supervision Maria used the time to ask questions concerning the policies of the organisation and to find out more about what to do in certain situations with the young people and when working with their families. Her supervisor responded at times with very specific information and direction. At other times, Maria was asked her opinion on a situation, and then her response was further discussed relating to a specific area of the work.

Maria always arrived to supervision with a list of items for the agenda. At times, this was drawn up in a panic just prior to supervision, with little thought given to preparation in between the meetings. But Maria was happy that she could think of things to talk about. Her supervisor was careful to facilitate Maria in reflecting on her actual practice and the rationale behind this last-minute approach. Through supervision, Maria became more self-aware. She realised that she had a responsibility to plan for the meeting in order to get the most from it. This would benefit her in a realistic manner within her practice.

Her supervisor helped Maria to identify the skills that she was using and to further develop her ability to cope with all the new experiences she was meeting in day-to-day practice. Through reflection on events within her area of work, Maria was guided to recognise alternative strategies for managing both young people and her reactions and interactions.

Using speculation, with her supervisor asking 'what if' questions, helped her to explore new approaches to practice in the safety of supervision. She no longer felt afraid to voice suggestions and opinions and participated more effectively in team meetings as a result. Her skill in advocating for young people was also developed through supervision. As she grew more self-aware, her supervisor was better able to challenge her around scenarios and thus encourage her to move out of her 'comfort zone' to consider new ways of working.

At one of their regular review sessions, her supervisor used feedback to identify changes in Maria and her practice. Through a mutual exchange of reflections on her practice, they were able to create a picture of Maria's development to date. She was both surprised and delighted by some of these changes. This process helped her to recognise that her confidence had improved significantly, although she also acknowledged her need to continue to develop. Using this information, they focused on identifying areas for Maria's ongoing development in the coming year.

Her supervisor assisted Maria in formulating a professional development plan. Maria's main objective was to become more competent in understanding the 'bigger picture' so that she could avoid her tendency to get bogged down in one aspect of a situation. They broke this overall objective into specific tasks that related to her daily practice and current workload. These included:

- Considering the children in her care within the context of their families.
- Examining the wider regional and national policies and legislation that inform practice.
- Looking at her skills and how transferable they are to other client groups and areas of work.
- Reflecting on her attitudes and how they impact on her decision making.

These areas were incorporated into the process of supervision over the coming months. This gave Maria a particular focus for her work and contributed to her increased motivation. She also began to use supervision in a more responsible way.

Maria – using supervision as a supervisor

Three years after graduation Maria successfully competed for and was recently appointed to the post of social care leader within the unit. She is aware of the wider organisational issues associated with working in the service and is familiar through her practice with the policies and procedures and their implication for effective service delivery.

Maria's experience in supervision has helped her to progress to this stage. In recent months she reflected on the skills necessary to achieve promotion to this senior post. She was encouraged by her supervisor to examine her motivation for seeking more responsibility and to identify areas she needed to develop further to be effective in the role. This ensured that Maria continued to work within a context of awareness around her ongoing development, achievements and needs. As part of her new role she has supervisory responsibilities for a number of other social care practitioners.

Maria has learned to use her supervision consistently to deal with the realities of her experiences. In this way she is able to voice her concerns and anxieties about her new role within supervision. Together with her supervisor, she identified the skills necessary for her to become an effective supervisor for other staff. The list included listening, reflecting, supporting, prompting, questioning, guiding, problem-solving, time-management and feedback skills.

Through discussion and prompting, Maria became aware that she already employs these skills in her everyday work. To be an effective supervisor, she would need to focus on her use of these skills and to develop a methodology for transferring them into her role as a supervisor. Attending the forthcoming training for new supervisors within the organisation will help this. In addition, Maria's ongoing supervision with her own supervisor will play a crucial part in her ability to become a good supervisor.

Working with her supervisor, Maria realises that one of her main anxieties as a new supervisor is that she will be expected to supervise staff members with whom she previously worked on a peer level. Her supervisor helps her to recognise that maintaining the balance between the three key aspects of supervision – accountability, support and learning – is the priority at this stage. She knows that it would be all too easy to slip into a supportive, empathic role and to fail to question, challenge or direct practice.

It is here that remembering the principles of the dual-focus approach will inform her practice as the supervisor. The important point to keep in focus is that the two facets of practice – the task and the person in the task – must both be examined and reflected upon.

In discussing her concerns with her supervisor, Maria is challenged to consider her own first impressions of supervision and subsequent actual experiences, and their impact on her attitudes to being a supervisor. Through her reflection, the importance of developing a clear framework within which she can commence and continue the process of supervision with her new supervisees is highlighted.

As she prepares for her first supervision meeting, Maria establishes a plan for this framework, identifying certain areas for inclusion, which she discusses with her supervisor:

- The need for both supervisor and supervisee to tune in to each other's expectations and experiences of the supervision process.
- The need to identify what is meant by professional supervision to ensure a shared understanding from the outset.
- The need to clearly explain and establish the ground rules, practicalities and policies relating to meeting for supervision.
- The drafting and signing of an agreed contract for supervision.
- The process and practice of recording a summary of the supervision together.
- The need to provide the proper environment for effective supervision. This includes an interruption-free zone with no external pressures to distract either person (no phones or mobiles, no emails or web-browsing, no callers, etc.).

In keeping with the principles of supervision, Maria feels sufficiently secure to discuss with her supervisor, on an ongoing basis, any concerns she may have regarding her own role as a supervisor. Through continuous reflection and challenge, Maria develops her knowledge, awareness and confidence as a supervisor in her new role. This is not always easy and at times she becomes aware of just how skilled her supervisors have been throughout her career to date. She realises that:

- She was facilitated to develop at her own pace.
- She was encouraged to question and also to consider her own opinions.
- She was supported and did not feel judged at times of doubt and confusion.
- She was challenged to improve in specific areas.
- She received regular feedback as a matter of course. This feedback was always presented clearly and was relevant to her practice – at times it was affirming and at other times it was corrective.
- She received direction and guidance.

Maria recognises that good supervision did not happen by chance. It required sustained, focused effort on behalf of the supervisor, realistic commitment by the organisation, and active, responsible engagement by the supervisee. Both supervisor and supervisee have a responsibility to make sure that the supervision they engage in is good supervision. To achieve this, they have to commit responsibly to honest, respectful communication, feedback and reflection.

CONCLUSION

Working in social care can be incredibly satisfying and also incredibly challenging. Supervision is seen as a reflective space to help identify the satisfactions and help manage the challenges. It provides opportunities to 'step back' from the immediate demands and complexities of daily situations and to review practice, responses and experiences. Furthermore, professional supervision is useful for helping practitioners to focus on themselves doing the work, to examine what they are aiming to achieve in specific involvements and interactions, to rethink approaches and interventions, to review their development and to ensure safe practice.

Used well, professional supervision contributes significantly to the development of accountable, competent, self-aware practitioners who display the ability to articulate and communicate their professional judgments across a range of settings to benefit those in their care. Working with people at times of vulnerability or need in their lives demands self-aware practitioners of the highest calibre who are in touch with their own strengths and limitations. Active and responsible participation in regular, structured supervision can contribute to meeting these demands at all stages of professional life.

13

Managing challenging behaviour

Eleanor Fitzmaurice

OVERVIEW

This chapter explores what is meant by 'challenging behaviour' in a social care context and outlines strategies for its management. Working with vulnerable and distressed service users may entail increased risk of verbal or physical aggression, with consequent effects on the social care practitioner's emotional and physical wellbeing. It is also important to remember that some service users may not channel their distress or anxiety into aggression towards others, but may harm themselves. Supporting service users who display challenging behaviour requires knowledge, insight, empathy, skill and consistent teamwork. Characteristics of effective service responses to managing challenging behaviour will be outlined in this chapter. An overview of issues of workplace health and safety will be provided in the concluding section.

Because people who use social care services do not form a homogeneous group, it is not possible to devise a set of instructions – a one-size-fits-all system – for the management of challenging behaviour in all social care settings. What this chapter aims to do is to point out generally applicable principles and strategies for managing situations where there is the risk of upset or injury to staff or service users due to challenging behaviour. Challenging behaviour is an individual's response to a system of relationships. Effective behaviour management requires consideration of the service user's individual characteristics and needs within the social and cultural context of the care organisation. Workers in these situations should be well trained and confident in their use of appropriate behaviour management techniques and should be able to rely on a robust team support system. Organisational systems should be flexible enough to respond to the differing and changing needs of service users and staff.

DEFINING 'CHALLENGING BEHAVIOUR'

Emerson (1995: 4–5) provided the classic definition of challenging behaviour as 'behaviour of such intensity, frequency and duration that the physical safety of the person or others is likely to be placed in serious jeopardy or behaviour which is likely to seriously limit or delay access to and use of ordinary facilities'. This definition was developed in the context of the needs of people with intellectual disabilities, but has subsequently been used in a wide range of social and health care contexts.

It is interesting to note that interpretations of this definition have altered over time. Challenging behaviour was initially assessed in terms of the degree to which it impeded a person's access to the ordinary, everyday settings that constitute normal social life. The *challenge*, therefore, lay in how a service should respond to the client's complex needs. The term is now used to mean 'problem' behaviour, disruption, hostility and potential violence.

The main forms of challenging behaviour have been identified as 'aggressive/destructive behaviour, self-injurious behaviour, stereotypy, and other socially or sexually unacceptable behaviours' (Male, 2003: 162). According to Kissane and Guerin (2010), after Qureshi (1994), a person is to be identified as having 'challenging behaviour' if their behaviour meets one or more of the following criteria:

- The behaviour causes repeated injury (bruising, bleeding, tissue damage), or repeated risk of injury, to self or others, and/or causes serious property damage.
- The behaviour seriously limits the use of, or results in the person being denied access to, ordinary community facilities.
- The behaviour causes significant management problems (intervention requires more than one member of staff for control and/or the behaviour causes daily disruption for the duration of at least an hour).

CAUSES OF CHALLENGING BEHAVIOUR

There are obvious dangers in attributing a general set of causal explanations to the behaviours demonstrated by heterogeneous groups of people. It may safely be stated that there are psychological, social, organisational and cultural influences associated with defining any individual's self-injurious or other-injurious behaviour. For example, people with severe intellectual disability may display aggressive behaviour if they are unable to indicate that they are in pain or distressed. An older person who has dementia may find it difficult to cope with a change of carer, routine or environment. A child with attention deficit hyperactivity disorder (ADHD) may have serious difficulty in making accommodations to the limits imposed by a structured classroom setting. None of these examples denotes an intractable predisposition towards aggressive or self-injurious behaviour. With patient, careful and empathic observation and assessment, conditions may be created for respectful management of the behaviour within a supportive relationship between the service user and the social care practitioner.

On a social level, adverse family situations may result in out-of-home placements for children and young people. Recovering from these experiences is a painful and complex matter. Young people often manifest a range of challenging behaviours, including self-injurious behaviours, as expressions of fear, anger and intense distress. As Kissane and Guerin (2010: 1) point out:

> Often a person who is presenting with challenging behaviours has communication difficulties and cannot articulate wants and needs. Those with a difficulty expressing themselves must be offered any tool available that might enable communication. Physical and mental illnesses need to be accurately diagnosed and treated or ruled out. Physical factors, such as constipation, stomach aches, headaches, addiction problems etc. can lead to physical discomfort and distress. A person may present with challenging behaviours as a result of physical discomfort and distress. For example, a person with limited verbal communication skills who has an earache may respond by hitting his ear, in order to communicate pain. A person with an intellectual disability and a mental illness may be distressed, confused and anxious and may respond by becoming verbally aggressive towards carers. Many people cannot report their subjective experiences due to limitations in communication and, therefore, symptoms of physical and mental illness are often misinterpreted.

The development of models of care that offer normalised, individualised and personalised support to clients has brought about significant change in how episodes of challenging behaviour are understood and managed. Mansell (1992) identified four essential aspects of service response to challenging behaviour:

1. *Prevention:* including the creation of an enriched and stimulating environment as well as the promotion of adaptive behaviour.
2. *Early detection:* including the observation and management of emergent problems.
3. *Crisis management:* involving contingency planning and skilled intervention.
4. *Specialised long-term support:* emphasising individualised help for clients and high levels of support for staff.

On a broad level, the gradual replacement of the medical model of care with a greater understanding of the social construction of ageing, disability, deviance and delinquency has led to a more humane and responsive delivery of social care services to all client groups. As a result, service users can now expect greater tolerance and respect for their complex individual needs and personalised support in managing those needs.

The factors that predispose individuals to harm themselves or others are complex, deep rooted and persistent. Service developments have increasingly taken account of the disempowering effects of institutional care. The move away from large institutions – in all aspects of care, including elder care and residential child care as well as services for people with disabilities – towards community-based services has resulted in more person-centred approaches based on strong therapeutic relationships.

The recognition that many challenging behaviours are a response to social and environmental factors has led to increased efforts to assess those factors in care environments that contribute towards, or hinder, the attainment of a good quality of life. It is widely recognised that this may best be assured through the adoption of empowering approaches to delivering social care. Cheryl Gibson (cited in Heumann et al., 2001: 9) defines *empowerment* as 'a process of recognizing, promoting and enhancing people's ability to meet their own needs, solve their own problems and mobilize necessary resources in order to feel in control of their own lives'. It may be easier to define empowerment in terms of its absence. Rappaport (1984) identifies certain key factors as indicative outcomes of *disempowerment*: a state of powerlessness, whether real or imagined; learned helplessness; alienation; and the loss of a sense of control over one's own life. In situations of perceived powerlessness, the client may engage in behaviours that secure personal, individualised attention, even if the consequences are negative or unpleasant.

Braye and Preston-Shoot (1995) express concern that service provision in itself may be oppressive, and point towards the development of a strong and active user movement in social care provision. The principles of respect, tolerance and self-direction are exemplified in the participation of clients in their own service design and delivery. Such participation is likely to assist individuals and their families in articulating their preferences, feelings and fears and thus reduce the likelihood of resorting to challenging behaviour to have their needs and wants met. Attempts to manage challenging behaviour in a culture of blame and power imbalance are more likely to reinforce the conditions and attitudes that caused the behaviours than to assist in their management.

While the Mansell report (1992) offered insights into the roots of challenging behaviour and appropriate service responses, it also highlighted the important issue of whether it is appropriate to use restraint in care settings for people with intellectual disabilities. The debate extends to other social care settings where the effective and ethical management of challenging behaviour is a key factor in the development of positive therapeutic relationships with clients. Stirling and McHugh (1997) point to the professional drive to find non-aversive strategies for managing challenging behaviour.

MANAGING CHALLENGING BEHAVIOUR

Since the original publication of the Mansell report, agencies have used a variety of approaches to the management of challenging behaviour, most of which require the training and accreditation of practitioners. These approaches tend to use combined strategies gleaned from the behaviourist perspective in psychology and from counselling approaches. Managing the environment so as to increase those stimuli that result in appropriate behaviour and reduce those that have negative outcomes is at the root of behaviour management strategies. Helping clients, through empathic support, to deal more appropriately with situations that trigger their negative emotional responses is an intrinsic part of this approach.

Examples of behaviour management approaches include:

- TCI (therapeutic crisis intervention) is used exclusively in the residential care facilities under the aegis of the Health Service Executive (HSE) and also in other social care agencies. All residential care staff in HSE centres must be certified TCI practitioners and there is a requirement for regular recertification of their credentials.
- CPI (Crisis Prevention Institute) provides a practical behaviour management programme, known as non-violent crisis intervention, used extensively in services for people with intellectual disabilities and in educational settings. It is practised in settings where clients tend to be confrontational, disruptive and/or aggressive.
- MEBS (multi-element behaviour support) is a non-aversive and highly individualised approach to working with challenging behaviour. It is primarily used in services that support people with intellectual disabilities and with autism spectrum disorders. The model is founded on a human-rights-based approach that emphasises person-centred planning.
- A-B-C (antecedent-behaviour-consequence) is based on functional behavioural assessment (FBA). This is a process primarily used to develop an understanding of a child's challenging behaviour, used mainly in educational settings. The goal of FBA is to identify the function of behaviour for the child, that is, why children behave as they do in specific situations. This approach is also used by many child and family support agencies, where observation and assessment of a child's behaviour are vital prerequisites for effective intervention.

Models of behaviour management are chosen to suit the ethos and practice requirements of specific care settings and service users, using insights, theories and approaches tried and tested by various professions such as nursing, psychology, social work and social care. These models share certain common characteristics.

Characteristics of behaviour management models

The adoption of a particular approach to behaviour management by an agency is an attempt to ensure that the safest possible work practices are followed, with positive implications for the continued emotional and physical wellbeing of all the people in that agency – staff and clients alike. While some behaviour may best be dealt with by the simple expedient of ignoring or redirecting it, it is not appropriate to ignore behaviour that is potentially abusive, destructive, threatening or dangerous. The decision to intervene in order to manage injurious behaviours involves professional judgment.

All models that address the management of challenging behaviour emphasise the following ten key characteristics, in order to ensure that decisions are taken that are considered, fair, respectful and likely to lead to positive and safe outcomes.

1. An ethos of respect for all members of the service community, including management, team leaders, staff and clients

This is at the centre of the duty of care, involving mutual responsibility for maintaining a respectful, supportive and therapeutic milieu. Each member of the service has rights and responsibilities in relation to the others. Codes of conduct – formal and informal – should emphasise respect for differing professional experiences and openness to diverse perspectives.

2. Endorsement and support of the behaviour management system by management

This involves a full undertaking by management of its responsibility to ensure that the workplace is as safe as it can reasonably be. Management must acknowledge the need for full availability of the resources necessary to deliver a professional, client-centred service and should commit to providing these resources. These include adequate staffing levels, physical and technical resources, relevant training and professional supervision, and time to plan, implement and evaluate appropriate procedures.

3. Effective risk-assessment procedures

Risk assessment aims to bring about a clear understanding of the specific behaviour that causes concern, to identify environmental triggers and to measure the frequency and intensity with which the behaviour occurs. Measuring the behaviour involves questions such as: How often and where does it occur? How long does it last? How do people in the vicinity normally react to it? How successful are current interventions? According to Scott (2008), 90 per cent of problematic behaviours in dementia care settings occur as a response to care practices or environmental factors. Identification and measurement of such factors in the care environment is essential to the assessment and management of risk.

Highly developed observational skills are necessary for accurate risk assessment. Even apparently minor factors in a service environment, such as excessive noise, heat or overcrowding, can contribute to a gradual increase in tension that can spill over into harmful behaviour. Practitioners need to be aware that, even when situations are calm, they should remain alert to triggers that may cause an outburst. A sudden change in a service user's demeanour, indicated perhaps through restlessness or extreme stillness, raised tone of voice or moody silence, can signal the onset of negative behaviour that may be verbal or physical, minor or extreme, self-directed or directed at others. It is at this initial point of observation that the effective practitioner is considering appropriate responses, assessing risks, noting the location of other staff and clients, and generally engaging in mental and physical preparation to manage the situation.

4. An individualised approach to understanding and relating to service users displaying challenging behaviour

Service users who believe that their concerns are being minimised or overlooked will tend to feel unhappy and possibly resentful, to the point of anger and frustration. It is important to acknowledge to service users that their individuality is respected and valued. The development of a strong positive relationship is therefore a major part of behaviour management. It includes taking the time to get to know the service user's preferences, moods and triggers in order to support the development of mutual trust and regard and to plan appropriate management strategies. Carter (2006: 103) recommends 'an individualised and flexible approach which provides for and specifically addresses the person's specific needs and the circumstances of the individual case'.

5. Self-awareness of staff

Reflective practice is the cornerstone of effective social care. Practitioners must be willing to constantly scrutinise their practice for its effectiveness in supporting service users. They must also acknowledge their own vulnerabilities, counter-productive reactions, tendencies to blame clients, reluctance to seek support and guidance and, possibly, ineffective use of supervision.

In particular, the management of challenging behaviour warrants continuous examination of the personal effects of managing high-risk situations. All interactions with clients have emotional implications for practitioners, none more so than those in which the situation is highly charged and laden with risk. Each challenging situation brings with it a plethora of reactions. For example, in a study conducted by Hastings and Remington (1994), staff working with people with severe or profound disabilities who showed challenging behaviour reported a number of emotional reactions, including feelings of anger, annoyance, anxiety and upset.

Smith (2005: 100), in an examination of the experience of fear in residential settings, asserts that 'Some workers will experience a "fracture of professional identity" and the potentially profound consequences of this in terms of their mental health and self-image should be appreciated.'

Williams and Gilligan (2011: 17) examined self-injury in thirty-four residential children's centres in Ireland, and highlighted the personal impact on practitioners:

> Some participants felt managing such traumatic situations had a deep effect on them personally. Almost all the interviewees explained how managing incidents of self-injury crossed the barrier from their professional lives into their personal lives impacting on their ability to do their job, their ability to 'switch off' from work and on their relationships with their families.

It is a personal responsibility and a professional imperative to acknowledge the effects of such challenging situations at work and to seek support and guidance in managing these effects. There is a danger that, otherwise, fears and distrust may take over the relationship, leading to containment of the behaviour rather than therapeutic personal development of the service user. Effective use of professional supervision is necessary to identify and address unhelpful emotional responses to situations characterised by high tension and confrontation.

6. Clear incident and response plans and reporting procedures

Reporting and recording systems are essential for identifying the type of challenging behaviour encountered in social care workplaces. Such identification helps agencies to prepare and implement timely and effective interventions. In particular, all incidents involving physical and/or psychological aggression should be accurately and promptly reported and recorded.

The International Labour Organisation (ILO et al., 2002: 26) recommends that report forms include the following information:

- Where the incident occurred, including a description of the physical environment
- The date and time of day
- The activity happening at the time of the incident
- Details of the victim
- Details of the alleged perpetrator
- The relationship between the victim and the alleged perpetrator
- An account of what happened
- Names of witnesses
- Outcome of the incident
- Measures taken after the incident
- Effectiveness of such measures
- Recommendations to prevent a similar incident from happening in the future.

The ILO also recommends that workers should be encouraged to report incidents where they are subjected to unnecessary or unacceptable levels of risk, regardless of whether a violent or dangerous incident has occurred. This is to counteract the possibility of under-reporting of such incidents.

7. Staff training

Agencies that support service users with particularly challenging behaviours tend to train all their frontline staff in one specific behaviour management approach. Generally, the approach chosen is in line with the ethos of the service; the ethical and legal implications of managing behaviour amongst the client groups that the agency supports; and the limits the agency sets on the extent to which staff may intervene in risky situations. The adoption of one unified approach in an agency has the benefit of ensuring that all staff members have an appropriate level of insight into, and competence in maintaining, a consistent, positive approach to managing challenging behaviour.

Whichever model of behaviour management is adopted, relevant staff training is a key factor in improving the quality of care offered to clients who demonstrate challenging behaviour. Williams and Gilligan (2011) found that staff who had received training in managing self-injury were helped to understand the reasons for the behaviour and learned practical ways to support the young people in their care. Significantly, training contributed to a reduction in fear associated with managing incidents. This is consistent with Allen and Tynan's (2000) finding that trained workers were more knowledgeable and confident than untrained workers when it came to managing challenging behaviour. McDonnell et al. (2008) also noted increases in carer confidence in managing challenging behaviour after training.

The type of training seems to be significant. Shore et al. (1995) found that an in-service training course that gave verbal instructions and explanations to staff was not effective at persuading staff to implement certain advocated approaches to managing challenging behaviour. Similarly, McDonnell et al. (2008) make the point that training workshops may not be sufficient for behavioural change in clients to occur. They recommend follow-up support and supervision in the workplace to increase the effectiveness of the training. Scott (2008) also advocates a combination of teaching, supervision and intense support for workers who regularly have to manage challenging behaviour.

Based on their research with management and staff of residential and day care settings in the south-east of Ireland, and with the families of service users who exhibit challenging behaviour, Kissane and Guerin (2010) maintain:

> Staff should have training in evidence-based treatment approaches and on-going supervision of practice of safe and effective ways to manage challenging behaviour. Better outcomes are associated with those services, which employ 'active support' in the areas of person-centred planning, activity planning and training and support of staff.

8. An effective and relevant behaviour management approach

Management of challenging behaviour must take place within a respectful, relational context. Effective behaviour management thus commences well in advance of any actual episode of challenging behaviour. The concept of positive behaviour support (PBS) is intrinsic to meaningful management of behaviour that threatens the safety and welfare of the person and those around them. PBS acknowledges the influence of both personal characteristics and environmental factors on behaviour. Carr et al. (2002: 4) describe PBS as 'an applied science that uses educational methods to expand an individual's behavior repertoire and systems change methods to redesign an individual's living environment to first enhance the individual's quality of life and, second, to minimize his or her problem behavior'.

An effective behaviour management approach, therefore, takes into account the individual's personal characteristics as they interact with the organisational environment and attempts to support the individual towards self-monitoring and self-management. It is essential that practitioners are able to:

- Identify the stages of a service user's gradual build up (or escalation) to a crisis.
- Quickly make use of individual and team responses that will help the service user to de-escalate.
- Use verbal and sometimes non-verbal interventions to manage behaviour that is in danger of escalating out of control.
- Use debriefing techniques appropriate to the service user's level of under-standing and self-awareness.
- Document the incident honestly, thoroughly, dispassionately and fairly.

McDonnell (1997) recommends three elements in a behaviour management approach: simple preventative strategies, a low-arousal approach to reducing aggressive behaviours and, only if necessary, socially validated physical inter-ventions designed to avoid pain. These should be underpinned by an under-standing of the nature and causes of aggressive behaviour. Staff, therefore, need a strong contextualised knowledge base as well as practical training in behaviour management strategies.

Simple preventative strategies rely heavily on practical management of the environment. Reducing excessive heat and noise, ensuring adequate physical space and removing potentially harmful objects are sensible attempts to reduce situational factors that might lead to an escalation of tension and violence. Distraction is also effective in the early stages of escalation.

Strategies to promote positive behaviour through fostering resilience are also important. Praising clients for good and helpful behaviour, increasing self-esteem by recognising talents and skills, and creating opportunities for praise and encouragement are all strategies for reinforcing the therapeutic relationship and supporting respectful communication.

Each individual who displays challenging behaviour should have a personal behaviour management plan. This is to ensure that practitioners do not simply react to isolated incidents, but deal with each episode as part of an overall management strategy, with clear goals and observable outcomes. Precise identification of which behaviours are to be managed, and how, is essential, as most clients will exhibit a range of behaviours and it is counterproductive to attempt to change all of them at once.

The *low-arousal approach* is an essential feature of effective situational management. Direct confrontation is likely to lead to escalation of the tension and anxiety that prompted the challenging behaviour in the first place. Effective communication skills are crucial components of the low-arousal approach. The ability to establish personal contact and maintain the therapeutic relationship with the service user, even when under considerable pressure, is a key feature of professionalism in social care. The quality of the rapport between the practitioner and service user needs to be sustained purposively from the moment that tension and anxiety are noted, throughout the entire episode and during the aftermath.

The use of *physical interventions* to prevent or control aggressive behaviour has long been a contentious issue in health and social care. The law recognises the need to take action using the minimum possible level of restraint, to prevent injury to the individual or to others and to prevent damage to property. Minimal force should be used when restraining clients whose behaviour has escalated to the point where they are a danger to themselves or to others. It is also essential that only those trained and certified as competent to use restraint engage in physical holding, due to the real risk of injury to the service user and to the practitioner.

Apart from the danger of inflicting injury on a service user, there is also the ethical question of whether using aggressive responses to challenging behaviour is appropriate, just or therapeutic. The decision to restrain a client should never be taken by a sole individual, but jointly by team members for reasons that are transparent and aimed at supporting the person through the crisis. All other strategies for managing the behaviour must have been tried before a decision to restrain is taken. Not all agencies advocate or allow the use of physical restraint; many prefer to use situation management techniques consistently and repeatedly in order to engage therapeutically with challenging clients.

9. A team approach

Teamwork is necessary to ensure the consistency, transparency, efficiency and effectiveness of interventions. The practitioner needs to feel supported by colleagues. Team members need to have confidence in each other's capabilities and maintain their rapport. Consistently high levels of tension can interfere with supportive interventions with the client, and the fear and anger often generated in critical incidents can prevent practitioners from supporting each other. Failure to acknowledge such tensions can lead to the breakdown of trust between team members, with negative implications for future teamwork.

10. Debriefing

According to the ILO et al. (2002: 26), debriefing should be made available to workers who experience workplace violence and should include:

- Sharing their personal experience with others to defuse the impact of violence.
- Helping those who have been affected by workplace violence to understand and come to terms with what has happened.
- Offering reassurance and support.
- Getting people to focus on the facts and give information.
- Explaining the subsequent help available.

Debriefing after a violent or threatening episode should (ideally) take place within the relationship of professional supervision. A pre-existing professional relationship that encompasses trust, support and challenge will facilitate the practitioner to come to terms with the conflicting emotions emanating from the personal experience of violence in the workplace. Many practitioners feel angry with the service user, with the agency and with management. There can also be feelings of guilt that such an incident happened while the service user was in the practitioner's care. There may be fear of a repeat incident or of appearing to be incompetent in the eyes of colleagues and management. All these emotions contribute to feelings of vulnerability and make it difficult to achieve a reasonable level of understanding of why the incident happened, the part the practitioner had to play in handling the situation and how more positive outcomes could be achieved in the future. Effective debriefing is therefore essential for the practitioner's continued psychological wellbeing. It is also an important part of the risk assessment strategy of the agency, as vulnerabilities are clarified and patterns of interaction explored for the part they play in creating tensions.

Maintaining a safe therapeutic relationship while managing risk is a serious challenge in social care. Agencies attempt to address their responsibilities towards service users and practitioners by adopting certain behaviour management approaches and training all staff to use them competently. For successful outcomes, such approaches need to be practised within a team context where mutual responsibilities are acknowledged and honoured. Professional supervision is a primary safeguard for practitioners' health and wellbeing, and for maintaining acceptable standards of professional practice. By paying attention to the continuous development of self-awareness and professional skills within a respectful team ethos, practitioners can engage meaningfully with the attempt to place the service user's wellbeing firmly at the centre of all interventions. It is apparent, therefore, that safe and competent management of challenging behaviour can be a catalyst for service users to develop positive strategies for seeking reassurance and support during their social care placements.

SAFETY AND HEALTH AT WORK: THE NATIONAL AND INTERNATIONAL CONTEXT

The Safety, Health and Welfare at Work Act 2005 addresses safety, health and welfare matters in all workplaces in Ireland. It places obligations on employers and employees to contribute to ensuring that their workplace and systems of work are safe. It is the employer's responsibility to assess risks and take reasonable but rigorous steps to avoid or control any that arise. Under law, employers should ensure that workers receive instruction and training in appropriate behaviour and risk-management strategies. A precise system of incident reporting must also be in place. Employees at risk of threatening or violent behaviour from clients should be able to avail of health checks. Counselling should be provided if needed.

While the Act relates to all workplaces, it has particular significance for professions where the risk of injury is high. According to the Health and Safety Authority (HSA, 2011), which provides data on reported workplace injuries, the employment sector involved in 'human health and social work activities' accounted for 20 per cent of all workplace injuries in Ireland in the year 2010/11. Social care is coupled with health care and social work in the statistics and it is difficult to separate out the specific aspects of the social care role, and the characteristics of social care settings, that lend themselves to high risk of injury. Service users with emotional and behavioural difficulties do pose significant risks for workers in the social care sector. Balancing therapeutic interventions with the need to maintain a safe workplace is a complex task.

Cooper et al. (2003: 3) point out the concentration of reported physical violence among 'certain occupations such as health care, police, social services, taxi drivers and drivers of public transport, hotel and catering employees, security personnel and teachers' across Europe. Chappell and Di Martino (2006) include health care, education, community services and social services in their listing of the occupational groups at highest risk.

Efforts to highlight internationally the risk of workplace violence are part of the ILO's commitment to promoting 'decent work'. Decent work, as the ILO (2003) defines it, is work that is productive and safe; ensures respect of labour rights; provides an adequate income; offers social protection; and includes social dialogue, union freedom, collective bargaining and participation. Historically ILO interventions in the area of workplace violence primarily focused on preventing gender discrimination in the form of sexual harassment. More recently the organisation has focused on other forms of workplace violence as an aspect of its 'decent work' agenda, in particular calling for the preservation of human dignity in the workplace.

Difficulties finding an accurate definition have hampered attempts to identify the extent of work-related violence. Some clarity has emerged with the European Commission's adoption of Wynne et al.'s (1997) definition of such events as 'incidents where staff are abused, threatened or assaulted in circumstances related to their work, involving an explicit or implicit challenge to their safety, wellbeing or health'. Similarly, accurate international measurement of the incidence and severity of workplace violence is difficult, as different countries and agencies measure different aspects of risk and violence. For Beech and Leather (2006: 29), 'the safest conclusion that can be drawn on the basis of officially reported incidents is that the numbers are a gross underestimate of the actual numbers of incidents'.

The European Agency for Safety and Health at Work (2002: 8) identified the following key factors in the effective reduction of work-related stress and injury: adequate risk analysis; thorough planning and a stepwise approach; combination of work-directed and worker-directed measures; context-specific solutions; experienced practitioners and evidence-based interventions; social dialogue, partnership and workers' involvement; and sustained prevention and top management support.

It is important to note that challenging behaviour is not confined to violent or aggressive behaviour (see Table 13.1). The HSA (2012: 14) defines workplace violence and aggression as occurring where 'persons are verbally abused, threatened or assaulted in circumstances related to their work'. Verbal abuse can often be as intimidating and upsetting as the risk of violence, and more protracted. Non-physical aggression can have an even more pervasive impact on the social care practitioner and the agency, as staff may not report incidents due to uncertainty and embarrassment. Inappropriate behaviour may continue unchecked, and the resulting impacts on the service user and the practitioner remain unacknowledged. The service user does not learn alternative appropriate ways of acknowledging and managing anger, while the practitioner may be reluctant to report the offending behaviour for fear that they may be accused of overreacting, exaggerating or in some way contributing to the inappropriate behaviour.

Table 13.1. Types of physical and non-physical violence

Physical violence	Non-physical violence
Assault causing death	Verbal abuse
Assault causing serious physical injury	Racial or sexual abuse
Minor injuries	Threats (with or without weapons),
Kicking	including physical posturing
Biting	Abusive phone calls
Threatening gestures	Threatening use of dogs
Punching	Harassment
Use of weapons	Swearing
Use of missiles	Shouting
Spitting	Insults, including name calling
Scratching	Bullying
Sexual assault	Innuendo
	Deliberate silence

Source: Bibby (1994)

Some service users may harm themselves. Williams and Gilligan (2011) describe typical self-injurious behaviours such as skin cutting, burning, skin picking and hair pulling. The reasons for self-harm are deep seated and complex and the situation is exacerbated by the fact that people who engage in this behaviour often cannot explain why. Caring for individuals who harm themselves brings with it a multitude of often conflicting emotional responses. Williams and Gilligan point towards the need for these effects to be acknowledged by staff and management, and for appropriate training and support to be put in place for workers.

It is important to remember that working in an environment that is characterised by high levels of tension and the risk of hurt to oneself or to clients places a significant burden of responsibility on a social care practitioner – responsibility for the health, safety and wellbeing of the client, responsibility for being an effective and committed co-worker and responsibility for dealing with the personal impact of the work in such a way as to remain capable of supporting clients effectively and with compassionate empathy.

THE COSTS OF WORKPLACE VIOLENCE

Beech and Leather (2006: 29) point out:

> Among those intrinsic work features which put an occupational group 'at risk' is the need to interact with members of the public who are in pain, frustrated, receiving bad news that confirms their worst fears, or who may have poor impulse or anger control as part of their problem, or who are in hospital against their wishes.

While this statement refers to workers in the health care sector, it is clear that working closely with certain client groups poses risks to personal safety that need to be assessed and managed for the safety of social care practitioners, other clients, members of the general public and the service user displaying the challenging behaviour. Installing appropriate and responsive procedures for assessing and managing risks in the workplace is a necessary support for practitioners in maintaining a positive, therapeutic and client-centred approach in their work.

Any behaviour that is aggressive or violent will have negative consequences for individuals, agencies and the broader society. Stress and injury caused by such behaviour also have a financial consequence in terms of absenteeism, premature retirement, frequent staff turnover, low morale and the negative effects on team membership, productivity and the potential benefits of service user placements. According to Cooper et al. (2003: 5):

> ... both physical and psychological violence have serious implications for health and well-being, with post-traumatic stress disorders and suicidal

thoughts relatively common in the most serious cases. Fear of violence in its own right may also have an adverse effect, involving a much larger proportion of the population than those who are directly affected by the violence. Exposure to violence manifests itself behaviourally, with negative implications for job satisfaction, productivity and group dynamics.

Cooper et al. (2003) also make the point that third parties may be affected by workplace violence, because of the negative effects on personal relationships.

THE DUTY OF CARE

All attempts to manage challenging behaviour in social care settings must happen within the context of the duty of care towards clients. This means taking reasonable care to avoid acts (or omissions) that could expose people, for whom there is an acknowledged responsibility, to a foreseeable risk of injury. Duty of care does not apply to only the helping professions: all employers must ensure that they provide and maintain a safe workplace, safe plant and machinery and safe operating systems; workers have a duty of care to each other; and agencies must take reasonable care to ensure the welfare of both staff and service users. In social care settings, however, an equal reciprocal responsibility for the maintenance of the duty of care may not reasonably pertain. Vulnerable clients cannot always be expected to understand or adhere to the maintenance of a code of conduct that is based on equal levels of knowledge, understanding and commitment. Social care practitioners thus have an undeniable duty of care to their clients, many of whom are vulnerable to exploitation and harm. Special attention, therefore, needs to be paid to managing, respectfully and safely, the challenging behaviour presented by these clients.

CONCLUSION

This chapter draws attention to key aspects of managing challenging behaviour in the social care workplace. All challenging behaviour is communicative and happens within a social context. Management of challenging behaviour, whether it involves self-harm or harm of others, must take into account the personal characteristics of the individual, based on thorough, comprehensive, holistic and impartial needs assessment, within the physical and social environment in which the care takes place.

Practitioners need the support of management, in acknowledging the effects of working in crisis situations and in adequately resourcing them in terms of training, staff resources and personal support. They also need to be supported in a team system that acknowledges strength and vulnerability and, through mutual respect, plans effective, consistent strategies for supporting people with challenging behaviour.

The importance of reflection through professional supervision cannot be underestimated. Within a respectful, collaborative supervisory relationship, the practitioner can be helped to identify and cope with the personal and professional challenges implicit in this often highly stressful aspect of social care practice. The principal function of professional supervision is to increase the practitioner's effectiveness in supporting the service user. Taking time to consider what it is that the individual is trying to communicate through this challenging behaviour and planning how to respond appropriately is a first step in promoting positive behavioural change in a working environment that respects individual differences and supports individual needs.

14

Social care management: theory and practice

Vicki Anderson, Judy Doyle and Patrick McGarty

OVERVIEW

Social care is a broad field of work and social care graduates can find themselves working in a wide range of professional roles. As it is increasingly recognised that service needs, social issues and societal problems cannot be resolved by single agencies or individual professions alone, social care practice invariably involves collaborating in teams with other professions and disciplines. Service users often have multiple needs that benefit from integrated service provision, rather than a fragmented series of encounters with disparate agencies. A teenager arriving on the door of a homeless shelter, for instance, may well not only need accommodation, but also have mental health problems and need financial advice. In addition, the underlying issues that result in service needs, whether it be, for example, domestic violence, substance abuse or homelessness, typically have complex causes, leading them to be termed 'wicked problems' (Conklin, 2006; Rittel and Webber, 1973). The different agencies and professionals involved with such 'wicked problems' often have radically different worldviews as well as different values and perspectives for understanding the problem (Conklin, 2006). This means that getting teams to work effectively in such circumstances is an even greater challenge than teamwork within a single organisation.

The aim of this chapter is to address management issues in social care practice arising from the complex context described above. The chapter will examine what is meant by the terms 'team' and 'multidisciplinary team'. It will consider ways to create a team, management theory and practice in social care, and leadership behaviours that make the most of teamworking.

INTRODUCTION

The pace of change in social care services in Ireland has been rapid in recent times and has affected everyone from managers, to frontline staff, to service users. Ongoing restructuring in relation to planning, organisation, funding and delivery of services has presented new challenges for social care practitioners, and the expectations on managers are many and varied. Government policies now emphasise accountability, quality, performance, value for money, outcomes and the integration of health and social care services in a dynamic work environment.

Health and social care services are not a conventional service industry, yet managers face the normal dilemmas of any industry in relation to staffing, resourcing and budgeting. The fact that social care managers operate within a legal, and increasingly structured, framework means that they need to be not only supervisors of professional good practice, but also monitors of compliance with agreed care procedures. In this context, the importance of human relationships in the workplace should never be taken for granted (Henderson and Atkinson, 2003). In particular, organising service delivery through teams and teamwork is most important, increasing the need for effective leadership. Strategic planning in health and social care recognises the contribution of teams in the sector – multidisciplinary teams rather than individuals are the building blocks of effective organisations and services.

One of the consequences of the growth of such teams is the potential for tensions based on the different values and norms that often arise from diverse professional backgrounds, conflicting allegiances, contrasting performance management regimes or differing financial and information management systems. While education and training in social care and social work now emphasise teamwork, many professionals still have only a limited understanding of the implications of teamworking, particularly when the team is multidisciplinary. Although a wide range of research has been conducted on effective management and leadership of teams, there remains little consideration of the application of such theories to social care settings.

WHAT IS A TEAM?

In its broadest sense, 'team' is an everyday concept familiar to everyone, but the term is often confused with other groupings. When asked, many people will define a team as a group of people, but if asked to list a range of groups they themselves are members of, only some of these will be a team. The list of groups is likely to include family, friends, church or other religious group, sports team, band, hobby group, fundraising committee, class or work colleagues perhaps. These are only a team if they have most or all of the following characteristics (Carpenter, 2011):

- A *definable membership*: a collection of three or more people identifiable by name or type.
- A *group consciousness or identity*: the members think of themselves as a group.
- *Commitment to a common purpose*: the members share some common task or performance goals.
- *Interdependence*: the members rely on one another to accomplish this purpose and hold each other mutually accountable.

- *Interaction:* the members communicate with one another, influence one another and react to one another.
- *Sustainability:* the team members periodically review the team's effectiveness.
- *Unity:* the members have the ability to act together as one.

Usually the tasks and goals set by teams cannot be achieved by individuals working alone. This may be due to limited time and resources or because few individuals possess all the relevant skills and expertise. Sports teams or orchestras clearly fit these criteria. Families, class cohorts and hobby groups generally do not. Just because a group has the title 'team' does not mean it is a team if it does not show most of the characteristics listed above.

Every workplace has groups that are called teams (senior management teams, project teams), but in reality the members may not share a common purpose, they may communicate poorly and not work interdependently. The entire workforce of any large and complex organisation is rarely a genuine team, but it is often described as such.

In summary, if a group of people are to correctly call themselves a team, they will be a small group with a mixture of skills, sharing a common purpose to achieve some specific outcomes for which they see themselves as mutually accountable.

WHAT IS A MULTIDISCIPLINARY TEAM?

In social care work, teams are regularly used to bring people with different expertise together to try to address difficult problems and improve services. Teams may be assembled to carry out a variety of roles on a short-, medium- or long-term basis. Effective teamwork will ultimately shape the quality of service delivered to service user groups. Examples of multidisciplinary teams include:

- An intercultural strategy for youth work is being developed through collaboration between youth work policy makers, practitioners such as youth and community workers, and representatives from minority ethnic communities and organisations.
- Domestic violence is typically addressed through collaborative approaches involving local refuges, Women's Aid and An Garda Síochána.
- The National Youth Health Programme is a partnership, between the National Youth Council of Ireland, the Health Service Executive and the Youth Affairs Unit of the Department of Education and Skills, for the purpose of providing a broadly based, flexible health promotion, support and training service to youth organisations and to ensure that young people's health is on the policy agenda.
- The Central Remedial Clinic is a non-residential national centre for the care, treatment and development of children and adults with physical disabilities.

Services provided involve professionals in clinical assessment, physiotherapy, hydrotherapy, speech therapy, occupational therapy, social work, psychology, nursing, dietetics, orthotics, technical services, orthopaedics, paediatrics, parent support, vision and hearing specialists, transport and catering.

- Primary care centres aim for a more integrated and comprehensive care service by bringing together in a single centre such professionals as GPs, public health nurses, social workers, child protection workers, physiotherapists and speech and language therapists.

These examples of multidisciplinary teams each unite people of diverse professional skills for a shared purpose of making a bigger difference in tackling complex issues such as domestic violence, racism, young people's health or enabling people with disabilities to develop their potential. The value of such teamwork to the service user is greater than the sum of the team's individual members (Carpenter, 2011; Martin et al., 2010). In social care environments, some of the strongest teams have developed a vision, direction, momentum and common purpose, working with the most difficult of service user groups.

The key distinction of a multidisciplinary team is that the members have diverse professional backgrounds, giving them quite distinct training, skills and roles. Often they also possess differing values, norms and understandings of the issues they are dealing with. Herein lies both the potential for mixed teams, but also the challenge in how to form them effectively. For all the enthusiasm about teamworking, there are times when it may be better not to use a team approach.

CREATING A TEAM – GETTING OFF TO A GOOD START

While the benefits of working together are well known, building teams and achieving effective teamwork can be difficult. Often people are thrown together and it is assumed they will naturally make a team. This is not the case and teamwork will not result in every instance. Various models of team formation recognise that a group has to develop to reach the point of mature teamworking. Tuckman and Jensen's (1977) much-cited version suggests the following stages of formation:

- *Forming:* when people come together and tend to be guarded and often excessively polite.
- *Storming:* members begin to fit into team roles often leading to conflict and the emergence of personal differences over such issues as how to work and whose ideas will dominate.
- *Norming:* ground rules and ways of working are established and trust begins to develop.
- *Performing:* being able to work at a high level, making decisions, openly disagreeing and valuing members' diverse ways of thinking and operating, even if this is frustratingly different from your own.

Getting a group off to a good start means allowing time to work through these stages and deliberately taking a group through the steps. Managers need to adapt their leadership approach to meet the different needs of the team at each stage. For example, they must be available to guide the team through some initial structured discussions that explicitly explore the purpose of the team, its primary task and the intended outcomes. Often people come together thinking they have a shared purpose, but then find they have quite different views on what they want the team to achieve. Other issues that need to be addressed include how to organise – What will be the working processes, such as making decisions or voicing disagreement, and the ground rules for how members will act towards each other? What role will individual members play and who will formally take the lead in the team? These points are important for any team, but they are heightened for interdisciplinary teams.

Among the barriers to effective multidisciplinary teamwork often highlighted are rivalries that can occur between the different professions. Interpersonal differences, lack of teamwork training and the competing priorities of members' employing organisations will also risk fragmenting a multidisciplinary team. So what can be done to help a team become high performing and really fulfil its promise of being more than the sum of its parts?

WHAT MAKES A TEAM HIGH PERFORMING?

High-performing teams are those that deliver strong results in an effective manner and also continue to be significant for the individual members. Some key features are:

- A well-defined purpose that is seen as significant by all team members.
- The expertise and characteristics of members of the team are complementary.
- The team initially allowed itself time to go through the stages of development – forming, storming, norming and performing – with the result that there is good trust and valuing of personal differences amongst members.
- The team has established good habits for making decisions and taking action.
- Regularly taking time out to review how the team is working, and being open to self-criticism.
- Effective ways have been developed for individuals and the team itself to continue to learn.
- There is a good balance between being supportive of individuals and encouraging questioning, challenging and experimentation.
- Individuals feel the team is making an impact and achieving results.

In addition, the high-performing team avoids what are termed the 'trappings of success' (Pedler et al., 2004), such as becoming complacent, keeping others out or being condescending to clients.

Thus, we can see that teamwork requires behaviours such as listening and responding constructively to views expressed by others; providing support and feedback; recognising the interests and achievements of others; and being open to challenging questioning.

TEAM ROLES

Teams work well when everyone has a complementary role. Ideally the composition and skill set of a team should ensure that there is appropriate diversity to undertake the necessary team roles. There are two different ways that team roles can be categorised: task roles and process roles.

Task roles are those to do with the content of the work and the functional expertise an individual brings. For example, a youth justice project might involve a garda, a family social worker, probation officer, teacher and community worker. Each will contribute their professional view and particular expertise, for example, knowledge of the law, education resources and sources of income.

Process roles are to do with the part each member contributes to help the team function and get the work done. One useful way of thinking about these roles comes from Belbin's (2012) work on teams. Belbin defines a team role as a tendency to behave, contribute and interrelate with others in a particular way. The behaviour-based model of team roles he developed suggests that effective teams need to have a range of participants who play nine very different roles within the team structure. No one person can have all the attributes, but individuals will tend to be stronger in two or three areas. Each role has particular strengths a team needs, but also particular 'allowable' weaknesses that can be compensated for by a well-balanced team.

Table 14.1. Belbin's team roles

Team role	Team contribution strengths	Allowable weaknesses
Plant	Creative, imaginative, unorthodox, solves difficult problems Team's source of original ideas	Ignores incidents Can dwell on 'interesting ideas' and be too preoccupied to communicate well
Implementer	Disciplined, reliable, conservative and efficient Turns ideas into practical actions Turns decisions into manageable tasks Brings method to team's activities	Somewhat inflexible Slow to respond to new possibilities Upset by frequent changes of plan

Team role	Team contribution strengths	Allowable weaknesses
Completer-finisher	Painstaking and conscientious Searches out errors and omissions Delivers on time	Anxious introvert; inclined to worry unduly Reluctant to delegate Dislikes casual approach by others
Monitor evaluator	Sober, strategic and discerning Offers dispassionate, critical analysis Sees all options Judges accurately	Lacks drive and ability to inspire others Lacks warmth and imagination Can lower morale by being a dampener
Resource investigator	Extrovert, enthusiastic and communicative Explores opportunities Diplomat with many contacts	Over-optimistic Loses interest as enthusiasm wanes Jumps from one task to another
Shaper	Challenging, dynamic, thrives on pressure Brings drive and courage to overcome obstacles Task minded; makes things happen	Easily provoked or frustrated Impulsive and impatient Offends other's feelings Intolerant of vagueness
Teamworker	Promotes team harmony; diffuses friction Listens Co-operative, mild, perceptive and diplomatic Sensitive but gently assertive	Indecisive in crunch situations May avoid confrontational situations
Co-ordinator	Good chairperson: clarifies goals, promotes decision making, good communicator, social leader, delegates well	Can be seen as manipulative Inclined to let others do the work May take credit for team's work
Specialist	Provides rare skills and knowledge Single minded and focused Self-starting and dedicated	Contributes only on a narrow front Communication skills are often weak Often cannot see the 'big picture' and dwells on technicalities

Source: Belbin (2012)

MANAGEMENT OF TEAMS

The staff team is the most valuable resource available to any social care agency. Management and leadership of a team, therefore, are vitally important in order for any organisation to achieve its objectives. Due to the individual nature of each team and its members, managing the team can prove to be the most challenging aspect of a manager's role.

Management is often a difficult notion to define. The role of a manager is influenced by the size, purpose and nature of the organisation in which they work. For example, a manager in a residential service catering for elderly people will have a very different role from that of a manager in a fast-food restaurant. Likewise, the role of the manager of a residential care unit may change depending on the size of the organisation. Larger organisations may call for a tiered approach to management by having frontline, middle and top managers, all with different roles and responsibilities.

'A manager is someone who works with and through other people by coordinating their work activities in order to accomplish organisational goals' (Robbins and Coulter, 2002: 5). This general definition allows for changes in the role of the manager to meet the goals of the particular organisation and also depending on the people the manager is working with or 'through'. Management can also be seen as a process, in that managers are viewed in terms of what they do on a daily basis.

Functions of management

The functions of management are commonly divided into the following: planning, organising, staffing, controlling and leading (Robbins and Coulter, 2002; Dessler, 2007; Tiernan et al., 2006).

Planning

Planning is the process of establishing goals and objectives and selecting future courses of action in order to achieve them. In other words, deciding what the organisation aims to achieve in the long term and working out the short-term actions that are most likely to help this achievement. For example, services for people with disabilities are increasingly focusing on supporting independence in the community. A change in objectives, from supporting people in a residential setting to supporting independence in the community, needs to happen over an appropriate period of time. A manager may decide initially that the service will run some programmes aimed at developing skills of independence. The next step would be assessing each service user's abilities before finally moving people to suitable accommodation and providing suitable support. Planning would also involve securing funding for the project, ensuring the service met necessary standards, employing staff, advertising the service and so on. Planning also includes very short-term services such as planning for activities in the coming weeks.

Organising

Once plans have been established it is necessary to allocate the appropriate resources to ensure achievement of those plans. Referring back to the above example, setting up a cookery class for the service users would require the organisation of a venue, funding and staffing. Much of the organisation can be done through delegation to team members.

Staffing

Staffing involves ensuring effective employees are selected and trained. The extent of a manager's involvement in the recruitment process will depend on the size of the organisation. At a more localised level, managers are responsible for allocating responsibilities and tasks. For example, what skills are required to run the cookery class? Which member of staff would be most suited to working in the class? Allocating jobs appropriately will ensure effective use of staff resources. Staffing will also involve support and motivation of staff, particularly in social care organisations.

Controlling

Controlling is the process of monitoring progress and, where necessary, taking action to ensure goals are met. Activities and the day-to-day running of the organisation need to be monitored in order to ensure that the overall goals are being met. When goals are not being achieved it is the manager's role to make the necessary changes. If, for example, the goal is to have 10 per cent of the residents living independently in the community by 2016, and only 2 per cent are making significant progress in developing their independence skills, the approaches being taken may need to be reassessed.

Leading

Leading involves inducing individuals or groups to assist in attaining the goals of the organisation. Leadership is discussed in greater detail below.

Research conducted by Doyle and McGarty (2012) found that a lot of a social care manager's time is consumed with large administrative workloads, much of which is linked to conformity with regulations, and inspection. The study highlighted many of the practical issues and concerns facing social care managers on a daily basis. Concerns were evident among social care managers that such management practices had adverse effects on the quality of care and the time available to interact with service users and to support staff in supervision and practice.

LEADERSHIP: A FUNCTION OF MANAGEMENT

What leadership entails is subject to change depending on not only the organisation but also varying contexts and stages of organisational development. It is helpful to think of leadership in three ways:

- *Leadership as position:* the formal position of authority – team captain, project leader, service director.
- *Leadership as function:* the broad activity of directing the organisation, recognising key challenges and mobilising action.
- *Leadership as practice:* what leaders do – the everyday actions they carry out in response to challenges; for example, how they use power, how they challenge or whether they work with a clear purpose.

Good leadership of teams is important for social care clients and organisations. One of the leading writers on leadership, Beverly Alimo-Metcalfe, suggests there are three rationales for leadership: a performance case, a business case and a moral case (Alimo-Metcalfe and Nyfield, 2002).

The *performance case* sees leadership as helping ordinary people to do extra-ordinary things. The hope is that, in a complex world, leadership helps people focus their effort by providing direction for their work, stimulating problem-solving behaviour, getting things done and dealing with multiple priorities. Leadership is then about rallying followers' energies and developing their capacity for higher levels of performance. This case for leadership is reinforced by Pedler et al. (2004), who take the view that leadership is about action in the face of challenge – that is, without leadership, less gets done and difficult issues go unaddressed.

The *business case* for leadership is backed up by evidence of the cost of poor leadership. Through poor leadership, organisations waste money and staff. Job changes are frequently provoked by the desire to get away from a poor boss – people leave their managers rather than their job. It is known that organisations lose money from absenteeism, but it is also likely that there is a connection with poor leadership. A Confederation of British Industry study (CBI, 2007) found that 72 per cent of absenteeism is attributed to stress. Two-thirds of this is attributed by staff to their boss. Poor leaders fail to help their staff deal with the stresses of work and, indeed, exacerbate stress through their behaviours.

This recognition of the inhumane consequences of poor leadership is the basis for the *moral case* for leadership. Bad leadership, whether in the form of bullying, inequity or inconsistency, can contribute to a poor working environment that is damaging for people. Yet just as bad is poor leadership that takes the shape of inaction, or abdication of responsibility. In fact, some would argue that leaders are servants and leadership is a service to others for which there is a moral responsibility not to decline.

The arguments presented suggest why social care staff might benefit from good leadership and that, likewise, service users benefit from the improved services that better leadership should produce.

THEORIES OF LEADERSHIP

Due to the importance and influence of good leadership, many theories have been developed to try to understand the characteristics of a good leader. Theories can be grouped into the following categories: trait, style, contingency and new transformational, each of which is summarised below.

Trait theories

The 1930s to 1950s were dominated by the belief that good leaders were those who had core heroic personality traits such as initiative, self-assurance, appearance, imagination, sociability and decisiveness; it was believed that leaders are born, not made. Stogdill (1948) outlined the following as essential leadership traits: intelligence, alertness, insight, responsibility, initiative, persistence, self-confidence and sociability. These 'Great Man' theories foundered because there was never any consistent agreement on what the essential traits of leadership were. Another issue was that many of the attributes outlined describe patterns of human behaviour rather than personality traits. Despite trait theories being discredited in many academic quarters, many managerial selection schemes and testing procedures still operate on a trait basis in identifying potential managers.

Exercise 14.1

What traits would you identify as necessary for a leader in a social care setting?

Style theory

In contrast to trait theorists, style leadership theorists argue that employees will work harder for managers who employ certain styles of leadership. Organisation psychologists in Michigan and Ohio State Universities in the 1950s identified two pillars of leadership behaviour: *employee-centred behaviour* that focuses on relationships and employee needs, and *job-centred behaviour* that focuses on getting the job done. Leaders who were mainly employee centred were said to be democratic and those who were mainly task focused, autocratic.

The Michigan and Ohio State University studies led to the development of two types of leadership behaviour – consideration and initiating. *Consideration* is leadership behaviour that involves employee participation in decision making and involves trust and support for the workforce. In contrast, *initiating behaviour* emphasises performance and goal attainment and expects workers to follow instructions (Northouse, 2010).

Further studies considered the combination of these behaviours at different levels, allowing for more leadership styles. Likert (1961) elaborated on a further model with four different styles of leadership: dictatorial, autocratic, democratic and laissez-faire. Each style has differing levels of concern for employees and for the tasks at hand.

Blake and Mouton (1985) further expanded on these theories, on the premise that different styles were most effective in different work settings. They developed a grid identifying five different styles of leadership with varying levels of concern for people and concern for production. For example, a leadership style that is task or production focused may be more suitable to a factory setting, where the output of product is the key organisational objective.

Exercise 14.2

You arrive to your job as manager of a residential care unit at 9.00 a.m. The two members of staff who were on the overnight shift report a very difficult shift involving challenging behaviours. Both are very tired as they received little sleep. One is particularly distressed about the events of the night. Both are due to leave at 11.00 a.m. You have a meeting at 10.30 a.m. and had planned to prepare for it this morning. What course of action would you decide on for the morning?

Contingency theory

While it is recognised that an employee-centred, participative and democratic style of leadership is favoured by most employees, proponents of contingency theory argue that one leadership style may not be effective in all circumstances, but is contingent on the particular situation. In other words, some leadership styles may be more effective in some situations than in others.

According to Fielder (1967), the style a leader should choose to be effective will depend on a number of factors, including the leader's personality, whether the leader is motivated by relationships or task completion, whether the leader has control and influence in the workplace, and by wider environmental factors such as organisation structure, characteristics of employees, the nature and complexity of the group's task, reward structure, nature of work contracts and external environment, all of which contribute to unique situations that ultimately influence leadership style (Northouse, 2010).

Contingency theory is the most complex theory, considering the most variables. On account of this complexity, it can be argued that it is the most adaptable to different situations. It is the first of the theories to consider the characteristics of the worker in addition to the organisation. Therefore, unlike some other theories, it focuses less on the leader and takes account of the influential factors. For example, two members of staff may respond differently to a particular leadership style. Likewise, the best leadership style for each team member may differ between situations.

Exercise 14.3

Consider the following two scenarios. Would you look for the same leadership approach from a manager in each case?

Scenario 1: A new service user enters your service presenting with challenging behaviour. Two members of your team have refused to work with this service user due to the challenging behaviour. They argue that, regardless of their relevant training to deal with challenging behaviours, they should not be expected to work in such conditions. You are working this weekend with both of these team members and you are apprehensive that you will need to work with the challenging service user alone. How would you like your manager to lead you and the rest of the team in this situation?

Scenario 2: A child is entering a residential setting in which you are working. You have been assigned as her key worker. A care plan needs to be developed for the child. What approach should a manager take to lead you in your key-working tasks?

New transformational theory

Contemporary leadership thought has changed to focus on activities and relations: on what leaders actually do across all levels of a hierarchy and the interrelationships between them and others. A differentiation is made between transactional and transformational leadership behaviours (Alimo-Metcalfe and Nyfield, 2002). Both are necessary for the organisation's performance, but it is transformational leadership that most influences followership. Transactional leadership is a familiar management style, whereby the manager makes transactions, exchanges resources, plans and monitors systematically. A core principle of transformational leadership is that people follow when they can see connections between their own sense of purpose and identity and the wider organisation's vision or purpose. Transformational leaders are those who help make those connections. People also follow leaders whose values and actions they respect, so transformational leadership qualities include integrity, consistency and equity, or modelling the way, as well as decisiveness and willingness to take risks. It is well summarised by Collins (2001b: 36) when he describes great leaders as 'a paradoxical blend of intense professional will and personal humility'.

CONCLUSION

Social care work aims to make a difference to people's lives through tackling some of the most difficult or 'wicked' problems. Effective management, with skilled leadership, can help teams to make a difference in vulnerable people's lives. Teams have an increasing role to play both within organisations and drawing from multiple organisations into multidisciplinary teams. A team will bring a wider range of skills together into more integrated service delivery and more comprehensive problem solving than any single agency or profession can achieve alone. When it works well, a team is more than the sum of its parts. Alongside the potential benefits of diverse professional backgrounds are the challenges that are posed by the mix of values, norms, status levels and ways of talking about, and understanding, the causes of the issues at hand. There is a danger of multidisciplinary groups punching below their weight and not fulfilling their potential as a high-performing team. Most social care professionals are aware that theory is often far removed from the cold face of practice. In social care environments the crisis of the moment can take over and force teams to react as opposed to interacting and working collaboratively.

Providing good team support, positive leadership and professional supervision are essential in order to ensure positive outcomes in social care practice. It is important that managers understand the difference between doing the right thing and doing things right as regulations may impose. Then, ultimately, the most important people, the service users, will truly reap the rewards of professional social care and management in practice.

15

Social care practitioners as agents, advocates and enablers of health promotion

Frank Houghton and Sharon Houghton

OVERVIEW

> Health promotion is the process of enabling people to exert control over, and to improve their health. (WHO, 1986)

This chapter explores some aspects of health inequality in Irish society. It outlines why and how social care practitioners can become involved in health promotion activity, in an active sense, but also through reflecting on the impact of their own health-related attitudes and practices. It makes some suggestions on working effectively with individuals, groups and communities to address health issues. There is more than one approach to health promotion and the chapter outlines some of the key paradigms. It concludes by pointing to some of the pitfalls and dilemmas involved, and suggests where practitioners and students might start to look for answers.

INTRODUCTION

Health promotion is of vital importance to the field of social care practice. The social care practitioner routinely works with some of the most marginalised and deprived people in society. As such, no other health and social care professional is better placed to understand the holistic health needs and resources of these excluded populations in their real-life context. Engagement by social care practitioners with health promotion is essential to confront and overcome the significant health inequalities that exist in Ireland. Social care practitioners are well positioned and trained to support individuals, groups and communities to identify their own health needs and concerns and respond to them.

INEQUALITIES IN HEALTH

Social care practice involves working with the most excluded and disadvantaged members of society. Service users may be people with mental health issues and/or physical impairments; they may be elderly or have learning or language difficulties. To varying degrees all of these groups are highly stigmatised in Irish society. A constant in the lives of most service users is the impact of poverty and relative deprivation.

The relationship between wealth and health is both startling and dramatic. Put simply, wealthier people live longer and are in better health than poor people. It is easy to assume this relates purely to differences between countries, with life expectancy in poorer and less industrialised countries being substantially less. This is true, but it is important to note that such differences are not purely between continents (Europe versus Africa) or countries (Ireland versus India), but within them.

Inequalities in health in Ireland are persistent, pervasive and startling, but Irish society has a long history of ignoring this (Aiach and Carr-Hill, 1992; O'Shea, 1997). Elsewhere we have suggested this absence of debate has been deliberately constructed by the Irish government (Houghton, 2005; Houghton and Houghton, 2013).

Health inequalities exist not only between the most excluded members and the rest of us, but throughout and between all levels of Irish society. The health and life expectancy of the most wealthy and educated, such as medical doctors, barristers and architects, tends to be better than that of nurses, teachers and social workers, which is in turn usually better than that of shop assistants, bus drivers and cleaners. Obviously the health of individuals in any of these groups may be better or worse than their social class or economic status would suggest, but as an occupational group (or class) this relationship holds. This finding is robust, and although the extent of the difference may change slightly depending on how you measure wealth (income, social class, occupational group or education) or health (morbidity or mortality), for almost all health conditions it is a constant.

It is worth briefly exploring some aspects of health inequality in Ireland to appreciate just how significant they are. For example, evidence suggests that all-cause mortality rates among those in the lowest occupational class are between 100 and 200 per cent higher than similar rates for those in the highest occupational class (Balanda and Wilde, 2001). These differences are particularly notable for conditions with acknowledged associations with deprivation and poverty; for example, the mortality rate from respiratory disease is more than 200 per cent higher among the lowest occupational class compared with the highest occupational class. Rates for mortality resulting from circulatory diseases are over 120 per cent higher, and injuries and poisonings are 150 per cent higher. The mortality rate from transport accidents demonstrates a particularly sharp differential on the basis of occupational class, being 354 per cent higher among the lowest occupational class compared with the highest occupational class (Balanda and Wilde, 2001).

Although these inequalities in mortality are significant, differences in mortality and morbidity are even more acute when particularly marginalised and deprived groups are examined. Such health inequalities are most apparent in Ireland when examining the health of homeless people (Condon, 2001; Costello and Howley, 1999; Focus Ireland, 2000; Smith et al., 2001), refugees and asylum seekers (Cairde, 2003; Fanning et al., 2001) and Travellers (AITHS, 2010, 2011).

The causes of these dramatic differences have been the subject of much debate. Some suggest the evidence of health inequalities is the result of imperfect measurement (known as an artefact of measurement). Others argue that healthier people are more able to take on challenging high-paid roles, while less healthy people are not able to do so (the natural selection/selection process argument). Both of these arguments have been found to be of very limited explanatory value.

Strong arguments have been made concerning the role of personal lifestyle in causing health inequalities. Risk behaviours that include smoking, high alcohol consumption, sedentary lifestyle, and high-fat and high-sugar diets are more common among people in lower socio-economic groups. Although these issues are undoubtedly important, it is inappropriate to separate behaviour from social and cultural contexts. An intense focus on such arguments can lead to victim-blaming and can appeal to (neo-liberal) governments looking to reduce both public expenditure and taxes.

Other arguments that have been put forward to account for health inequalities include the life course model (whereby future health may be predicted based on early life circumstances) and the psycho-social model (which explores the impact of issues such as relative deprivation on self-esteem, stigma and marginalisation). It has been strongly and convincingly argued that health inequalities are the result of material disadvantage. Poorly educated people from more deprived backgrounds are more likely to be unemployed or working in insecure jobs. They are also more likely to be employed in hazardous occupations and working in unsafe environments (Tones and Green, 2005; Naidoo and Wills, 2009).

For further reading on health inequalities, we suggest Public Health Alliance (2007), Barrington (2004), Wilkinson and Marmot (2003), Balanda and Wilde (2001) and O'Reilly (2011).

SOCIAL CARE PRACTITIONERS: THEIR ROLE IN HEALTH PROMOTION

Aspects of the social care practitioner role are vital in understanding the pivotal importance of health promotion to social care practice. Many practitioners routinely support service users in tackling issues such as alcohol or drug misuse. The life circumstances and health status of service users may be adversely affected by smoking, educational disadvantage and exclusion. Social care practitioners are concerned with combating disadvantage, as well as with empowerment and community development. These are all crucial elements of modern health promotion.

Contemporary Western biomedicine (often described as pharmacotherapy) is entrenched in a set of biomedical beliefs that, although successful in many spheres, are limited. Under the biomedical approach, the clinical focus is reductionist (it focuses on the constitutive components of the body) and mechanistic (the body is treated as a machine and only the 'broken' piece is fixed). The medical approach also focuses on the causes of illness (pathogenesis) rather than the causes of health (salutogenesis); uses a system of opposites (allopathic); and assumes that the mind and body are separate entities (dualistic). Under biomedical approaches people are not treated in a holistic manner that explores their general wellbeing and circumstances. Instead, individual health issues are examined and attempts made at treatment in a narrow and focused manner (Tones and Green, 2005; Naidoo and Wills, 2009).

Dahlgren and Whitehead (1992) have outlined the manifold influences on health and wellbeing across differing scales (see Figure 15.1). Biomedical approaches routinely ignore personal, family, cultural, socio-economic and environmental contexts. Given their training, social care practitioners are not as blind to wider circumstances and will want to explore and understand these crucial factors.

Figure 15.1. Factors that impact on personal health

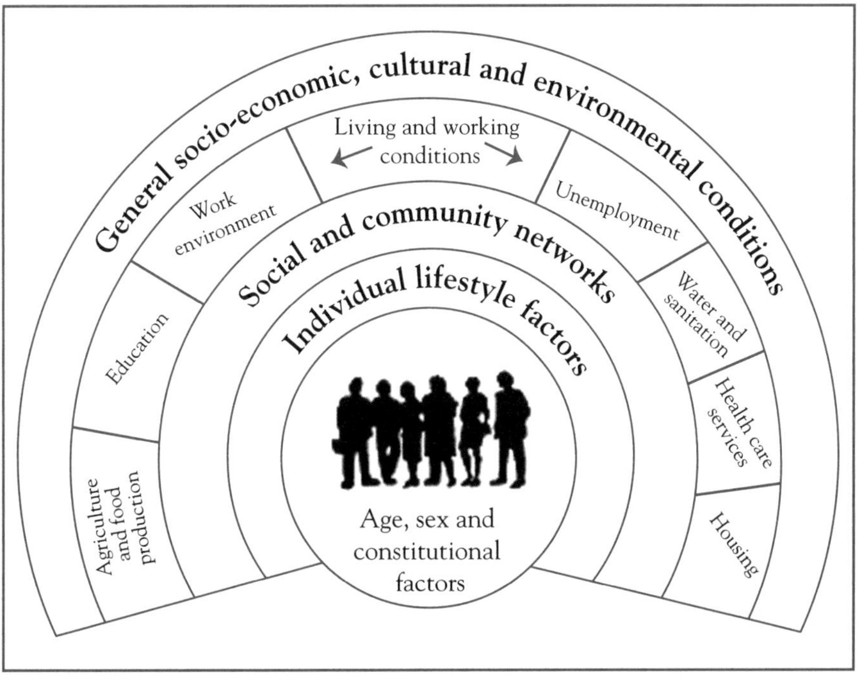

Source: Dahlgren and Whitehead (1992)

Agents of health promotion

Experience suggests that social care practitioners routinely engage in health promotion activities. They often feel poorly trained in this field and do not conceptualise themselves as formally fulfilling this role (Kelly and Houghton, 2009). This is unfortunate and potentially severely limiting. Social care practitioners are unique among health and social care professionals in often spending an extended length of time in the life-space of service users. They are optimally placed to understand and respond to wider health issues faced by service users in their real-life contexts. They are also ideally placed to understand significant issues such as literacy (including health literacy) and language difficulties.

For further reading on health promotion, we suggest Naidoo and Wills (2009) and Tones and Green (2005).

Working with individuals

Social care practitioners may find themselves working in a variety of contexts where they have opportunities to promote health. This may be in a one-to-one context with a service user, perhaps as a key worker. A practitioner may operate *in loco parentis* in a residential setting. Practitioners need to reflect on their role in terms of the broader provision of 'life education'. This might cover issues such as nutrition and exercise, as well as perhaps dealing with more obvious health issues such as mental ill-health, addiction or acute illness. For example, a practitioner could not only complete a course such as Cook it!, which combines the development of nutritional knowledge with culinary skills, but could also train as a Cook it! instructor, competent, experienced and skilled in passing on this knowledge to service users (Health Promotion Agency, 2008).

It is essential that social care practitioners develop a competence and comfort level in discussing all aspects of health and wellbeing. Some aspects can be potentially embarrassing at first (for all concerned), as they cover topics deemed personal, intimate or taboo. It is vital that in your professional role as a social care practitioner you do not shy away from these sensitive topics. Service users may try to elicit essential information or advice from you on a variety of topics, including sex and contraception. Coy answers, or obvious discomfort, in discussing these or related topics may not only result in a missed health promotion opportunity, but may leave a service user highly vulnerable.

Working with groups

Social care practitioners routinely work in group settings. This provides a valuable opportunity to promote health and has the added advantage of involving multiple service users. Vignette 15.1 presents an example of a successful group-based health promotion project.

> *Vignette 15.1. Skin, smoking and nutrition*
>
> Social care practitioners can introduce health promotion issues through their routine work with service users. An excellent example of this was observed through a placement visit. It involved a social care student working with a group of teenage girls from a relatively deprived area in a social/educational service context. The student was a trained beautician and used her skills to capture the interest of the group of teenage girls she was working with. The teenage girls involved were interested in make-up and having 'good skin'.
>
> Rather than simply lecturing the service users on the importance of diet, the student supported a project in which the service users themselves explored the biology of the skin and the importance of diet and nutrition. They also explored the impact of smoking and aspects of personal hygiene on skin. The service users then produced posters on their findings for other groups to examine.
>
> Through this health-promoting project the service users developed IT skills, which enabled them to go online and explore information, and a high degree of group cohesion. The group also developed writing and art skills in creating their posters, as well as an educational resource for other service users. To celebrate the successful conclusion of the project, the social care practitioners offered a make-over to all participants.

Working with communities

Social care practitioners may increasingly find themselves involved in community development roles. This might involve areas undergoing redevelopment or regeneration, or alternatively working with particularly disadvantaged and vulnerable groups. For clear, concise and succinct information on community health promotion, see Donald (2006). Working with communities necessitates particular skills, such as networking. As for individual work, community development may involve a significant amount of capacity building. Vignette 15.2 provides a brief overview of how social care practitioners can support and empower Travellers to become community health workers employed to promote health in their communities.

> *Vignette 15.2. Empowering Travellers to promote health in their communities*
>
> An encouraging model of contemporary health promotion work in Ireland can be seen in the training of Travellers as community health workers. Ample evidence of the poor health status of this minority group is available. The Health Service Executive (HSE) and education and training providers have developed packages to support Travellers to train and then be employed as community health workers with a specific remit of working within and across

their communities. Such training and education programmes often start by addressing literacy and numeracy skills before moving on to tackle topics associated with health, health promotion and community development. Social care practitioners, often working alongside nursing and educational staff, have been crucial in supporting Travellers in these challenging programmes.

Social care practitioners have also often had a formal role as support staff for Traveller community health workers in bimonthly meetings of regional Traveller Health Units. These meetings often involve relevant HSE staff (such as public health nurses and area medical officers, and staff of mental health, primary care and maternity services) and representative Traveller community health workers. An equal number of Travellers and HSE staff is usual, to maintain balance. Such meetings are often rather intimidating and formal, although great efforts are made to minimise this. Social care practitioners often accompany Traveller community health workers to such meetings (rather like a key worker) and have helped to arrange relevant training, covering such areas as minute taking, public speaking and self-efficacy, where appropriate. Such a supporting role can be temporary and success in empowerment can result in the role becoming redundant. It is both impressive and encouraging to see a Traveller community health worker formally announcing at such a meeting that they no longer require a support worker to accompany them. This is particularly impressive when they are sitting at the same table as senior area medical officers, superintendent public health nurses and numerous other health service staff and administrators.

SOCIAL CARE PRACTITIONERS AS MENTORS, GUIDES AND ROLE MODELS

It is important to remember that the explicit professional role of social care practitioners in the context of health promotion is only one dimension of their role. Practitioners may find themselves working with vulnerable groups such as young people or people with a learning impairment. As such they may be working with impressionable service users. It is imperative that practitioners are aware of the impact their actions, conversations and attitudes may have on those they are ostensibly trying to help.

Social care practitioners, through their professional role, are often engaged as mentors and guides to at-risk service users. They may also be role models, whether they are aware of it or not. Let us take the issue of smoking among staff in a youth service. Even if staff are not sharing cigarettes with service users (providing access to first-hand smoke) or exposing service users to second-hand smoke (passive smoking), what message does it send if staff are seen or known to smoke? Smoking has been variously found to be perceived as cool, sexy, adult and rebellious.

As for the inequalities in health examined earlier, smoking and smoking-related diseases demonstrate a clear social gradient. Poorer people are more likely to smoke and to die early from smoking-related diseases. Another significant issue to emerge in recent years is the reversal in the gender gap among young smokers. Although traditionally young men smoked at a higher rate than young women, smoking is now slightly more prevalent among the latter. If your aim is to eradicate or reduce some of the health inequalities in Irish society, it is worthwhile thinking about the acceptability of smoking among social care practitioners. For a brief overview of the health impacts of smoking, see Fact file 15.1.

Fact file 15.1. Ireland and smoking

- Smoking is estimated to cause approximately 7,000 deaths in Ireland each year, chiefly through illnesses such as lung cancer, heart disease, stroke and emphysema.
- Smokers reduce their life expectancy by, on average, between ten and fifteen years.
- 50 per cent of smokers die from smoking-related diseases.
- Around 30 per cent of all cancer deaths in Ireland are attributed to smoking.
- Lung cancer is the most common form of cancer and 90 per cent of lung cancers are caused by smoking.
- It costs the Irish state €1 billion per year to provide health services for smokers.
- People are usually under age when they become addicted to nicotine.
- By 2030 tobacco is expected to be the single biggest cause of death worldwide, accounting for about 10 million deaths per year.
- Tobacco is one of the greatest causes of preventable and premature deaths in human history.

Source: Ash Ireland (ash.ie)

Similarly, dangerous levels of alcohol consumption and binge drinking are the norm among young people in Ireland. To compound this difficulty, alcohol consumption is routinely glorified and embellished in social situations. Unguardedly discussing alcohol consumption, either in the past or in anticipation of the future, may legitimise and promote intoxication, as well as normalising routine high levels of alcohol consumption. For an examination of the impact of alcohol, see Fact file 15.2.

Fact file 15.2. Ireland and alcohol

- The European Union is the heaviest drinking region in the world.
- The Irish spend more of their income on alcohol than any other European country.
- The Irish are the most frequent binge drinkers in Europe. Recent evidence suggests that one-quarter of Irish adults engage in binge drinking weekly.
- Over half of Irish drinkers have been identified as having a harmful drinking pattern.
- Between 1980 and 2009 alcohol consumption in Ireland increased by 18 per cent. This figure is double the increase noted in the United Kingdom in the same period and, in Europe, is second only to the increase noted in Finland.
- A significant volume of research clearly indicates that children and adolescents in Ireland are routinely drinking alcohol.
- Evidence suggests that children in Ireland are starting to drink alcohol at an earlier age. The age of initiation into alcohol consumption has been identified as an important risk factor for alcohol dependence.
- For Europe as a whole, alcohol is the third most adverse risk factor for premature death and ill-health.
- Alcohol is known to increase the risk of more than sixty serious medical conditions, including cancers and gastrointestinal conditions.
- Between 2000 and 2004 alcohol caused an estimated 4.4 per cent of all deaths in Ireland.
- Alcohol was responsible for 4,321 deaths in Ireland between 2004 and 2008. For 2008, this equated to eighty-eight deaths per month.
- Alcohol has been identified as a contributory factor in half of all suicides in Ireland. A recent Irish study noted that alcohol was thought to be a major contributing factor in 823 suicides in a five-year period from 2000.
- Research from 2010 identified that alcohol was consumed in 40 per cent of cases of self-harm in Ireland.
- Alcohol misuse has also been identified as increasing the risk of children requiring special care. Evidence suggests that where children were referred to care primarily because of parental alcohol addiction, there was a tendency for such children to get 'stuck in care'.
- International literature indicates that alcohol problems in adults are associated with 16 per cent of child abuse and neglect cases.
- Between 1995 and 2008 alcohol-related admissions to acute hospitals doubled.
- Alcohol is associated with 2,000 beds being occupied in acute hospitals in Ireland every night. This represents an estimated 10 per cent of bed days, totalling almost 3.5 million bed days from 2000 to 2004.
- 28 per cent of all injuries presenting to Irish A&E departments in 2003/4 were recorded as being attributable to alcohol.

- Alcohol was the primary drug responsible for 7,866 admissions to specialised addiction treatment centres in 2010. This figure represents an increase of 43 per cent in just five years.
- Based on figures for 2007, it is estimated that alcohol-related illness costs the Irish health care system €1.2 billion per year.
- Other alcohol-related costs include the costs of crime, lost economic output and road traffic incidents. Based on 2007 figures, these have been estimated to cost €1.19 billion, €527 million and €530 million respectively in Ireland.

Source: Alcohol Action Ireland (alcoholireland.ie)

It is equally worth practitioners reflecting on their role as a mentor and role model in relation to other crucial health issues such as exercise and the impact of a sedentary lifestyle, diet and nutrition, and drug misuse.

SOCIAL CARE PRACTITIONERS: REFLECTING ON HEALTH AND HEALTH BEHAVIOURS

Before engaging in health promotion it is important for social care practitioners to be aware of their own health beliefs and health behaviours. What does health mean to you? Are you healthy? The World Health Organization (WHO, 1946) suggests that health may be defined as 'a state of complete physical, mental and social well-being and not merely the absence of disease or infirmity'. Although this definition is important in that it moves beyond the traditional focus of the medical model towards a more holistic and rounded approach, its emphasis on complete wellbeing across these domains is perhaps unrealistic. Most people have some slight health issue, however minor, most of the time.

The WHO definition mentions mental, physical and social wellbeing, but neglects other dimensions of health such as sexual, emotional and spiritual health. It also neglects wider dimensions of health, such as societal, environmental and global health (Naidoo and Wills, 2009). How healthy are you across these six internal (mental, physical, social, sexual, emotional and spiritual) domains? Do you feel that you are in control of your health and have the capacity to make any necessary changes to your lifestyle?

It is useful to critically monitor and explore our own health behaviours. International evidence suggests that people routinely underestimate the negative health behaviours they engage in, while overestimating their positive behaviours. For example, people typically underestimate their weight, the amount of calories they consume, the amount of alcohol they drink and the number of cigarettes they smoke. Conversely, they usually overstate the amount of exercise they engage in, as well as the number of fruit and vegetable portions they consume per day.

One of the most useful methods of exploring the lifestyle habits of both oneself and others is to keep a diary recording the issues in question. This might be a food diary, or an alcohol or exercise diary. Although this can be time consuming and potentially tedious, it is for many people a worthwhile and often revealing experience.

APPROACHES TO HEALTH PROMOTION

Before considering taking action on health promotion it is worthwhile (if not essential) to explore some of the general approaches to health promotion that exist. There are five main approaches to health promotion (Tones and Green, 2005; Naidoo and Wills, 2009):

- The *medical approach* aims to reduce morbidity and mortality through engaging with high-risk groups or whole populations. A routine focus of this approach is the use of medical interventions, such as screening and immunisation. This approach is expert-led and people are expected to be passive and conforming patients.
- The *behaviour change approach* focuses on personal responsibility and aims to encourage people to adopt healthy lifestyles. It can involve both individual counselling and mass-media campaigns. This approach is also expert-led and assumes a dependent recipient. It can lead to victim-blaming; for example, where people who smoke or are overweight are blamed and stigmatised for their ill-health.
- The *educational approach* aims to increase both knowledge and skills about healthy living. It involves information given through such media as posters and leaflets. It can also involve individual and small group activities to develop life skills that support a healthy lifestyle, such as culinary skills and developing nutritional knowledge.
- The *empowerment approach* aims to support and develop individuals and communities to explore and respond to their perceived needs. Central tenets of this approach are training and support as well as community facilitation, advocacy and networking.
- The *social change approach* aims to address the stark health inequalities that exist in society based on factors such as class, gender, race, ethnicity or geography. This approach may be termed radical health promotion and aims to deliver positive changes in the economic, social and physical environment. Although often involving community action and consultation, this approach entails high-level changes in policy and legislation, and as such is a top-down approach.

It is important to be aware of the differences between these approaches as they involve radically different philosophies, methods and underlying power relations.

Practitioners should reflect on these models in the context of other elements of their social care training or practice, such as the social and medical models of disability. Similarly, it is worth examining the importance and absence of empowerment in these varying approaches, as well the tension between top-down/expert-led models and grassroots philosophies.

HEALTH PROMOTION PARADIGMS

Caplan and Holland (1990) suggest that there are four fundamental health promotion paradigms, based around two dimensions: the nature of knowledge and the nature of society. The first dimension assumes knowledge is a continuum from subjective to objective. The second is based on assumptions concerning the nature of society and runs from radical change to social regulation. When combined, these two dimensions create four quadrants in which sit approaches to health and health promotion. The four paradigms are: radical humanist, radical structuralist, humanist and traditional. Each of these quadrants has specific views on the nature of health, the role of 'expert knowledge' and how to achieve change (see Figure 15.2).

Figure 15.2. Four health promotion paradigms

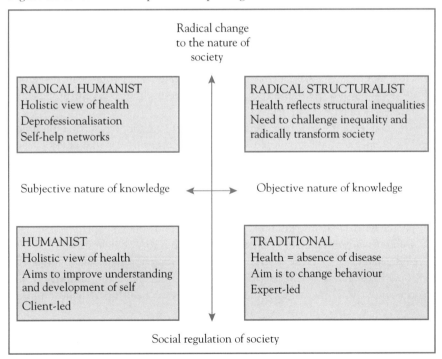

Source: Naidoo and Wills (2009)

PITFALLS, DILEMMAS AND DEBATES

This chapter has introduced some of the basic tenets of health promotion. As you can see, it is a contested terrain, with many unresolved ethical and practical issues and debates. Even a cursory examination of the pitfalls, dilemmas and debates in the field of health promotion would be a book in itself. Instead, we list a number of questions for reflection that also introduce the literature on this area.

- People generally, and the media often, tend to examine health by exploring the origins and causes of disease. This may be termed a disease causation or pathogenic paradigm, based on the medical approach to health and illness. Why not instead focus on what keeps people healthy? This focus on health-promoting attitudes and environments is called the salutogenic approach (Antonovsky, 1984; Sidell, 1997).
- How much do you assume that your health status is outside your control? Is your health governed by factors such as your genes, environment, social class or occupation? (Davison et al., 1997)
- How much of health promotion focuses on medical approaches to health that serve to undermine your feelings of control and competence in maintaining your own health? (Illich, 1976)
- Health promotion and health education have served to expand the influence of medicine into numerous spheres of ordinary life. To what degree has this served to medicalise an increasing proportion of 'everyday life'? (Illich, 1976)
- To what extent is health promotion used to regulate and control people and populations? (Scrambler, 1991; Goffman, 1968; Illich, 1976; Zola, 1991)
- How much do you accept that your mental state affects your health? (Dubos, 1991) What are the implications of this for yourself and in your professional role as a social care practitioner?
- To what extent should we 'encourage' people to adopt healthier lifestyles? When does advice become pressure? How important is freedom of choice and voluntarism around health issues? (Tones, 1997; Dines, 1997)
- How do we avoid paternalism and maintain individualism and self-determination in promoting health? (Beauchamp, 1997). How do we navigate this territory when working with particularly vulnerable groups, such as people with a learning disability, older people and young people?
- Different cultures may have different approaches to, and definitions of, health and wellbeing. Specific training on these issues for particular groups can sometimes serve to inadvertently locate this 'problem' within minority groups (Peberdy, 1997). How aware are you of your own health paradigms and how open are you to exploring and accepting others?
- How much should health promotion focus on being comprehensive (trying to include everyone) or on being selective (trying to focus on particular populations)? (Coombes, 1997)

- How will you evaluate a health promotion initiative? Are there different approaches to evaluation? What factors and ideologies influence which methods and outcomes are used in such evaluations? (Beattie, 1997)

CONCLUSION

Social care practitioners have an ethical obligation to promote the health of the clients, groups and communities they are working with. Ideally they should be able to empower and support service users and wider communities in identifying and responding to their health needs, subject to the wishes and concerns of service users themselves. Social care practitioners need to consciously identify and position themselves as health promoters. This will facilitate their access to a wider literature on models of action, as well as helping focus and direct their activities.

Social care practitioners may achieve a wider impact in health promotion by working at a policy level, ranging from national and international policy to regional, local and organisational policy. Evidence suggests that many agencies in the social care field do not have formal health promotion policies (Kelly and Houghton, 2009). The absence of such organisational focus and commitment to this issue makes health promotion initiatives all the more difficult to implement and sustain.

It is important to remember that morbidity and mortality are not static. It is equally important to understand the dynamic nature of social care practice. Demographic changes, combined with national and international developments, can have a dramatic impact on the profile of vulnerable populations. We are currently faced with an increasingly overweight and sedentary population over-eating a diet high in fats, sugars and salts. Deprived local environments are often obesogenic, being typified by a host of fast-food outlets and poor provision for active transport or recreation and play. Conditions such as type 2 diabetes are increasingly seen among young people, including teenagers and even younger children. This condition was once referred to as mature onset diabetes as it usually affected older people, particularly pensioners. This epidemic is looming and such developments inevitably concentrate on the deprived and marginalised populations.

Social care practitioners cannot afford to ignore these developments and must continually monitor emerging health trends and issues. As it is impossible to accurately predict the future health issues that will face service users, practitioners require an openness and commitment to continuous professional development around health issues (see Vignette 15.3 for information on how you might access health information to explore an issue).

Additional recommended reading: NYHP (2000), Ryan et al. (2006) and Wren (2003).

Vignette 15.3. Finding information on health and health promotion

As well as becoming familiar with hard copy and online resources (such as Ebrary, ScienceDirect, Wilson Web and EBSCO), it is always worthwhile exploring an issue comprehensively by examining other sources.

Taking the issue of alcohol, it would be important to determine which government departments and agencies might be able to provide valuable information on this topic. The most obvious government department dealing with this issue is the Department of Health (dohc.ie), which lists its publications on its website (free to access, download and print). You should also consider other government departments or agencies that might be useful, for example the Health Research Board's online library (hrb.ie); the health promotion section of the Health Service Executive (HSE) (healthpromotion. ie); and the Department of Children and Youth Affairs (dcya.gov.ie). It is also worth exploring the output of agencies from other countries, such as the Centers for Disease Control and Prevention in the US (cdc.gov).

Looking at intergovernmental agencies, many health and health promotion topics are covered by the European Union (ec.europa.eu/health-eu/index_en.htm) and the World Health Organization (who.int/en or euro. who.int/en). The Institute of Public Health in Ireland (publichealth.ie) is a cross-border body established under the Good Friday Agreement and is particularly useful, as is the Health Well, which is also a cross-border initiative (thehealthwell.info).

It is usually fruitful to explore non-governmental organisations or charities that might have addressed the topic. For alcohol, Alcohol Action Ireland provides valuable and freely available information (alcoholireland.ie). It can also be useful to look at bodies that have a strong reputation for research involving health topics; for example, the Economic and Social Research Institute (esri.ie), Department of Health Promotion in NUI Galway (nuigalway.ie/hpr) and Children's Research Centre in Trinity College, Dublin (tcd.ie/childrensresearchcentre). Such groups routinely make many of their reports available for free over the Internet.

When examining health information, it is also useful to consider freely available online journals that may not be included in the journal databases held by your library. One obvious example is the *Irish Medical Journal* (imj.ie). Many health journals are available for free online, particularly if their funding comes from the US government. It is often worth visiting PubMed Central (PMC), which is a free archive of biomedical and life sciences journal literature at the US National Institutes of Health's National Library of Medicine (ncbi.nlm.nih.gov/pmc/).

16

Emancipatory social care practice

Majella Mulkeen

OVERVIEW

This chapter sets out an emancipatory project for social care in the Irish context. The term 'emancipate' means to free from bondage and oppression, to liberate. Many of the individuals with whom social care practitioners engage experience domination, oppression and exploitation as a result of poverty, exclusion, marginalisation or discrimination. Many students enter social care courses with a commitment to some kind of social reform or change, a concern for social disadvantage and those who experience it. Emancipatory practice is primarily concerned with operating in ways that further a society without domination, exploitation and oppression (Fook, 2002). The chapter is best read in conjunction with Chapter 6, which discusses how Irish society is characterised by inequality and suggests a framework for thinking about and integrating equality into social care practice.

This chapter examines emancipatory values in social care practice and the critical context provided by Irish equality legislation. Theoretical and policy debates on the formation of an emancipatory project in social care are examined alongside the role of broader egalitarian movements in challenging the more conservative approaches. Concepts such as empowerment and equality are discussed so as to critically embed them in social care practice. Readers are introduced to strategies at an individual/organisational level that can enhance self-awareness, knowledge and skills in emancipatory practice.

INTRODUCTION

The value of non-discrimination in social care practice is based on the belief that service users should be protected from unfair treatment or disadvantage on a variety of grounds, including age, gender, disability, ethnicity, sexual orientation and family status, when they are receiving services. This position is compatible with the dominant liberal approach to equality in Irish public policy, which seeks to create fair competition and equal opportunities by making it an offence to treat people less fairly in employment or when accessing services (Crowley, 2006; Hanlon, 2009).

An emphasis on egalitarian, anti-oppressive or emancipatory values in social care shifts attention from individual experiences of discrimination to the social processes involved in discrimination, racism, poverty, sexism and misogyny, homophobia and other social harms (Baker et al., 2009; Thompson, 2011; Morrison and Horwath, 1999). An egalitarian, anti-oppressive or emancipatory approach seeks to integrate individual social care practice with a wider socio-political concern with inequality. Such approaches highlight the persistent and significantly unequal outcomes experienced by some groups (such as people with disabilities, women, older people, children and ethnic minorities) in the benefits accruing from income, health, education and employment (Hanlon, 2009). An emancipatory practice seeks to work at not only the individual and organisational levels but also, crucially, the broader policy level to counter the alienation, marginalisation and social exclusion that are features of these unequal outcomes.

WHY SOCIAL CARE SHOULD DEVELOP AN EMANCIPATORY PROJECT

There are compelling reasons why addressing inequality is central to best practice in the social professions:

1. If practitioners are to understand the people they work with, it is essential that they understand how inequality and discrimination have played a part in their lives to date and continue to do so (Thompson, 2012). It is important to be aware of the structures of society that contribute to people feeling powerless to change their situation and to understand why people may sometimes act in a helpless manner and feel they have no influence over their lives (Allen and Langford, 2008).
2. To work effectively and ethically in social care, it is essential that practitioners' actions or inactions do not contribute to inequality in the lives of those they work with (Thompson, 2012). The emotional aspects of dealing with inequality mean that it is virtually impossible for practitioners not to be subjectively involved to some degree in how they interact with people different to themselves, reflecting as they do their own expectations and socialisation. Social class, position, ethnicity, gender, sexuality and ability all influence how people see and understand the world and may restrict their ability to develop practices that are inclusive and emancipatory.
3. Inequality and discrimination is inevitably an issue for care practitioners in their transactions with powerful institutions, such as state bureaucracy (Allen and Langford, 2008: 22). Such transactions often demonstrate the existence of institutional discrimination. The MacPherson report, produced in Britain in the aftermath of the murder of black teenager Stephen Lawrence, offers the following definition of one form of institutional discrimination – institutional racism (Home Office, 1999: 6.34):

The collective failure of an organisation to provide an appropriate and professional service to people, because of their colour, culture, or ethnic origin. It can be seen or detected in processes, attitudes and behaviour which amount to discrimination through unwitting prejudice, ignorance, thoughtlessness and racist stereotyping which disadvantage minority ethnic people.

For Barnes (1991: 1), in writing about the experiences of people with disabilities, institutional discrimination 'is apparent when services are ignoring or meeting inadequately the needs of disabled people. It is also present when these agencies are regularly interfering unnecessarily in the lives of disabled people in ways and or to an extent not experienced by non-disabled people.'

Where institutional discrimination occurs, awareness means being skilled at both recognising its existence and developing a capacity to challenge it.

4. Treating people equally must take into account their differences and respond to their needs, circumstances and background accordingly. While human beings are deemed to be equal because of shared features and similarities, different cultures define and structure these features of our humanity differently (Commission on the Future of Multi-Ethnic Britain, 2000). Treating people equally requires social care practitioners to take into account both their similarities and their differences.

5. The role of the social care practitioner is a double-edged one, consisting of elements of care and control. It can lead to either potential empowerment or oppression (Thompson, 2012). Care work itself is contested – particularly by the disability movement, which has challenged the notion of 'care', arguing that people who need support in their daily lives have been constructed as dependent, thus depriving them of their right to live more independently (Morris, 2005).

6. Social care practitioners are often in positions of power where they may gatekeep resources, or where reports they write will have a significant impact on a person's life (Allen and Langford, 2008: 24). Practitioners, through unwitting prejudice, ignorance and thoughtlessness, may ignore or fail to meet the needs of those they have responsibilities towards and/or interfere unnecessarily in their lives.

The challenge for social care practitioners is to act not as mere functionaries of the agency, following policy and procedure without any questioning or reflection as to the impact of decisions and actions on those with whom they work (Thompson, 2012). In the next section we examine the structural manifestations of oppression.

DISCRIMINATION AND OPPRESSION

Discrimination occurs at the level of personal prejudice and is manifest in an individual practitioner's interaction with clients, where prejudice and inflexibility of mind can stand in the way of fair and non-judgmental practice. Discrimination at a personal level is embedded in the culture of a society (Thompson, 2012). Cultural practices in a society can operate to privilege dominant lifestyles, values and identities, while labelling others in a manner that encourages hostility, discrimination and exclusion.

Discrimination also occurs at the structural level: the network of social divisions and associated power relations. Such power relations are oppressive because dominant groups are able to derive systematic benefit from their subordination of others through a variety of means, including economic exploitation, cultural imperialism and actual or threatened violence (Young, 2011). Typically, those on the receiving end of oppression will suffer some inhibition of their ability to develop and exercise their capabilities and express their needs, thoughts and feelings. For every oppressed group, there is a group that is privileged in relation to that group. Members of the privileged group may not necessarily be aware of any conscious intention to oppress others (Young, 2011).

Inequality and discrimination are sewn into the fabric of society. In 2011, 15 per cent of TDs in Dáil Éireann were women, while women accounted for just over one-third of members of state boards and less than one-fifth of members of local authorities (CSO, 2012f). Immigrants are more likely to report working in jobs below their skill level, and are less likely to be in a permanent position. They receive lower gross earnings than Irish nationals, and job applicants with 'foreign' names are less likely to be called for interview (ESRI, 2011).

Census figures on care work in Ireland measure only unpaid care for adults and children with disabilities. Caring for children, apart from children with disabilities, is the main form of care work undertaken in the country, but this work is not enumerated as work in the census. The European Community Household Panel (ECHP), however, does calculate such forms of care work. ECHP figures show that 40 per cent of women aged sixteen years or older have some care responsibilities (mostly for children), compared with 16 per cent of men (cited in Lynch and Lyons, 2008). While the omission of care of children as work in census calculations may be unintentional, it demonstrates a deeply patriarchal set of assumptions to hide women's unpaid work in this way (Lynch and Lyons, 2008: 10). The above are examples of how oppressive structures are sewn into the fabric of 'how things get done' in Irish society, resulting in exclusion and marginalisation. Practices of exclusion and marginalisation arise from the values of a society, of professional groups and of individuals.

While many social care students experience a transformation in their values, outlook and commitments as a result of their practice learning and education, it can be a personal and professional challenge to appreciate that one is not completely free of prejudice (Mulkeen, 2012b). The term 'critical practice' is often used to refer to the capacity to integrate four levels of knowledge and action. These are: a critically reflective use of self, a sound skills base, a value base that respects others as equals, and an open approach to practice in a socio-political context where discrimination and diversity are socially constructed (Brechin, 2000: 35).

A lack of sensitivity and an unwillingness to change dearly held views are likely to result in unconscious, unintentional but nevertheless damaging discriminatory behaviour. A concern with outcomes rather than intentions can help social care practitioners to focus on what is happening in any situation. A useful starting point for practitioners in developing strategies to promote equality is an awareness of how their values impact on their professional practice. A second strategy is an understanding of equality strategies already in existence that may support their efforts. The next section addresses the relevance of equality legislation to social care practice.

EQUALITY LEGISLATION

Social care practitioners can use their knowledge of equality legislation to support the development of emancipatory practice by being aware of the legal protections available to them as workers and by being able to advocate on behalf of those less powerful, where necessary. Crowley (2006) notes that Irish equality legislation reflects an emphasis on difference and diversity, addressing as it does nine separate grounds for the prohibition of discrimination: age, gender, sexual orientation, marital status, family status, race, religion, membership of the Traveller community and disability. Identity is significantly determined by one's gender, sexual orientation, skin colour, national identity, religion and so on, and can in part be shaped by experiences of discrimination and exclusion, such as sexism, racism, homophobia and ageism.

The use of legislation to underpin rights and to prohibit discrimination is an important part of any strategic action to promote equality in a society. The Employment Equality Acts 1998 and 2004 prohibit discrimination in all aspects of employment. The Equal Status Acts 2000 and 2004 prohibit discrimination in the provision of goods and services. Below we examine key definitions in the legislation and offer a critique of its effectiveness.

- *Discrimination:* discrimination occurs if a person is treated less favourably than another person is treated, has been treated or would be treated, on the basis of any of the nine grounds listed above.
- *Indirect discrimination:* this is defined as discrimination by impact or effect. It occurs where an apparently neutral provision puts a person belonging to one of the discriminatory grounds at a particular disadvantage. For example, in a case taken by the Psychiatric Nurses Association on behalf of a number of female claimants in 2006 (*O'Donnell and Others v Health Service Executive*

NW Area, DEC-E2006-023), the equality officer concluded that the roster, which required the claimants to work six or seven consecutive days and on occasion thirteen to sixteen days, impacted more heavily on the claimants as women and primary carers and was indirectly discriminatory on the gender ground (Equality Authority, 2006: 13).

- *Harassment:* both the Employment Equality Acts and the Equal Status Acts prohibit harassment and sexual harassment. In the case of sexual harassment and harassment on any of the nine grounds, it is defined as conduct that has the purpose or effect of violating a person's dignity and creating an intimidating, hostile, degrading, humiliating or offensive environment for the person.
- *Reasonable accommodation:* the Acts place a significant positive duty on employers and service providers to reasonably accommodate the needs of people with disabilities.
- *Positive action:* the Acts allow employers and service providers to put in place positive action measures to promote equal opportunities and full equality in practice across all nine grounds, with a view to removing existing inequalities that affect opportunity. It recognises that individual effort alone will not address the inequalities in access to employment experienced by members of the discriminated group.

In 2010 there were 796 individual referrals to the Equality Tribunal under the Employment Equality Acts. The majority related to discrimination on the grounds of race, disability, gender and age (Equality Tribunal, 2011: 7). In the same year there were 196 individual referrals under the Equal Status Acts, most frequently invoking the disability, Traveller and race grounds. The Equal Status Acts prohibit discrimination in accessing goods and services (Equality Tribunal, 2011: 10).

Social care practitioners can expect that their engagement with members of groups who experience discrimination and inequality will in part be shaped by their experiences of being excluded, ignored and treated less fairly.

Critique of legislation

While legislation has played a significant role in highlighting how pervasive discrimination is in Irish society, it does have a number of drawbacks that hinder its effectiveness. Two aspects are briefly addressed here:

1. The Equality and Equal Status Acts are retrospective in their application and depend on individuals to enforce their rights. An incidence of discrimination must occur and then an individual must take a civil case challenging this discrimination to the Equality Tribunal. Rights are thus generally enforced on a case-by-case basis. The development of a legally based statutory duty on the private and the public sector to promote equality alongside the individual

enforcement model would be of enormous significance to the groups who experience discrimination and inequality (Crowley, 2006: 108–9).
2. The positive action provision in the legislation at present is voluntary. A requirement on employers and service providers to take positive action where significant imbalances in equality outcomes are identified would ensure a targeting of resources and initiatives (Crowley, 2006: 113).

The legislation has been successful in raising awareness of the pervasive nature of discrimination and it has given people who experience discrimination a means of legal redress. Cases can be brought to the Equality Tribunal without the costs or the anxiety associated with vindicating one's rights in the courts. The process is accessible and social care practitioners can act as advocates in supporting people to vindicate their rights, either informally through the mediation service or by taking a case. In line with the development of case law challenging discrimination, there has been a move in social care to challenge more conservative values and develop a more emancipatory approach in the Irish context.

EMANCIPATORY THEORY IN SOCIAL CARE

There has been some attention to emancipatory theorising in social care in the Irish context. Recent work by Hanlon (2007a, 2007b, 2009), Mulkeen (2012a, 2012b), O'Connor (2006), O'Doherty (2006) and O'Toole (2009) offer a critique of traditional social care values and practice; development of a structural analysis of social care; and pointers towards the theoretical and practice frameworks for an emancipatory approach. Work by Murray and Urban (2012) on equality and diversity makes a valuable contribution to the early childhood sector and provides useful tools applicable in the social care sector.

O'Connor (2006: 102–3) identifies the broad focus of social care education as stimulating and enriching for learners but argues that if pursued without a clear social care project it is a significant stumbling block for the profession. In his view, without integration it may resemble a large 'V', with activity going in opposite directions. A commonly used definition of social care, from the Joint Committee on Social Care Professionals (JCSCP, 2002: 13), is:

> ... the professional provision of care, protection, support, welfare and advocacy for vulnerable or dependent clients, individually or in groups ... achieved through the planning and evaluation of individualised and group programmes of care, based on needs, identified where possible in con- sultation with the clients and delivered through day-to-day shared life experiences.

This definition has an exclusive focus on 'vulnerable or dependent clients' to the neglect of the contexts in which people become and/or remain 'vulnerable' or 'dependent'. It ignores the role that social divisions play in the maintenance of dependence and vulnerability, given the evidence that social class, ethnicity, disability and gender are crucial factors that shape inequality and resultant dependencies.

All service users engaged with social care practice are members of groups that are to some extent marginalised in Irish society. Practice needs to take into account the enormous power differences between people. For example, social care practitioners coming from a settled rather than a nomadic background are positioned more powerfully in Irish society than Travellers with whom they may work. Their role as social care practitioners is likely to give them more power in their interactions. Social care practitioners who do not have obvious impairments are positioned more powerfully in society than people with impairments due to the disabling nature of our society. The social care practitioner is often in a more powerful position socially than those they work with but this awareness may be lost when the focus is on supporting individual problem-solving capacities (O'Doherty, 2006).

Although the day-to-day needs of clients are vitally important, if social care practice is limited to these then it addresses the symptoms only. In this situation social care practitioners may risk becoming 'one-dimensional practitioners' (O'Connor, 2006: 88). Practice that focuses on the individual and the everyday may neglect the centrality of the state's response as a critical determinant of the quality and type of social care practice possible in any specific setting. Social care practitioners who do not have at least an implicit appreciation of the nature of inequalities, and of how they impact on the lives of service users, are lacking a basic knowledge required to do this work.

Effective practice is not merely about meeting interpersonal care needs 'on the ground'. It is also about how these needs are met and whether they empower or reinforce relations of oppression (Hanlon, 2009: 9). Social care practitioners committed to supporting people to enact their rights will seek accountability for how decisions are made, how resources are deployed, how difference is accommodated and how relations of love and care are supported (Baker et al., 2009; Hanlon, 2009). This is a significant challenge in social care practice. Hanlon (2009: 10–11) applies the five-dimensional model of equality developed by Baker et al. (2009) to social care practice as follows.

1. *Power and representation* refer to equalities of power, voice and decision making. Because power inequalities are institutionalised within caring professions (Hugman, 1991), practitioners need to question the nature of power relationships within their organisations.
2. *Resources* refer to the unequal distribution of a wide variety of resources required to live a decent life. Practitioners need to question how decisions about the allocation of resources are made. In what ways are social inequalities and social needs taken into account when allocating resources? For example, what time and money is spent on different users and for what reasons?

3. *Respect and recognition* refer to equalities of status. Respect is arguably the most fundamental of social care values. Respect and recognition raise questions about prejudice and judgment in the relationships between staff and service users. It is vital to the therapeutic value of social care that practitioners do not reproduce relationships that denigrate, and that they challenge beliefs that do, including racism, misogyny and homophobia.

4. Equality of *working and learning* in social care means ensuring that practitioners pay attention to the developmental, educational and learning opportunities and experiences of service users.

5. *Love, care and solidarity* are also common inequalities that many people experience, particularly those who access social care provision. The fact that some people do much more of the burdensome caring work in society is a primary example. Another is where some people have little or no access to ongoing loving and supportive relationships, such as children in care and people in mental health institutions and prisons. Although Irish social care has a deeply troubling history of abuse and neglect, it can still make an enormous contribution to developing and supporting relations of love and care, although to do so may require significant changes in practice.

O'Toole identifies gender as one aspect of a structural analysis of social care (see Chapter 8). Her work focuses on gendering processes in social care with reference to the language of care itself, how femininity and masculinity is constructed within social care practice and the need to examine how gendered social relations permeate interactions and interventions between social care practitioners and service users. A study of inquiry reports into intra-familial abuse argues that an analysis of the gendering processes that underlie understandings of and responses to neglect, violence and abuse can make child protection policy and practice more effective (Mulkeen, 2012a).

Anti-bias approach

The challenge now is to incorporate the discourse of equality into social care education and professional practice. The anti-bias approach adopted by the early childhood sector in Ireland provides valuable insights and tools adaptable for social care (Murray and Urban, 2012: 121). Its starting point is that children develop biases against people of other skin colour and cultures than their own and against people with abilities different to their own when they are very young.

The anti-bias approach is built on four sequential goals for both adults and children. In particular the goals for adults working in early childhood could usefully inform practice in social care. These goals are to: be conscious of one's own culture, attitudes, values and how they influence practice; be comfortable with difference, have empathy and engage effectively with families; critically think about diversity, bias and discrimination; and confidently engage in dialogue about issues of diversity, bias and discrimination so as to challenge individual and institutional forms of prejudice and discrimination (Derman-Sparks and Olsen Edwards, 2010).

In these sentiments are the seeds of a debate about the nature of social care practice, heretofore socially conservative, to which educational and professional associations can contribute. Inclusion of insights and approaches informed by user-led movements, partnership and empowerment can generate opportunities for social care practitioners to broaden their remit and challenge unequal power relations.

Emancipatory movements and partnerships

Traditionally charity- or 'expert'-led models of care were the basis of social provision, where experiences were invariably oppressive and practices exclusionary. For example, services for people with a disability were traditionally medically oriented, seeking to diagnose and treat people. They were largely provided by religious charities and excluded the voice of people with a disability.

With the rise of the disability rights movement, new analyses emerged centring on rights rather than charity (Toolan, 2003; McDonnell, 2007). The challenge of user-led movements arises from an analysis of power and oppression by the people directly affected by inequality. These voices from below became significant forces for change in the theories used to understand the world and the practices utilised to intervene in people's lives. The most well-known and effective movement for change in the twentieth century in Ireland and across the world is the women's movement. Women with experiences of unequal pay, exclusion from the labour market, rape, sexual abuse and violence and many other discriminatory and oppressive practices have long led campaigns and initiatives to challenge such inequalities (O'Connor, 1998).

Irish Travellers were represented by settled people for many decades using a model of assimilation that sought to ensure Travellers became settled and that ignored cultural practices central to Travellers' identity. Since the 1980s the growth of Traveller-led organisations such as the Irish Traveller Movement, and the development of a partnership approach between settled people and Travellers in organisations such as Pavee Point, have challenged established ways of thinking and acting towards Travellers. Emancipatory work with Travellers is premised on the belief that real improvement in Travellers' living circumstances and social situation requires the active involvement of Travellers themselves. Non-Travellers have a responsibility to address the various processes that serve to exclude Travellers from participating as equals in society (Kenny and McNeela, 2006).

The disability movement can be defined by distinguishing between organisations *for* and organisations *of* people with disabilities. Organisations for people with disabilities are concerned with disability issues but are largely staffed by able-bodied people working in partnership with national and local government, such as the National Disability Authority and the Brothers of Charity Services. In contrast, organisations of people with disabilities are run exclusively by and on behalf of people with disabilities and are informed by the social model of disability, which places emphasis on the disabling environment as a barrier to participation and the exercise of one's rights, rather than solely on individual impairments (Barnes, 1991). The challenge to the service provision model has been a significant force in bringing about change for people with disabilities in Irish society and has influenced professional practice and the development of partnership models in this field.

Partnership is a process whereby people directly experiencing oppression establish partnerships with those not directly affected but committed to challenging exclusion, domination and marginalisation. As such, it attempts to alter the balance of power within such relationships. While a partnership may not mean that participants always have equal power, it does imply recognition and open discussion about how power is distributed and used. People who lack power may become adept at resisting or subverting the expectations of them – often in subtle and even unconscious ways. Within the context of social care practice, such approaches may not easily change, even if they are offered alternative ways of having influence through partnership working (Tew, 2006: 38). A partnership must result in the redistribution of some of the power held by the more powerful group and requires the employment of external resources to support the capacity of the less powerful group to participate as equal partners.

Troubling values in social care empowerment

There is often a woolly and sometimes contradictory usage of the term 'empowerment' in social work and social welfare (Pease, 2002). It may be used to denote mutual support and collective action undertaken by disadvantaged and marginalised groups. In a much more individualised sense, it may also be used to describe people who manage to rise out of positions of helplessness and confusion to (re)claim control over their lives and discover their 'inner strengths'.

Tew's (2006) work on power in social work is a useful contribution to discussions of power and empowerment in social care practice. There is a tendency for vested political or professional interests to define empowerment for relatively powerless people, thereby retaining their status as 'experts' and their ability to exert influence over others' lives. Often, the operation of power may be a double-edged or contradictory process: oppressive or limiting in some respects and productive or protective in others. Tew suggests a working definition of power as 'a social relation that may open up or close off opportunities for individuals or social groups' (2006: 39), where 'opportunities' may involve anything from accessing resources and social or economic participation, through to developing personal identities and capabilities, to expressing needs, thoughts and feelings, and to renegotiating relationships.

EMANCIPATORY STRATEGIES FOR PRACTITIONERS

In the context of emancipatory practice in social care, much of what has been addressed in this chapter is dependent on the practitioner first developing self-awareness aligned with critically reflective practice. The following steps draw on the work of Thompson (2011) and Braye and Preston-Shoot (1995):

- *Developing and owning a personal commitment.* The process of unlearning prejudice and assumptions and relearning understanding is essential for competent practice.
- *Being personally responsible* for ensuring that good practice prevails is central to professionalism but often neglected. Familiar excuses such as a lack of policy, procedure or resources are not acceptable.
- *Letting go of the culture of 'knowing best'* by addressing practices such as speaking for others, gatekeeping resources and deriving role security from such actions is an essential starting point in emancipatory practice.
- *Recognising the impact of internalised oppression* requires a willingness to ensure that people with whom partnerships are operating have the support to be equals in such an arrangement.
- *Critically reflective practice*, developed from the work of Schön (1991a, 1991b), emphasises reflecting on the typically 'messy' professional situations in which social professionals engage. Critical reflection helps to check assumptions that can be discriminatory and avoid reliance on 'common sense'.
- *Challenging the actions of others* where it is oppressive in its outcome is necessary. Discriminatory behaviour by others must be challenged tactfully and constructively.
- *Being sensitive to language and images* is critical because they play a pivotal role in constructing reality.
- *Openness and demystification* practices ensure decisions are taken in an open and transparent manner. Where events, decisions and planning take place behind closed doors, the scope for oppressive practices is significant.
- *Humility* is required, as oppression and inequality are complex and ever-changing, with new challenges to our understanding and practice arising all the time.

CONCLUSION

This chapter has sought to engage with questions of equality and how social care students and practitioners can develop an emancipatory social care project. In doing so it outlined the rationale for addressing inequality and discrimination in social care practice and the critical context provided by the Irish equality legislation. Recent theoretical developments in the social care field in Ireland were highlighted for their contribution to the development of an emancipatory project in social care. Movements and partnerships in the fields of disability, mental health, ethnicity and gender were examined in the light of their impact on social care practice. Concepts and practices such as empowerment and a substantive model of equality need to be critically embedded in social care practice. The chapter addressed strategies at both an individual and an organisational level that can provide practitioners with the tools to enhance their self-awareness, knowledge and skills. Such a process can inform personal and professional strategies to challenge inequality and develop an emancipatory project for social care practice in Ireland.

Part IV

17

Residential child care

John McHugh and Danny Meenan

OVERVIEW

This chapter has two aims: first, to outline the residential child care system in Ireland and, second, to identify and discuss some aspects of working in residential care settings. In outlining some of the key features of residential child care, we emphasise the vulnerability of the young people who use such services and the challenges for those who practise in them. The professional skills required of practitioners are identified, as are some of the key personal attributes that contribute to effective care practice. The complex nature of the day-to-day work is explored and the importance of self-care is emphasised. The discussion is by no means exhaustive, but should act as a stimulus to further reading and research.

Working with children in residential care is challenging but rewarding. It may be beyond an individual, group, agency or government to provide perfect care in perfect settings, but all involved in residential care provision must strive to develop and maintain the best possible care.

TOWARDS AN UNDERSTANDING OF RESIDENTIAL CHILD CARE

The Constitution of Ireland (*Bunreacht na hÉireann*) is the basis of Irish law. Article 42.5 pledges the government to provide care for children who, for whatever reason, cannot be cared for by their parents:

> . . . in exceptional cases, where parents for physical or moral reasons fail in their duty towards their children, the state as guardian of the common good, by appropriate means shall endeavour to supply the place of the parents, but always with due regard for the natural and imprescriptible rights of the child.

This commitment has been elaborated on and further consolidated through the implementation of the Child Care Act 1991, the Irish government's ratification in 1992 of the UN Convention on the Rights of the Child and publication of the *National Children's Strategy* in 2000. The Health Service Executive (HSE, 2011b:

119) notes: 'HSE Children and Family Services have responsibility for children whom they place with relatives or with foster carers or in residential placements, as provided for in the Child Care Act 1991 and the Child Care Regulations 1995'.

Ferguson and O'Reilly (2001) explain that social service intervention in a case of child protection is a result of concern being raised by an interested party. Under the Child Care Act 1991, the HSE has a statutory duty to promote the welfare of children who are not receiving adequate care and protection. Upon notification, an investigation is carried out by a social worker in consultation with a social work team. Where further investigation or intervention is necessary, the primary focus is always on attempting to maintain the child within their family. The HSE may do this by providing a 'family support worker' to work with the family on issues of concern in their own home. The family support worker is answerable to the social worker, who maintains regular contact with the family (Ferguson and O'Reilly, 2001: 101). Where it is deemed impossible to maintain the child in the family, they may be taken into the care of the HSE ('alternative care') under the provisions of the Child Care Act 1991.

There are a number of procedures that the HSE can use when dealing with children who are at risk or who are in need of care. It may apply for orders that give the courts a range of powers, including decisions about the kind of care and the access to the children for parents and other relatives:

- *Emergency care order:* maximum of eight days in care.
- *Interim care order:* maximum of eight days in care but may be extended.
- *Care order:* can continue until the child reaches the age of eighteen.
- *Supervision order:* maximum of twelve months but may be renewed.
- *Interim special care order:* maximum of twenty-eight days but may be extended.
- *Special care order:* maximum of six months but may be extended.

A child taken into care may be placed either in foster care (possibly with their extended family) or in a residential child care setting. The purpose of residential care is to provide a safe, nurturing environment for children and young people who cannot live at home or in an alternative family at that time. The residential care home aims to meet, in a planned way, the physical, educational, spiritual and social needs of each child.

The Department of Children and Youth Affairs (DCYA) was established in 2011 following a government decision to bring together a range of functions that were previously the responsibilities of the Ministers for Health; Education and Skills; Justice and Law Reform; and Community, Rural and Gaeltacht Affairs. The new department is focused on the transformation of Ireland's children and family services, including the creation of a new specialist agency. In November 2012 the government approved the drafting of the legislation necessary to establish the new Child and Family Support Agency. Child welfare and protection services currently operated by the HSE include family support and alternative care services such as residential child care homes. The planned reform aims to move away from a complex and fragmented approach towards improved service delivery and clearer accountability within a single dedicated state agency, overseen by a single dedicated government department. This independent agency, separated from the health service and under the direction of the DCYA, is to have a children's rights-based approach; it is underpinned by legislation and incorporates a new alignment of key children and family services.

In March 2012 there were 6,236 children in care; 2,248 of whom entered care during 2011. The total number in care rose by almost 20 per cent in the four years to 2012, in line with national population growth. Approximately 90 per cent of those in alternative care are in foster care, with less than 10 per cent in residential care homes. There is a long-term trend towards higher rates of foster care provision: this proportion increased from 66 per cent in 2001 to 90 per cent in 2010.

Children's residential centres are not immediately obvious as they are found in domestic homes in housing estates on the outskirts of towns and villages. They can typically have between two and six children, usually in their teens. The children and young people often attend local schools and take part in local sporting and community activities. Staff work on a shift basis providing round-the-clock care. Each young person in the centre is allocated a key worker. Children's residential centres are inspected by the Health Information and Quality Authority (HIQA) against the *National Standards for Children's Residential Centres* (DoHC, 2001a) and the inspection reports are published on an anonymised basis.

Residential children's centres are run directly by the health service, by voluntary bodies or by private companies. The average number of children per unit is three to five and the cost of residential care is high. Unpublished figures from the HSE reported in the *Irish Times* on 5 February 2009 indicate that €135 million was spent on the provision of residential care for about 400 children and young people, an average of €337,500 per child per annum, with private care costing up to €420,000 per child. In contrast, the cost of foster placements in 2007 was €98 million, or about €21,000 per child per annum.

There are several reasons why children may be in alternative care. They may be suffering abuse or neglect; their parents/guardians may be unable to cope due to illness or disability; or their parents/guardians may be absent for a variety of reasons (for example, they might have left, have died, be in prison, or the child might be an unaccompanied asylum seeker). In some cases children are taken into care because of emotional or behavioural problems. Care may be for short periods to give their parents the chance to recover from illness or another traumatic event. Some children are admitted into the care system with the voluntary agreement of their parents.

The most common reasons for children to be taken into care are to protect them from neglect, parental incapacity, children's emotional behavioural problems or physical abuse (see Table 17.1). Contrary to media or popular portrayals, comparatively few children are placed in care as a consequence of sexual abuse, involvement in crime or domestic violence, although these may be associated, if not primary, criteria.

Table 17.1. Principal reasons for admission to alternative care

Primary reason for admission to care	Emergency court order	Other court order	Admitted voluntarily	Total	%
Abuse	202	265	305	772	35
Physical abuse	35	55	79	169	8
Sexual abuse	4	20	9	33	1
Emotional abuse	32	21	34	87	4
Neglect	131	169	183	483	22
Child problems	30	52	261	343	15
Emotional/behavioural	13	29	164	206	9
Abusing drugs/alcohol	4	4	18	26	1
Involved in crime	0	0	5	5	0
Pregnancy	0	1	6	7	0
Physical illness or disability	3	3	14	20	1
Mental illness or intellectual disability	1	6	9	16	1
Other	9	9	45	63	3
Family problems	108	179	816	1,103	50
Parent unable to cope/housing/finance, etc.	16	43	421	480	22
Abusing drugs/alcohol	39	77	146	262	12
Domestic violence	8	14	12	34	2
Physical illness or disability	3	1	27	31	1
Mental illness or intellectual disability	24	16	94	134	6
Separated child asylum seeker	0	5	4	9	0
Other	18	23	112	153	7
TOTAL	340	496	1,382	2,218	100
Reason unrecorded				30	
Total admitted to care				2,248	

Source: HSE (2011b)

It is generally accepted that all children in care have experienced a degree of life trauma by virtue of the fact that they have been separated from their birth family. The emotional impact of early life trauma is well documented. Fahlberg (1994) suggests that children who have experienced early life trauma may present with particular emotional or behavioural difficulties. Children with such difficulties often find it hard to cope with the necessary structures in place in residential services. The Eastern Health Board (EHB, 1998) found that some children may run away from residential care or be removed for presenting with chaotic violent behaviours or drug misuse. These children often end up homeless and are deemed to require a more secure form of accommodation. A number of cases have been before the Irish courts in relation to the lack of facilities available for such children.

The difficulties experienced by the HSE in finding 'suitable' placements for homeless children with behavioural difficulties has led to the development of a small number of special care and high-support services (see Table 17.2). Special care units are HSE-managed secure residential facilities for young people aged between twelve and seventeen years who are detained under a High Court order for a short period of time for their own safety and welfare. The children and young people cannot leave the facility of their own accord. Special care units 'provide the child or young person with a model of care and appropriate interventions which are based on relationships, containment and positive reinforcements in order to stabilise the persistent and extreme situation' (CAAB, n.d.).

Table 17.2. Types of children's residential care centres in Ireland

Type of facility	No.
Community-based children's residential	114
Special care units	3
High support	10
Hostel/emergency beds	11
Special arrangements	6
Leaving and aftercare	6
Other	11

Source: HIQA (2009)

High-support units have a higher ratio of staff to young people. The young people have access to education on site or to training tailored to their needs, and they usually have enhanced access to assessment and sometimes therapy provided on site by specialist staff. High support differs from ordinary residential care in that the units offer higher staff ratios, on-site education as well as specialised input such as psychology services (DCYA, 2013).

YOUNG PEOPLE IN RESIDENTIAL CARE

As we have seen, children and young people enter residential care for a number of reasons, such as abuse, neglect or foster care breakdown, or they may live in unsafe environments where their protection cannot be guaranteed. Many young people in residential care can experience deep-seated feelings of loss, separation and abandonment. They may carry the baggage and scars of multiple placements and transfers of bases, where they have not had opportunities to build trusting relationships or invest in emotional security.

Fahlberg (1994: 160) discusses how unresolved separations can interfere with the development of future attachments. She suggests that the new attachments that young people make are not meant to replace the old attachments – they can co-exist. This is also true for young people in residential care. For a number of young people, prior negative experiences with adults and other caregivers have led them to develop their own coping mechanisms. These may prevent the development of further attachments, either out of loyalty to birth parents or as a means of self-preservation. The role that residential workers play in the lives of young people in care is of vital importance. The smallest aspects of everyday caring can make a difference and have a great impact. In this process, the job of the residential social care practitioner has many elements: teacher, mentor, role model, listening-friend and advocate, to name a few. It is essential that the practitioners understand how to maintain a high level of professionalism in this complex care environment. They need to be able to work efficiently and to engage with the various agencies involved in care provision.

The role the residential care practitioner plays may be a far cry from the other adults these young people have known throughout their short lives. Some may have had to learn to be self-reliant due to extended periods of neglect. They may not trust adults readily. For many, the apparent containment of a mainstream residential centre, with its rules and responsibilities, can prove difficult to adhere to and can lead to points of conflict. For some young people, residential care may be the best option, as living in a foster care placement may constantly remind them of the dysfunctionality of their own families, adding to their pain and frustration. Residential care can also be seen by the young person as a temporary base, away from their home, where they can explore specific issues that caused their family life to break down.

While there are many common factors that lead young people into care, everyone in residential care has their own unique set of circumstances. Each young person is an individual and should be treated accordingly. Residential workers often find it difficult to come to terms with the fact that some young people will present particular behaviour as a way to avoid an exploration of the reasons for their admission into care. The presenting behaviour becomes the focus, with the underlying reason for the behaviour not receiving attention. This situation can leave the practitioner feeling frustrated and may sometimes lead to feelings of self-doubt. Where the social care practitioner is unable to identify or explore the core reason for behavioural problems, it is essential that they recommend referral to an appropriate discipline such as psychology or child and adolescent mental health.

All residential workers must understand that some young people in residential care may *never* fully discuss their true feelings or how the emotional impact of their past experiences has affected them. The simplest triggers – a song on the radio, a phrase someone uses, the smell of a particular perfume or cologne – may bring memories flooding back. These can be the precursor to a violent outburst or a retreat into their inner space. The important thing is to let these young people know that there is someone who will be there for them when they feel that they are ready to talk. This is a personal path that some young people may take many years to travel.

RESIDENTIAL CHILD CARE SKILLS

So what are the skills needed to equip social care practitioners for their role in residential child care settings? For Clough (2000: 23), one of the challenges of working in residential child care is to define what is specific and distinctive about it. He suggests that in residential houses there is a mix of physical care, holding and the development of self. Residential care should provide a good place to live, where residential workers can respond in everyday activities in ways that are therapeutic and life enhancing.

Research that involved talking to social care practitioners in residential care about the key skills and attributes for working with young people (Meenan, 2002) identified the following attributes:

- Non-judgmental
- Team member
- Good communicator (oral and written)
- Good listener
- Problem-solving abilities
- Patient – remaining calm in a crisis
- Awareness of self
- Caring nature
- Assertive
- Open to learning new things
- Understanding
- Creative and imaginative
- Sense of humour.

Words such as 'rewarding', 'demanding' and 'challenging' have been used to describe working with young people in residential care. Some practitioners see their work in residential care as more of a vocation than employment. They emphasise staying focused and being consistent and dedicated, even in the most difficult times, to help make a difference in young people's lives, rather than just coming to work as a means to an end.

Residential care can be a mind-opening experience for many social care practitioners. Many initially find it difficult to comprehend what some children and young people have already experienced in their short lives – more than many other adults, including staff themselves, will experience in a lifetime. Practitioners have talked about finding it difficult to rationalise how adults can treat children and young people with such contempt and cause so much pain. Residential care has 'opened their eyes' to personal trauma and behaviour that they never knew existed.

So how does one prepare oneself to work in this environment? Many practitioners would welcome the development of the theory related to this work. A professional entering residential child care experiences a very sharp learning curve that requires quick thinking and ingenuity on a daily – sometimes hourly – basis. For many, the theory studied at college does not always match the reality of working in a residential centre, but it can provide insights into why some young people behave the way they do. Smith (2009) identifies psychodynamic theory, behaviourist approaches and developmental models as providing insights that can be useful to understanding relationships and behaviours that exist in residential child care. Attachment theory and resilience can also be useful in approaching the care relationship, with solution-focused brief therapy and social learning models having a valuable contribution to make.

Professional training provides opportunities to develop and practise skills and heighten self-awareness. These opportunities, coupled with relevant theory, promote a reflective approach to social care practice. It is the responsibility of the individual practitioner and of the service provider to ensure that all staff are both aware of and equipped for their professional role.

Practitioners need to afford young people in residential care the opportunities to explore issues and learn from life experiences and, indeed, to make mistakes. Practitioners also have to realise that as a consequence of young people's experiences prior to admission, some in residential care find it beyond their ability to break the spiral of negative or offending behaviour, no matter how many supports are provided.

Social care ethics direct practitioners to support and be proactive in young people's development, safety and journey to adulthood. It is an integral part of the job to network with other agencies while remaining cognisant of confidentiality and children's right to privacy. They must document and accurately record any information that will help and enable the choices and opportunities for the young person.

WORKING IN RESIDENTIAL CHILD CARE SETTINGS

The needs and problems of many children in care are complex and difficult to serve appropriately. Or more correctly, their needs are deceptively simple, but delivering the right response is deceptively complex (Gilligan, 2001: 1). This section examines life and work across the range of residential child care settings.

Children and young people who live in residential care have faced, and bring with them, exceptional problems and difficulties. These may include neglect, abuse (physical, emotional, sexual), family breakdown, separation and loss or betrayal of trust. They may be in their first care placement or may have moved several times from one care setting to another. They may have a clear understanding and acceptance of what is happening in their life or may be confused, anxious or angry. They may be open to talking about their situation or may not yet be able to express what they are feeling. They may have an ability to quickly form relationships with new people or they may prefer to cut themselves off from any kind of relationship that involves trusting others. Their behaviour may be 'normal' and stable or unpredictable and even dangerous.

According to Chakrabarti and Hill (2000: 9), 'it is the responsibility of residential staff and carers, acting on behalf of society at large, to promote these children's well-being and to minimise the negative consequences of separation'. This overall aim is usually broken down into a number of professional tasks that permeate all aspects of life in residential care. They include: developing and working with care plans and placement plans, relationship building, and key working.

Care plans and placement plans

The Child Care (Placement of Children in Residential Care) Regulations 1995 require that a written care plan is in place either before or immediately after a young person is placed in residential care. A distinction is made between the overall long-term plan for the care of the young person and the more immediate plan with regard to the time the young person is in the centre. The overall care plan takes account of the young person's educational, social, emotional, behavioural and health requirements, whereas the placement plan focuses on how the residential care setting intends to meet those needs.

The social care practitioner must have a clear understanding of the needs of young people generally. Knowledge of developmental psychology, attachment, behaviour management and health and safety will help in responding to the needs of particular children and young people. Practitioners need to have skills and knowledge, drawn from a number of different disciplines, ranging from the directly practical – nutrition, recreation and health care, for example – to personal, people-centred skills such as care and control, communicating with children, counselling and family work, backed by in-depth and detailed knowledge of child development (Residential Forum, 1998: 11).

It should be noted that life in care for the young person may be far less clear than that reflected in the care plan or placement plan. Their unique story may have a lot of pain, hurt and confusion. The success of their placement largely depends on the trusting relationships built with the people with whom they share this part of their life. But the care plan can be a useful tool to assess progress and bring some overall clarity to the complex task of working with children in care.

Relationship building

The caring relationship is at the heart of good and effective professional social care. But relationships in residential care settings, as in life generally, are often complex. They change and develop over time and involve sharing ourselves with others at various levels – emotionally, physically and professionally. Relationships are entered into rather than created. While there is no easy formula for creating an effective relationship with positive outcomes, Rogers (cited in Murgatroyd, 1996: 15) suggests that professional caring relationships have three basic qualities that the worker needs to be able to communicate if the relationship is to be successful:

- *Empathy:* the ability to experience another person's world as if it were one's own without ever losing that 'as if' quality.
- *Warmth:* accepting people as they are, without conditions, and helping them to feel safe.
- *Genuineness:* a way of being with other people built on open communication and respect.

In residential care settings, working with children and young people who have not experienced positive, trusting relationships can make the task of relationship building even more challenging. Trying to define and analyse relationships may not be of much help in developing skills in relationship building. Think of important relationships in your own life: they are usually described in terms of actions and feelings rather than defined through words or terminology. Thus, 'relationships are developed through the most mundane and routine of tasks from reading a story at bedtime, to repairing a puncture in a pushbike, or providing hugs or reassurance when a child falls over, as well as through sharing critical episodes and crises' (Residential Forum, 1998: 9).

Professional social care work in residential child care settings is about creating and maintaining meaningful relationships through everyday activities. As Gilligan (2001: 56) suggests, 'it is often the little things that carers do that register with and reassure children. It seems that, through these little things, the carers somehow communicate interest and concern and help the child feel connected to the carer.'

Social care practitioners must be equipped for this kind of work. A thorough knowledge of the procedures, policies and legislation that provide the framework the caring agency operates in is necessary. Practitioners also need to have a theory base that gives them an understanding of people, systems and practices: 'The nature of relationship-based work is that it gives rise to many questions. The purpose of theorising is to promote thinking so that practice is improved' (Residential Forum, 1998: 12). Perhaps the most challenging aspect of working with young people in residential care is sharing life: sharing experiences, perspectives, feelings, emotions and beliefs. This aspect of professional practice demands a high level of self-knowledge, which can be gained through personal development.

Key working

Key working is a system for providing individualised social care through named persons. The key worker is the person who has responsibility and accountability for the care of the service user and for decisions relating to their situation. The key worker does not have sole responsibility for the care of the young person, but does co-ordinate and ensure that the young person's care plan is progressed and that the young person's life in the centre is supported positively and with individual care. Petrie et al. (2006) point out that key working can take place at various levels: an administrative role that ensures that an individual child's records and paperwork relating to their ongoing care are accurate and well maintained; and as a core person in the young person's life, with a meaningful relationship in which the child knows that the key worker knows them. It can also be a combination of both these roles.

Key working involves (SCA, 1991):

- Mutual trust and respect.
- The social, physical, intellectual, cultural, emotional and spiritual aspects of the service user's development and wellbeing.
- Creating a sense of purpose and change.
- Partnership between the key worker, other service providers and those who are the users of their services.
- Planning – utilising the abilities of individuals and groups in the arena of problem solving.
- Changing social environments, including, for example, challenging racist, sexist and ageist attitudes and behaviours.

More specifically, HSE and IAYPIC (2009) list practical aspects of the key worker's role, including regular check-in meetings, 'life-story work' and remembering special occasions, keeping in contact with family and social worker, advocating with and for the young person, preparing reports and maintaining records, developing life skills and planning for the future, and preparing for moving on from residential care.

The residential care centre is a busy place, with all the activities of daily living: breakfast, school, games, clubs, TV, Internet, homework, cleaning and cooking. There is the added complication that it is not a family unit; rather, a team of social care practitioners takes on the parenting role. As Burton (1993: 48) puts it, 'I am not saying that the worker is a parent to the child . . . the worker remains a worker throughout, but we are using inner resources and knowledge – the most personal and tender and vulnerable areas of our inner selves – to do the work.' In the context of the residential care centre, the relationship between practitioner and young person is clearly of vital importance, but it can be difficult to develop and maintain significant relationships in an environment interrupted by shiftwork patterns, or where high staff turnover puts an end to developing attachments and relationships.

Another factor that may impact negatively on quality personalised care and relationship building is the sheer amount of activity within and around the residential centre. This may include official business regarding the care and related issues of the children and young people, staff meetings, new admissions, aftercare, and daily living tasks and issues, for example, school, hobbies and interests, shopping, eating and so on. The primary role of the key worker is to help make sense of this experience of living for the individual child or young person. Key working has been found to 'improve personalised care, relationships, the clarity of the residential tasks and helped to improve other aspects of life in the establishment . . . for the staff as well as for the resident' (Clarke, 1998: 31).

The key worker is usually given particular responsibility in relation to a child, for example to accompany them to appointments or to liaise with relevant professionals, agencies, school and family. For this to take place, emphasis is placed on developing a positive, professional caring relationship between the young person and the key worker. The key worker needs to have a clear understanding of the theory that underpins the work, for example, attachment theory, the hierarchy of need, developmental psychology and so on. They must also develop competency in a range of skills relating to communication, active listening, advocacy, boundary maintenance and confidentiality. A practitioner who takes on the role of key worker should receive and use supervision and may need further training depending on the specific needs of the child. It is expected that the key worker will attend reviews of children for whom they are responsible.

Times of transition or change in a young person's life often bring with them anxiety, insecurity and feelings of vulnerability. The key worker can have an important role at such times. In preparing to leave a care setting, the young person may be supported, empowered and gain confidence through clear guidelines around moving on and outreach. The key worker plays a vital role at this time and can provide further support through planned aftercare.

It is clear that the role of key worker in the residential care centre is central to the quality and effectiveness of care experienced by the young person: 'enduring relationships with committed people become very important for young people growing up in care. It is from these relationships that their "secure base" may emerge' (Gilligan, 2001). Enduring relationships are important in enabling any of us to negotiate our way through difficult periods of our lives. Young people in care have a special need for experiencing such relationships, as their home base is at best fragile and perhaps disintegrated. Developing a trusting, mutually respectful relationship with an adult can give the young person some of the tools to begin building that secure platform for future life experience.

RESIDENTIAL STAFF

The issues of self-awareness and professional boundaries are always contentious for those who work in residential care. There is always a need to remain safe, but provision of a high quality of care can sometimes leave individual staff in vulnerable situations. Communication among the team is a very important aspect in residential work. Sharing ideas, consulting with others, ensuring a consistent and continuous approach with all staff and following agreed protocols and policies cannot be emphasised enough.

Practitioners in residential care must be aware of what they bring as individuals to residential work – their own prejudices, beliefs and values. Their professional motivation is based on a belief that they have something to offer the young people they work with. But practitioners' personal experiences and life events should not colour their vision or lead them to make particular judgments just because they feel they know better or have experienced a similar emotional trauma. Practitioners in residential care must always retain an open outlook and see each young person as an individual who will react differently in a variety of similar situations. They must work at an appropriate pace and level of understanding to help children and young people to deal with their issues.

Many residential staff are faced with situations that are challenging, sometimes emotionally, sometimes physically. These situations force them to think more laterally and constructively about their professional roles and relationships. Residential teams usually comprise a variety of individuals who have stories to tell and experiences to share. There should always be opportunities to grow and develop, both personally and professionally. Strong elements of trust and open communication between team members are necessary, as each individual practitioner needs to feel a sense of support and security from others at times of heightened anxiety or aggression within a centre. Knowing that someone is there to assist through particularly difficult situations and that there is support afterwards can be the factor that gives residential staff the focus necessary to respond appropriately to the complex needs and behaviours of the young person in care. Structures, routines, consistency and clarity of actions are all important aspects of team cohesion.

At an organisational level, the shift system, if not organised properly, can allow different staff members to work in significantly different ways. If the same rules are not applied by all staff in a consistent manner, this can potentially lead to confusion and frustration for the young people, as well as difficulties in staff relations. Failure to maintain equilibrium of approach can be reminiscent of the previous experiences of some young people. They may quite naturally play off one set of staff against the other. Communication is vital and properly structured handover meetings between shifts reduce the opportunities for manipulation and potential conflict. Centres with a high staff turnover may reflect the previous turmoil in some young people's lives and reinforce the inconsistency and lack of constancy in their lives.

Residential staff at different points in their careers – students on placement, newly qualified staff, practitioners with many years of life experience, and others with years of work experience – all agree that one has to work in residential care to experience its emotional rollercoaster. They also stress how rewarding, worthwhile and enjoyable it is to make a positive contribution to the lives of children and young people in care.

Self-care

One of the most important issues about working in residential care is the issue of self-care. Of course, this is an issue not solely for social care practitioners in residential settings, but given the pressure and stress that this type of work creates, it can be an area that is neglected.

Self-care in the professional context means that every individual must take responsibility for their own needs and wellbeing. Monk (2011) argues that, as 'healing agents', practitioners must strive to prevent the emotional, psychological, physical and spiritual impacts of stress that arise in the course of their work or elsewhere. They cannot provide adequate and appropriate care for others, particularly troubled children and young people, if they do not make time to look after themselves. It could be said that as you are the only person who is constantly with you, you must always be the one to care for yourself.

Self-care in this environment is closely linked to self-awareness. Individuals must remain acutely aware of their limitations and levels of tolerance and anxiety. The ability to recognise incidents of high anxiety in oneself may take some time to master but, if practitioners are not careful and continue to work, oblivious to their mood and ignoring the indicators, this may lead, in time, to feelings of complete exhaustion and occupational burnout.

Many people do not recognise that they are suffering from stress. They think feelings of rushing adrenalin and high anxiety are part of the job, and in some circumstances are the stimulus that keeps them going. Failure to recognise that you are under pressure can often lead to additional issues in the workplace. For some people, this could mean making rash decisions or reacting in an unaccustomed manner that may lead to the further deterioration of a situation that can spiral out of control. The young person can end up feeling, and reacting, defensively and neither side is willing to back down due to the fear of losing face.

Everyone wants to do their best for the young people and can become quite attached to them, even to the young people who constantly challenge them and stretch their patience to the limit. People generally get support and guidance from other team members and the longer-serving members of the team often find themselves in the position of mentor and emotional supporter during times of upset and frustration.

Good support through supervision is vitally important for all residential staff. Supervision should not be a place that just evaluates a practitioner's plan of work for their key child and organises their next time off. It is an opportunity to explore the impact of particular situations and events and how they have affected the practitioner on all levels as well as a chance to plan how they will deal with similar situations better. At times, people will avoid exploring specific issues in supervision, as they often fear letting their guard down. They wonder how their manager will view them if they really say what they are feeling or thinking. It is healthy to explore all the emotions that negative situations may generate; individuals can remain emotionally stunted if they do not fully express the issues that contribute to their frustrations and distress.

In meeting the needs of residential staff, it may be useful to make use of the services of an external clinical supervisor who can provide a place where the safety valve can be opened and personal issues can be released and explored. Many staff have found this method of self-exploration in a non-work environment very therapeutic and have stated that it gives them the opportunity to explore specific issues and frustrations in a freer manner, without feeling professionally vulnerable. All practitioners need to have this opportunity to explore the specific issues that residential care can throw at them, since without it, their vision may be clouded, their opinions misjudged and their work with young people tinged with misunderstanding. These feelings are often stronger after an aggressive outburst, where a lot of anger is displayed and even physical assaults take place.

No one comes to work to be assaulted or verbally abused, but the fact remains that in residential care it can be an occupational hazard. While such incidents cannot always be prevented, they must never be condoned. When children and young people have been traumatised, they can act out in aggressive and unpredictable ways. For many, it is an open expression of their inner turmoil, which one manager described as being akin to a volcano before it erupts. It is unhealthy for anyone, particularly troubled young people, to repress anger and hurt, as they will often erupt when least expected.

Children and young people are naturally active and boredom can lead to frustration and an inappropriate response to the simplest of requests. Residential staff need to be proactive in promoting ways that allow and facilitate young people to let off steam. Social care practitioners in residential care have the responsibility to ensure that this happens in a safe environment and that a steady stream of activities facilitates this.

As in all professions, people have a certain working style or forte that leads them to work in particular environments. Some prefer to work with younger children, others with adolescents. Some enjoy the revolving door of a short-stay or assessment centre as opposed to the longer commitment of medium- to long-term care. Whichever environment a practitioner works in, be it mainstream, high support or secure care, other professionals are there to support and help them, both inside and outside the service. In addition, practitioners should not feel undervalued or intimidated by the seniority of other professionals. Residential child care practitioners have the best knowledge of the young people in their care; after all, they are with them almost every day, experiencing the variety of emotions that are displayed. It is important that they share this knowledge clearly and confidently, as they are important contributors in the decision-making process and can influence the development of plans for the young people under their care.

CONCLUSION

This short introduction to the world of residential child care has attempted to outline a context for this area of service delivery, to provide some basic facts and figures and to reflect something of the experience of working in this field. It can be easy to be overwhelmed by the raft of legislation, reports, enquiries and guidelines in this area, but it is important to have an understanding of the changing framework within which residential care is provided in order to focus on the quality of the professional caring relationship between practitioner and young people.

Readers are encouraged to relate the issues here to their practice experience and/or further reading with a view to developing their ability to work with children and young people in residential care settings. The challenge must surely be to move from learning *about* to learning *with* children in care in order that this sometimes necessary response can be of the best possible quality.

18

Social care and the older person

Carmel Gallagher

OVERVIEW

This chapter examines policy, services and issues related to social care for older people in Ireland. Following a brief discussion of population ageing in Ireland and the implications of an ageing population for service provision, it outlines the welfare model for social care services for older people in Ireland and describes the principal policy developments in care services for older people since the 1960s. The provision of residential care for incapacitated older people is examined and recent legislative initiatives to improve quality of care are discussed. Different types of residential care – public, private and voluntary – are described and examples are given of residential settings. Turning to day care service provision, the chapter outlines aims, examines policy issues and describes day centres. It highlights the issue of improving quality in care settings and examples are given of good practice and innovative projects. Quality initiatives are analysed in the context of a social care model of service provision. Consideration is given to the implications of a social care model for education and training of staff. The chapter concludes by advocating a positive vision of the possibilities for living a full life in later years and the challenges involved for social care practitioners in achieving this.

INTRODUCTION

When social care is discussed in relation to older people, it is often associated with tailored services that aim to meet personal and social needs of frail, chronically ill or confused older people. Ageing or senescence is associated with a decline in physiological effectiveness that affects us all sooner or later and is an intrinsic part of growing old. While disease affects only certain members of the older population, many diseases are related to age. The combination of senescent changes such as hearing loss or deteriorating eyesight, and a greater risk of illnesses such as stroke or heart disease, makes the older person more vulnerable and dependent. The realities of old age have come to be seen by contemporary governments as presenting problems that require solutions.

There has been a significant increase in the proportion of older people in the populations of many Western countries. Ireland has been an exception to this trend and is, in fact, a young country in comparison with its European neighbours (O'Shea, 2006). In 2006 Ireland had the lowest proportion of older people in its population among European Union countries: 11 per cent of the population was aged sixty-five or over, compared with an EU-27 average of 16.8 per cent (CSO, 2007: 10). In the 2011 census the proportion of older people in the population was 11.6 per cent, indicating a slight upward trend (CSO, 2012e). Population projections by the Central Statistics Office suggest that, by 2036, older people may make up 20 to 23 per cent of the population. This shift in population profile will have major implications, particularly for pensions and other services that older people use or rely heavily on, such as health and long-term care (Fahey et al., 2007).

Given the preference of older people to be cared for at home (O'Hanlon et al., 2005) and the central role of the family in the provision of day-to-day care, policy has been focused on support and advice for carers, the development of domiciliary services such as home help, and on improving the range of services and quality of care provided in day and residential centres. Traditionally many social care services for older people were provided by voluntary organisations, with nuns from religious orders providing much of the expertise. With the decline in the number of religious, these services have increasingly come under the remit of the health service. The voluntary sector continues to play an important role at the local level in the provision of many day care services and supported housing projects. In the development of these services, the health and housing authorities seek to work in partnership with voluntary bodies where possible. In residential care, the private sector has played an expanded role within a framework of legislative regulations and state subvention. Thus, a mixed economy of welfare model is evident in the provision of social care services for older people.

Community care services for older people are underdeveloped and have no legal basis. The NESF (2005: iv) report *Care for Older People* commented that the community care system for older people is 'crisis driven, lacks sufficient co-ordination and resources and does not afford older people the choice, independence and autonomy they seek and deserve'. Current difficulties in public finances, particularly since the onset of the economic recession in 2008, have led to severe curtailment of the domiciliary care services and supports necessary to give effect to principles of 'ageing in place'.

Important community care services are already thinly spread. For example, 'meals on wheels' are provided almost entirely by voluntary groups to less than one per cent of the elderly population; there is an acute shortage of paramedical and therapeutic services; and there are very few day care places available across the country (O'Shea, 2006: 16). Home help service provision is very low in Ireland by international standards. The HeSSOP II study (O'Hanlon et al., 2005) estimated that take-up of home help services among the over sixty-fives was 6 per cent in the Western Health Board and 9 per cent in the Eastern Health Board. This compared with a rate of 19 per cent in Sweden. An Irish longitudinal study on ageing (TILDA) found that only 3.5 per cent of people aged over fifty had received state-provided home help services in the past year (Barrett et al., 2011a: 204).

It is increasingly acknowledged that the older population is a more heterogeneous group than is often suggested. Most 'young elderly' (usually thought of as the 65–75 age group) are fit and active and the vast majority of older people live independent lives. Decline in physical function may be of little consequence to older people until they cross some threshold that prevents them from carrying out necessary activities. Indeed, older people contribute to the quality of life of family and kin through being involved in a long-term chain of support, including emotional support and care for ill and dependent relatives. There is evidence of older people giving considerable amounts of practical and emotional support in daily living, mainly to family but also to friends and neighbours (Barrett et al., 2011a; Gallagher, 2008; Phillipson et al., 2001).

POLICY DEVELOPMENT SINCE THE 1960s

Until the 1960s social service provision for older people in Ireland was limited to a number of core income maintenance schemes and a rather stigmatised system of residential care for infirm and chronically ill elderly people with limited means. Since the 1960s a number of key government reports have shaped policy and services for older people in Ireland:

- The 1968 *Care of the Aged Report* was a seminal document that addressed the needs of older people as a distinct group in a coherent way. It signalled a move away from institutionalised care to care in the community, based on the belief that 'it is better, and probably much cheaper, to help the aged to live in the community than to provide for them in hospitals or other institutions' (Interdepartmental Committee on the Care of the Aged, 1968: 13).
- *The Years Ahead: a policy for the elderly* (DoH, 1988) formed the basis of official policy for older people in Ireland until the mid-1990s. It advocated a strong service-delivery model relating to health and social care services for older people at home, in the community, in hospitals and in long-term care. The role of key health professionals and social care providers was emphasised and reflected the growth in professional health and welfare services since the *Care of the Aged Report*.
- *Shaping a Healthier Future: a strategy for effective healthcare in the 1990s* (DoH, 1994) represented a challenge to this service-oriented approach. It made two key points: one cannot assume that services have an inherent value (it is necessary to evaluate the health and social gain they produce); and it is essential to have consumer participation in the planning of services and in ensuring the accountability of service providers.

- *Adding Years to Life and Life to Years* (DoHC, 1998) was launched in 1998. It addressed health promotion for older people, in its broadest sense, acknowledging the impact of environmental and social factors on the quality of life of older people, and the contribution that many sectors outside the health sector make.
- *Quality and Fairness: a health system for you* (DoHC, 2001b) highlighted quality of life as a central objective and proposed a number of comprehensive actions to meet the needs of older people into the future. These included health promotion; dementia services; clarification on eligibility and subvention arrangements for long-term care; provision of additional community nursing unit places; extension of the remit of the Social Services Inspectorate to include inspections of residential care for older people; and preparation of national standards for community and long-term residential care (O'Shea, 2006: 16).

The introduction of the Home Care Package Scheme in 2001 was another important development that sought to provide a more comprehensive mix of support services for older people with high dependency needs who wished to remain at home. The scheme involves the provision of home care based on the individual needs of the person and can include nurses, home care assistants, home helps, physical therapy and occupational therapy (DoHC, 2009). While there has been considerable investment in this scheme in recent years (11,565 home care packages were made available in 2007), it is not a national scheme and is not established in law (Considine and Dukelow, 2009). The challenges of sustaining such discretionary schemes at a time of budgetary constraints were underlined with the announcement in 2012 of significant cuts in both home care packages and home help hours across the country (Wall, 2012).

As a result of these and other policy developments, the range of social care services now provided for today's older population – covering income maintenance, health care, domiciliary care, housing and residential care – is wider than any previous generation of older people would have imagined. The family continues to be placed at the centre of social care provision but there is a lack of policy coherence in the supports available to families to help them to care for their elderly relatives at home. Commenting on supports for both domiciliary care and residential care for older people in Ireland, Timonen and Doyle (2008: 86) state:

> . . . the Irish care regime is yet to make the transition to a state of joined-up thinking about the different components of this regime. Formal and informal care are still viewed as opposites, rather than complementary areas that should be able to interact in a manner that eases the transition between the home and institutional care for the older person in need of care.

RESIDENTIAL CARE

The provision of long-stay care for older people who can no longer be cared for at home for social and medical reasons gives insight into how society perceives both the needs of, and the possibilities for, very frail and incapacitated older people in terms of their wellbeing. We will examine the different types of long-term care available before considering the quality of care that infirm older people receive. The Interdepartmental Committee on the Care of the Aged (1968) differentiated between the types of institution providing extended care for older people. The county home model of institutional care was to be replaced by a number of different types of geriatric and welfare facilities: general hospitals, geriatric assessment units, long-stay units and welfare homes.

Despite the trend for new facilities to be much smaller in size and part of a continuum of care, the legacy of the policies of the 1950s and 1960s – where all dependent older people were gathered together in one county home – can still be seen in the considerable number of large, institutional geriatric hospitals and homes in all parts of the country.

The Years Ahead (DoH, 1988) recommended a wider range of facilities to meet the low- to medium-dependency needs of frail older people. These included: sheltered housing with back-up day care facilities; boarding out of older people under the supervision of the health boards; multipurpose homes (as developed in Donegal); and community hospitals with a range of services to include assessment and rehabilitation, respite, day care, short-term care and long-term care. There was little reflection on what type of life might be aspired to in extended care facilities. Furthermore, while the report clearly recognised the role that private nursing homes play in caring for older people, and the right of older people to avail of such care as a matter of choice, its recommendations were confined to a licensing and inspection system with minimalist standards.

Shortcomings in the subvention scheme, which had been in place since the early 1990s, led to the development of a new scheme for assessing and charging for long-term care in Ireland. The Fair Deal Nursing Home Support Scheme was introduced in 2009 as a means of funding long-term care for older people (The Nursing Home Support Scheme Act 2009). Under the scheme, older people in need of long-term care contribute according to their means to the cost of their care and the state pays the balance. This applies whether the nursing home is public, private or voluntary. People are required to pay 80 per cent of their assessable income and 5 per cent of the value of any assets, collected posthumously when their estate is being settled. Contributions do not exceed 15 per cent of the value of the family home (HSE, 2013). The state expected to pay close to €1 billion in the Fair Deal scheme in 2012 (Oireachtas, 2012a). Almost 8,000 applications were approved in 2011 under the scheme, which was an approval rate of 75 per cent (Oireachtas, 2012b). The sustainability of the Fair Deal scheme as currently structured remains a challenge in the light of the serious problems in the public finances.

LEGISLATION AND IMPROVED QUALITY OF CARE

Introduction of a regulation and inspection system under the Health (Nursing Homes) Act 1990 resulted in improved levels of care in private nursing homes (EHB, 1999: 86). Since the introduction of this legislation, the role of the private sector in particular has been expanding, with the Health Service Executive (HSE) contracting private nursing home beds to meet its obligations. However, concern has arisen over quality of care in some residential and domiciliary care services.

An RTÉ *Prime Time Investigates* documentary, screened on 30 May 2005, highlighted substandard conditions and patient neglect at Leas Cross, a private nursing home in Swords, Co. Dublin, where the HSE had contracted beds. A subsequent report into the home by geriatrician Professor Des O'Neill concluded that there had been systematic abuse and failures at many levels, including management and clinical leadership. In addition, policy, administrative and legislative shortcomings were identified in delivering quality care to incapacitated older people.

New legislative standards were introduced in 2009 applying to all residential settings (public, private and voluntary) where older people are cared for and for which registration is required (DoHC, 2009). Independent inspection of all residential care services for older people by the Health Information and Quality Authority (HIQA) commenced in the same year. The new regulatory framework reflects current expectations and ideas about quality of care and quality of life and was underpinned by research that examined the views of service providers and service users. Key quality-of-life domains were identified based on what residents in long-stay care themselves valued (Murphy et al., 2006). These included:

- Independence, privacy and self-expression.
- Confirmation that their life contains meaning and hope in the same measure as before.
- Homely atmosphere and person-centred routines that emphasise choice and empowerment.
- Aesthetically pleasing physical environment.
- To be connected to other people and to be able to maintain relationships with family and friends.
- To have meaningful and purposeful activity that they themselves are involved in planning and arranging.

The new standards include requirements in relation to consultation and participation; civil, social and political rights; care plans; and autonomy and independence. For example, Standard 18.2 states: 'The resident is given opportunities for participation in meaningful and purposeful activity, occupation or leisure activities, both inside and outside the residential care setting, that suit his/her needs, preferences and capacities' (DoHC, 2009). The importance attached to these aspects of care is highlighted in the care settings described later in this chapter.

SOCIAL CARE SETTINGS

There are approximately 20,000 residents aged sixty-five or older in long-stay residential care in Ireland, representing just under 4.6 per cent of the total elderly population. It is estimated that 31,000 (or 7 per cent) of the elderly population living at home need high or continuous care. Statistics from the Department of Health and Children indicate that 72 per cent of residents are in the high or maximum dependency category. Chronic physical illness (33 per cent) and mental infirmity or dementia (24 per cent) are the main reasons for admission into long-stay care. Just over 12 per cent of older people in long-stay care have been admitted for 'social reasons' (O'Shea, 2006: 12–13).

A survey of long-stay care settings showed that the vast majority of residents are aged seventy-five or older, with just over 40 per cent aged over eighty-five (Murphy et al., 2006: 114). The survey also showed that the largest units are the public geriatric homes/hospitals, which have a mean capacity of ninety-two beds. Private nursing homes have the lowest mean number of beds at thirty-nine (Murphy et al., 2006: 113).

Two models of public residential care that have become increasingly popular are community hospitals and community nursing units. They provide a contrast to the old-style geriatric hospital/home in size, range of services and emphasis on health and social gain. Community hospitals are designed to provide a broad range of services, including long-stay care; assessment and rehabilitation; convalescent care; day hospital and/or day care services; respite care; and information, advice and support for those caring for older people at home. Community units are small nursing units catering for up to fifty people and have a day care centre attached. They differ from the traditional model in many respects, including location (less isolated), architectural style, provision of individualised programmes of animation, a wider range of recreational activities on offer and more emphasis on being part of the community. The resources required to build and to refurbish existing units have been slow to materialise (Ruddle et al., 1997; ERHA, 2001: 3). Indeed, in January 2012 the HSE announced that, for budgetary reasons, 555 public beds in community nursing units would be removed (HSE, 2012a).

Notwithstanding this lack of progress, nursing homes built or refurbished in recent decades generally incorporate good design and strive to enhance health and social gain for all residents. A new model of residential care, the Teaghlach model (based on the family home), has been piloted in Clonakilty Community Hospital in West Cork (see Example 18.1). A brief description of a voluntary nursing home in Dublin is given in Example 18.2.

Example 18.1. Teaghlach model

Clonakilty Community Hospital was a 194-bed hospital serving West Cork. It provided continuing care, respite care, palliative care, community support and a dementia-specific unit. The Teaghlach model developed as a pilot initiative in 2008 and involved the transformation from a hospital model to home-like, small-scale living grouped into households. The aim was to change the culture from a task-oriented institutional model to one that supports older people to continue to direct their own lives in an interactive social environment where both residents and staff are valued and thrive. Preliminary research findings suggest that residents are happier with the new care environment (Linehan and Lynch, 2009).

Example 18.2. Voluntary nursing home

An example of a nursing home in the voluntary sector is St Gabriel's in Raheny, Dublin. This purpose-built nursing home was opened in 1991 by a religious order of nuns, the Poor Servants of the Mother of God, to replace an older residential home in the inner city. It does not have a specific catchment area and admissions are determined by the management, but most residents come from the adjoining areas. St Gabriel's also provides respite and day care.

St Gabriel's has fifty-two individual en-suite rooms on two storeys. Residents on the first floor are reasonably mobile, while there is accommodation on the ground floor for those who are more incapacitated. Each room is individually arranged by the resident with memorabilia, including photographs, pictures on the wall and items of personal furniture. The day rooms are spacious and bright and there is a central conservatory. The use of glass creates a bright and sometimes sunny interior. In addition to a dining room, there are small kitchens attached to the sitting rooms, where residents may make a cup of tea. There is an oratory where daily Mass is said, which is attended by both residents and day care users.

An activity programme, run by an activities co-ordinator, is displayed on a noticeboard each day/week. Activities at various times include Sonas, bingo, a reminiscence programme, quizzes, pampering sessions and computers. St Gabriel's relies on volunteers to provide some of its activities, including reception staffing, fundraising and visitation of residents who have limited mobility and few visitors.

DAY CARE SERVICES

The main objectives of day centres, as set out in *The Years Ahead* (DoH, 1988), are:

- To provide a midday meal, a bath, physiotherapy and a variety of other social services.

- To promote social contact among older people and prevent loneliness.
- To relieve caring relatives, particularly those who have to go to work, of the responsibility of caring for older people during the day.
- To offer social stimulation in a safe environment for older people.

A report by the National Council on Ageing and Older People on the development of day services classified them in the following way (Haslett, 2003):

- *Day care centres* provide a range of medical, therapeutic and social services, such as nursing, physiotherapy, bathing and chiropody. Of vital importance in the continuum of care, particularly for people with reduced mobility, day care is funded by the health service and is usually attached to geriatric hospitals, community hospitals/units or voluntary nursing homes. Staffed by health care professionals, day care centres are designed to support independent living and to give respite to carers. Referrals are usually made by public health nurses, GPs or on discharge from hospital.
- *Dementia-specific day care centres* are designed to give stimulation and care to people with dementia and to provide a break for their primary carers.
- *Day centres* and *social clubs* are mainly managed by locally based voluntary/parish groups and are grant-aided by the health service. Their focus is social and recreational and they usually provide a meal.

Most day centres/social clubs start out having only a social mandate, but due to a chronic lack of day care centres many end up providing services to a wide spectrum of older people (Haslett, 2003: 175):

> Social club/day centres are providing increasing levels of service in the areas of personal care, paramedical treatments and even nursing. They are providing relief to family carers and the safe environments needed to avail of these services. They are, in fact, fulfilling many of the classic day care objectives while, at the same time, catering for a constant flow of more active people.

Haslett found that day services are hugely beneficial to the many different categories of older people attending a variety of day care environments (2003: 167):

> Apart from the tangible health and social benefits conferred by the delivery of services in all categories of centres, these older people and their family carers become part of a wider network of caring. They are known to, and looked out for by, not only a range of service providers (e.g. members of voluntary committees, managers, care attendants, drivers and volunteers), but by each other. The social capital gains achieved through mutual support, co-operation, empathy and trust are very real.

A report by the Society of St Vincent de Paul (SVP, 2011) found that its day/activity centres were highly valued by older people for companionship, camaraderie and friendship as well as for the food, recreational and paramedical services provided. Yet, despite the evident benefits of day centres and social clubs, the reality is that the majority of older people choose not to attend such services.

It has been argued that the emergence of individuality and independence in later life poses serious challenges for day service providers (Graham, 2004). Survey evidence from the North West Health Board indicates that 75 per cent of older people do not attend day centres mainly because they see no need or have no interest in doing so. It has been suggested that it is necessary to establish day services that are about lifestyle enhancement and that are highly individualised, targeted to need, non-stigmatising, able to take advantage of community resources and interests and driven by the choices and interests of the older person (Graham, 2004).

There are encouraging signs that many clubs and day centres are adopting principles of empowerment and facilitating more active participation by service users in the choice and running of activities (Gallagher, 2008). The success of the active retirement movement testifies to the desire of many older people to be actively involved in choosing and running their own social activities. For example, an impressive range of activities provided through Summerhill Active Retirement Group in Co. Meath comprises health initiatives, personal care services (including chiropody and aromatherapy), exercise and fitness programmes, intergenerational and intercultural programmes, teaching knitting in local schools, lifelong learning initiatives and events (including IT classes, mentoring programmes, art and drama), volunteering opportunities, holidays and exchanges, providing a Senior Help Line, a laundry service, a Millennium bus, and a resource centre (Nally and Walsh, 2004).

Examples 18.3 and 18.4 present brief descriptions of day centres in Donegal and Dublin that strive to enhance health and social gain for participants.

Example 18.3. Rural day centre

Rathmullan Social Activity Centre in Co. Donegal is run by the local Society of St Vincent de Paul (SVP) and grant-aided by the HSE. Established in 2006, it opens two days a week and is staffed by a full-time manager/cook, part-time FÁS and Rural Social Scheme participants as well as SVP volunteers. A three-course lunch is served and activities include bingo, Scrabble, cards, exercises and computer classes. A research study conducted by SVP recorded the views of service users at the day centre: 'In conversations, as part of our research consultations, the people there told me how much they enjoyed their day at the Centre, what a difference it made to their lives and how they loved to be able to catch up with their neighbours and friends and how good the lunch was!' (Walsh, 2012: 12). It is not just people in the oldest age group who use the centre but other local residents avail of the lunch as well and it is regarded as a valuable resource in the community.

Example 18.4. Urban day centre

Clareville Day Care Centre opened in Glasnevin, Dublin, in 2000. It is a purpose-built centre in the grounds of the Clareville Court sheltered housing complex. The centre involved co-operation between Dublin City Council, which is responsible for social housing for older people, the HSE and the local community. Service users come from both Clareville Court and the general community and the centre can cater for about eighty people every day. The manager and public health nurse decide on admissions and people are allocated a set number of days and collected by bus. Those who can come independently can use the centre five days a week if they wish. There are eight staff (three full time and five part time) and twelve volunteers. The service users are encouraged to be involved in decisions about the running of the centre and to help out in small daily tasks.

Facilities include treatment, assisted bathing and a laundry service. The public health nurse and chiropodist attend regularly. There is a full meals service and a wide range of activities to suit what residents themselves want. There is a philosophical discussion group, the Socrates Café, which meets every Tuesday. Other activities are relaxation and exercise class, bingo, computer classes, art, table quiz and bridge. There is a regular evening music session, Mass once a month and a weekly bus trip to a local shopping centre. The staff make a special effort to mark the seasonal festivals of Christmas, Easter, Halloween and St Valentine's Day. Every year there are outings organised, an art exhibition of work done in the centre and a community week held in the summer.

QUALITY INITIATIVES IN RESIDENTIAL CARE

Recognising that older people have a capacity for continued learning and creativity, many initiatives have been undertaken to provide meaningful activity programmes in care settings. Activities such as drama, art, storytelling, craftwork and creative writing have been introduced successfully in day and residential settings and have challenged perceptions that passive leisure and entertainment such as bingo or sing-songs are sufficient to satisfy older people (Gallagher, 2008: 96).

Projects involving the introduction of arts activities in care settings have been undertaken in recent years. Age & Opportunity promotes the Creative Exchanges programme, which aims to make creativity intrinsic to life in care settings. It provides FETAC-approved training to care staff who work in care settings (ageand opportunity.ie/creative-exchanges/how-creative-exchanges-organised).

Healthy ageing initiatives that involve an emphasis on maintaining physical and mental fitness have been introduced to many residential and day centres. The Go for Life campaign is a joint initiative of Age & Opportunity and the Irish

Sports Council and runs in partnership with the HSE. It promotes physical exercise and sport to suit all ages and levels of fitness. In 2011 Go for Life worked with 35,000 older people, of whom 1,500 were trained as physical activity leaders who run sports and physical activity sessions among their own groups (ageandopportunity.ie/physical-activity-sport).

An example of an innovative project that empowers and enriches the lives of older people is the Socrates Café in Clareville Day Care Centre in Dublin (see Example 18.4). This breakfast club was set up in December 2011 and is structured as a discussion forum where philosophical questions and issues of general interest to the participants are discussed under the direction of a facilitator. The participants are mainly residents of Clareville Court sheltered housing, day centre users, staff and other interested participants. The Socrates Café captures the idea of older people and staff learning together in an atmosphere of mutual regard and openness to learning. A small research project evaluated the Socrates Café and found that every participant was unreservedly positive about it.

The need for new thinking in relation to activities in residential homes was demonstrated by the findings of an Irish research study (Walsh, 2004), which compared community-dwelling older people with nursing-home residents (largely concentrated in private nursing homes) in terms of their cognitive, sensory and sensorimotor abilities. The study found a high degree of idleness among residents of nursing homes, typified by long periods spent in the television room and little conversation. The author was critical of the institutional environment, which he argued encouraged dependency and discouraged the activation of self-care and independent skills and induced a norm of 'batch living'. He also examined the availability of four different activities in seventeen nursing homes: exercise, painting, parish activities and Sonas. He found that each of these activities was available in only one nursing home out of the seventeen.

A more recent survey of 322 long-stay facilities for older people (Murphy et al., 2006) found a wider range of organised activities available. Listed in order of highest to lowest availability, they included visits from schools, music, physical exercise, bingo/cards/board games, arts, complementary therapies, Sonas, dancing, gardening and Snoezelan therapy. In addition, library facilities were available in most of the settings surveyed. The authors commented that while there is a significant amount of activity taking place, the opportunity to participate in meaningful activity is much more circumscribed; for example, only one-third of community/district hospitals allowed residents to participate in household tasks.

These research reports suggest that there is considerable variation in the quality of the social and recreational environment in different types of facility.

SOCIAL CARE MODEL

There is a growing recognition that services for the dependent elderly should follow other services, such as those for people with intellectual or physical disabilities, by adopting a social care model in preference to a medical one in meeting their users' needs. The largest group of employees in residential care settings are nurses and care attendants. It remains a challenge to develop cultures of care that emphasise individuality and a holistic approach to wellbeing in contrast to a medical model that is more task-oriented, focused on problems and deficits and based on routines designed for efficiency.

A social care model can be observed in the move away from large institutional settings with a hospital atmosphere to smaller homely units, and the increasing emphasis on purposeful activity and links with the community. An encouraging development has been the employment of activities co-ordinators in many residential care homes and geriatric hospitals. It was pointed out over a decade ago that the implications for training had not been fully worked out, given the traditional staffing structures of such services (Gallagher and Kennedy, 2003). While this remains a concern, there have been some positive educational developments.

A training initiative for staff taking on the relatively new position of activities co-ordinator was developed by Dublin Institute of Technology (DIT) in 2005. The part-time programme, 'Developing a Social Care Value Based Activities Programme for Older People', gives an excellent foundation for anyone working in the area of activities, providing the knowledge, skills and confidence required to run a successful and sustainable activity programme. The course involves thirty class contact hours and leads to a DIT Certificate (Level 7) in Continuing Professional Development. The philosophy of the course is the recognition that older people, regardless of age or infirmity, should have opportunities for meaning-ful interaction and continuous development and learning. The programme includes an introduction to drama, art and music; principles of professional practice; spirituality; Marte Meo/communication/multisensorial approaches; dementia care; Go for Life/physical exercise; psychological and social transitions and challenges; programme planning, assessment and evaluation; and older people and community. Participants are encouraged to reflect on their own practice. The programme also helps to create informal learning networks and to disseminate good practice among frontline staff.

Another educational initiative was the development of the BA in Social Care Practice (Older People) in the DIT in 2010. This is a Level 7 degree tailored to staff working directly with older people. The uptake has been disappointing, however, suggesting that the sector is not yet ready for training at this level.

CONCLUSION

Services for dependent older people have developed from the institutional model of the county home – still dominant in the 1960s – to smaller, more homely units where routines are designed to be more 'normal', where stimulating recreation is provided and where links with the outside community are cultivated. Expectations in relation to what a dependent older person might want in a residential unit have changed from an emphasis on physical care to meeting psychosocial, emotional and spiritual needs. Achieving quality and high standards is now supported by legislation. There are many innovative examples of good practice involving the arts and educational projects in care settings, participation by service users themselves in the programmes provided in care centres and more interagency co-operation in creating healthy ageing opportunities for older people in the community.

It is clear that positive ageing is enhanced by attention to suitable housing, a safe environment and amenities and facilities for social and recreational activities. The contribution that older people make and can make in their own communities is increasingly being recognised. Traditional ideas about older people as 'good causes', while worthy and helpful in past decades in eliciting a humane response to deprivation, have been challenged by groups representing older people, who rightly aspire to a more participative role in society. The potential of older people to use their accumulated skills and experience in voluntary work and intergenerational learning is being increasingly recognised (Murphy, 2012).

Underpinning all these developments must be a vision of what the possibilities are for living a full life during the later stages of the life course, or of what constitutes good human functioning for older people, whatever degree of dependency they may experience. Challenges remain in relation to how good practice can be introduced and sustained, both in residential and day services, and how acceptable and dependable community services should be provided. A key issue is that of education and training for staff working with older people.

19
Social care and family support work
Colm O'Doherty

OVERVIEW

This chapter shows how social care practice can support families in a changing Ireland. Its purpose is twofold: first, to provide a framework for social care practice that delivers a range of services to meet the needs of parents and their children in their local communities; and, second, to identify a new agenda for practice that promotes generalised wellbeing and social cohesion.

Beginning with an account of changing family types and practices in contemporary Ireland, the reader is then introduced to models of family support and social care practice responses aimed directly at promoting the wellbeing of children, parental capacity building and wider society. The chapter identifies the social care practice approaches that are in keeping with the aims and values of family support work.

UNDERSTANDING FAMILY

'Family support' seems such an innocuous phrase: of course we should support families, and all families need and deserve support. But what is a family, how do we define it, and which families need support? Are all families, or only some, in need of support? Who decides, and how? What happens when the family is detrimental to children and parents? How does family support work then? (Phillips, 2012)

The grand narrative of traditional family life, espoused by the 1937 Constitution, has been increasingly replaced by the construction of many different truths, produced by many different actors, reflecting the social identity of family life in contemporary Ireland. I have suggested elsewhere (O'Doherty, 2007: 39) that the family unit now operates as a social franchise under whose auspices individuals are free to live for themselves.

To be successful, any franchised venture must appeal on some level to potential customers. Membership of a social franchise, such as the family, is more likely to be encouraged if individuals see the franchise as operating on principles that are responsive to their needs. The challenges, changed operating environment and principles affecting this new franchise are detailed in Table 19.1.

Table 19.1. A new social franchise: the changing Irish family

Drivers for change	Challenges	Principles
• In 2011 there were 1,179,210 families in Ireland: 12 per cent more than five years earlier. Families are defined as couples with or without children, or lone parents with children • The number of children in families increased by almost 140,000 from 2006 to 2011 • The number of lone parents increased by 14 per cent between 2006 and 2011. In 2011 there were 215,300 families headed by lone parents (87 per cent by lone mothers) in Ireland • In 2011 there were 4,042 same-sex couples living together: 230 with children • The long-running trend of families having fewer children slowed between 2006 and 2011. The average number of children was 1.38, down from 1.41 in 2006 but a less pronounced drop than those seen in censuses from 1997 to 2006 • In 2011 544,357 people reported having a nationality other than Irish	• Changing work practices and high unemployment mean that geographical location, employment status, range of skills and self-identity are open to change in the flexible new economy. Due to the economic crash, unemployment has risen to 15 per cent • Changes in intimate life: increased availability of birth control, visibility of gay and lesbian relationships, divorce and global development of feminism • Challenges in parenting: parents must earn their authority over children while facing an uncertain future • Personal debt: 1.82 million adults have less than €100 a month to spend after bills are paid	Relationships set up under this franchise must be capable of: • Promoting emotional and sexual equality • Acknowledging mutual rights and responsibilities in relationships • Facilitating co-parenting • Negotiating authority with children • Fulfilling obligations towards older family members

Sources: CSO (2012e), ILCU (2012), O'Doherty (2007: 39)

UNDERSTANDING SUPPORT

A major government-funded research initiative in the United Kingdom to inquire into the informal and formal supports that parents need to help them look after their children effectively found (Quinton, 2005: 156):

'Support' is a very general term. It is easy to respond to a problem by saying that we should 'put in more support', without being at all clear what we mean or what we want to achieve. Support for parenting is complex to assess, to get right and to deliver because of the balance between the neglect of family problems and intrusion into family life, not to mention ideas of what satisfactory parenting is, how and when this needs support and who should decide that.

In practice, families and children can benefit from different types of family support (see Table 19.2).

Table 19.2. Varieties of family support

Categories	Types of support	Integration
Formal Personal social services delivered by social care or social work personnel Structured individual or group support from a family or resource or health centre (e.g. Springboard) Structured support from health personnel such as public health nurses	*Basic practical support* Help with child care arrangements; for example, a neighbour who is not working might provide afterschool care for a working neighbour	*Provision of commissioned/ collaborative services* A family support centre provides services on behalf of another agency; for example, purposive mixing of family centre staff with professionals from other agencies to provide a specific service in order to run a group, with shared input and responsibility
Semi-formal Groups geared towards particular parenting activities such as nutrition Personal development groups Parenting programmes Luncheon clubs Groups for parents of children with specific needs or disability	*Emotional support* Listening and communicating. Listening is a skill that requires cultural awareness and understanding	*Provision of complementary services* Family centres and other agencies provide separate services to the same families to meet different needs; for example, commissioned working (by health service) and family centres acting as a venue for other service providers (e.g. public health nurses) to work with the family
Informal Cultural activities (music classes, drama groups, literary groups, sport, outdoor pursuits) that are accessible to parents and children in their locality (Jack and Gill, 2003)	*Esteem support* Communicating to a person that they have value. The person may be valued for being kind or fair, brave or bold, a good parent or a good friend in their dealings with others	*Provision of an integrated service* Family centres and other agencies have an explicit joint plan of work for the provision of family support services where they can call on each other to provide inputs to the family

Sources: CSO (2011a, 2012e), ILCU (2012), O'Doherty (2007: 39)

UNDERSTANDING PARENTING

Parenting is a difficult but essential and rewarding social task that carries a range of formidable responsibilities. In the twenty-first century men and women who are parents frequently negotiate their parenting role. Approaches to parenting are variable and open to debate and in the contemporary world are being shaped by various forces such as advice, politics, finding oneself, risk, inequality, children's rights and good value.

Advice

So-called 'expert' advice on parenting may complement and in some instances replace the advice and practical support previously offered by extended family members. Expert advice can be offered by psychologists, doctors, feminists, economists, academics, nurturant fathers and government agencies through different media pathways.

Research by Davis (2012) into fifty years of motherhood manuals calls into question the value of advice from expert sources. She spoke to women about the advice given by child care 'experts' who had published books on parenting and found that experts presented their advice in the form of orders. The levels of behaviour expected of mothers were often unattainably high.

Along with the more traditional parenting advice columns of the print media there has been a growing popularity of parenting websites. The *Irish Times* has a parenting section in its weekly *Health Plus* supplement. Websites such as mykidstime.ie, netmums.com, mumsnet.com, magicmum.com and rollercoaster.ie dispense advice and offer support networks to parents (mainly mothers) who may be feeling overwhelmed, stressed or isolated by the demands of raising children. According to a user of the Mumsnet website, 'It's like an "invisible" circle of friends . . . always there when you need them for advice, support or information' (mumsnet.com/talk).

Politics

In the UK a new policy initiative will see the National Health Service adopt a two-pronged approach to parenting. New parents are to be given advice on issues from teething to tantrums, including tips on nappy changing and baby talk. Under this initiative, a £3.4 million digital information service already provides free email alerts and text messages. In addition, free parenting classes will be available to parents of children under five years in three trial areas, to be rolled out nationally if effective, and relationship support for first-time parents will also be offered in pilot projects. The British Prime Minister, David Cameron, has said it is 'ludicrous that parents receive more training in how to drive a car than how to raise children. This is not the nanny state; it is the sensible state' (*Observer*, 2012).

Finding oneself

An observable feature of life in the twenty-first century is the 'project of the self'. Individualisation, the process whereby a person maps out an identity and life plan for themselves rather than for their wider community or family, may not be harmonious with the self-denying responsibilities of parenting.

[handwritten margin note: ? Good role Model for self-care ?]

Risk

Parenting involves managing the risks generated by natural hazards, the effects of social change, economic forces, scientific development and technological change.

Inequality

Child poverty is a serious problem in Ireland. According to the *Survey of Income and Living Conditions 2010* (CSO, 2012d), one in five children in Ireland is at risk of poverty. Those who fall into the at-risk-of-poverty or relative poverty category are persons whose income is below 60 per cent of the national median (middle range) income. In 2013 this equates to a disposable income of €10,831 or less. Children are heavily exposed to consistent poverty. A total of just over 8 per cent experienced this form of poverty in 2010, in contrast to just under one per cent of the population aged over sixty-five. The consistent poverty measure looks at those persons who, in addition to being at risk of poverty, are also suffering enforced deprivation (for example, not possessing proper shoes or eating proper meals). Income inequality increased sharply between 2009 and 2010, with the gap between the top and bottom 20 per cent of income earners growing by 28 per cent.

Children's rights

The 1937 Constitution favoured the rights of parents over the rights of children. This constitutional alignment underpinned the state's overreliance on parents to vindicate the rights of children and contributed to an under-investment by the state in family support services. On 10 November 2012 the Children referendum asked voters to re-balance the rights of children and parents: in a low turnout of 33.5 per cent, 57.4 per cent voted Yes and 42.6 per cent voted No. This result means that Article 42.5 in the Constitution is replaced by a new Article 42A, under which:

- The state recognises and affirms the natural and imprescriptible rights of all children and undertakes, as far as is practicable, through its laws to protect and vindicate those rights.
- The state, as guardian of the common good, shall by proportionate means, as provided by law, in exceptional cases where parents, regardless of their marital

status fail in their duty towards their child to such an extent that the safety or welfare of any of their children is adversely affected, endeavour to supply the place of the parents, but always with due regard for the natural and imprescriptible rights of the child.

- Legal provision will be made for the adoption of any child where the parents have failed for a specified period of time in their duty towards the child and where the best interests of the child so require.
- Legal provision will be made for the voluntary placement for adoption and the adoption of any child.
- Legal provision will be made so that in the resolution of all proceedings concerning the welfare and protection of children the best interests of the child will be the paramount consideration.
- Legal provision will be made for securing the views of children in child welfare and protection proceedings. Account will be taken of the age, maturity and capability of each child and their views will be weighted accordingly.

With the passing of the referendum, the state is in a position to engage children, as entitled citizens, in the co-production of new family support services.

Good value

A recent review (Furlong et al., 2012: 2) of the effectiveness of behavioural and cognitive/behavioural group-based parenting programmes concluded:

> Parenting programmes that are delivered in group settings have the potential to help parents develop parenting skills that improve the behaviour of their young children. This review provides evidence that group-based parenting programmes improve childhood behaviour problems and the development of positive parenting skills in the short-term, whilst also reducing parental anxiety, stress and depression. Evidence for the longer-term effects of these programmes is unavailable. These group-based parenting programmes achieve good results at a cost of approximately $2500 (€2217) per family. These costs are modest when compared with the long-term social, educational and legal costs associated with childhood conduct problems.

UNDERSTANDING FAMILY WELLBEING

Family wellbeing is promoted when the relationship between families and wider society is characterised by respect for the family as a social asset and an essential social welfare organisation. The idea that parents and carers need support should not be seen as strange – a stranger idea is that parents and carers do *not* need support. But what kind of support? When and why might support be needed? How should it be provided and by whom? (Braun, 2001: 243)

All families benefit from being supported and esteemed by their immediate community and wider society. What weaves all family types together is the thread of relationships. The quality and tone of internal and external relationships are at the heart of family life and family wellbeing is influenced by the interplay between children's developmental needs, parenting capacity and wider family and environmental factors.

It is useful to examine theories which help us to understand: the mutual interdependence of people and their environments (ecological theory); the role of formal and informal social support networks; and the importance of social capital in promoting social cohesion.

- *Ecological perspective:* the ecological understanding is 'borrowed' from biology and refers to the mutual interdependence of plants, animals, people and their physical environments. Within the ecological perspective, the child, child's family and the environment in which they live influence one another in a constant process of reciprocal interaction. The ecological perspective links the wellbeing of parents and children to the characteristics of the environment they inhabit.
- *Networks:* Gilchrist (2004) sees the benefits of community and social networks as an alternative user-friendly source of help during crisis points for those seeking assistance with risky or embarrassing problems who do not wish to resort to professional (sometimes stigmatised) service provision. Social networks supply informal care over and above the care provided by family and friends. In addition to these practical benefits, social networks provide their members with opportunities for positive emotional engagement.
- *Social capital:* social capital (O'Doherty, 2007) is a community resource, the 'social glue' that creates social cohesion. It is formed by creating opportunities for people to develop trusting relationships through participation and engagement in mutual support organisations such as family support services and community development projects. Participation in cultural, recreational and sporting activities with other people helps to overcome barriers of mistrust and build social capital.

UNDERSTANDING FAMILY SUPPORT SERVICES

Broadly speaking, family support services in Ireland can be categorised according to their function and governance structures.

Family resource centres

Family resource centres provide focused but flexible programmes that enhance the self-esteem and potential of individuals and actively increase the capacity of local communities to become self-reliant and self-directed. Typically such centres deliver a mix of services to meet child and family needs at different life stages.

Operating under a voluntary management committee structure, generally comprising representatives from target groups in the community, these centres provide open access to members of a community or neighbourhood. This open access or universal framework approach means that information and support can be seen as everyone's entitlement, thus taking away the stigma of asking for it.

Family resource centres were first established in the early 1990s on a pilot basis under the then Department of Social Welfare. An evaluation of the pilot programme (Kelleher and Kelleher, 1997) crucially recommended that funding be mainstreamed for the centres by the Department of Social Welfare and not the Department of Health, which carried the main responsibility for personal social services. This meant that family support services were not integrated with health and personal social services. In 2003 the Family Support Agency (FSA) was established and given responsibility for the Family and Community Services Resource Centre Programme (FRC). In 2010 responsibility for the FSA transferred from the Department of Community, Equality and Gaeltacht Affairs to the Department of Children and Youth Affairs. The FSA core-funds 107 family resource centres in local communities around Ireland, as part of the FRC programme (FSA, 2012).

The operating budget for all family resource centres in 2010 was €36.7 million. The objective of the centres is to build social capacity and social capital formation. They seek to create an environment that welcomes, supports, empowers and encourages people to belong and participate in their community's development and to develop services and facilities that will improve the quality of life and respond to the needs of all ages (SMWCDSA, 2006: 69). They provide a framework for the development of an interpersonal economy that fosters skills, competencies, capacities and connections that lead to the establishment of social networks.

The general aims of family resource centres (Neville, 2012) are:

- To help combat disadvantage by supporting families.
- To be actively involved in anti-poverty initiatives and social inclusion projects.
- To attempt to encourage local people to participate in the centre and its work: from the designing and planning of an FRC to its establishment; by acting as volunteers, creating the opportunity for community involvement and activism.
- To 'empower and facilitate groups or individuals experiencing exclusion to take control of their own lives and address their needs' (FRC National Forum, 2006: 10) through community development.
- To build relationships and social networks in communities.
- To facilitate positive working relationships between the voluntary sector and statutory agencies in an area; for example, by setting up new community groups or influencing social policy (FSA, 2007: 1).
- To enhance the self-esteem of individuals in the community and so increase the potential for change within a community.

Supports and services typically provided by family centres include:

- *Support* for individuals, women's groups, men's groups, immigrants, luncheon clubs for elderly citizens, etc.
- *Child care:* preschools, playschools, summer camps, homework/breakfast clubs, youth clubs/drop-in centres.
- *Counselling* for individuals and families, on relationships, separation, bereavement, stress, bullying, domestic violence, debt, substance abuse, etc.
- *Community and adult education:* parenting programmes, IT skills, preparation for interviews, return-to-work programmes, personal development work, committee skills, employment law, cookery, etc.
- *Cultural and artistic opportunities:* arts and crafts, musical tuition, drama, etc.
- *Sports and recreational activities:* athletics, football, basketball, snooker/pool, outdoor pursuits, etc.

In addition to the direct provision of supports and services, family resource centres act as gateways for individuals and groups to access formal services from public health nurses, social workers, local authorities, youth justice and crime agencies, chiropodists, speech therapists, physiotherapists, legal aid, meals on wheels, GPs, education providers, and the Money Advice & Budgeting Service (MABS). In this way each family centre can act as a *one-stop shop*. Their location and integrity help to maximise access to centres and underpin links and partnerships with other agencies. Open access family centres that provide universal services (available to everybody) have the dual advantage of reducing stigma and increasing the acceptability of specialised mainstream helping services.

The gateway function of family centres can enhance the co-ordination of local services. An evaluation of the Shanakill Family Resource Centre in Tralee (O'Doherty, 2003) established that it operates as a gateway to outside agencies and organisations that can deal with problems and difficulties beyond the scope or expertise of the centre's staff. Similarly, a study of family centres in the UK (Tunstill et al., 2007: 87) found:

> First, centres acted as a gateway for families to access other services, which could be alternative, supplementary or subsequent to those on offer in the family centre. A second aspect of co-ordination was the provision of a gateway for professionals in other agencies to access families using the family centres who might need the service of other agencies.

An evaluation of the work of family resource centres (FSA, 2010) similarly found that they act as a focal point for onward referrals to mainstream service providers.

An Irish Congress of Trade Unions (ICTU, 2012) report looked at changes in employment and services in the voluntary and community sector between 2008 and 2012 and found a contraction of 35 per cent in the sector. Government figures show that from 2008 to 2012, funding for family resource centres has been reduced by 17 per cent. But, for approximately €2.50 per child per day, family support services provide food, education and personal development opportunities for children whose circumstances place them at risk of long-term social exclusion, with a series of attendant social costs. This severe budgetary reduction will increase levels of inequality in Irish society: services provided through family support centres effectively redistribute income from the better-off to those with limited means.

Springboard

Springboard is a community-based programme that aims to support vulnerable families in the home, school and community. The then Department of Health and Children established it as a pilot in 1998, with fifteen projects across the country; the number has since increased to twenty-two (Phillips, 2012). Springboard projects are located in high-stress neighbourhoods where there is a marked incidence of factors that contribute to the reception of children into care. Each project has its own history and developmental pathway. The expectation was that the projects would:

- Identify the needs of parents and children in a specific area and focus on safeguarding children in families where child protection concerns exist.
- Target the most disadvantaged and vulnerable families in an area and focus on improving their parenting skills and child–parent relationships.
- Develop programmes of family support services in partnership with different agencies in an area.
- Develop programmes of family support services in partnership with key groups, individuals and families in the community.
- Provide direct services through a structured package of care, intervention, support and counselling to targeted families and children, and to families within the wider community.

Home-Start

Home-Start is a voluntary organisation committed to promoting the welfare of families with at least one child under five years of age. Volunteers offer regular support, friendship and practical help to young families in their own homes, helping to prevent family crisis and breakdown. Home-Start is a high-impact, low-cost early intervention service, which operates a volunteer-based model that is focused on parents first, and then on children. It is a non-discriminatory service that provides support to all parents regardless of social class, financial status, religion or ethnicity. Home-Start's aim is to prevent families falling into crisis and breakdown.

The organisation provides weekly home visits through trained volunteers who all have parenting skills themselves. These volunteers provide a listening ear or reassurance in a non-judgmental way; this helps break down that sense of isolation and loneliness and address social isolation and maternal emotional wellbeing. Co-ordinators support up to twenty volunteers, who in turn support up to thirty families with children under five. Services also include family mornings and personal development courses.

Home-Start supports the hard-to-reach families, who are often reluctant to use services, particularly state services (Home-Start, 2008). Projects operate in Blanchardstown, Lucan, Swords, Tallaght, Athenry and Cork city.

HSE family support services

The Health Service Executive (HSE) is obliged under Section 3 of the Child Care Act 1991 to provide family support services to promote the welfare of children not receiving adequate care and attention. Despite this obligation, child protection rather than family support has dominated and continues to dominate the practice activity of Irish social workers. Since the passing of the 1991 Act, statutory family support services have remained underdeveloped and patchy. While the philosophy of the 1991 Act is that families and children should be supported and that children should be brought up in their own families, the HSE has no dedicated family support programme to date.

A new organisational platform that could deliver a range of services, targeted at different levels of need, within a framework of prevention is being planned. It is the government's intention to establish a Children and Family Support Agency in 2013. The new agency will provide integrated family support and child protection services. The existing Family Support Agency will be merged into the new agency.

The issue of different priorities is a major factor in the differing perspectives of social workers and family support practitioners. Social work services in the HSE are, in the main, characterised by a style of practice that is legalistic, formal, procedural and managerial. Research by O'Doherty (2004) into the national statutory child care system highlighted how key stakeholders in the system (social workers, child care managers) privilege child protection work over family support initiatives. Social work is locked into a power-laden investigative approach that struggles to meet the complex needs of families.

While family support is underdeveloped in the HSE overall, some service development has taken place. For example, a successful, if limited (in terms of staffing), Kerry Family Support Service has been operated by the HSE Southern region since 2004. The service dealt with 44 families and 114 children between 2010 and 2011 and aims to 'improve the quality of family life by broadening parents' knowledge, skills and confidence so that they are better equipped to manage behavioural, emotional and developmental problems as presented by their children' (Kerry Family Support Team, 2012).

SOCIAL CARE AS COMMUNITY PRACTICE

What kind of education and training is required for family support work? Social care professionals are increasingly making the link between service delivery work and social intervention in communities (O'Doherty, 2007, 2008a, 2008b). This translates into a holistic practice model where social care practitioners engage with the whole person, the whole system and the whole community. A holistic social care practice model that can be employed in family centres, Springboard projects and specialised family support services comprises three interlocking components: values, practice strategies and working methods.

Social care practitioners interested in becoming policy and practice pioneers in family support interventions will need to embrace a professional *value system* that promotes social justice, participation, equality, learning and co-operation. Social justice requires that people be enabled to claim their human rights, meet their needs and have greater control over the decision-making processes that affect their lives. Participation involves the facilitation of people in issues that affect their lives. Family support practitioners manifest the value of equality by challenging and resisting discrimination against and marginalisation of individuals and communities. The learning that results from people taking action to tackle social, economic, political and environmental problems should be acknowledged and practitioners should adopt a co-operative approach to working with service users and other professionals.

The *practice strategies* will aim to enable, encourage, empower and educate people. The *working methods* employed by social care practitioners engaging in family support work are dictated by a broad range of tasks implicit in the process of strengthening and assisting families. These include providing resources, providing information, helping groups, education and training, establishing groups, establishing networks, policy work and community-based artwork.

A human rights approach to family support work

The very essence of social care practice is its focus on promoting wellbeing by enabling full participation in work and mainstream society. Levels of wellbeing are related to health, relationships and work-role satisfaction. This practice approach draws on a human-rights-based approach to family support. The United Nations (UN, 1994) states that 'the family is the basic unit of society'. Social care as community practice should focus on rights rather than on need. The principles underpinning a human-rights-based approach are:

- *Legitimacy:* solutions are based on the human rights recognised in international law.
- *Accountability:* governments and public institutions are answerable for their acts or omissions in relation to their duties.

- *Empowerment:* communities and individuals know, claim and defend their rights and know their responsibilities.
- *Participation:* solutions maximise the participation of the community; participation must be active, free and meaningful.
- *Equality:* non-discrimination and prioritisation of vulnerable groups. The prioritisation of vulnerable groups and the principle of non-discrimination are expressly included in all human rights theories. Equality is fundamental to all human rights: social, economic, cultural and political (European Anti-Poverty Network Ireland, 2008a: 10).

In human rights terms, the professional activity of social care practitioners is directed towards maximising opportunities for people to determine the conditions of their own lives so that they can fully develop their capacities. Capacity building involves a great deal more than priming individuals to contribute to the material economy through the labour market. There is a body of evidence to show that, in an overall sense, citizens have not benefited from the high priority afforded to the material economy in Ireland and other similarly affluent countries (Cullen, 2006; Halpern, 2005; Helliwell and Putnam, 2005; Layard, 2005).

Riley's study of twelve middle- and low-income countries found that they build social capital in a different way (2008: 3). Through the pursuit of what is called *social growth* or *social development*, rather than economic development, low-income countries found ways to build their own forms of social capital, even though their people had little capacity for spending on things other than the basic necessities of life and their governments lacked the revenues to fund costly programmes.

Jordan (2007) makes a strong argument for social care practice to reassert the value of the interpersonal economy, that is, the value produced in relationships. Such an approach would focus on boosting the interpersonal economy, which creates value through relationships of empathy, equality and justice. The value of the interpersonal economy is realised through its role in the creation of higher levels of social capital in communities and wider society. Social capital, an intangible resource generated through collective interaction, builds greater community cohesion and social integration. It improves people's lives by engaging them in mutually supportive activities that are beneficial to them and their communities. This kind of service development is vitally important in an Ireland where social cohesion is being undermined by growing inequality, the challenges of diversity, crime, substance abuse and mental ill-health.

CONCLUSION

This chapter began by highlighting the challenges facing families in contemporary Ireland. It moved on to explore family support provision and concluded by making the case for social care practice that safeguards and promotes the wellbeing of children, communities and families.

20

Social care in services for people with a disability

Karen Finnerty

OVERVIEW

This chapter introduces concepts, practices and beliefs that have significantly influenced the nature and development of services for people with disabilities in Ireland. It aims to provide an understanding of the development of services and an appreciation of current and future issues. While you may find some of the content challenging and contrary to what you have previously learned or experienced about disability, it is hoped that the chapter will provide you with a broader understanding of the area, and help you to situate your concept of disability services and supports in their proper context – in the mainstream of ordinary daily life.

The chapter opens by discussing what is meant by 'disability' and how it is defined. An understanding of definitions is important as, whether accurate or not, they have an ongoing influence on attitudes and decision making in relation to people with disabilities and the design and delivery of the services that they receive. An examination of how services developed in Ireland lays the groundwork for an understanding of models of service delivery: the medical/traditional model; the social model; and, more recently, a policy shift towards services that are individualised in terms of their design, delivery and funding. The chapter concludes with a discussion of the major changes under way in the sector and the role of the social care practitioner in disability services in the future.

WHAT IS DISABILITY?

What do you think of when you hear the word 'disability' – a person in a wheelchair, a person with a guide dog, a child with Down syndrome? It may surprise you to know that disability can be understood as existing along a continuum, and that any of us who experience particular difficulties may be considered 'disabled'. For example, we tend not to think of a person with a chronic or long-term illness as being disabled, nor are many of us aware that 13 per cent of the population (595,335 people) have a disability (CSO, 2011c). Is it acceptable to speak of 'the disabled' as a distinct and homogeneous subset of Irish society – separate and different to the rest – defined by terms such as 'handicapped', 'disabled' or 'impaired'?

Although many people consider the words 'disability', 'handicap' and 'impairment' to be interchangeable, the World Health Organization (WHO, 1980, Section 27.29.14) developed a three-tier definition based on particular descriptions of these terms:

> An *impairment* is any loss or abnormality of psychological, physiological or anatomical structure or function; a *disability* is any restriction or lack (resulting from an impairment) of ability to perform an activity in the manner or within the range considered normal for a human being; a *handicap* is a disadvantage for a given individual resulting from an impairment or a disability, that prevents the fulfilment of a role that is considered normal (depending on age, sex and social and cultural factors) for that individual.

The medical orientation of this WHO definition, with its stress on incapacity and reliance on terms such as 'normal' and 'abnormal', has provided support for the view that people with disabilities are different from the rest of the population – different in a way that is negatively valued and so justifies the distinctions between us and them: the normal and the abnormal.

As a result of its medical focus, the 1980 WHO definition was aligned with what is known as the *medical model of disability* and was widely accepted by health bodies and governments for many years. Disability activists rejected it, arguing that disability is not caused by chance, nor is it limited to impairment. While acknowledging the reality of what is referred to as 'impairment', they argued that the disability was a social construct, created through society's response to the impairment and by its failure to put sufficient supports in place to ensure that the person with the impairment achieved the same quality of life as other members of society. This perspective is known as the *social model of disability*, since the problem is based in society and its attitudes and in how people respond to people with disabilities.

The medical and social models found some common ground during the 1990s in what is known as the *biopsychosocial model*. This model sought to understand disability from the perspective of the biological, psychological and sociological systems of the individual (Engel, 1977) – that is, from the perspective of the whole person and their environment. In 2002 the WHO published the International Classification of Functioning, Disability and Health (ICF), which incorporated the thinking of the biopsychosocial model. The ICF contains a universal classification of disability and health and provides a standard language and framework for the description of health and health-related states (WHO, 2002: 3):

The International Classification of Functioning acknowledges that every human being can experience a decrement in health and thereby experience some disability; [it] mainstreams the experience of disability and recognises it as a universal human experience.

Notwithstanding the ICF framework, a legal definition of disability has posed problems for many countries and has generated much debate. There is no universal legal definition of disability, nor is there any single one in any European country, and definitions vary depending on the area under discussion, such as employment, social welfare entitlements or income matters (Degener, 2004).

Ireland has also struggled with the definition. The Employment Equality Act 1998 defined disability along similar lines to the 1980 WHO three-tier definition with its medical focus and language. A 1996 report from the Commission on the Status of People with Disabilities entitled *A Strategy for Equality* brought some clarity to the matter, defining disability to include 'children and adults who experience any restriction in their capacity to participate in economic, social or cultural life on account of a physical, sensory, learning, mental health or emotional impairment' (1996: 11). The Disability Act 2005 used a definition closely aligned to that contained in *A Strategy for Equality*:

Disability in relation to a person means a substantial restriction in the capacity of the person to carry on a profession, business or occupation in the State or to participate in social or cultural life in the State by reason of an enduring physical, sensory, mental health or intellectual impairment.

This 2005 definition is now the most frequently cited and accepted definition of disability used in Ireland (Keogh, 2011).

INCIDENCE OF DISABILITY IN IRELAND

After many years of inadequate information the need to gather accurate statistics for service planning was addressed in 1995 with the establishment of the National Intellectual Disability Database (NIDD). The database provided for an annual review of the numbers of people receiving and waiting for services and was followed in 2003 by a similar database for the physical and sensory disability area (NPSDD). In addition, the census of population included a question on disability for the first time in 2002. The 2006 census contained a full section on disability, and the Central Statistics Office (CSO) also undertook a major survey on disability in 2006 (CSO, 2010). The 2011 census, which included specific questions focused on disability, classified disability (for the purposes of data gathering) as:

- Blindness or serious vision impairment
- Deafness or serious hearing impairment

- A difficulty with basic physical activities such as walking, climbing stairs, reaching, lifting or carrying
- An intellectual disability
- A difficulty with learning, remembering or concentrating
- A psychological or emotional condition
- A difficulty with pain, breathing or any other chronic illness or condition.

Figure 20.1 indicates some relevant statistics.

Figure 20.1. Overview of Ireland's disability-related statistics (2011)

National Census of Population 2011

- 13 per cent of the population, or 595,335 individuals, have a disability.
- 244,739 people have a difficulty with 'basic physical activities'.
- 96,004 people have a psychological or emotional condition.
- 92,060 people are deaf.
- 57,709 people have an intellectual disability.
- 51,718 people have a sight-related disability.
- 56,087 people with disabilities who are aged over 65 years live alone.
- Among people with disabilities in the 16–49 age group, 16 per cent have completed no higher than primary education (compared with 5 per cent for the general population).

National Intellectual Disability Database

- 27,324 people were registered on the database at the end of 2011.
- 26,831 people were receiving services (98 per cent).
- 271 people who required a service were not receiving one.
- 222 people did not require or wish to receive a service.
- 26,744 people availed of at least one day programme/service.
- 8,214 people were in full-time residential care (30 per cent).
- 17,916 people lived at home with parents, siblings, relatives or foster parents (66 per cent).
- 214 people living in a psychiatric setting were waiting to be moved to a more appropriate home.

National Physical and Sensory Disability Database

- 25,170 people under 66 years of age were registered on the database at the end of 2011 (responsibility for people over age 66 lies with the Department of Health).

- 53 per cent of people registered on the database were male and 47 per cent were female.
- 21,583 people were receiving one or more therapeutic intervention/rehabilitation services (86 per cent).
- 823 people were availing of residential services.
- 13,804 people availed of a day service and/or support with a daily activity outside the home.
- 7,197 people were in need of personal assistance and/or support services.
- 16,343 people were in need of at least one technical aid or appliance (65 per cent).

Sources: CSO (2011c), Kelly (2012), Doyle (2012)

SERVICE DEVELOPMENT IN IRELAND

Prior to the Industrial Revolution people with disabilities lived in the community into which they were born. Prosperity and urbanisation in the eighteenth century attracted people from rural areas to towns and cities. As the urban population grew, so did the number of 'vagabonds' and 'beggars', and consequent concern among citizens. The authorities in Dublin responded to this concern in 1773 by opening the Dublin House of Industry, where those regarded as social 'undesirables' were incarcerated. Such institutions (generally known as workhouses) catered for many social problems and, within a short time, had allocated separate space for people with mental health difficulties, then termed 'lunatics' and 'idiots'. This system continued to expand until, by the time of the Famine, 163 workhouses had been built in Ireland, where the destitute received meagre food and lodging in return for work done.

The reinforcement of difference based on health and social status and the practices of segregation continued to grow during the 1850s and by the close of the nineteenth century there were twenty-two district 'lunatic asylums'. Some of these institutions were the forerunners of today's services for people with mental health difficulties, such as St Patrick's Hospital, Dublin (Robins, 1986). In 1869 the Stewart Institution for Idiotic and Imbecile Children was opened in Dublin. Its original aim was to train children with learning disabilities so that they would be able to return to their homes and families by the time they reached the age of eighteen. But the children did not return to their homes and, as numbers grew, few vacancies arose. Meanwhile, numbers in the district asylums had swollen, and a suggestion was made that auxiliary asylums be created for 'incurables'– primarily people with learning disabilities. In 1926 a Catholic order of nuns, the Daughters of Charity, turned the workhouse school in Cabra, Dublin, into a home and school for children with 'mental handicap'. Over the following three to four decades religious orders opened at least ten similar institutions around Ireland, and during the 1950s several non-denominational organisations were also founded.

In 1955, on the initiative of a mother whose son had a learning disability, the first day-service for children with learning disabilities was founded. This service and many other community-based services evolved from the pioneering work of parents and family members who rejected the belief that children with disabilities should be 'put away'. Instead, they advocated for the provision of services 'in community' – in small locally based settings. While the advent of community-based services did not result in the closure of the large institutions, it did influence how institutional care was provided and changes began to occur within these settings (for example, the building of small group homes, albeit often within the grounds of the institution).

Despite these improvements, most children and adults with disabilities had to avail of segregated services away from their own neighbourhoods – often transported in buses labelled as ambulances with signage referring to children and to the name of a charity. Children who were considered capable of education attended 'special' schools, while others attended 'special care' services. The public image that was projected was of benign organisations that protected and cared for unwell and vulnerable people of limited potential.

For very many of these young people, surrounded as they were by negative stereotypes and the imagery of incapacity, the beliefs and attitudes of significant others acted as a brake on their achievements and personal growth. They experienced home, community and service environments where their learning and daily life experience was restricted by the low expectations that others had of them. As they grew into adulthood they attended segregated day services where a combination of limited resources and low expectations resulted in a focus on group activities and repetitive monotonous tasks that contributed little to personal development or learning. In the absence of necessary education, training and supports, and with limited experience of ordinary life, many failed to reach their potential. Their lack of progress was seen to justify the original negative view of their capacities. A continuous cycle of low expectations, denied opportunities and limited life experiences had been created. While Western societal attitudes had generally improved, people with disabilities were still not generally regarded as having a status equal to that of their non-disabled peers (Collins, 2001a).

SERVICE RESPONSES TO PEOPLE WITH DISABILITIES

Traditional/medical model

As noted above, the provision of education, training and care services for people with disabilities occurred very often in segregated settings separated from meaning-ful interaction with non-disabled peers and from the richness of experience that exists in the mainstream of ordinary life. Service provision on this basis is known as the traditional model of service provision. In this model, the service was frequently self-contained with all needs – physical, social, medical and educational – catered for by the organisation, very often from 'cradle to grave'. Hierarchical management systems operated, with executive management at the top, controlling expenditure and decision making, and people with disabilities (often referred to as clients or patients) and their families at the bottom, in receipt of services but almost always without any influence in relation to decision making, how services were designed or how funding was spent (Figure 20.2).

Figure 20.2. Traditional service model

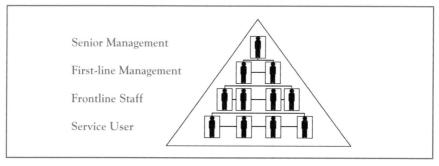

Source: O'Brien and O'Brien (1989)

Another significant aspect of the traditional model was the influence of the medical profession. As disability was primarily seen as a 'medical problem' that could only be assisted in a hospital or therapeutic setting, medical professionals very often held positions of power in disability services. The traditional model also became known as the medical model of service delivery. What is significant about the medical model is that it operated within the classic understanding of medicine – the diagnosing and treating of illness and injury and the preservation of health – and the accompanying acceptance that the medical professional 'knows best'.

The medical model significantly disempowered people with disabilities in that the decisions of medical, clinical and indeed other organisation personnel nearly always took precedence over the wishes or views of the people being served and their families. In fact, within the medical model, for many years people were not consulted about or involved in decisions that had very significant impact on their lives.

The behaviour and language of the medical approach contributed to a process that failed to distinguish the person from the disability. The fact that the person with a disability was a unique individual with likes and dislikes, skills and abilities, wishes and dreams and a capacity to learn was all too frequently lost as powerful labels conveying imagery of incapacity – 'the cripple', 'an epileptic', 'the disabled' – became dominant in their lives and in the perceptions of society at large. Such labels supported the development of low expectations, ignored the potential of the person and validated the inadequate responses of society and service providers to their needs.

Social model

As understandings and definitions of disability were increasingly questioned and rights issues gained prominence, the 1980s and 1990s saw a shift from the thinking that informed the traditional/medical model towards the recognition that disability is 'created' by society and that the social model represents a more appropriate response.

The social model recognises that people may have 'impairment', but contends that people become 'disabled' by a society that actively or passively excludes them from full participation. It locates the cause of disability not in the person who experiences the impairment, but in society's response: a response expressed in the language used to describe the person; in the supports provided to enable him or her to live a full and meaningful life; and in how the person is restricted or supported to exercise power over the everyday decisions of his or her life. This shift in thinking reflected earlier experiences of the struggle for equality and rights, particularly in the United States, and was driven by people with disabilities. These activists redefined 'disability' and full inclusion in society as human rights issues.

Reflecting wider international and European influences, people with disabilities in Ireland began to reframe their situation in the 1990s in terms of human rights. The need to move from a medical to a social approach was endorsed by the findings of A Strategy for Equality, which stated (Commission on the Status of People with Disabilities, 1996: 9) that:

> ... a given level of impairment or degree of restriction does not necessarily lead to disadvantage: It is the societal response (in terms of attitudes and expectations as well as the services and facilities made available), which has an important impact on the extent to which impairment or disability lead to disadvantage.

To clarify a more appropriate societal response, John O'Brien, an American activist and writer on disability issues, developed a model of service that, rather than segregating individuals, acts as a facilitator to ensure that people are linked to and can participate in their own community. O'Brien's Basic Strategy (Figure 20.3) distinguishes between the person, the service and the community. The person's network of friends and family is recognised as being of particular importance and the person's community is seen both as a resource and as the environment that the person needs to be connected to. The primary role of the service becomes one of supporting and safeguarding individuals within their own social network, creating and developing new opportunities in their own community. This type of service is person-centred and informed by the individual's needs and choices, as opposed to the more traditional management approach where services and activities are primarily group-based and may lack relevance for individuals.

Figure 20.3. O'Brien's Basic Strategy

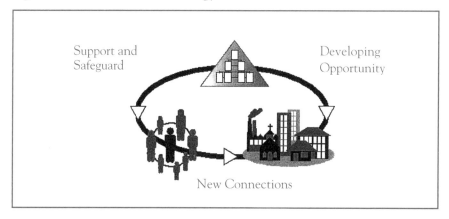

Source: adapted from O'Brien and O'Brien (1989)

The social model has roots in the concept of social role valorisation (SRV), which focuses on human relationships, human interaction, interdependence and inclusion. Wolf Wolfensberger (1934–2011), originator of SRV, described it as 'the application of what science can tell us about the enablement, establishment, maintenance and/or defence of valued social roles for people' (1983). The major goal of SRV is to create or support roles in society that have social value, as holding valued social roles enhances the opportunity to secure what Wolfensberger (1983: 6) called the 'good things' in life:

> The 'good things' include home and family; friendship; being accorded dignity, respect, acceptance; a sense of belonging; an education and the development and exercise of one's capacities; a voice in the affairs of one's community and society; opportunities to participate; a decent material standard of living; and opportunities for work and self-support.

With regard to services that support people with disabilities, O'Brien and O'Brien (1989) describe 'five valued experiences' that they consider all people seek – experiences consistent with the 'good things' in life described by SRV theory. These experiences are: having relationships, exercising choice, making a contribution, sharing ordinary places and having the experience of being treated with dignity and respect (Figure 20.4). They propose that services for people with disabilities should be designed on the basis of these five valued experiences and that, when service provision operates on the basis of providing people with the five valued experiences in a consistent and meaningful fashion, five service accomplishments are achieved: community participation, promoting choice, supporting contribution, community presence and encouraging valued social roles.

Figure 20.4. The five valued experiences and service accomplishments

VALUED EXPERIENCES FOR PEOPLE

SERVICE ACCOMPLISHMENTS

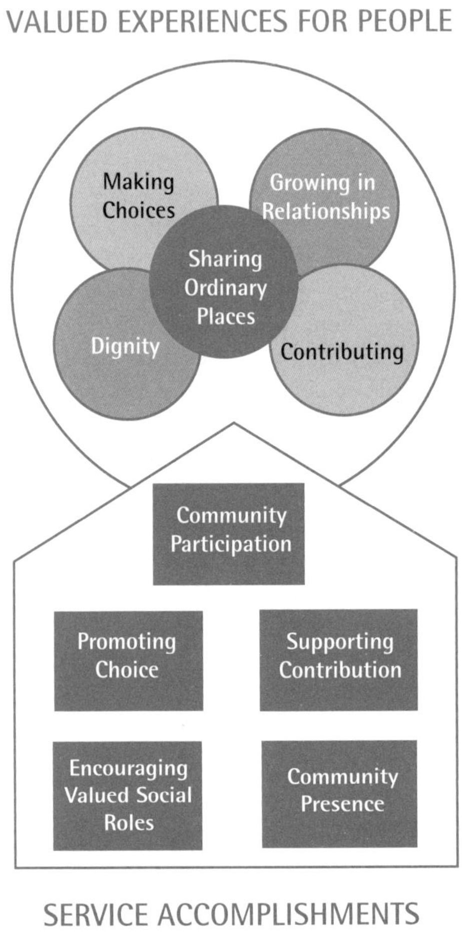

Source: adapted from O'Brien and O'Brien (1989)

It is clear that a desire for the good things in life is universal. As people are valued differently by society and as devalued people are more likely to be treated badly and lose out on the 'good things', it is imperative that we understand the importance of supporting the development of valued social roles for people who are socially devalued and those at heightened risk of becoming devalued. How many people with disabilities get to exercise the opportunity to marry and have children? Do people with disabilities have friendships outside their disabled peer groups? Do people actually participate and 'belong' in their community to the extent that it matters if they are not present? What percentage of people with disabilities are afforded the opportunity to work and develop their competencies and potential? Consider the following:

- People with disabilities are twice as likely as other citizens to experience poverty (NDA, 2005).
- People with disabilities are only half as likely as their non-disabled peers to have employment (CSO, 2011c).
- The greatest barrier to participation (community) for people with disabilities is the physical environment (57 per cent), followed by the weather (53 per cent) and lack of sufficient income (40 per cent) (Doyle, 2012).
- 37 per cent of people with disabilities in private households have difficulty socialising in public places, moving about in their local area and availing of local services such as banking (CSO, 2010).
- 29 per cent of people with disabilities are impeded by the condition of footpaths in their local community (CSO, 2010).
- 21 per cent of respondents in a survey on attitudes said they would object if children with intellectual disabilities or autism were in the same class as their child (NDA, 2011).
- 20 per cent of the general population have some level of discomfort with a person who is experiencing mental health difficulty living in their neighbourhood (NDA, 2011).
- People with a chronic illness or disability were much less likely than others to be a member of a club or association, to talk to neighbours most days or to have had an afternoon or evening out for entertainment in the previous fortnight (Gannon and Nolan, 2007).
- 73 per cent of people with disabilities report that the emotional effect of disability is a significant challenge for them (Doyle, 2012).

With such sobering statistics, can anyone argue that people with disabilities are fully valued members of society? More importantly, what can be done to address these matters? A starting point is to consider relevant policy and legislation.

SOCIAL POLICY, LEGISLATION AND DISABILITY

The Commission of Enquiry on Mental Handicap (1965) recommended that 'health authorities should accept responsibility for coordinating the activities for all the organisations involved and should encourage the development of the voluntary organisations'. This recommendation greatly influenced the current system of service provision, where the state provides funds but service delivery is largely left with the voluntary sector (the organisations formed by parents' and friends' groups and by the religious orders during the 1950s and 1960s to provide services to people with disabilities). These voluntary organisations are funded primarily through government sources but also engage in their own income-generating activities.

The Review Group on Mental Handicap Services (Government of Ireland, 1990) recommended that the term 'mental handicap' should no longer be used to describe people with intellectual disabilities; that general learning disability should be differentiated from intellectual disability; and that residential services should be located in ordinary community settings. It also formally acknowledged that people with intellectual and general learning difficulties had potential for learning that was previously not recognised. This report was a major influence on how services developed during the 1990s.

Since 1996, when A *Strategy for Equality. Report of the Commission on the Status of People with Disabilities* was produced, significant policy and legislative developments have influenced how the area of disability has evolved and will continue to evolve into the future. Table 20.1 outlines some of the major policy and legislative changes. A comprehensive review of policy and legislative changes is beyond the scope of this chapter, however, the information in Table 20.1 highlights how fast this area has changed and indicates the breadth and depth of some of these changes (see fedvol.ie; www.nda.ie; hse.ie or gov.ie for further information).

The policy and legislative changes outlined in Table 20.1 are consistent with the social model approach and address one of the most significant barriers to its implementation: how services are funded and structured. For example, Keogh (2011), in the disability policy review, describes how the majority of services to people with intellectual disabilities and, to a lesser extent, services to people with physical or sensory disabilities are provided in segregated settings. While many services state that they are 'person-centred', they are inadequately focused on meeting the needs of individuals. The report also notes that while service provision may be described as 'community-based' there is a great difference between community *presence* (living in a house in the community) and community *participation* (being an active member of the community that you live in). The disability policy review established through consultation that people with disabilities were unhappy with the amount of choice they had over the services they received; they wanted 'flexible supports to suit individual needs' and to 'do ordinary things in ordinary places'(Keogh, 2011: 10).

Given the significant change required to address these issues, and the policy and legislative developments mentioned earlier, questions arise as to what service structures will look like in the future and the role of social care practitioners in these new service structures. The remainder of this chapter is devoted to discussing these two matters.

Table 20.1. Disability-related policy and legislation, 1996–2013

Year	Name	Details
1996	*A Strategy for Equality. Report of the Commission on the Status of People with Disabilities*	People with disabilities led the development of this major strategy document, which made 404 recommendations and called for the delivery of quality services within a rights, rather than a charity, framework
1998	Employment Equality Act	Outlaws discrimination in employment matters on nine grounds, including disability
	Education Act	Provides the legal basis for the equal treatment of children in education, including children with disabilities
2001	*Quality and Fairness: a health system for you: primary care strategy* (DoHC)	Identifies four goals for the health system: better care, fair access, responsive and appropriate care, and high performance in service delivery
2004	Equality Act	Changed the basis for determining discrimination on the grounds of disability in the workplace
	Education for Persons with Special Needs (EPSEN) Act	Provides for an inclusive educational environment for students with special educational needs
	National Disability Strategy (Government of Ireland)	Seeks to improve the status and quality of life of people with disabilities Continues to be the overarching government policy on disability in Ireland and has five main components: Disability Act 2005; EPSEN Act 2004; sectoral plans for particular government departments (Government of Ireland, 2006b); Citizens Information Act 2007; and an annual investment strategy
2005	Disability Act	Provides for: the assessment of health and educational needs; the allocation of resources; an appeals process where needs are not being met; access to public buildings, information and services; public sector employment; and departmental plans focused on disability

Year	Name	Details
2006	*Towards 2016: ten-year framework social partnership agreement 2006–2015* (DoT)	Lists a number of priority actions relating to disability, including actions in the training and employment area
		Adopts the Lifecycle Framework, an approach that positions 'the individual' as the centrepiece of social policy
	A Vision for Change: report of the Expert Group on Mental Health Policy (DoH)	Sets out a comprehensive policy on mental health service provision for seven to ten years
		Includes a section specific to mental health and disability
2007	Citizens Information Act	Established the Citizens Information Board and provided for a Personal Advocacy Service for people with a disability
	Health Act	Established the Health Information and Quality Authority (HIQA), which has statutory responsibility for standards (safety and quality) in health and social and personal services
	UN Convention on the Rights of Persons with Disabilities (UN CRPD)	Aims 'to promote, protect and ensure the full and equal enjoyment of all human rights and fundamental freedoms by all persons with disabilities and to promote respect for their inherent dignity' Ireland signed the Convention in 2007, but (as of June 2013) has not ratified it, citing the lack of appropriate legislation on 'capacity' as the major barrier to full ratification (see 2012 below)
2009	*National Quality Standards: residential services for people with disabilities* (HIQA)	Quality standards developed by HIQA and presented to service providers, who were requested to implement them on a voluntary basis
2011	*Report of Disability Policy Review* (Keogh)	The government's value-for-money (VFM) reviews were driven by the fiscal challenges and the need for austerity measures as agreed with Europe. This document was the first step in the VFM review of disability service provision
		Suggested a range of policy changes, which were incorporated into the VFM report published in 2012 (see below)

Year	Name	Details
2011	*Time to Move on from Congregated Settings: a strategy for community inclusion* (HSE)	Focuses on 4,000 adults with disabilities living in institutional settings (residences of ten or more people) Establishes the number of congregated settings and the number of people living in them, and develops a plan for supporting residents 'to live full inclusive lives at the heart of family, community and society'
2012	*New Directions. Review of HSE day services and implementation plan 2012–2016* (HSE)	Seeks to modernise HSE-funded day services for people with disabilities, embracing principles of person-centredness, access, accountability and quality
	Value for Money and Policy Review of Disability Services in Ireland (DoH)	Establishes that current service systems are deficient in terms of both quality and quantity, and that people with disabilities are seeking more choice and control over the services they receive Makes key recommendations in areas such as programme objectives, economy and efficiency, effectiveness, governance and accountability, and information
	Assisted Decision-Making (Capacity) Bill	Aims to reform the law on mental capacity, taking into account the Law Reform Commission's report on vulnerable adults and the law The passing of this law will clear the way for Ireland to ratify the UN Convention on the Rights of Persons with Disabilities
2013	*National Standards for Residential Services for Children and Adults with Disabilities* (HIQA)	A revised version of those published in 2009, the 2013 version was developed following an extensive consultation process with stakeholders
	Value for Money and Policy Review of Disability Services in Ireland: National Implementation Framework (DoH)	Sets out the reporting and monitoring structure for the implementation of the VFM review (DoH, 2012)

THE FUTURE DEVELOPMENT OF SERVICES

The above review of relevant policy and legislative developments indicates the four pillars that will underpin services for people with disabilities into the future and that represent powerful drivers for change. The four pillars are: the rights of people with disabilities, the delivery of person-centred services, the mainstreaming of service provision, and service quality. When considered together they clearly amount to more than the sum of their individual parts and signify fundamental change for disability services in Ireland.

Rights of people with disabilities

The rights of people with disabilities are enshrined in the UN Convention on the Rights of Persons with Disabilities, which came into force in 2008. Although Ireland became a signatory to the Convention in 2007, the need for legislation on mental capacity has been a factor in delaying its ratification. Mental capacity, from a legal perspective, is about making decisions for oneself and having such decisions respected in all areas of life. In Ireland, disability activists have called for certain principles to be enshrined in the proposed legislation, including a presumption of capacity by all; a recognition of the 'will and preferences' of the person; and the creation of appropriate mechanisms (such as advocacy and peer supports) to assist people in making their own decisions. Only when all support mechanisms have been exhausted should a decision be taken on behalf of the person and such decisions should be based on their will and preferences rather than on the basis on what is considered 'in their best interests' (Timmins et al., 2012). The necessary legislation, the Assisted Decision-Making (Capacity) Bill, was included in the government's legislation programme for spring 2013 and the government has indicated that the UN Convention will not be ratified by Ireland until the mental capacity legislation is in place.

The general principles of the UN Convention are: respect for the inherent dignity of the person; the right to individual autonomy, including the freedom to make one's own choices, and the independence of persons; non-discrimination on grounds of disability; full and effective participation and inclusion in society; respect for difference and acceptance of human diversity; equal opportunity; accessibility (with regard to the environment, transport and information); gender equality; respect for the evolving capacities of children with disabilities; and the right of children with disabilities to preserve their identities.

While the UN Convention provides a welcome statement of rights, accessing those rights is a different matter. Many people who have a disability require personal support in overcoming barriers to their views being heard, to their wishes being complied with, to their rights being respected and to their entitlements being given to them – and the process and practice of advocacy has evolved in response to this issue. *A Strategy for Equality* (Commission on the Status of People with Disabilities, 1996: 106) states:

> Advocacy is concerned with getting one's needs, rights, opinions and hopes taken seriously and acted upon. It allows people to participate more fully in society by expressing their own viewpoints, by participating in management and decision-making, and by availing of the rights to which they are entitled.

The Citizens Information Act 2007 established the Citizens Information Board (CIB), the statutory agency responsible for supporting the provision of information, advice and advocacy to the public on a broad range of social and civil services. The 2007 Act empowers the CIB to 'support the provision of, or to provide directly, advocacy services to individuals, in particular those with a disability, that would assist them in identifying and understanding their needs and options and in securing their entitlements to social services' (CIB, 2012). In 2011 the CIB established the National Advocacy Service for People with Disabilities to provide independent, representative advocacy services specifically for people with disabilities.

Person-centred services

Person-centred service is a way of working with individuals that supports each person to live a life of their own choosing; and research has shown it to have a positive impact on the quality of life of people with disabilities, with benefits in the areas of community involvement, contact with friends and family and exercising choice in life matters (Institute for Health Research, 2005). At the heart of a person-centred approach to planning services lies 'an appreciation of the person as a unique individual, requiring that all planning is based on supporting each individual to lead his or her life as and how he or she wishes' (NDA, 2004: 11).

Although many organisations claim that they are person-centred in their approach, there is little evidence from research to support this. To be truly person-centred the service must be clearly and *measurably* working in accordance with key principles, which include:

- Planning is undertaken from the perspective of the individual and his or her life – it is not planning from the perspective of the service provider.
- The process is creative – asking what is possible rather than limiting the person to what is available.
- Planning takes into account all resources available to an individual, not just those on offer within the service.

The person-centred planning approach requires serious and genuine commitment and co-operation by all involved in the process, and recognition that planning in this way is an art not a science – best viewed as an organic, evolving process. The objective is not the development of a plan but making a real difference to a person's life (NDA, 2004).

The Health Information and Quality Authority (HIQA) has stated that a person-centred approach is 'one where services are planned and delivered with the active involvement of people who use services' and has described person-centred service in residential care in the following terms (HIQA, 2013: 63):

> People living in residential care are actively involved in determining the services they require and are empowered to exercise their rights including the right to be treated equally in the allocation of services and supports, the right to refuse a service or some element of a service, and to exit a particular service in favour of another one or in order to live independently. People make their own choices, participate in the running of the services and contribute to the life of the community, in accordance with their wishes.

Mainstreaming of service provision

Mainstreaming of service provision refers to a reorganisation of service delivery so that people with disabilities can access services and supports using the resources and facilities generally available in the community. For example, education and training are provided in ordinary school and training settings, and employment services are provided through the state agencies that serve the general population, as are housing and welfare services and supports. Bank-Mikkelsen (1976: 3) described mainstreaming as:

> The full acceptance of people with disabilities offering them the same conditions as are available to other citizens; it involves an awareness of the normal rhythm of life – including the normal rhythm of a day, a week, a year, and the life-cycle itself. It involves the normal conditions of life – housing, schooling, employment, exercise, recreation and freedom of choice. This includes the 'dignity of risk' rather than an emphasis on 'protection'.

The main purpose of mainstreaming is to support the development of a more socially inclusive society; a society that does not segregate or treat people differently on the basis of disability, social disadvantage or personal characteristics. Although the concept has a long history (Wolfensberger, 1972; Nirje, 1985), it gained particular prominence in 1996 in *A Strategy for Equality* (Commission on the Status of People with Disabilities) and was given government acknowledgment and backing in the national health strategy: *Quality and Fairness* (DoHC, 2001b).

The disability policy review (Keogh, 2011: 54) and the report on value for money (DoH, 2012: 16) also specifically refer to mainstreaming as a cornerstone of social inclusion, the former noting that 'mainstreaming is about people with disabilities having access to the same services as the general population'.

Towards 2016 (DoT, 2006) is a clear example of mainstreaming being incorporated into government and social policy. It specifically states that people with disabilities should be supported to benefit from measures that apply to their peers in the non-disabled community. For example, children with disabilities are treated as children first and should benefit from all measures aimed at children. Similarly, older people with disabilities should be supported to access the same services as their peers without disabilities. Already there is evidence of mainstreaming with regard to the work of government departments, including the Departments of Justice and Equality, of Education and Skills and of Social Protection. Full implementation of mainstreaming requires not just acceptance of the principle but also the provision of the necessary supports to enable people with disabilities to participate fully (NDA, 2006; Keogh, 2011).

Service quality

Service quality is primarily determined by two factors: *service effectiveness*, which is concerned with the extent to which important outcomes are achieved for those who use the service; and *service efficiency*, which is concerned with the optimal use of resources.

Although a variety of systems for service quality measurement and enhancement have been available in Ireland since the early 1980s, until recently there was no statutory basis for the monitoring of quality in services for people with disabilities. This issue was addressed in the Health Act 2007, which made provision for the inspection of disability services by HIQA, and was followed in 2009 by HIQA's publication of national quality standards for residential services for people with disabilities. While adoption of the standards was not compulsory, service providers were requested to implement them on a voluntary basis. HIQA published revised standards in January 2013, which take statutory effect from September 2013 (when inspections are scheduled to commence).

The HIQA (2013: 3) standards are based on the premise that:

> People with disabilities, both adults and children, have the right to be safe, to receive person-centred, high quality services and supports and to have access to the services they need in order to maximise independence and choice and enable them to lead a fulfilling life. This basic right is fundamental to their wellbeing and healthy development.
>
> … To empower and enable adults and children with disabilities to achieve these rights, services must adopt a person-centred approach which supports the delivery of high quality, safe and effective care and supports to people with different abilities. This approach should involve good leadership, skilled and experienced staff and the effective management of resources.

The 2013 standards are presented as eight themes: individualised supports and care; effective services; safe services; health and development; leadership, governance and management; use of resources; responsive services; and use of information. Each theme has a number of specific 'standards'. For example, a standard under individualised supports and care is: 'each person exercises choice and control in their daily lives in accordance with their preferences'. Detailed sub-criteria on each standard are provided to assist in making the judgment as to whether the standard is present (good evidence present), partially present (some improvement needed) or not present (significant improvement needed).

With regard to service efficiency, a government-commissioned value-for-money (VFM) review incorporating a review of disability policy was completed and published in 2012. The policy review (Keogh, 2011: 12) articulated a vision for disability services: 'To realise a society where people with disabilities are supported to participate fully in economic and social life and have access to a range of quality supports and services to enhance their quality of life and well-being'. Two goals, underpinned by specific principles and values, are proposed for achieving this vision: 'full inclusion and self-determination for people with disabilities' and 'the creation of a cost-effective, responsive and accountable system which will support the full inclusion and self-determination of people with disabilities'. The VFM review (DoH, 2012) proposes a fundamental change in approach to the governance and funding of disability services in Ireland, with a move from the dominant group-based service delivery model to a person-centred model of individually chosen supports. This is to be achieved by implementing a system of *individualised budgeting* that links funding provision directly to the services that each individual service user requires and receives.

The three main forms of individualised budgeting are: direct payments are made to the person with a disability who purchases and manages their own services; an independent broker supports the person to purchase and manage their funding and services or does so on their behalf; and service providers receive funding for each service user that is clearly linked to the assessed needs of each individual, and the agency is required to account for the services provided and the funds spent.

THE SOCIAL CARE PRACTITIONER IN DISABILITY SERVICES

The role of the social care practitioner in disability service provision has never been particularly well defined. In the traditional service model, the forerunner to the social care practitioner role – child care worker or care assistant – was generally understood as a role of paternalistic care. Working mainly within the confines of the residential or day service facility, the worker was primarily engaged in physical care and welfare activities, very often in a subordinate position to nursing and clinical staff.

As the influence of the social model has grown, the social care practitioner position has developed into a more holistic role that engages with the social, occupational and emotional needs of service users in addition to their physical care and welfare. Key features of this more enhanced role include supporting people with disabilities to: make informed choices, undertake personal development and learning activities, and participate in all aspects of community life. In addition, as the role has developed and gained a more equal status with other professionals, the social care practitioner has become better placed to act as an advocate for the individuals they serve – a role of particular importance in the context of the forthcoming changes in service funding and delivery.

With regard to the professionalisation of the social care role it is important to note that the disability policy review (Keogh, 2011) suggests that professionals can shape services in ways that are not always based on the needs of service users as identified by themselves or their representatives. 'Disability service provision is strongly influenced by a "professionalised" model of provision. This model has professionalised need, such that needs are assessed from the point of view of what health and social care professionals can offer and what services can offer' (Keogh, 2011: 11). Regrettably there is considerable truth in this statement. For many years, particularly under the traditional model, 'professionals' were the decision makers in the lives of people with disabilities and the views, wishes and desires of service users and their families were often ignored. Today, social care practitioners, as emergent professionals, must deal with this legacy, not least because of the forthcoming ratification of the UN Convention on the Rights of Persons with Disabilities and the policy and legislative developments outlined earlier. These demand a different construct of power than that traditionally associated with the professional role (Finnerty, 2012). While in a general sense, professionals are granted decision-making power by virtue of professional status (Gibson and Schroeder, 2002), in working to deliver on the new vision for people with disabilities social care practitioners will be required to recognise, understand and honour service users' right to make their own decisions about their lives.

Supporting people with disabilities to achieve their goals can require the social care practitioner to work intensively with individuals for extended periods of time, and the quality of the relationship that develops between the practitioner and the person with a disability is a key success factor. Research has established that the development of a robust and engaged relationship can lead to significant outcomes for service users that include successfully working through difficult or traumatic experiences, enhancing connections with family and reducing social isolation (Finnerty, 2012). While the building of this type of relationship can occur within the simplicity of everyday life activities, it is a sophisticated process that requires considerable time, skill, insight, knowledge and judgment, in addition to the ability to work with empathy and care. It requires social care practitioners to be person-centred in their focus, to be individualised in their approach, to treat each service user with dignity and respect regardless of circum-stances, to actively support service user autonomy, to support service users to advocate for themselves and to advocate for them where necessary. Developing this type of relationship and working so intimately in the life-space of the service user also requires sophisticated management of the professional boundary, an approach that recognises and addresses a service user's needs on an individual basis and that facilitates appropriate emotional connection.

Perhaps the most fundamental question to be asked with regard to the social care practitioner in the future is 'Who will the employer be?' With the move to individualised budgets, the employer could be a service provider organisation as at present; it could be a person with a disability acting alone or through a represen-tative or broker; it could be an agency similar to those currently operating in nursing and elder care; or the social care practitioner could be self-employed offering services in the same manner as other self-employed clinical professionals.

While a great deal of work and reorganisation of structures and funding mechanisms will be necessary to get to a point where these options are realities for all people with disabilities, there are already instances of these approaches being implemented. For example, some service provider organisations have established pilot projects on individualised budgets where service users exercise choice over the services they receive; some people with physical disabilities receive direct payments and employ their own personal assistants; a small number of parents have secured direct funding in order to purchase the supports that their children require; and there are international examples where systems of brokerage have been operated successfully.

The employment landscape is also likely to be affected by the recommendation that disability services be commissioned using a competitive procurement process (DoHC, 2012: 42) and by the entry of commercial service providers into a disability sector that had a total spend of €1.7 billion in 2011 (DoH, 2012: 49).

Although the number of social care practitioners employed in disability services is difficult to establish, 3,000 of the estimated 23,866 people working in disability service provision in 2009 were classified as 'health and social care professionals' and a further 6,000 were classified as 'other patient and client care' (DoH, 2012: 57). Despite the impending changes, the disability sector remains a very large employer and, irrespective of delivery structures and funding mechanisms, is likely to provide employment opportunities for social care practitioners far into the future.

CONCLUSION

The disability sector is changing so fast that in the last thirteen years the area has been impacted by no fewer than seven Acts of the Oireachtas, eight significant review/policy documents, a major disability strategy and a UN convention. One of the most important changes to occur in disability service provision in the past thirty years has been the move from the medical/traditional model to a social model. Recent policy developments point towards a removal of barriers to full implementation of the social model with the implementation of individualised budgeting. This funding shift has very positive implications for people with disabilities but also affects people working in services including social care practitioners.

Social care practice is an emergent profession in many sectors and no less so in services for people with disabilities, where it is emerging at a critical juncture in the development of services. This offers a great opportunity to develop a role that is unique and truly person-centred: a professional role that understands the importance of relationships and is prepared to invest in their development; that is robust in supporting rights; that is open to listening; and that works in partnership. The social care professional of today and into the future will need to support autonomy and independence, skilfully manage emotions and boundaries, work autonomously, understand and apply quality standards, connect to community and be committed to the full inclusion and participation of people with disabilities on their own terms.

21

Travellers in Ireland and issues of social care

Tamsin Cavaliero and Hannagh McGinley

OVERVIEW

This chapter provides an overview of the Irish Traveller community, examining origins, culture, issues that affect Travellers and legislative developments. It also provides a small amount of information on the Roma community in Ireland. It is important to note that the term 'Roma', as defined by the Council of Europe, refers to Roma, Sinti, Kale and related groups in Europe, including Travellers and Eastern groups (Dom and Lom), and covers the wide diversity of the groups concerned, including persons who identify themselves as 'Gypsies'. In Ireland, since the late 1980s, there has also been a rise in a non-traditional group of travelling people, known as New Age Travellers.

This chapter outlines demographic information on the Traveller population, in Ireland and elsewhere; examines key issues for the Traveller community, with a focus on health and education; suggests some of the main implications for social care practice; and concludes with a list of key Traveller organisations and a summary of the main legislative actions that have impacted on the lives of Travellers in Ireland.

WHO ARE THE TRAVELLERS?

Irish Travellers (Pavees or Mincéirs as they refer to themselves) are an indigenous group of people traditionally resident on the island of Ireland. While Travellers are often presented as a distinct group, it is important to recognise that they are not an homogeneous group and are perhaps better viewed as 'a community of communities' (Commission on the Future of Multi-Ethnic Britain, 2000: 34). As with the wider sedentary population, hierarchies of status exist in the community. The extended family is the pivotal unit of organisation.

According to Pavee Point, reflecting the Irish population as a whole, half of all Irish Travellers live in four counties: Cork (8 per cent), Dublin (23 per cent), Galway (11 per cent) and Limerick (7 per cent) (Ó Riain, 1997: 9); counties Galway and Limerick have particularly high concentrations. While the majority of Irish Travellers live in Ireland, they also reside in the United Kingdom and in the United States. In the US, the largest population (circa 2,500) of Irish Travellers is in Murphy Village (named after its founder), outside the town of North Augusta in South Carolina, with other communities near Memphis, Tennessee, and smaller communities in Georgia, Alabama and Mississippi.

The Equal Status Act 2000 defines Travellers as a 'community of people who are commonly called Travellers and who are identified (both by themselves and others) as people with a shared history, culture and traditions, including, historically, a nomadic way of life on the island of Ireland'.

Travellers have their own distinct language, which is known as Cant or Gammon, but which academics often refer to as Shelta. Traveller culture emerged as an oral tradition, which has contributed substantially to Irish culture, in particular music and storytelling.

Due to the oral tradition of Traveller society, history was passed on by word of mouth as opposed to being documented in the written context, making it difficult to establish origins for the group. According to the *Oxford English Dictionary* (1989), the name Tynker appears in records as early as the twelfth and thirteenth centuries, referring to those of a particular dialect and social group in Scotland and England.

Numerous theories as to the origins of the Irish Travellers have been suggested, including that Irish Travellers are descendants of royal chieftains of the wandering cattle-herding clans. Other suggestions include Travellers as descendants of those dispossessed during Oliver Cromwell's military campaigns or people displaced during *An Gorta Mór* (the Great Hunger or Famine). In response to the Famine, and throughout the nineteenth century, many Irish Travellers emigrated to Britain, the US and Australia (McDonagh and McVeigh, 1996). In 2011 a joint study between the Royal College of Surgeons and Edinburgh University found that Travellers are a distinct ethnic minority who were separated from the sedentary Irish community at least 1,000 years ago (Hough, 2011). This, along with the fact that two separate groups of Irish people migrated to the US during the Famine, disproves the theory that Travellers are descendants from the Famine era.

CHARACTERISTICS

Family

The extended family operates as the pivotal unit of social organisation in the Traveller community. The vast majority of Travellers practise endogamous marriage (marriage within their community) but marriage outside the community is not unheard of. It is a common perception that Travellers frequently practise consanguineous marriage (marriage between cousins) but accurate information is hard to obtain. A report produced by the Traveller Consanguinity Working Group

(TCWG) in 2003 stated that 'studies have estimated that between 19% and 40% of Traveller marriages are between first-cousins'.

Travellers tend to marry at a younger age than the general population, with young women marrying around the age of seventeen and young men around nineteen. Travellers often had large families: research conducted in 1997 suggested that the average number of children for each family was eight (Ó Riain, 1997); however, the propensity for such large families has been diminishing. Traveller family life is often organised along traditional gender divisions with the women being the primary carers.

The most common Traveller names are Cash, Cawley, Collins, Connors, Corcoran, Delaney, Doran, Doherty, Doyle, Joyce, Lawrence, Maughan, McCann, McDonagh, McGinley, McInerney, Mongan, Murphy, O'Brien, O'Driscoll, O'Donoghue, Quilligan, Reilly, Stokes, Sweeney, Toohey and Ward (Griffin, 2008: 283).

Nomadism

In Irish, Travellers are called *an lucht siúil*, which translates as 'the walking people' (Ní Shúinéar, 2004). Traditionally Travellers practised a nomadic way of life; the majority of Travellers tend to be more sedentary nowadays for reasons that include the introduction of trespass legislation in 2002, which criminalises Travellers if they practise a nomadic way of life; the curtailing of traditional stopping places; the increase in educational attendance; and the reduction in traditional forms of employment. It is important to note that while many Travellers may live in one place they tend to have a nomadic perspective, which differs from sedentary ways of viewing the world.

The Irish Traveller Movement estimates that around 25 per cent of all Travellers are mobile at any given moment (Donahue et al., 2007: 5). Travellers practise nomadism to maintain social networks (visiting family and friends), for seasonal employment and for pilgrimage. Pavee Point (2011a) has suggested that the Housing Miscellaneous Act 2002 has had a significant impact on the mental health of the Traveller community in that it has curtailed travelling and the extent to which members of the Traveller community relate to their extended family.

Religion

The majority of Travellers are Roman Catholics; their particular interpretation and practice of Catholicism may differ slightly from that of the sedentary population with an emphasis on traditional cures and holy sites. Many Travellers make pilgrimages and visit sites of healing such as holy wells or visit holy places such as Lough Derg, Knock and Lourdes.

Ethnicity

Members of the Traveller community in the UK are officially recognised as belonging to a distinct ethnic group. This is not the case in the Republic of Ireland, with the result that Travellers in Northern Ireland have their distinct ethnic status acknowledged, whereas those in the Republic of Ireland do not. The United Nations Committee for the Elimination of Racial Discrimination has called for the 'Irish Government to work more concretely towards recognising the Traveller community as an ethnic group' (Irish Traveller Movement, 2011). At the United Nations Periodic Review in 2011, the Minister for Justice and Equality, Alan Shatter, said that the Irish state was seriously considering this issue (Pavee Point, 2011b).

ROMA

The Roma community comprises the largest ethnic minority group among European Union member states. According to estimates made by the Roma Support Group and Pavee Point, Roma make up approximately 0.07 per cent of the Irish population, numbering 3,000. Roma are distinct from Irish Travellers but, like Travellers, were originally a nomadic people. The majority are now settled.

Roma began to arrive in Ireland in the nineteenth century and, following the collapse of communism in Eastern Europe in the late twentieth century, significant numbers sought asylum here. Of the Roma residing in Ireland, approximately 90 per cent originated in Romania, with the remainder mostly coming from other EU member states: Poland, Slovakia and Hungary. While the majority of Roma practise Pentecostalism, there are also Orthodox and Roman Catholics in the Roma community. Their lack of English is a major barrier to accessing services. Like the Traveller community, Roma have suffered from discrimination. Policies aimed at receiving asylum seekers fail to take into account the extended family needs of Roma. The Roma in Ireland are considered the most disadvantaged migrant community, with lower levels of life expectancy, higher infant mortality rates and higher levels of poor-nutrition-related illnesses compared with the wider Irish society (Pavee Point, 2011b).

In 2011 the Irish government, in accordance with directives issued by the Council of Europe, launched *Ireland's National Traveller Roma Integration Strategy* (DoJE, 2011). The European Commission's (2012a) communication on Roma identifies four areas of strategic importance to overcoming Roma exclusion: employment; education; poverty and social exclusion; and poor health and housing.

TRAVELLER DEMOGRAPHY

According to the All Ireland Traveller Health Study (AITHS, 2010), the number of Travellers on the island of Ireland is 40,129 (Republic of Ireland: 36,224, Northern Ireland: 3,905). There are differences in the demographic make-up of the Traveller community and the general population, as shown in Table 21.1.

Table 21.1. Irish and Traveller populations

Age group	Irish population	Traveller population
Over 65 years	11%	3%
Under 25 years	35%	63%
Under 15 years	15%	42%

Source: AITHS (2010)

It is difficult to ascertain numbers of Irish Travellers residing in Britain as they are not yet specifically defined as a separate ethnic grouping on census forms. Pavee Point estimates there are 15,000 Irish Travellers living in Britain and 10,000 Irish Travellers living in the US (Ó Riain, 1997: 9; McDonagh and McVeigh, 1996).

DISCRIMINATION AND SOCIAL DISADVANTAGE

Members of the Traveller Community experience either direct or indirect forms of discrimination on a daily basis. They also experience social disadvantage in terms of poverty, social exclusion, health status, infant mortality, life expectancy, literacy and education, training levels, access to decision making, political representation, gender equality, access to credit and accommodation and living conditions (Watson et al., 2012). Following pressure from national Traveller organisations, the Press Council's code of practice now highlights the Traveller community as a group to be cognisant of when publishing material that might cause serious offence or provoke hatred (McGaughey, 2011: 16).

Employment

The majority of (male) Irish Travellers are self-employed, traditionally as craftsmen, tinsmiths, horse traders, entertainers and seasonal labourers. As Ireland moved from a rural to an urban society, many of the traditional skills were no longer considered to be of value. Despite these changes in society, many Travellers, while no longer practising the same occupation, have proved to be adept at adjusting to fluctuations in the market and continue to organise work activities in similar ways through the continuation of trading. It is estimated that 20 per cent of market traders in Ireland are from a Traveller background (McCarthy and McCarthy, 1998: 51).

Unemployment levels are high amongst the Traveller community with 84 per cent unemployment: 87 per cent amongst men and 81 per cent amongst women. At 57 per cent, Travellers' participation in the labour force is nearly five percentage points lower than that of the general population: Traveller women are significantly more likely to be working in the home (33 per cent compared with 18 per cent for the general population); Travellers also experience a rate of permanent sickness or disability at 4.4 per cent – more than double that of the general population (CSO, 2012c: 32).

Accommodation

Travellers live in a variety of housing situations, including official and unofficial halting sites, group housing schemes, local authority housing, private rented accommodation and their own private property. By far the largest number of Travellers live in houses (73 per cent), but a significant number (18 per cent) live in trailers, mobile homes or caravans and 7 per cent (2,753) do not have access to basic services such as running water (AITHS, 2010).

With the introduction of the Housing (Miscellaneous Provisions) Acts 1992 and 2002, nomadism was severely curtailed through the use of evictions and the criminalisation of trespass on public and private land. Despite the Traveller Accommodation Act 1998 requiring that all local authorities produce accommodation plans, lack of adequate deterrents in the form of incentives or penalties resulted in the failure of the local authorities to provide suitable accommodation. Suitable accommodation requires planners to take into consideration aspects of Traveller culture such as nomadism, work practices (scrap collection requires areas for materials to be stored at the homeplace) and extended families residing together.

One of the main reasons that local authorities do not meet the accommodation needs of Travellers is due to objections from local residents to the building of culturally appropriate accommodation. A recent study found that 80 per cent of the population would be 'reluctant' to buy a house next door to a Traveller (MacGréil, 2010).

Health

Travellers of all ages continue to have much higher mortality rates than people in the general population. Traveller men now live, on average, fifteen years less than men in the general population and Traveller women live, on average, eleven and a half years less than women in the general population. Pavee Point has noted that the levels of mortality for the Traveller community today are, for women, the same as for sedentary women in the 1960s in Ireland and, for men, the same as for the sedentary population in the 1940s in Ireland. Deaths from respiratory diseases, cardiovascular diseases and suicides are significantly higher in the Traveller community when compared with the general population.

Traveller organisations are pressing for an ethnic identifier to be included in health data systems in order to accurately monitor Traveller health and provide information on the services that Travellers access. Based on the findings of the AITHS, the Traveller Health Advisory Committee and the Health Service Executive have identified the following priority areas: mental health, suicide, men's health, addiction/alcohol, domestic violence, diabetes, cardiac health, and the linking of Traveller Health Unit work to primary care teams and networks.

Mental health – suicide rates

Suicide among Travellers is significantly higher than amongst the sedentary population – in 2005 it was over five times higher (Walker, 2008). For the total population, male suicide is four times as common as female suicide, but for Travellers, male suicide is over nine times as common as female suicide. The largest concentration of suicides among the Traveller community is among those aged under thirty (over 65 per cent); the comparable figure for the sedentary population is 34 per cent. The 25–29 age group is most vulnerable to suicide within the Traveller community (Walker, 2008). Of those who die by suicide, 52 per cent have never married, with a further 15 per cent being separated or widowed.

Genetic disorders

There are a number of autosomal recessive genetic disorders that are more prevalent in the Traveller community than in the general population. For example, one in eleven Travellers carry the altered gene causing galactosemia (an inability to metabolise sugar) as compared with one in 107 of the sedentary population. Other genetic disorders include glutaric aciduria type I, Hurler's syndrome, Fanconi's anaemia and type II/III osteogenesis imperfecta (TCWG, 2003). Traveller babies are given the newborn screening test immediately on birth in order to facilitate early diagnosis. In response to the increased carrier frequency of certain genetic disorders, a voluntary, confidential genetic counselling service is provided through the National Centre for Medical Genetics.

In 2000 the Traveller Consanguinity Working Group was established to explore the possible link between consanguineous marriage and higher rates of autosomal recessive genetic disorders. Its findings suggest that, while consanguineous marriage is common in many parts of the world, Travellers tend to face misunderstanding and prejudice from certain sections of the sedentary population in relation to this practice. It identified the practice of endogamous marriage (marriage within the Traveller community), rather than consanguineous marriage, as the cause for the high frequency of altered genes.

Primary health care

Research shows that marginalised populations experience poor health and restricted access to adequate health care (Kenny and McNeela, 2003). According to a recent study, the level of trust by Travellers in health professionals is 41 per cent, half that of their sedentary counterparts (AITHS, 2010).

In the early 1990s Traveller organisations began to apply an innovative approach to health care borrowed from the developing world, known as primary health care (PHC). During the last two decades the numbers of projects applying the approach have increased significantly. The PHC model works in partnership with communities in order to highlight inequality and arrive at mutually acceptable solutions. Enshrined in the PHC model are values of empowerment, partnership and advocacy, community participation and intersectoral collaboration. Research indicates that for Travellers, as for other ethnic minorities, a key part of culturally appropriate practice is the genuine involvement of minority members in the delivery and provision of services (Kenny and McNeela, 2003). The model works by recruiting and training women as community health workers who then identify local health needs within the community and work alongside local health care providers.

Traveller women

Traveller women face double discrimination as they experience the inequality that women in society meet with, combined with the discrimination of being a member of the Traveller community. The now defunct National Consultative Committee on Racism and Interculturalism highlighted the fact that many Traveller women are more easily recognisable than Traveller men, and so more likely to experience the impact of discrimination from the wider sedentary population (Pavee Point, 2011a: 36). Women, as the primary carers in the family, are more likely to come into contact with service providers and members of the settled community through schools, social welfare, doctors and other service providers, and experience significantly more discrimination as a result.

While violence against women is not limited to particular communities and affects women of all ages, race, ethnicities, religions and levels of social class, there are particular issues that need to be taken into consideration when thinking about service provision for Traveller women. Many fear contacting the gardaí and statutory services because of the history of discrimination they have experienced at the hands of the general population. They may also fear being ostracised from their own community for bringing in service professionals who are, as well as being practitioners, members of the sedentary community. It is important that practitioners are aware of these issues and make provision for diverse needs that may include diet, hygiene, family formation, information, literacy, religion and culture. Exchange House Travellers Service delivers a domestic violence programme aimed at children, young people and women entitled *Sunia geel* ('Take care of yourself'). The specific groups identified by the project are Irish Travellers, Sinti, Roma and Muslim migrants in Europe.

Criminal justice system

Globally, indigenous ethnic minorities are overrepresented in the prison system: this is also true for members of the Traveller community in Ireland. Travellers comprise 4.6 per cent of the prison population, but only 0.9 per cent of the Irish population. Traveller men are five times more likely, and Traveller women eighteen times more likely to be imprisoned than their sedentary counterparts. The factors that contribute to the overrepresentation of ethnic minorities in prison are social disadvantage, economic disadvantage, marginalisation and dis-crimination. A study conducted by the Irish Chaplaincy in Britain of Irish Travellers in prison in the UK concluded that 'Irish Travellers suffer unequal hardship in prison. Poor levels of literacy, mental illness, limited access to services, discrimination and prejudicial licence conditions for release, disproportionately affect Traveller prisoners' (MacGabhann, 2011: 84). It should also be noted that 99 per cent of the Traveller population is not in prison.

CONFLICT

Conflict is apparent in all societies, within and between communities. Its causes may originate outside the community as a form of pressure that leads to internal stresses. MacLaughlin (1995: 50) has suggested that the shift from a rural-based to an urban-centred community saw the development of large Traveller encamp-ments, which have become a significant factor in the friction that escalates between communities. Historically Travellers responded to conflict by moving on, but, with the curtailment of nomadic practices by the Housing (Miscellaneous Provisions) Acts, this is no longer a viable option.

Conflict within the Irish Traveller community is complex and, at times, affects delivery of all services. A recent initiative has been piloted through the Midland Traveller Conflict and Mediation Initiative (MTCMI). This project, funded by the Department of Justice and Equality and the Joseph Rowntree Charitable Trust, was launched in 2009 and supports engagement and co-operation between statutory agencies in counties Laois, Offaly, Longford and Westmeath. Research has suggested that the absence of policing; substandard and overcrowded living conditions; and the effects of oppression are some of the main contributing factors for the escalation of conflict within the Traveller community (MTCMI, 2009).

TRAVELLERS AND SOCIAL CARE

Travellers are overrepresented in young people leaving state care in the Republic of Ireland, accounting for 9 per cent of those leaving the care of the health service and 12 per cent of those leaving the care of the special schools system (Kelleher et al., 2000). Lack of trust between Travellers and public bodies is of particular concern in relation to social care practitioners and social workers. Fear based on historical reasons, particularly of losing children into care (Warde, 2009), may contribute to the lack of engagement between Travellers and social care practitioners. Practitioners may be apprehensive of visiting Traveller families, which can result in the neglect of Traveller children's needs (Cemlyn, 2008).

In response to the particular needs of the Traveller community, Travellers Family Care, a voluntary organisation funded by the Health Service Executive under Section 10 of the Child Care Act 1991, was established. The organisation provides residential and family support services for Traveller families and their children. The Shared Rearing Service recruits, trains and supports foster families from the Traveller community for Traveller children from across the country who need alternative family care when they cannot remain in their families of origin.

Research indicates that Traveller clients are more positively disposed towards Traveller child care workers and foster carers who are able to promote ethnic self-respect and understanding in culturally appropriate ways. In addition, Travellers are now trained and working as primary health care workers, family support workers and child care workers.

Exchange House is a multidisciplinary service provider that offers family support, youth services, addiction services and education services to members of the Traveller community. Services are provided to men and women, Traveller families, and Traveller young people and children, many of whom are in crisis. Exchange House also delivers a national service through training, provision of expertise and partnerships with other organisations providing services to Travellers in Ireland.

Early years

There has been a concerted focus on the development of child care services in Ireland, in particular early intervention for children who experience disadvantage, through the promotion of preschool in general and the introduction of the free preschool year in 2010. In addition, outreach programmes have been developed or expanded, including Lifestart family visitors, Toybox projects and Playbus schemes. These initiatives are designed to raise awareness amongst Traveller parents of play and engaging in play activities with their children as important aspects of the early years education process. While these initiatives are welcomed, it is important to recognise the value of early years' experience in the home and to acknowledge the vital role that Traveller parents play as experts in their own children.

The *Preschools for Travellers National Evaluation Report* (DES, 2003c) has recommended that all preschools should actively work on policies and procedures to encourage equality. An evaluation of Toybox initiatives in Northern Ireland (McVeigh, 2007) advocates increasing use of Traveller storytellers, Traveller education community resources and a broader focus that recognises the expertise of Travellers.

Youth

The majority of the Traveller population is concentrated in the younger years. Specific issues facing Traveller youth include early school leaving, high levels of suicide (particularly amongst young men) and a drop-off in participation rates in education among Traveller women aged fifteen to seventeen years. Pavee Point (2012) has called for a culturally sensitive space within services for young Traveller women with services tailored accordingly. The National Youth Council of Ireland has produced guidelines for engaging with Traveller youth as part of its *Access All Areas: a diversity toolkit for the youth work sector*.

TRAVELLERS AND EDUCATION

Poor literacy has been a salient characteristic of Travellers' education, contributing to cycles of disadvantage. When parents' literacy is poor they are not able, for example, to support children with homework, to read letters from school or to follow medication instructions. Many of the older generation of Travellers received little education. The education they did receive was usually in segregated classrooms or schools, where Traveller culture and history was practically invisible, and accounts from Travellers abound with discrimination and racist name-calling that, not surprisingly, have affected how some Travellers engage with the education system.

In 2006 the government launched the *Report and Recommendations for a Traveller Education Strategy*, which advocated an anti-bias and intercultural dimension to promote integration rather than segregation (DES, 2006). Nevertheless, budget cuts in 2011 led to a number of supports being withdrawn, including the removal of all forty-two visiting teacher for Traveller posts; the withdrawal of resource teacher posts for Travellers at primary level; the withdrawal of teaching hours for Travellers at post-primary level; and significant reductions in provision of Traveller school transport. In addition, all senior Traveller centres were closed. A joint statement by the Irish Traveller Movement, National Traveller Women's Forum and Pavee Point highlighted that these cuts were 'disproportionate' (Pavee Point, 2011a).

While Traveller children now enjoy almost full participation at primary level, their participation rates at second level are far below those of their sedentary counterparts. The Traveller education strategy notes that 85 per cent of Traveller children transfer to post-primary school, but that the drop-out rate amongst Travellers at second level is nearly 40 per cent higher than that of the sedentary population (DES, 2006: 3). A 2006 survey indicates that only 2 per cent of Travellers have completed the senior cycle of second-level schooling (DES, 2006). The 2006 *State of the Nation's Children* report found that 'almost half of the total Traveller population of Ireland are under 18 years of age and that approximately 6 out of every 10 Traveller children (58.9%) lived in families where the mother had either no formal education or primary education only' (OMC, 2006b).

Initiatives aimed at addressing issues faced by Travellers in the education system have been developed at regional and national level, including the production of a DVD by Pavee Point entitled *Pavee Parents: Primary Concerns*. In 2008 the Irish Traveller Movement piloted an intercultural programme called 'Yellow flag'. Its objectives were to assist and support schools in the area of intercultural education, to involve the local community, to promote diversity and to improve the whole school environment for all students, staff and parents.

Adult education

FÁS, the national state training agency, recognises Travellers as a distinct group and delivers Traveller-specific training and employment programmes such as Community Employment, Local Training Initiatives (many targeted specifically at Traveller women) and Jobstart schemes.

Roma in education

Approximately 30 per cent of Roma children living in Ireland attend school. Research indicates that 85 per cent of the Roma population are illiterate and 95 per cent of Roma women living in Ireland cannot read or write in any language (Lesovitch, 2005). Particular support is available for Roma adults through dedicated further education provision by the City of Dublin Vocational Education Committee. All adult Roma are entitled to education in the same way as their Irish peers, although there may be some limitations if they are not EU citizens.

GOVERNMENT POLICY

Travellers are highlighted as one of Ireland's most vulnerable groups under the Europe 2020 strategy (European Commission, 2012b). The *National Reform Programme for Ireland* acknowledges that targeted social inclusion programmes will be aimed at Travellers (DoT, 2012). The national social partnership agreement *Towards 2016* (DoT, 2006) sets out priority actions for Travellers in the areas of accommodation, education outcomes, opportunities for employment and communication between Travellers and the settled community. It also led to the establishment of the National Traveller Monitoring and Advisory Committee in 2007. Despite these advances, the refusal of the Irish government to acknowledge Irish Travellers as an ethnic group contributes to a continued lack of coherence and clarity in policy towards Irish Travellers.

Relevant legislation

1963 Commission on Itinerancy recommended assimilation

1983 Report of the Travelling People Review Body recommended integration

1988 Housing Act – statutory recognition of Traveller-specific accommodation

1991 Prohibition of Incitement to Hatred Act

1992 Housing (Miscellaneous Provisions) Act – Section 10 gives local authorities the power to move unofficially camped Travellers

1993 Unfair Dismissals (Amendment) Act – Travellers are named specifically

1993 Roads Act – local authorities and gardaí can remove temporary dwellings in certain circumstances

1994 *Shaping a Healthier Future: a strategy for effective health care in the 1990s* – contains a section on Traveller health

1995 White Paper on Education entitled *Charting our Educational Future* – integration and full participation by Traveller children

1995 Casual Trading Act – market traders must apply to local authorities for a licence for any market

1995 *Report of the Task Force on the Travelling Community* acknowledges distinct culture and identity of Traveller community

1997 Control of Horses Act – restriction on ownership of horses

1998 Housing (Traveller Accommodation) Act – local authorities required to meet current and projected needs of Traveller community; increased powers of eviction

1999 Employment Equality Act

2000 Equal Status Act

2001 Youth Work Act

2002 Housing (Miscellaneous Provisions) Act – criminalises trespass on private and public land

2005 *National Action Plan against Racism*

2010 *Our Geels: All Ireland Traveller Health Study*

CONCLUSION

Travellers' experiences of institutions and sedentary organisations have been challenging and this may lead to lack of engagement or sporadic involvement. It is imperative that social care practitioners understand their own cultural biases and value judgments. Acknowledging the expertise in the Traveller community while reflecting on practice, combined with an understanding of the structural forces in Irish society that have facilitated the marginalisation, deprivation and discrimination experienced by the Traveller community, are vital to engaging and supporting authentic relationships with members of the Traveller community.

Traveller organisations

Exchange House National Travellers Service

Organisation of Traveller and sedentary people working together to provide services to the Traveller community, many of whom are in crisis. This multidisciplinary service provider offers family support, youth, addiction and education services to members of the Traveller community in the Dublin area, as well as delivering a national service through training, provision of expertise and partnerships with other organisations providing services to Travellers in Ireland. (exchangehouse.ie)

Irish Traveller Movement

National network of organisations and individuals working within the Traveller community. (itmtrav.ie)

Mincéirs Whiden

Ireland's only all-Traveller forum was formally founded in 2008. It aims to promote an understanding and recognition of Travellers as a minority ethnic group in Irish society who are proud and confident of their identity. It seeks the full participation and inclusion of Travellers in the economic, social, political and cultural life of Ireland. (minceirswhiden.org)

National Traveller Women's Forum

The national network of Traveller women and Traveller women's organisations from throughout Ireland. It recognises the particular oppression of Traveller women in Irish society and works to address this issue through the provision of opportunities to Traveller women to meet, share experiences, ideas and develop collective strategies and skills to work towards the enhancement of their position in society. (ntwf.net)

Pavee Point

A non-governmental organisation committed to the promotion and realisation of Travellers' human rights. A partnership of sedentary people and Travellers, who work together regionally, nationally and internationally to ensure that Irish Travellers and their counterparts are recognised and respected, that their human rights are implemented, and that inequalities and discrimination faced by Travellers are named and addressed. (paveepoint.ie)

22

Working with young people: discourse, policy and practice

Maurice Devlin

OVERVIEW

Much social care work is carried out with young people. This raises the question of how the work relates to other types of service or provision that are also concerned with young people. Recent years have seen a proliferation of what might be termed 'youth services' and sometimes the boundaries between the different services are not readily clear, especially to external observers. The very terms 'youth' and 'young people' (like the terms 'child' and 'children') can be understood and defined differently in different legislative or policy contexts, or in different professional settings and services. This chapter outlines some of the main approaches to working with young people before focusing on the approach that is specifically known (and defined in Irish legislation) as 'youth work'.

DISCOURSE AND LANGUAGE

While different approaches to working with young people may be based on different legal provisions and different organisational and administrative structures, they also reflect differences at the more fundamental level of ideas. Differences in legal codes, policy frameworks and professional practices relating to young people exist not only because young people are a heterogeneous group with diverse needs and circumstances, but also because there is a variety of ideas and assumptions in society about the nature of youth (in general) and the needs of young people (in general). In understanding how these different ideas relate to each other, and how they come to be reflected in different forms of policy and provision for young people, it is useful to make use of the sociological concept of *discourse*.

In common usage, discourse means much the same as 'discussion' or 'debate'. In social theory, its meaning is more complex. Drawing substantially on the thinking of the influential French philosopher Michel Foucault (1970, 1972), Stuart Hall (1997: 6) offers the following definition:

> Discourses are ways of referring to or constructing knowledge about a particular topic or practice: a cluster (or *formation*) of ideas, images and practices, which provide ways of thinking about, forms of knowledge and conduct associated with, a particular topic, social activity or institutional site in society.

The phrase 'ideas, images and practices' captures the essence of discourse. A discourse refers not just to a way of thinking about a given topic or to a set of images based on such thinking, but also to a practice or set of practices (ways of *behaving*) shaped by or complementary to such ideas and images. Discourse has a 'materiality', meaning that when we talk about, for instance, the 'discourse(s) of youth' or the 'discourse(s) of adolescence' in contemporary Ireland, we refer not just to prevalent *ideas* about young people but to practices and institutions associated with, and in themselves reproducing, those ideas. Aspects of young people's needs or behaviour will be interpreted differently according to the assumptions underpinning different discourses, and views as to appropriate responses will vary accordingly. Payne et al. (2009: 11) give a practical example of how discourses work:

> For example, there are a number of ways of understanding teenage binge drinking. It might be a failure of parental socialization of weak-willed individuals, or an example of commercial pressures to spend money in conventional entertainment, rather than encouraging participation in positive educational experiences in youth clubs, or a legitimate letting off steam in active young people. Different ways of understanding, or combinations of explanation, might lead to different ways of dealing with the problem in a town centre, and helping a young person who has become dependent on alcohol.

In studying different ideas, images and practices relating to young people, it is important to be aware of language itself. All three of these aspects of discourse – ideas, images and practices – are directly implicated in the very nature of language. A central insight of recent sociological studies of discourse is how language, rather than passively communicating ideas or information from one person (or group) to another, actively contributes to the construction and reproduction of meaning; it 'channels and shapes communication, and hence the meanings derived from it ... Any one system of thought or communication necessarily allows for some things to be communicated and excludes others' (Fook, 2012: 72–3). Parton (2009: 220) suggests that 'words do not simply describe things, they do things and thus have social and political implications'.

From this perspective, it is not an insignificant matter whether we habitually refer to people aged thirteen to seventeen years as 'young people', 'youth', 'youths', 'kids', 'adolescents', 'teenagers', 'minors', 'juveniles' or even 'boys' or 'girls'. The different words may literally refer to the same age group in the population (in other words they may have the same *denotation*), but tend to be loaded with different ideas and images (they carry different *connotations*). It is open to adult members of society to select as appropriate from this 'lexicon' when they communicate different ideas and images about the young, or develop and deliver what they consider to be appropriate responses to young people's needs. For a discussion of why there might be such a wide variety of ways of referring to young people, how this relates to young people's social status and how young people do notice and care about how they are described and portrayed, see Devlin (2006).

PROFESSIONAL DISCOURSES OF YOUTH

Discourses about young people are embodied in the schooling system, youth work services, social work and social care services for young people, the juvenile justice system, employment legislation and other aspects of the law. They underpin the 'youth (or teen) industries' such as young people's television and radio, online entertainment, social networking sites, fashion and popular music. In all cases, there are complex institutions that embody sets of ideas about young people, and practices – patterns of behaviour, rules, roles and responsibilities – associated with the young people and the adults involved. The ideas, images and practices may not be consistent and may vary considerably from one profession, institution or 'site' to another, or even within the same site, reflecting an ambivalence about young people in contemporary societies. Referring to the complexity of the law with regard to definitions of youth (that could equally be applied to 'childhood'), Berger and Berger (1976: 236, 239) say that the:

> . . . law always reflects the society in which it has its being and . . . in this particular area the ambiguities of the law reflect the ambiguities of the society's conception of youth . . . [In modern society] it is unclear when youth begins and when it ends. And it is far from clear what it means while it is apparently going on.

Because there is a prevailing ambivalence in society as to 'what is going on' during young people's transition into adulthood, different professional practices have emerged over the last century and a half, the period during which the transition from childhood to adulthood has been systematically extended by social, economic and technological change. These practices are rooted in different basic assumptions about the nature of youth, and may draw on different academic disciplines (which themselves have emerged and developed over the same period) or different branches of the same discipline (such as developmental, social or clinical psychology).

For example, formal educational practice – the profession of teaching – has traditionally approached young people in a particular way. It has a specific word that has most commonly been used to define young people and position them within educational systems and structures: they are 'pupils'. This term captures the traditionally unequal relationship between teachers and the taught: a pupil historically (and etymologically in its Latin origins) meant a ward or an orphan and in some legal contexts still carries the meaning of being in the care of a guardian. As teaching evolved into a modern profession, it drew both on the classical thought of ancient philosophers and on the emerging discipline of educational science, itself closely related to the growth of psychology. Influential figures such as William James (1842–1910) and John Dewey (1859–1952) worked intellectually and professionally at the interface of philosophy, psychology and education.

While formal education is something in which all children and young people are expected (and required by law) to participate, social work and social care have developed as professional responses to the needs of young people (and adults) with particular difficulties or problems. These practitioners also have their own characteristic ways of thinking and acting – their own discourses – in relation to the young people with whom they work. They also have their own ways of referring to the people with whom they work – 'clients' and 'service users' are common terms – and a body of theoretical and empirical knowledge on which they draw, often giving particular attention to insights from adolescent psychology. Indeed, the use of the term 'adolescent' is more common in these professions than in some others such as formal education and youth work.

As in education, contemporary social work and social care often adopt a critical stance with regard to some of their traditional assumptions and practices, and attempt to build more equitable relationships between those providing services and those availing of them. For example, social work with young people in the United Kingdom has been accused, by social workers themselves, of taking place 'in the shadows of the new "popular punitivism" and authoritarian interventions' (Grier and Thomas, 2009: 68). A recent study of social work with young offenders in the UK provides a hypothetical case study of a professional intervention in the life of a teenage boy, John, and challenges the narrowness and disempowering nature of the assumptions on which such interventions can rest (Haines, 2009: 294–5):

> Throughout John's short teenage years, no one has listened to his story, taken his problems seriously or acted constructively to improve his situation. A lack of critical practice has failed John. Interventions have focused on John's offending, failing to address the problems underlying his behaviour. Instead, John has been perceived as a problem and an offender: the system has responded to him accordingly. As a result, John, an average 15-year-old child, sits alone and afraid in custody awaiting his fate.

Haines (2009: 300) argues that social work with young people in trouble with the law should move away from a view that they are inherently different from others of their age, and should be based on a fundamentally positive attitude to the nature of youth:

> In thinking about work with young offenders, therefore, we must start from thinking about youth and about linking interventions with young people in difficulty into the range of provisions or activities that exists for all young people ... international conventions establish the principle that interventions with young people, including those who have committed an offence, should be based on the premise of 'normalisation' ... this means reversing the trend of criminal justice interventions that have been recently developed in youth justice.

It is possible that the differences between the various professional discourses relating to young people are diminishing over time. This trend may be encouraged by an increasing emphasis in some countries on an 'integrated' approach to working with children and young people, involving practitioners from a range of professional backgrounds working closely together. This has been the main direction of development in the UK in recent years and is reflected in a range of vocational and professional training programmes (Edmund and Price, 2012; Oliver and Pitt, 2011). In Ireland, integrated services for children and young people are also increasingly prioritised at local and national level, as reflected in the establishment in 2011 of the Department of Children and Youth Affairs, led by a full cabinet minister. Other countries, including the United States, Canada and Australia, have also seen a convergence, to some extent, of professional approaches to working with young people (Fusco, 2012). In other respects, significant differences persist, as becomes clear when we look in detail at youth work in Ireland.

WHAT IS YOUTH WORK?

Like the other types of educational, developmental or welfare-based approaches to working with people – what are sometimes collectively called 'social professions' (Banks, 2004, 2012) – the term 'youth work' is open to contrasting, and sometimes conflicting, interpretations. While there is still plenty of room for discussion and debate about what youth work is or should be, a good starting point is the legal definition. Youth work, in Ireland, is unusual among the social professions in that there is a law that says what it is; Section 3 of the Youth Work Act 2001 describes youth work as:

> A planned programme of education designed for the purpose of aiding and enhancing the personal and social development of young persons through their voluntary involvement ... which is – (a) complementary to their formal, academic and vocational education and training; and (b) provided primarily by voluntary organisations.

This definition may be imperfect (Spence, 2007) and have the rather technical or instrumental character of legal language, but it nonetheless encapsulates key points or principles that would command widespread agreement among people involved in youth work in Ireland today. The first is that youth work is, above all else, an educational endeavour and should complement other types of educational provision. Indeed, it is also called 'out-of-school education', which is misleading as it can sometimes take place in school buildings. It is now more common to refer to it as 'non-formal' or 'informal' education.

Second, young people participate in youth work voluntarily: they can take it or leave it, a situation markedly different from their relationship with the formal education system. This means they have a different type of relationship with the adults who work with them. This difference is reflected in the words used to describe them: youth workers generally refer to the young people they work with as 'participants' or 'members', or just as 'the young people'.

Third, youth work is mostly carried out by organisations that are non-statutory or non-governmental as well as non-profit. It is in the nature of these voluntary organisations that many, in fact most, of the adults who work with them do so on an unpaid basis. Throughout its history, Irish youth work has relied enormously on voluntary effort, both individual and institutional. This continues to be the case although, as we will see, recent years have seen the emergence of enhanced roles for the state and for full-time professional staff in the provision of youth work services.

THE EMERGENCE AND DEVELOPMENT OF YOUTH WORK

The key points highlighted above make it clear that contemporary youth work – despite areas of overlap discussed later in this chapter – is different in significant ways from social care work with young people. By definition, the latter's principal focus must be the care of the young person. This is related to their education but is not the same as it; and children and young people do not as a rule volunteer to put themselves in care.

Youth work and social care work (and social work) were part of the broad philanthropic movement of the nineteenth and early twentieth centuries, which was concerned with 'rescuing' (or controlling) needy, destitute and troublesome children and young people, whose numbers and visibility increased substantially as society industrialised and urbanised. The particular direction that care work took was shaped by its links with the industrial and reformatory school system and with provision for young offenders (Lalor et al., 2007: 290). The direction taken by youth work (and its emergence as a separate area of practice) was due to the fact that the early combination of philanthropy and 'moral panic' (Cohen, 2002) gradually merged with other impulses that associated young people not just with the problems of the present, but with the promise of the future and with the potential to defend and promote certain political, cultural or religious values and beliefs.

Social movements involving young people (and largely directed by young people) have been found throughout Europe since the Middle Ages (Zemon

Davies, 1971). The first voluntary youth groups and organisations in Ireland in the nineteenth and early twentieth centuries – including the various Scouting and Guiding organisations and the early Boys' and Girls' Clubs – might also be seen as part of a broad youth movement, albeit one with adults exercising key leadership roles. They were closely associated with other movements of the time concerned with promoting national aspirations or religious ideals. Ireland is certainly not the only country where youth work (and other work with young people) had its origins in voluntary activity but, in Ireland, the emphasis on voluntarism took on a particular character because of the fraught nature of the historical relationship with Britain and the fact that the great majority of the country's population, particularly south of the border after independence, was Roman Catholic. In this context, voluntarism was, among other things, an expression of the principle of *subsidiarity*, which was emphasised by Catholic social teaching (Devlin, 2010). According to this principle, the state should only have a supportive ('subsidiary') role in providing for people's care, welfare and education, and the primary responsibility should be vested in families, communities and voluntary associations. In Ireland, historically, the churches set up most such associations and therefore many of the longest-established youth organisations have religious affiliations.

In youth work, as in other areas of social policy (including primary and secondary education and the Irish hospital system), the state's main role in the past has been to fund and support the non-governmental sector to be the main direct provider of services. Thus, almost all the existing youth work services in Ireland are delivered by voluntary organisations. The main ones at national level are the uniformed organisations (Scouts, Guides, Boys' and Girls' Brigades), Foróige, Youth Work Ireland and (in the Dublin Archdiocese) Catholic Youth Care. These organisations were set up, mostly independently of each other, over a period of more than a century. A significant development took place in 1967 when the largest organisations came together to form a representative or umbrella body, the National Youth Council of Ireland (NYCI). The next year, Bobby Molloy TD was appointed as the first parliamentary secretary with responsibility for youth and sport (the role of parliamentary secretary was the precursor of what is now known as a minister of state or, informally, junior minister), and in 1970 the Department of Education began to distribute the first formal youth service grants to the voluntary sector.

The main exception to the pattern of voluntary (or non-statutory) predominance has been in Dublin, where the City of Dublin Youth Service Board (CDYSB) was established as a subcommittee of the City of Dublin Vocational Education Committee (CDVEC) on the instructions of the Minister for Education in 1942. This development was a response to the severe problem of youth unemployment in the city at the time. Although this represented direct intervention on the part of the state, the development had the active encouragement of the then Archbishop of Dublin, Dr John Charles McQuaid (Devlin, 2010). The early focus of the organisation (initially called Comhairle le Leas Óige, or

Council for the Welfare of Youth) was on the provision of practical skills training for the young unemployed. Over the years it broadened its range of services to include funding, support and training for youth clubs and volunteer youth leaders and, particularly since the 1980s, for community-based youth projects employing full-time paid workers.

The arrangement whereby the Department of Education disbursed grant aid through its Youth Affairs Section to the voluntary youth work sector (and the small statutory sector) has changed relatively little since the outset, although the relevant government department is now the Department of Children and Youth Affairs and the Youth Affairs Section is now a 'Unit' within the department. The amount of funding involved increased enormously over the years, particularly since the establishment of the National Lottery in 1986. Two of the main funding lines are the Youth Service Grant Scheme (mostly for 'mainline youth work') and the Special Projects for Youth (or SPY) Scheme. The latter is intended to enable the employment of full-time paid staff to work with disadvantaged young people.

The Youth Affairs Unit also funds a network of youth information centres and supports a number of other initiatives related to youth work (for example, Gaisce – the President's Award; north–south and international youth exchanges; the national youth arts and health programmes; and the Child Protection Unit for the youth work sector). In 2011 the total youth affairs budget was more than €61 million, the vast majority of which was drawn from National Lottery proceeds. Youth work also benefits from health service funding (€8.3 million in 2011). Most of the Garda Youth Diversion Projects funded by the Irish Youth Justice Service are run by youth work organisations, who received €8.85 million for this purpose in 2011. In many cases, youth work organisations are in receipt of funding from multiple sources.

Different funders inevitably have different expectations regarding process, product and 'outcomes' (they may be operating out of different discourses of 'youth'); this raises important questions about the interface between youth work as it is defined in law and other types of youth service (Powell et al., 2012).

PRINCIPLES AND PRACTICE: WHAT DO YOUTH WORKERS DO?

According to practitioners and policy makers, youth work rests on a number of key principles. The first three listed below are enshrined in legislation (Youth Work Act 2001, Education and Training Boards Act 2013):

1. It is primarily concerned with the education and development, personal and social, of young people.
2. It relies on the voluntary engagement of young people: they are not compelled to attend or to take part.
3. As an important part of civil society or what is sometimes called 'associative life' (through which citizens come together to work collaboratively to achieve

shared objectives), the role in youth work of voluntary organisations, and individual volunteers, is vital.

We can add a number of other principles to these, reflecting existing policy and practice (DES, 2003b: 13–15; NYCI, 2006; Devlin and Gunning, 2009; OMCYA, 2010). For example:

4. Young people are full and active partners in youth work, participating meaningfully in making decisions and in programme planning and implementation.
5. Youth work should aim to empower young people and give them a voice, individually and collectively, and it should uphold and promote the rights of children and young people as citizens (such as those set out in the UN Convention on the Rights of the Child).
6. Youth work should aim for openness and inclusiveness and for the active promotion of equality; no individual young person, and no group of young people, should feel excluded or diminished in a youth work context.
7. Youth work has a community dimension and a social purpose; it has benefits for adults as well as young people; it strengthens social solidarity and contributes to positive social change.
8. Youth work, like all good education, should be experienced as both challenging and enjoyable, both fulfilling and fun, both enriching and uplifting, for young people and for adults.

How do youth workers go about implementing these principles? Above all, youth work is *educational*. As the *National Youth Work Development Plan* (DES, 2003b: 13) puts it, 'education is by definition a planned, purposeful and conscious process (whereas "learning" may or may not be planned and purposeful, and may or may not be conscious)'. This means that youth workers approach any activity or programme, any situation or eventuality – structured or unstructured, expected or spontaneous – by asking themselves what opportunities it presents to further the education and development of young people, individually and collectively.

This is why youth work can be educational in both 'non-formal' and 'informal' ways. It is non-formal in that it does not usually take place in schools or follow a predetermined curriculum. It is informal in that it rests crucially on a relationship between adults and young people that strives for optimum mutuality, cordiality and conviviality and makes the most of spontaneous 'daily life activities' (Youth Service Liaison Forum, 2005: 13). It sees these principles as central to its concerns rather than as distractions from some more 'serious' purpose.

What do youth workers do? *How* they do things is at least as important as the things they do. This is often described in terms of 'process' and 'product' (or 'task'). It is not helpful to see these in terms of a polarity, where an emphasis on one must inevitably be at the expense of the other. It is better to see them as different dimensions of the youth worker's role, each enriching the other (Devlin and Gunning, 2009). For this to happen, it is important that workers and young people have the space, opportunity and support to reflect consciously and purposefully on what they have learned and what they have yet to learn, and how they might go about doing this. Much theory and practice in youth work (and related areas such as community development and adult education) has been influenced by the idea of learning as a cycle that moves through stages of experience, reflection and conceptualisation and then onto further, enriched experience and experimentation, which begins the cycle again (Kolb, 1984; Smith, 2001). But however youth workers envisage their work with young people, its key purpose is likely to be seen in educational and developmental terms.

As regards the activities and programmes to which youth workers bring this approach, the range is very wide. Figure 22.1 lists some of the main possibilities.

Figure 22.1. Youth work activities and programmes

- Recreational and sporting activities and indoor/outdoor pursuits, uniformed and non-uniformed.
- Creative, artistic and cultural or language-based programmes and activities.
- Spiritual development programmes and activities.
- Programmes designed with specific groups of young people in mind; for example, young women or men, young people with disabilities, young Travellers or young people in other ethnic groups, young asylum seekers, or young lesbian, gay, bisexual and transgender people.
- Issue-based activities (related to, for example, justice and social awareness, the environment, development education).
- Activities and programmes concerned with welfare and wellbeing (health promotion, stress management, or relationships and sexuality).
- Intercultural and international awareness activities and exchanges.
- Programmes and activities focusing on new information and communication technologies (ICTs).
- Informal learning through association, interaction and conversation with youth workers and other young people.

The important point is that the overall approach to the programme or activity, and the principles informing the interaction with young people, are consistent with those indicated above. Many of the areas involve specialist ability or professional expertise (for example, outdoor pursuits and sports, information technology, artistic and creative work) and many young people avail of such learning and leisure opportunities independently of youth work. What makes youth work different is that such activities are engaged in, not just for their intrinsic value or interest, but also for their contribution to young people's personal and social development and to broader community and societal development. Many worthwhile and innovative programmes involve youth workers and other professionals working collaboratively, as, for example, in youth arts where youth workers and artists are often jointly involved (Devlin and Healy, 2007).

In keeping with the principles outlined above (especially 5 to 7) youth work often focuses on particular groups of young people who share certain identities, circumstances or needs. In many cases they have collectively been the victims of social inequalities, based on such factors as gender, class, disability, race, ethnicity or sexuality. Such work clearly has an important role to play in addressing the developmental needs of individual young people who may be facing particular difficulties related to their material circumstances and lack of equal opportunities for leisure and socialising, and who may be dealing with prejudice and discrimination and the impact this can have on confidence and self-esteem. However, youth work also has the potential, even the responsibility, to raise awareness in society as a whole of the nature and impact of such inequalities and to involve young people themselves in working to challenge and change them, and not just the young people directly affected. This is not a novel insight. More than a quarter of a century ago the National Youth Policy Committee made the point forcefully (NYPC, 1984: 116):

> If youth work is to have any impact on the problems facing young people today, it must concern itself with social change. This implies that youth work has a key role in enabling young people to analyse society and in motivating and helping them to develop the skills and capacities to become involved in effecting change.

RECENT POLICY DEVELOPMENTS

The National Youth Policy Committee (NYPC) was appointed in 1983 and issued its final report in 1984. Its proposal for a comprehensive national youth service with a legislative basis was broadly accepted in a White Paper published the following year (Government of Ireland, 1985), but a general election and change of government intervened before the national youth policy was implemented. A similar pattern has been repeated several times, whereby political and administrative change has delayed or frustrated the execution of youth work plans or policies (Devlin, 2008). The 1984 report of the NYPC remained influential and its proposals can clearly be seen to have contributed to the shaping of the Youth Work Act 2001.

As we have seen, the Youth Work Act 2001 defined youth work as essentially a part of the broader education system. It provided that the Minister for Education would have statutory responsibility to ensure the development and co-ordination of youth work programmes and services at national level (now the responsibility of the Minister for Children and Youth Affairs) and that vocational education committees (VECs) would have a similar responsibility at local level. It specified that voluntary organisations would remain the primary direct *providers* of youth work. If 'subsidiarity' was a key governing principle of Irish youth work policy and provision in the past, then 'partnership' was central to the Youth Work Act, as it has been to so much recent Irish social policy (Fanning, 2006: 14). The main partnership in this case is that between the statutory and the voluntary sectors.

After the Act was passed each VEC (except where it already had youth work staff) was funded to employ a youth officer, whose role was to support the provision of youth work by voluntary groups and organisations. But the most important structural provisions of the legislation, giving VECs a statutory obligation to provide youth services, have never been formally implemented or 'commenced'. The merger of the existing thirty-three VECs (in 2013) into sixteen education and training boards, whose functions include supporting 'the provision, coordination, administration and assessment of youth work services' (Education and Training Boards Act 2013, Section 10), has, for the first time, placed youth work on a secure statutory footing.

One element of the Youth Work Act 2001 that was formally implemented was the reconstitution of the National Youth Work Advisory Committee (NYWAC), first established under the Youth Work Act 1997. NYWAC's membership comprises representatives of government departments, statutory agencies and the Irish Vocational Education Association and nominees of the 'prescribed national representative organisation' for the voluntary sector. The National Youth Council of Ireland was explicitly named in the Act as having that status for the first three years, after which it was renewed by statutory instrument.

In 1999 the first NYWAC approved a proposal from the National Youth Council of Ireland that it prepare proposals for a national youth work development plan, to complement and build on the amending youth work legislation then in preparation. The Minister of State for Youth Affairs endorsed the idea, and over the next two years NYWAC engaged in a comprehensive process of research and consultation, which resulted in a set of recommendations for a plan that was eventually approved by the government. Launched in 2003 as the *National Youth Work Development Plan 2003–2007* (DES, 2003b), it was constructed around four broad goals and a number of related actions.

The four goals were:

- To facilitate young people and adults to participate more fully in, and to gain optimum benefit from, youth work programmes and services.
- To enhance the contribution of youth work to social inclusion, social cohesion and active citizenship in a rapidly changing national and global context.
- To put in place an improved infrastructure for development, support and co-ordination at national and local levels.
- To put in place mechanisms for enhancing professionalism and ensuring quality standards in youth work.

The related actions (implemented) were:

- Appointment of a national assessor for youth work in the Department of Children and Youth Affairs.
- Significant increases in funding for the youth work sector in the years immediately after the plan's launch (with a levelling off subsequently and a more recent reduction in common with other sectors).
- Annual development fund providing additional support for local clubs and groups.
- Support for 'single worker projects' to recruit additional staff.
- Major review of funding in the youth work sector.
- Revision of the code of good practice on child protection in youth work (DES, 2003a) and establishment of a Child Protection Unit to offer support and training to youth organisations. In 2012 a review was commenced of the code of good practice to bring it in line with the revised *Children First* (DCYA, 2011) child protection guidelines and to take account of the fact that legislation was before the Oireachtas to place the *Children First* guidelines on a statutory footing.
- Development of codes and guidelines on various aspects of youth health and welfare.
- Establishment of the North/South Education and Training Standards Committee for Youth Work.
- Implementation of the National Quality Standards Framework (NQSF) for youth work, setting out standards to be attained by all staff-led youth work projects and organisations in receipt of funding from the Youth Affairs Unit (OMCYA, 2010).
- Implementation of a similar (but less onerous) standards framework for volunteer-led youth groups (DCYA, 2013).

Responsibility for youth work at national level now rests with the Department of Children and Youth Affairs (DCYA), established in 2011. This was effectively an upgrading to departmental status of the Office of the Minister for Children and Youth Affairs, originally established as the Office of the Minister for Children in 2005 and expanded to incorporate Youth Affairs in 2008. It was an executive office of the then Department of Health and Children. The DCYA has respon-sibility for a wide range of policy areas and services for children and young people (see Figure 22.2). In early 2013 it is preparing to introduce a successor to the national children's strategy and, complementary to that, a youth policy frame-work that will deal with youth work and other youth services. This framework, along with the Education and Training Boards Act 2013, will set the context for the development of youth work in Ireland for the foreseeable future.

Figure 22.2. Organisational structure of the Department of Children and Youth Affairs

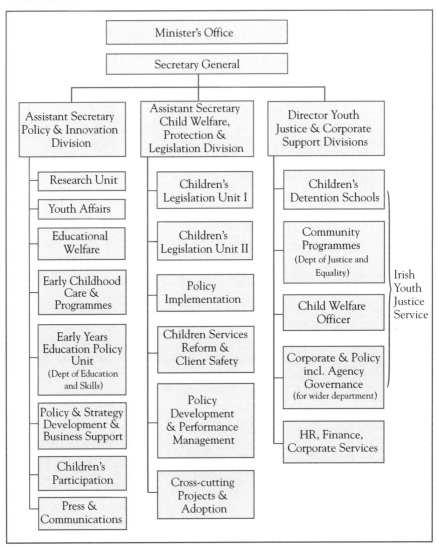

Source: DCYA (July 2012): dcya.gov.ie/documents/Organisation/OrganisationChartJuly 2012.pdf

PROFESSIONALISM, PROFESSIONALISATION AND TRAINING

Is youth work a profession? The answer is not as straightforward as it might seem. Youth work has changed enormously over time, and the people doing it are now much more likely to be working on a full-time paid basis and to have to give an account of themselves to line managers, boards of management and funders. This in itself is suggestive of a process of professionalisation. Exact figures are hard to come by, but it has been estimated that there are approximately 1,400 full-time paid youth workers in Ireland (Indecon, 2012: 45) and the real number could be substantially higher. It is also generally recognised that youth work has become an increasingly complex and challenging job and that a substantial process of advanced training and education is necessary to be able to do it properly.

A number of third-level institutions offer professional programmes in youth work (NUI Maynooth, University College Cork, Dundalk Institute of Technology, University of Ulster). Given the increasing number and range of services for young people, it is likely that other institutions will begin to offer programmes. These institutions now fall under an all-Ireland framework for the sectoral approval or endorsement of their youth work training programmes, carried out by the North/South Education and Training Standards Committee (NSETS), established as part of the *National Youth Work Development Plan*. In turn, NSETS works closely with its counterparts in England, Scotland and Wales, helping to ensure a common approach to training and workforce concerns and enhancing student and worker mobility.

It is not legally required that a person possess a particular qualification to do the job of youth work (as is the case in the more established and regulated professions) but, in practice, employers are now likely to stipulate that applicants for posts hold a professionally endorsed qualification. Employer interests are represented on the NSETS committee, as is the DCYA and the Department of Education for Northern Ireland (as well as all the other major stakeholders), meaning that the endorsement process has a wide currency in the sector. This might be seen as another significant indication of professionalisation.

Possessing an endorsed qualification does not bear any relation to the salary earned by the worker, and different organisations continue to use different pay scales depending on the funding available to them. It remains the case that most of the people who do youth work are volunteers. There are perhaps as many as 40,000 volunteers in the youth work sector (Indecon, 2012: 44) and they carry significant responsibilities in their engagement and interaction with young people. Good will is not enough to make for successful youth work practice, whether on the part of paid staff or volunteers. This is why youth organisations have provided volunteer training programmes for many years, and more recently the National Youth Work Advisory Committee and the National Youth Council of Ireland have developed a common national induction programme for volunteers in youth work organisations (NCYI, 2010). The concept of *professionalism*, referring to high standards, responsibility and accountability, need not (and should not) be limited to paid workers.

Youth work is not just a *vocation*, although almost inevitably the people who do it have a particularly strong sense of personal commitment to the work and to the wellbeing of young people. It is a *profession*, in the sense that all those who do it, both volunteer and paid staff member, are required and obliged, in the interests of young people and of society as a whole, to carry out their work to the highest possible standards and to be accountable for their actions.

CONCLUSION

This chapter has introduced the concept of discourse and suggested that there may be a number of different discourses relating to the nature of youth, reflected in different professional approaches to working with young people and meeting (and even defining) their needs. It has focused in particular on the policy and practice of 'youth work', defined in Irish law as a distinctive type of educational and developmental work with young people, based on their voluntary participation and primarily carried out by voluntary organisations. It has also briefly considered the issues of professionalism and professionalisation in youth work.

It is clear that while in certain significant respects youth work and social care practice are different, in other respects they have important things in common, such as a fundamental ethical commitment to the wellbeing of children and young people; a concern with giving a voice to those they work with; a particular focus on disadvantaged individuals and communities; and the use in certain cases of similar activities and methods. They are both part of the 'social professions' (Banks, 2012), all of which face particular challenges in this late modern or postmodern era, in an Ireland that has experienced such diverse and rapid social change. Despite such changes, involvement in the social professions presents practitioners with a valuable opportunity to make a positive impact on the lives of the individuals they work with and to contribute to making society a fairer and better place for children and young people.

23

Homelessness

Mairéad Seymour

OVERVIEW

This chapter examines the issue of homelessness with specific reference to the role of the social care practitioner. The definition, nature and extent of homelessness in Ireland are outlined and an overview of the risk factors and common 'pathways' into homelessness for young people and adults is presented. The social care practitioner is required to respond to the needs of homeless people in line with the law and vision outlined in national homeless policy approaches. It is with this in mind that an overview of homeless legislation and policy is provided, extending from the Housing Act 1998 to the Housing (Miscellaneous Provisions) Act 2009 and the most recent government response to homelessness contained in the *Homelessness Policy Statement* (DECLG, 2013). The chapter concludes with an account of the challenges for social care workers when working with homeless people.

DEFINING HOMELESSNESS

There is limited agreement about how homelessness is defined, nationally and internationally. While the image of the unkempt individual huddled under a blanket in a public doorway may be the stereotype, in reality, sleeping rough, or 'rooflessness', is the narrowest definition of homelessness. Homelessness manifests itself in various forms, from families staying in bed and breakfast accommodation or young people staying in homeless hostels, to adults residing involuntarily with family or friends because no other accommodation options are available to them. Homelessness is best understood not as a static situation, but as a process whereby 'individuals and households may move between being homeless, poorly housed and adequately/well housed' (Anderson and Tulloch, 2000: 3).

The European Observatory on Homelessness has developed a typology of homelessness and housing exclusion based on the premise that there are three main domains that constitute a home: the physical domain (having an adequate dwelling, or space, over which a person or family can exercise exclusive possession); the social domain (being able to maintain privacy and enjoy relations); and the legal domain (having a legal title to occupation) (FEANTSA, 2007). The absence of any of these three domains can be said to define homelessness. The typology outlines four housing situations in a continuum of homelessness: rooflessness, houselessness, insecure housing and inadequate housing (see Table 23.1).

Table 23.1. European Typology of Homelessness and Housing Exclusion (ETHOS)

Roofless	People living rough.	Living in the streets or public spaces, without a shelter that can be defined as living quarters.
	People in emergency accommodation.	People with no usual place of residence who make use of overnight shelter, low-threshold shelter.
Houseless	People in accommodation for the homeless.	Where the period of stay is intended to be short term.
	People in women's shelters.	Women accommodated due to experience of domestic violence and where the period of stay is intended to be short term.
	People in accommodation for immigrants.	Immigrants in reception or short-term accommodation due to their immigrant status.
	People due to be released from institutions.	No housing available prior to release. Stay longer than needed due to lack of housing. No housing identified (e.g. by 18th birthday).
	People receiving longer-term support (due to homelessness).	Long-stay accommodation with care for formerly homeless people (normally more than one year).
Insecure	People living in insecure accommodation.	Living in conventional housing but not the usual place of residence due to lack of housing. Occupation of dwelling with no legal tenancy; illegal occupation of a dwelling. Occupation of land with no legal rights.
	People living under threat of eviction.	Where orders for eviction are operative. Where mortgagee has legal order to repossess.
	People living under threat of violence.	Where police action is taken to ensure place of safety for victims of domestic violence.
Inadequate	People living in temporary/ non-conventional structures.	Not intended as place of usual residence. Makeshift shelter, shack or shanty. Semi-permanent structure, hut or cabin.
	People living in unfit housing.	Defined as unfit for habitation by national legislation or building regulations.
	People living in extreme overcrowding.	Defined as exceeding national density standard for floor space or useable rooms.

Source: FEANTSA (2007)

The official legislative definition of homelessness in Ireland is contained in the Housing Act 1988. Under the Act, a person is considered homeless by the relevant local authority if (emphasis added):

(a) There is no accommodation available which in the opinion of the authority he, together with any other person who normally resides with him or who might reasonably be expected to reside with him, can reasonably occupy or remain in occupation of, or

(b) He is living in a hospital, county home, night shelter or other such institution and is so living because he has no accommodation of a kind referred to in paragraph (a) and he is, *in the opinion of the authority*, unable to provide accommodation from his own resources.

The words 'in the opinion of the authority' are noteworthy because they give power to the local authority to decide if an individual is deserving of assistance.

'Youth homelessness' refers to young people (under eighteen years) who are out of home independently of their parents or guardians. The definition adopted in the *Youth Homelessness Strategy* (DoHC, 2001c) refers to homeless youth as:

Those who are sleeping on the streets or in other places not intended for night-time accommodation or not providing safe protection from the elements or those whose usual night-time residence is a public or private shelter, emergency lodging, B&B or such, providing protection from the elements but lacking the other characteristics of a home and/or intended only for a short stay . . . Young people who look for accommodation from the Out-of-Hours Service and those in insecure and inappropriate accommodation with relatives or friends are also included in this definition.

The Out-of-Hours Crisis Intervention Service is an emergency service that provides accommodation to young people when no other option is available and it is not possible for them to return home (see dcya.gov.ie).

THE NATURE AND EXTENT OF HOMELESSNESS

Under Section 9 of the Housing Act 1988, local authorities are required to undertake an assessment of housing need at least every three years. In conjunction with this exercise, an assessment of the number of homeless people in each area is also undertaken. An assessment based on an extract of data relating to the number of households approved for social housing on 31 March 2011 (Housing Agency, 2011) identifies that, of 98,318 households in need of social housing support, homelessness forms the basis of need for 2,348 households (2.4 per cent). The figure of 98,318 households is based on the number of households who cannot be accommodated through the existing stock available to housing authorities. It excludes households who are already in local authority accommodation or voluntary co-operative or rental accommodation scheme (RAS) accommodation. Homeless households who are not registered for social housing or who attend homeless services are also excluded and it is therefore unlikely that the figure captures the full extent of homelessness in Ireland.

A more comprehensive approach to identifying homeless people in Ireland was included for the first time as part of the 2011 census. The enumeration process recorded the number and profile of individuals who resided in accommodation for homeless people on the night of 10 April 2011, as well as those who were sleeping rough (CSO, 2012a). The Department of the Environment, Community and Local Government (DECLG), homeless people and organisations working with CSO staff identified the accommodation included in the count of homeless people. In order to validate this selection process, accommodation providers were contacted to confirm that they currently offered services to homeless people. All properties included in the count were confirmed as providing accommodation to homeless people by contacting the proprietor of the relevant agency. Data on rough sleepers was collected by the Dublin Region Housing Executive in Dublin and by local field workers in other areas. The data generated represents a major development in improving knowledge on the extent and profile of homelessness at national level. Previously, such information was only available on the homeless population in Dublin, following periodic week-long assessments of homelessness undertaken by the Homeless Agency (Williams and Gorby, 2002; Homeless Agency, 2006, 2008). Such assessments, based on a comprehensive methodology, recorded details of those identified as homeless in A&E departments, individuals sleeping rough or using emergency accommodation, food and day homeless services, and street outreach services, as well as those on local authority homeless lists.

The Central Statistics Office (CSO, 2012a) reports that 3,808 people in Ireland were recorded as homeless in the 2011 census. Of those, over 60 per cent (2,375) were recorded in the Dublin region, supporting existing research that homelessness is predominantly an urban phenomenon (O'Sullivan, 2006). Eighty per cent of homeless people in Dublin and 83 per cent in the rest of Ireland were identified as Irish nationals. Non-Irish nationals were slightly overrepresented in the homeless population (15 per cent) when compared with the proportion they represent in the general population (12 per cent) (CSO, 2012a).

Single adults tend be overrepresented in homeless populations in part because they are deemed to be of lower priority in terms of housing need than other homeless groups such as families with children (Burke, 2008). Of the 3,351 recorded homeless individuals aged fifteen and older in the census data, over two-thirds (67 per cent) were single and the marital status of a further 17 per cent was identified as separated or divorced.

The international literature (National Coalition for the Homeless, 2009; SAMHSA, 2011) points to a high prevalence of males in homeless populations and this was borne out in the Irish statistics, where 67 per cent of homeless people were recorded as male and 33 per cent as female (CSO, 2012a).

Almost three-quarters (73 per cent) of the homeless population recorded were aged between twenty and fifty-nine years and a further 10 per cent were aged sixty years or older. Those in the 0–19 age group accounted for 17 per cent; of these cases (641), 457 related to children aged fourteen or younger. In total, 498 children were identified as homeless within family units. Of these family units, 64 were headed by couples and 185 by lone parents (CSO, 2012a).

Emergency accommodation, such as bed and breakfast and hostel accommodation, is the most common form of sleeping arrangement for homeless people in Ireland (43 per cent), followed by long-term homeless accommodation (26 per cent), transitional accommodation (15 per cent) and mixed accommodation (9 per cent) (CSO, 2012a). A heavy reliance on emergency accommodation reflects the dearth of services to assist individuals to move out of homelessness. The result is that many homeless people spend long periods in emergency homeless services and this is particularly significant given that 'the lack of "move-on accommodation" . . . hinders and sometimes impedes reintegration' (FEANTSA, 2005: 26).

Sleeping rough is considered to be the 'most extreme form of homelessness' (Anderson and Christian, 2003: 114) and enumerating those who sleep rough within a particular timeframe is difficult, not least because of the extremely transient nature of their existence. A total of 1.6 per cent (64 cases) of those identified as homeless on census night were sleeping rough and of these rough sleepers, 59 were located in Dublin (CSO, 2012a).

The Homeless Agency (2008) notes that since 1999 there has been a steady decline in the numbers of people who self-report sleeping rough: the level of rough sleeping in 2008 was 40 per cent of the level recorded in 1999. It attributes the substantial decrease to improvements and investment in outreach and emergency services. An exception to this downward trend is the growth in the proportion of non-Irish nationals who are reporting rough sleeping in recent years. Existing research suggests an increase from one in ten reporting a foreign nationality and sleeping rough in 2005 to two out of every five individuals sleeping rough in 2008. A particular concern for homeless services is that non-Irish nationals are likely to experience additional challenges in exiting rough sleeping due to language barriers and restrictions related to the habitual residence condition (a condition that requires claimants to prove that they are habitually resident in Ireland in order to claim social welfare payments).

A substantial proportion of homeless adults in Ireland experience long-term homelessness. The available data on the long-term nature of homelessness is based primarily on Dublin and ascertained from the findings of the *Counted In* report (Homeless Agency, 2008). It found that just over 84 per cent of respondents reported being in homeless services for more than six months, with almost one-third of the total being in homeless services for more than five years.

BECOMING HOMELESS

Structural issues such as poverty and unemployment, coupled with an inability to access appropriate housing, have been consistently forwarded as contributory factors to homelessness (Gould and Williams, 2010). However, as O'Sullivan (2008) argues, structural reasons do not explain why only some households who experience impoverished circumstances become homeless as a result. It is increasingly acknowledged, therefore, that the risk factors associated with homelessness are complex and involve a number of structural, institutional, family and individual issues (see Table 23.2).

Table 23.2. Risk factors for becoming homeless

Structural factors	• Shortage of affordable housing. • Low income and poverty.
Institutional factors	• Being in local authority care. • Being in the armed forces.
Family background factors	• Experience of family homelessness in childhood. • Family breakdown and disputes. • Being in reconstituted families with step-parents. • Sexual or physical abuse in childhood or adolescence. • Experiencing premature death of parents or step-parents. • Having parents or step-parents with drug or alcohol problems. • Having a mother aged under 25 at birth of first child.
Individual factors	• Using drink or drugs at an early age. • Getting involved in crime at an early age. • Offending behaviour and/or experience of prison. • Having difficulties at school and lack of qualifications. • Lack of social support networks. • Debts, especially rent or mortgage arrears. • Causing nuisance to neighbours. • Drug or alcohol misuse. • Poor physical or mental health.

Source: Anderson and Tulloch (2000: 48)

Family conflict, abuse, substance misuse, mental health problems, criminality and victimisation are all associated with increasing the likelihood of becoming homeless (Barrett et al., 2011b; Fitzpatrick et al., 2013; Fitzpatrick et al., 2000). It is equally the case that many of these issues occur for the first time, or are exacerbated, as a *consequence* of becoming homeless (Lawless and Corr, 2005; Tyler and Johnson, 2006). In addition, although households may experience a range of risk factors in the lead-up to becoming homeless, a single 'trigger' or event is usually related 'to finally pushing them into homelessness' (Anderson and

Tulloch, 2000: 50). Triggers range from leaving home after an argument, to eviction from accommodation or a financial crisis, through to leaving prison or state care (Aviles de Bradley, 2011; Fitzpatrick et al., 2000; Mayock and O'Sullivan, 2007; Seymour and Costello, 2005). Overall, the evidence suggests that the multiplicity of risk factors associated with homelessness requires a diverse and nuanced health and social care response to meet the needs of homeless people.

Routes into homelessness

Of themselves, risk factors tell us little about the processes by which individuals become homeless. The need for a more sophisticated analysis to explain homeless causation has been advocated (Anderson and Christian, 2003) and recent research has focused attention on the process by which factors combine and create pathways into homelessness (Mayock and Carr, 2008; Mayock and Sheridan, 2012; Mayock and O'Sullivan, 2007; Warnes and Crane, 2006). Anderson and Tulloch (2000: 18) suggest that pathways fall under three age-related categories: youth pathways (15–24 years), adult pathways (20–50 years) and later life pathways (50+ years).

Youth pathways

Research on homeless young people in Dublin (Mayock and Vekić, 2006) and in Cork (Mayock and Carr, 2008) identified three different but interrelated pathways into homelessness. Mayock and Carr (2008: 36) explain that 'while typologies [pathways] provide a useful tool for framing and understanding the complex transition to homelessness, not all young people fit neatly into the pathways identified'. In these circumstances, young people were assigned to the group most representative of their life circumstances and experiences. The three common pathways that emerged from a total of seventy-seven biographical interviews across the two studies were:

- *Care history pathway*: a distinct pathway for one group of young people emanated from their history of state care. Their experiences were characterised by separation from their family, multiple placements, placement breakdown and social isolation. In turn, they sought alternative sources of support, including anti-social peer groups that sometimes led them to drug use and criminal activity (Mayock and O'Sullivan, 2007). The combination of failed care placements and lack of a nurturing environment were identified as placing them at increased risk of homelessness.
- *Household instability and family conflict pathway*: another group consisted of young people who lived mostly with family or extended family, but their negative experiences at home eventually culminated in them leaving home. The negative experiences described were broadly similar to those in the

international literature (Thrane et al., 2006; Tyler and Johnson, 2006) and included frequent moves as children, family problems for several years, trauma, conflict related to a step-parent in the home, assault, parental drinking, inconsistent parenting and unfair treatment.

- *Negative peer associations and 'problem' behaviour pathway*: this group of young people consisted of those who described how risk behaviour, drinking, drug use and negative peers led to them being 'kicked out' of home and to contact with the police. Most of this group also outlined events and circumstances that left them vulnerable, including serious illness or death of a family member, and tension and conflict in the home (Mayock and O'Sullivan, 2007).

A fourth pathway, described as 'abusive family situation', was also identified in the Cork-based study (Mayock and Carr, 2008).

Adult pathways

In contrast to youth homelessness, pathways into adult homelessness are more often attributed to a lack of suitable and affordable accommodation at a time of crisis (Pillinger, 2007) and financial matters such as mortgage arrears/repossession, rent arrears/abandonment or eviction (Anderson and Tulloch, 2000). The breakdown of a marital or other intimate relationship can give rise to additional housing needs if one household splits into two. Relationship breakdown associated with domestic violence creates a differentiated pathway into homelessness, as does leaving institutional care, long-term hospitalisation or imprisonment. A final pathway relates to homelessness linked to addiction or physical and mental health difficulties.

Mayock and Sheridan's (2012: 1) study of the homeless journeys of sixty women aged from eighteen to over fifty years found that women's entry into homelessness is often 'a culmination of a complex range of experiences, which, together, resulted in housing instability and subsequent homelessness, very often on several, separate occasions'. Over one-quarter of the women had a history of state care and a majority experienced childhood deprivation, instability, abuse and neglect. Violence was often experienced in the context of intimate partner relationships and acted as a trigger to homelessness in many cases. Alcohol and drug use were prevalent among the women and frequently contributed to housing instability. Mayock and Sheridan (2012: 16) argue that some of the reasons for women's homelessness are likely to differ from those of men and suggest that greater attention be given to 'gender-specific dimensions of homeless situations and experience'.

Distinct causes and pathways into homelessness have been identified amongst the elderly. Warnes and Crane's study of 131 homeless individuals aged fifty years or older in England found that there were 'five "packages of reasons" that created distinctive "pathways" into elderly homelessness' (2006: 412). While many of the pathways were common to all adults, the death of a close relative or friend was identified as an age-specific pathway amongst this cohort. Those with dependency needs were particularly vulnerable following the death or infirmity of their carer. Other pathways for the elderly are likely to include retirement from longstanding employment with accommodation, domestic violence and mental health problems, including dementia (Anderson and Tulloch, 2000).

These youth and adult pathways clearly indicate that homelessness is an issue that permeates all spheres of social care work across all age groups and settings. As a result, practitioners are likely to have a role to play in responding to or preventing homelessness amongst those at risk, whether their work is based in a community or residential setting or in mainstream or homeless services.

RESPONDING TO HOMELESSNESS: LEGISLATION AND POLICY

Statutory responsibility for assisting people who are homeless was assigned to the local authorities under the Housing Act 1988. Local authorities were tasked with developing a priority scheme for letting dwellings to those unable to access accommodation from their own resources. They also had the power to give direct financial and other assistance to homeless people or to fund approved agencies to provide and manage homeless accommodation options. Despite these measures, the Act has had limited impact in reducing homelessness. One of the main limitations was that it did not place a statutory duty on local authorities to house people who are homeless.

The Housing (Miscellaneous Provisions) Act 2009 provides a statutory basis to address the needs of individuals experiencing homelessness in Ireland. Section 37(1) of the 2009 Act provides that a housing authority shall, in respect of its administrative area, adopt a homeless action plan to address homelessness within a specified time period. The Act strengthens the informal consultation arrangements outlined in many previous homeless strategies, and makes provision for the formation of a homelessness consultative forum (consisting of representatives from the local authority, Health Service Executive [HSE] and homeless service providers) and a statutory management group in each area. Most significantly, it gives a legislative basis to homeless action plans and their implementation.

In recent years, government policy on homelessness has moved increasingly towards an emphasis on tackling long-term homelessness. The strategy document *The Way Home: a strategy to address adult homelessness in Ireland 2008–2013* (DEHLG, 2008) identified the elimination of long-term homelessness (defined as an individual occupying emergency accommodation for longer than six months), and the minimisation of homelessness through effective preventative policies and services, as key policy objectives.

In February 2013 the government launched a *Homelessness Policy Statement* outlining six key aspects to its response to homelessness in Ireland: preventing homelessness, eliminating the need to sleep rough, eliminating long-term occupation of emergency accommodation, providing long-term housing solutions, ensuring effective services and providing better co-ordinated funding arrangements. Central to this policy approach is the goal of eliminating long-term homelessness by 2016 through the implementation of a 'housing-led approach' (DECLG, 2013). Such an approach focuses on accessing permanent housing with appropriate support to sustain tenancies as the main response to all forms of homelessness. In so doing, it moves away from a reliance on the use of short- and medium-term responses to homelessness in the form of emergency hostel or shelter-type accommodation.

Youth homelessness policy

Under Section 5 of the Child Care Act 1991, the HSE has a statutory responsibility to provide for children aged under eighteen years who become homeless. The strategic approach to youth homelessness is set out in the *Youth Homelessness Strategy* (DoHC, 2001c). The goal is to reduce, and if possible eliminate, youth homelessness through preventative strategies and, where this is not possible, to ensure that a comprehensive range of services aimed at reintegrating the child into their community are provided as quickly as possible. The objectives to prevent homelessness include the development of multiagency services and multidisciplinary teams to target young people at risk, and a strengthening of aftercare services for children leaving foster care, residential care, centres for young offenders and other supported accommodation. Where homelessness occurs, the objectives focus on minimising the impact on the child through the provision of accessible emergency services, the development of a care plan and the appointment of a key worker for the child or young person.

The HSE is the lead agency responsible for implementing the strategy and the Child Welfare and Protection Unit at the Department for Children and Youth Affairs (DCYA) monitors the implementation via the Youth Homelessness Strategy Monitoring Committee (YHSMC). In December 2011 it was announced that the Centre for Effective Services (CES) had been engaged to undertake a high level review of the *Youth Homelessness Strategy*. The aim of the review is to establish the extent to which the strategy has been successful in achieving its aims, to identify barriers to its implementation, and to make recommendations on a new implementation framework to address youth homelessness in Ireland.

Access to key services in the areas of family support, drugs, mental health and appropriate care placements continue to present challenges to the goal of preventing young people from becoming homeless in the first instance (DoHC, 2005; Social Services Inspectorate, 2003). The dearth of services further increases the risk of homelessness in already vulnerable young people, particularly those with a history of care or social service involvement. A number of services have been developed to assist homeless youth since the implementation of the strategy, but there is a continued overreliance on the use of emergency accommodation and limited opportunities for long-term placements to move young people out of homelessness. The importance of moving young people off the streets at the earliest opportunity is central to minimising the risk of long-term homelessness and of becoming immersed in the homeless culture of the streets, including risk behaviour and criminality (Hagan and McCarthy, 1997), and its associated dangers such as exploitation and victimisation (Mayock, 2008; Thrane et al., 2006).

CHALLENGES FOR SOCIAL CARE PRACTITIONERS

The challenge for social care practitioners in the years ahead will be to develop their practice in line with the policy goals and strategies for preventing and eliminating long-term homelessness amongst adults and young people. Homeless prevention work encompasses a wide range of social care tasks and is not restricted to work with homeless young people or adults. Ensuring that vulnerable individuals and families are supported in a way that diminishes their risk of homelessness, either through direct work with them or by accessing support services on their behalf, is an important preventative role executed by social care practitioners. Preventing homelessness can also entail working with those in state care, acute hospitals or prisons to reduce their vulnerability to homelessness on their return to the community. The challenge for social care practitioners is to work effectively on an individual or collaborative interagency basis to minimise the crises that often leave individuals and families without stable housing.

Necessity may bring many homeless people into daily contact with services but, for some, the profoundly negative social and psychological effects of homelessness (Bentley, 1997; Vandemark, 2007) will impact on their ability or willingness to engage with services (Crane and Warnes, 2005). Others may resist the intervention of services because of the stigma associated with being identified as homeless (Cleary et al., 2004; Harter et al., 2005), because of previous negative experiences with homeless services (Hoffman and Coffey, 2008) or because they have chosen to manage their homeless existence without service intervention (Osborne, 2002).

Some subgroups of the homeless population, such as young people and people with mental health, substance abuse or related problems, are likely to present additional challenges to practitioners. Homeless young people are required to navigate the pathway to adulthood and experience the challenges associated with it while also coping with the absence of a stable home. In negotiating this pathway, they require support on the one hand and independence on the other (De Winter and Noom, 2003), leaving a challenge for service providers 'to strike a balance between recognising and respecting young people's social and cultural worlds, and at the same time, setting rules that help to protect [them]' (Mayock and O'Sullivan, 2007: 238).

Working with people with mental health and substance abuse problems is another challenging role that requires a balance between meeting the day-to-day needs associated with being homeless and also having due regard for the difficulties related to the addiction or health-related problems. Challenges reported by practitioners include the need to detect and recognise the signs and symptoms of different drugs, to deal with the multiple needs of homeless drug users, to motivate service users, to address preconceptions about homeless drug users and to have regard for staff and service user safety (Lawless and Corr, 2005).

The heterogeneity of risk factors and pathways into homelessness provides strong evidence of the need to avoid making assumptions about the needs of homeless people or attempting to impose interventions based on assumptions (Kidd et al., 2007). It is in this context that social care practitioners must be mindful of the incontestable right of homeless individuals to choose or reject intervention and to be accorded respect for their decision.

CONCLUSION

This chapter set out to provide an overview of homelessness, particularly focusing on the policy and practice issues relevant to the role of the social care practitioner. Homelessness by definition and context is a complex phenomenon that requires careful exploration and analysis. A nuanced understanding of homelessness that recognises the diversity of the profile and needs of the homeless population provides an important baseline from which to develop practice in the area of preventing and responding to homelessness. Homelessness has been the focus of numerous social research agendas, but there has been limited evaluation of the effectiveness of services for homeless people or opportunities for them to be involved in a meaningful way in informing policy and service development and delivery. In practice, as in research, the voice of the service user must remain paramount, particularly when working with some of the most vulnerable and marginalised individuals in society.

24

The juvenile justice system

Eileen Farrell

OVERVIEW

This chapter examines the legislative and philosophical changes that have taken place in youth justice in Ireland and will highlight the key governmental agencies that have been given responsibility for working with young offenders. It begins with a brief discussion of why children and young people offend, then outlines the key legislation and discusses responses to such offending behaviour. There are two distinct possible pathways: a juvenile justice route that emphasises a diversionary and restorative justice approach, and a health service/welfare route that emphasises a care and protection approach for non-offending children who are considered at risk of harm due to their high-risk behaviour (IYJS, 2012b). This chapter focuses exclusively on the first of these: the juvenile justice route. It outlines the philosophy that underpins restorative justice and highlights how this philosophy has been incorporated into the juvenile justice process through community-based initiatives and sanctions.

WHY DO YOUNG PEOPLE OFFEND?

International research indicates that it is most common for criminal behaviour to begin at the age of ten years and peak at seventeen years (Cashmore, 2011). There have been many theories developed to provide an understanding of why young people offend. Explanatory factors include a person having a genetic predisposition; biological factors as a result of diet or substance misuse; or neurological factors such as a learning disability, attention deficit hyperactivity disorder (ADHD) or acquired brain injury. The Irish Penal Reform Trust (IPRT, 2012) reports that four in ten young people on remand in custody in Irish detention centres have learning difficulties. Others argue that factors that influence criminality can include a desire for financial gain and/or status (strain theory), an individual's lack of self-control (social control theory) and engaging in criminal activity by choice (rational choice theory).

Research indicates that young people who experience poverty, emotional turmoil or social exclusion are at greater risk of committing a criminal offence. Anderson and Graham (2002: 33) provide an insight into children who offend in

Ireland and have found that children in custody 'experienced numerous negative and traumatic events in their lives. High levels of family breakdown, abuse, homelessness, substance misuse and educational failure ... a history of failed foster and residential placements was prevalent'. Research conducted in the United States by Thornberry et al. (2001) identified a link between abuse and juvenile offending. They found that young people who experience abuse during childhood and into adolescence are more likely to commit juvenile crime than those children who experience abuse during childhood only. They also found that where abuse began in adolescence it increased the likelihood of juvenile offending. A study conducted in Australia by Stewart et al. (2008) reported similar findings.

In a study entitled 'The Class-Cultural Dynamics of Crime, Community and Governance in Inner-City Dublin', Ilan (2011: 1) notes that many residents in an inner-city community ('Northstreet') had 'developed a rough cultural code in response to their experiences of poverty and social exclusion'. Traditionally these communities have tolerated certain types of criminal behaviour and are mistrustful and hostile towards institutions such as An Garda Síochána and other services that represent the state's authority.

It would appear that young people living in areas of social and economic disadvantage are at an increased risk of becoming involved in criminality. Young people with intellectual disability are also disproportionately represented within the criminal justice system.

LEGISLATIVE FRAMEWORK

Children Act 1908

The Children Act 1908, a landmark document for the care of children in Ireland, was passed in Westminster while Ireland was under British colonial rule. At the time it was seen as a progressive piece of legislation (Seymour, 2006; Kilkelly, 2006). It attempted to apply a unified system of law to deal with children's issues. A key aspect of the legislation was the provision for juvenile offending. It established juvenile courts and Section 107 made provision for the supervision of young offenders by the Probation Service. Other provisions such as the payment of a fine, compensation or costs by an offender and the detention of a young offender where deemed appropriate (Kilkelly, 2006). This Act remained largely unchanged until the 1990s in Ireland.

UN Convention on the Rights of the Child

The Convention on the Rights of the Child (UNCRC) was adopted by the United Nations in 1989 and ratified by Ireland in 1992. It states that children should be detained only as a last resort and, in such cases where children are imprisoned, for an appropriately short period of time. It prohibits the imprisonment of a child for life. It requires states to establish an age of criminal responsibility below which it is presumed that children are not legally and morally culpable for their actions (Kilkelly, 2006). It also requires them to have a variety of options available, such as probation, diversion projects, alternative care providers and vocational and educational training programmes, 'to ensure that children are dealt with in a manner appropriate to their well-being and proportionate both to their circumstances and the offence' (Kilkelly, 2006: xviii).

Children Act 2001

The Children Act 2001 can be viewed as one of the most important pieces of legislation to be enacted in Ireland. Its objective was not only to replace the almost century-old Children Act 1908, but also to bring about a significant ideological shift regarding best practice in relation to working with young offenders. The 2001 Act aims to promote the use of community-based sanctions as an alternative to detention. It employs the principles of restorative justice to encourage young offenders to address their anti-social or offending behaviour and change it so they can positively contribute to society and reduce reoffending. The focus of the act is on the welfare, treatment and rehabilitation of young offenders.

Responsibility for the Act is shared between the Minister for Children and Youth Affairs and the Minister for Justice, Equality and Defence. The Minister for Justice, Equality and Defence has responsibility for:

- The three children detention schools at Oberstown, Lusk, Co. Dublin.
- All policy and law relating to young offenders, including crime prevention, reduction and detection, criminal proceedings, diversion programmes and community sanctions (including community projects).
- An Garda Síochána, the Probation Service and the Irish Prison Service (St Patrick's Institution), which all have a juvenile justice responsibility within their brief (IYJS, 2012b).

AGE OF CRIMINAL RESPONSIBILITY

The Children Act 2001 increased the age of criminal responsibility from seven to twelve years. Section 52(1) states that 'it shall be conclusively presumed that no child under the age of twelve is capable of committing an offence'. This means that children who have not reached the age of twelve years cannot be charged with an offence. There are two exceptions:

- Children aged ten or eleven can be charged with murder, manslaughter, rape or aggravated sexual assault (as amended by the Criminal Justice Act 2006).
- Where a child under fourteen years of age is charged with an offence, no further proceedings can be taken without the consent of the Director of Public Prosecutions.

Although children younger than twelve years of age are prohibited under the 2001 Act from being charged and convicted of a criminal offence, they do not enjoy total immunity from action being taken against them. Section 53 of the Act, as amended by Section 130 of the Criminal Justice Act 2006, places an onus on gardaí to bring children younger than twelve years of age to their parents or guardian, if they have reasonable grounds for believing the child has committed an offence. The Children Act 2001 also makes it possible for children under twelve years of age who commit criminal offences to be dealt with by the Health Service Executive (HSE) and not within the criminal justice system.

THE CHILDREN COURT

A juvenile court system was established by the Children Act 1908. These courts had the power to deal with children who had come into conflict with the law up until the age of seventeen years. Section 71 of the Children Act 2001 replaced the juvenile courts with what is now referred to as the Children Court. The Children Court has the power to deal with both offending and non-offending children up to the age of eighteen years.

The 2001 Act directs that the Children Court should be held in a different building to courts for adults. Where this is not possible, the sitting of the Children Court must be in a different part of the building or at different times to other court proceedings. The Act also stipulates that the child should be kept apart from adult defendants (other than adult co-defendants) and that the amount of time that children have to wait for proceedings to take place be kept to a minimum.

Protection of the child's identity

Section 41 of the Children Act 2001 ensures that a child's identity is protected and that all cases are heard in camera, meaning that the only people permitted to attend the court proceedings are those who are directly involved with the case such as the officers of the court: the judge, the court clerk, gardaí, solicitors involved in the case and the duty probation officer. The child's parents or guardians and adult relatives of the child along with bona fide members of the press may also be present but no members of the public are permitted. The Act also places restrictions on the reporting, publishing or broadcasting of any information about the child that could result in the child being identified.

Parental responsibility

The Children Act 2001 obliges parents or guardians to be present at all of their child's court appearances. They are required to attend, participate and comply with all court requests and directions; for example, they may be requested to participate in a family conference in respect of their child. Parents may also be asked to pay compensation for offences committed by their children and they may be ordered by the court to exercise control over their children. The Children Court also has the power to adjourn proceedings and issue a warrant for the arrest of parents or guardians who fail to attend court proceedings 'without a reasonable excuse'.

RESTORATIVE JUSTICE

The Children Act 2001 introduced the concept of restorative justice to juvenile justice in Ireland. The philosophy at the centre of this tradition is the notion of responsibility and atonement or pay back. According to Zehr (2002: 27), 'restorative Justice is a process to involve, to the extent possible, those who have a stake in a specific offence and to collectively identify and address harms, needs and obligations, in order to heal and put things as right as possible'. Restorative justice is provided for in the Children Act 2001 by way of having the victim present at a formal caution or family welfare conference. In both settings, the victim of the offence is given the opportunity to have a face-to-face meeting with the offender or have their views presented to the offender through a mediator or by letter. The hope is that the offender will realise that the offence is not merely against the law but that their actions impact adversely on others. This process challenges the offending behaviour and offers the offender an opportunity to apologise and repair the damage. This may be done via an action such as replacing the stolen goods, repairing damage to property or through compensation (An Garda Síochána, 2012).

IRISH YOUTH JUSTICE SERVICE

In 2005, following a review of the juvenile justice system, the government agreed that reform was needed. Amendments were made to the Children Act 2001 in the form of the Criminal Justice Act 2006, and the Irish Youth Justice Service (IYJS) was established. This new service was given responsibility for leading and driving reform in the area of juvenile justice in Ireland. The remit of the IYJS is guided by the principles of the Children Act 2001 and it has established the following goals (IYJS, 2012c):

- To provide leadership and build public confidence in the youth justice system.
- To work to reduce offending by diverting young people from offending behaviour.
- To promote the greater use of community sanctions and initiatives to deal with young people who offend.
- To provide a safe and secure environment for detained children that will assist their early reintegration into the community.
- To strengthen and develop information and data sources in the youth justice system to support more effective policies and services.

The IYJS funds organisations and projects providing services to young offenders who may be involved with An Garda Síochána, the Probation Service and the Courts Service. It is also responsible for the development and management of an integrated children detention school service (IYJS, 2012a).

AN GARDA SÍOCHÁNA

According to Seymour (2006), it is the policy of An Garda Síochána not to prosecute juvenile offenders unless their previous offence(s) or current offence is considered serious enough to warrant such an action. An Garda Síochána has a number of strategies available to it when working with young offenders.

Good behaviour contracts and anti-social behaviour orders

Part 12A of the Children Act 2001 legislates for good behaviour contracts (GBCs) and anti-social behaviour orders (ASBOs) as amended by Part 13, Section 257A-(2) of the Criminal Justice Act 2006. According to the 2006 Act, children behave in an anti-social manner if they cause, or in the circumstances are likely to cause, to one or more persons who are not of the same household as the child: (a) harassment, (b) significant or persistent alarm, distress, fear or intimidation, or (c) significant or persistent impairment of their use or enjoyment of their property.

These measures were introduced in March 2007 amid much controversy. They were strongly criticised by many, including the Irish Penal Reform Trust; children's rights groups such as the Children's Rights Alliance; and Youth Work Ireland. Hamilton and Seymour (2006: 62) suggest 'the introduction of anti-social behaviour orders create a legal mechanism which facilitates the imposition of the majority conception of order within the community on its more marginalised members such as children and young people'.

The key features of ASBOs for children that differ from those for adults are the series of stages before an ASBO can be sought (including a 'behaviour warning', a GBC and referral to the Garda Diversion Programme); involvement by parents is required, particularly in the case of a GBC; and an application for an order can only be made by a Garda superintendent in the Children Court (DoJE, 2012a).

Garda Diversion Programmes

The Children Act 2001 formally established the Garda Diversion Programmes. These had been in existence on an informal, non-statutory basis since the 1960s. The scheme permits gardaí to deal informally with offenders younger than eighteen years of age who have committed a criminal offence. There are members of the force who have received specialised training to work with young people who offend and their families. They are referred to as juvenile liaison officers (JLOs).

To be considered eligible for the JLO process, youths must satisfy a number of criteria. They must be at least ten years of age and be under seventeen years of age but this can be extended to the age of eighteen years. They must take responsibility for their behaviour (there must be an admission of guilt) and they must also give consent to be cautioned and, where appropriate, to supervision by the JLO. A case may be regarded as unsuitable if the child does not accept responsibility for the behaviour or if the child is offending persistently.

Garda Diversion Programmes aim:

1. To provide an alternative to court for young people who have offended. Instead of a formal charge and prosecution, the child is cautioned (they receive a warning in relation to their behaviour). This can be an informal or formal caution. An informal caution may be given to the young person in their own home or in the garda station by the JLO. A formal caution, which is given in accordance with Sections 26 and 29 of the Children Act 2001, may also be given for more serious offences. Where the caution refers to a more serious offence it must be given by a garda inspector or a more senior-ranking garda. The young person's parents or guardian must be present when a caution is given.
2. To divert young people from further offending. A young person who is given a formal warning is also placed under the supervision of the JLO. The young person is not obliged to attend meetings, but is aware that their behaviour is being monitored by An Garda Síochána.
3. The young person will not receive a criminal conviction for the offence.

Garda Youth Diversion Projects

Garda Youth Diversion Projects (GYDPs) are funded by the Irish Youth Justice Service. They work with young people aged twelve to eighteen years. They are community-based and offer a multiagency approach to youth crime prevention. The projects endeavour to divert young people away from anti-social and/or criminal behaviour. They do this through modelling pro-social behaviours and by engaging the young people in pro-social activities that facilitate personal development. They also promote civic responsibility and improve long-term employability prospects through education programmes.

The projects also work with young people who may not have committed an offence but are significantly at risk of becoming involved in anti-social and/or criminal behaviour. The child is referred to a project by a JLO; however, a child can also be referred by another garda, another agency, a community worker or a family member. In 2012 there were 100 GYDPs nationwide (An Garda Síochána, 2012).

THE PROBATION SERVICE

The Probation Service is an agency within the Department of Justice and Equality. Its role is to work with offenders to assess their risk of offending and/or harm; to challenge offending behaviour and motivate behavioural change; to supervise offenders in the community as directed by the courts; and to support offenders making the transition from prison or places of detention into the community (Probation Service, 2012a).

Young Persons' Probation (YPP)

Following the commencement of the Children Act 2001, the Probation Service established a specialist division in 2006 known as Young Persons' Probation (YPP). The role of YPP is to work exclusively with children and young people aged twelve to eighteen years who come before the courts or those detained in St Patrick's Institution or the children's detention centres. The YPP works from a child-centred approach and takes the view that all decisions must be in the best interest of the child (O'Leary and Halton, 2009). The work of the YPP involves facilitating family welfare conferences, preparing pre-sanction assessments for the courts, supervising offenders in the community who are referred by the courts, supervising offenders released conditionally from custody, attending sittings of the Children Court and offering advice to the court as requested (Probation Service, 2012e).

The Children Act 2001 stresses that the detention of juvenile offenders should occur only as a last resort when all community-based sanctions have been exhausted. Therefore, it is imperative that the seriousness of the offending and the risk of further offending are assessed. Part 9 of the 2001 Act provides the Children Court with ten community sanctions as an alternative to detention when dealing with juvenile offenders. Nine of these involve the input of the Probation Service. In 2011 there were 947 community sanctions made by the Children Court that involved some form of YPP supervision (Probation Service, 2012d).

The Probation Service may become involved in the criminal justice process between the prosecution of an offender and the trial. Probation officers may be required to hold a family conference. These are based on the principles of restorative justice. A family welfare conference may occur at the direction of the court (see Figure 24.1).

An action plan made as a result of the family conference may include: an apology to the victim, financial or other reparation to any victim, and initiatives within the child's family and community that might help to prevent reoffending (Probation Service, 2012b).

Figure 24.1. The role of the Children Court and the Probation Service in family welfare conferencing

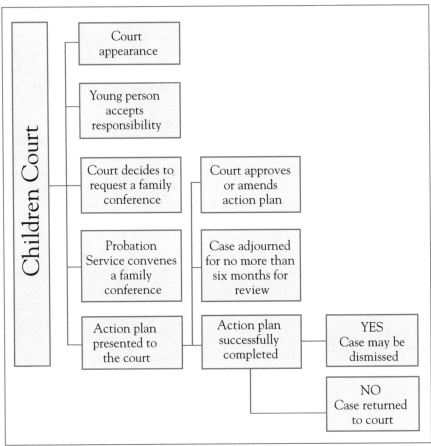

Source: Probation Service (2012b)

During 2011 the Children Court made 914 requests for pre-sanction reports to be prepared by YPP. A pre-sanction report provides the court with a detailed personal profile, offending history and an assessment of the risk of reoffending. The pre-sanction assessment and report may be used by the court to assist in deciding on an appropriate sanction (Probation Service, 2012b). As the principle of the Children Act 2001 is minimal detention with an emphasis on community-based sanctions, there is a need to establish the level of risk, the seriousness of the crime and also the likelihood of reoffending.

ASSESSMENT OF RISK

O'Leary and Halton (2009: 98) maintain that with such an 'array of community sanctions available under the Children Act, particular demands are placed on the professional in terms of determining a recommendation that meets the seriousness of the offence, the suitability of the offender to the various penalties and the likelihood of the offender reoffending'. As a result, YPP has adopted the Youth Level of Service/Case Management Inventory (YLS/CMI) to inform the assessment of a young person's likelihood of reoffending.

Risk factors can be classified as static and dynamic. Static risk factors do not change, whereas dynamic risk factors can. Static risk factors may include historical characteristics such as age, prior offence history, the age at which prior offences were committed and the number of prior arrests or convictions. Dynamic factors include drug or alcohol use, poor attitude (for example, low remorse and victim-blaming), low educational/vocational attainment and anti-social attitude. These dynamic risk factors can be addressed through interventions made by the Probation Service, An Garda Síochána and Garda Diversion Programmes. As these attitudes decrease, the level of risk of reoffending can also decrease and therefore it is important that a risk assessment is conducted every six months to establish any changes.

Community sanctions available to the Children Court

The Children Act 2001 provides for an array of community sanctions that are at the disposal of the Children Court. These vary in severity, length and requirements, ranging from restriction of movement to intensive probation supervision (see Figure 24.2).

Children's detention schools

Children detention schools are used to detain children who have criminal charges and or convictions. The Children Court can remand a child in custody or while awaiting trial for criminal charges. Children may also be detained in a detention school following a conviction where the Children Court has found that a community sanction is not appropriate. There are currently three detention schools: Trinity House School, Oberstown Boys' School and Oberstown Girls' School. They are all located on the same campus at Oberstown, near Lusk, in north Co. Dublin. Section 158 of the Children Act 2001 states that the detention schools must provide appropriate education and training programmes with the aim of reintegrating the children back into the community with the skills necessary to lead a pro-social lifestyle and reduce their risk of reoffending.

The IYJS is responsible for overseeing the development of a new national children's detention facility on the Oberstown Campus. In 2012 the government

Figure 24.2. Community sanction orders available to the courts under Part 9 of the Children Act 2001

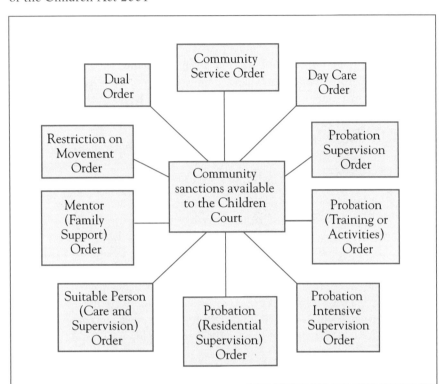

Source: Probation Service (2012c)

confirmed that €50 million in capital funding is being provided to deliver the facility, designed to bring to an end the practice of detaining 16- and 17-year-old boys in St Patrick's Institution. This facility is scheduled to open in 2015 (IYJS, 2012c).

St Patrick's Institution

St Patrick's Institution is a closed, medium-security place of detention located on the North Circular Road, Dublin 7, adjacent to Mountjoy Prison. It has the capacity to accommodate 217 young men between the ages of sixteen and twenty-one years, who may be on remand (awaiting trail) or sentenced prisoners. During 2011, 1,481 young men were committed into custody, of whom 90 were aged sixteen, 141 were aged seventeen, and the remainder (1,250) were aged between eighteen and twenty-three (IYJS, 2012b).

In June 2012 the Inspector of Prisons, Judge Michael Reilly, presented his inspection report to the Minister for Justice and Equality, Alan Shatter. The report (DoJE, 2012b) was critical of the management, staff and facilities available to the children and young adults detained in St Patrick's Institution. The report expressed concern that the rights of the children and young adults detained in St Patrick's were in some cases being ignored or violated. This was not the first time that St Patrick's had received condemnation. Other children's rights interest groups have criticised the facility over many years, including the UN Committee on the Rights of the Child, European Committee for the Prevention of Torture and Inhuman or Degrading Treatment or Punishment, Irish Penal Reform Trust, Children's Rights Alliance and Fr Peter McVerry Trust (Ombudsman for Children's Office, 2011).

CONCLUSION

In Ireland, the notion of rehabilitation is embedded in the legislation that governs Irish juvenile justice. This has led to a significant change in how Irish society engages with young people who come into conflict with the law. This chapter has sought to give an overview of the juvenile justice system in Ireland. It highlighted the philosophical and legislative changes that have taken place in Ireland, and the roles of the Children Court, An Garda Síochána, Garda Diversion Programmes and the Probation Service in juvenile justice. It outlined the work of the various agencies involved in working with young people who offend and the community sanctions that are at the disposal of the Children Court.

25

Social care in a multicultural society

Celesta McCann James

OVERVIEW

Ireland has become a country of immigration, with movement, relocation and resettlement occurring for thousands of individuals. Emigration among Irish nationals has also increased sharply in recent years, with 87,100 people emigrating over the twelve months to April 2012. During the same twelve-month period the number of immigrants remained stable at around 53,000 (CSO, 2011b). The 2011 census revealed that 17 per cent of the present population of Ireland, or 766,770 people, were born outside the country, and over half a million people are speaking a language other than English or Irish at home (CSO, 2011a). Trends such as these have resulted in definitions and experiences of 'modern Irish society' being challenged and changed. Irish society has become more diverse with 188 countries being represented in the non-Irish-national population (CSO, 2011d). There has been an associated increase in the perception of 'difference' in relation to, for example, skin colour, clothing or religion.

'Multiculturalism' describes an ideology and subsequent social policies or institutions that imply a recognition and validation of ethnocultural minorities, as well as the promotional acceptance of difference, including societal structures that support ethnic organisations and common concerns, such as human rights or fear of racism. In order to put the discussion of social care provision and multiculturalism into an Irish perspective, this chapter presents modern trends in immigration and identifies policy issues and current responses that support or neglect the care needs of immigrants. Having outlined social care provision for immigrants, the chapter will then contextualise key concepts related to a multicultural society: ethnicity, racism and, in particular, institutional oppression. By recognising the effects of oppression on social institutions, the chapter will help to clarify challenges that face the social care profession. A model for strategic change will be presented that offers an integrated approach to best practice for all those involved in social care practice in a multicultural society.

It is acknowledged that any discussion on multiculturalism in Ireland is incomplete without reference to Travellers. Their specific contribution to, and participation in, Irish society is discussed in Chapter 21.

INTRODUCTION

'Immigrant' is the term generally used to describe those individuals or groups of individuals who come from another country and are granted legal permission to live in a host country. Most definitions imply a permanent or semi-permanent residency to a specific country, regulated by state legislation regarding rights to employment, education, health services and so on. In comparison, the term 'migrant' is applied to individuals who are primarily motivated by economics and who usually move within or from their own country with the purpose of seeking employment. Migrants may move to a number of places, doing seasonal work or living temporarily in any given location. The terms 'immigrant' and 'migrant' are used interchangeably in Irish literature, with only minor differentiation, if any, being highlighted (for example, Feldman et al., 2008).

For many Irish citizens, previously accustomed to a single, dominant culture, the exposure to different traditions, customs and routines is an unfamiliar reality. New faces, identities and practices appear in shops, schools and the media, at recreational facilities and local pubs and, sometimes, next door. Among the newcomers are both those seeking economic and/or social opportunities and those seeking asylum and refuge. Ireland is legally and socially obliged to admit refugees, if and when their case is proven. It also has a political and moral duty to ensure that immigrants have access to appropriate legal, social, health and educational services.

Some political and media speculation has fuelled hostility towards immigrants, portraying them as 'illegal' or 'bogus' non-nationals and unworthy of social assistance that is not rightfully theirs, thereby costing the Irish taxpayer unfairly and unjustly. In her research into the link between migrants and social resources in the Dublin 15 area, Ní Chonaill (2007) found that while some Irish people view migrants' presence and participation as acceptable when resources are abundant (jobs, housing), views are very different when resources are perceived as scarce (school places). Ní Chonaill's research parallels findings from Balibar (1991) and Lewis (2005), which also indicate that refugees and migrants are blamed for scarcity in social resources.

This discourse distracts attention from the Irish government's failure to plan and provide for adequate public services. Lorenz (1998) notes that this perceived misappropriation of taxpayers' money is not limited to existing definitions commonly associated with commercial transactions (such as having paid into insurance funds as a precondition for getting benefits), but through cultural criteria such as not being 'of the same kind'. Analysis by the IZA and ESRI (2011) indicates that migrants do not use welfare in Ireland more than native Irish do. Indeed, some use significantly less welfare. There are structural mechanisms in place such as the residency requirement and the contributory nature of benefits that keep immigrants out of the welfare system for an initial period.

Closer inspection of Irish statistics reveals that the majority of immigrants are Irish returning from abroad or Europeans from other European Union countries.

In total, the number of non-Irish nationals in 2002 was recorded at 224,261 persons. By 2006 this had increased to 419,733, representing an increase of 87 per cent. The growth in the number of non-Irish nationals has continued, albeit at a slower pace, and their number stood at 544,357 at the time of the 2011 census (CSO, 2012b).

EMERGING TRENDS IN IMMIGRATION AND CARE PROVISION

Recent years have produced a growing body of research evidence on changing migration patterns in Ireland. In addition to migration between European Union countries, specific attention has been given to the upsurge of individuals and minority groups who enter Ireland either as refugees or as asylum seekers. The Office of the Refugee Applications Commissioner (ORAC, 2010: 6) defines a refugee as:

> A person who, owing to a well-founded fear of being persecuted for reasons of race, religion, nationality, membership of a particular social group or political opinion, is outside the country of his or her nationality and is unable or, owing to such fear, is unwilling to avail himself or herself of the protection of that country; or who, not having a nationality and being outside of the country of his or her former habitual residence, is unable or, owing to such fear, is unwilling to return to it.

In comparison, an asylum seeker is defined as (ORAC, 2010: 6):

> A person who seeks to be recognised as a refugee in accordance with the terms of the 1951 Geneva Convention relating to the status of refugees and related 1967 Protocol, which provides the foundation for the international protection of refugees.

According to ORAC (2010), in 1992 there were just thirty-nine applications for asylum in Ireland; by 2002 this number had risen to 11,634. In 2005 applications decreased to 4,323 and by 2010 the number was down to 1,939. From 1992 to 2010 a total of 85,000 applications were processed. This change has been accompanied by serious economic and social challenges, particularly experienced in the east of the country, where major responsibility for the needs of asylum seekers falls to the Eastern region of the Health Service Executive (HSE).

Implications for social care provision coincide with wider political, social and economic concerns where parity of opportunities is conditional on social policies and legislation that define entitlements. Government reports show that immigrants are twice as likely to be experiencing consistent poverty and deprivation as Irish nationals (Government of Ireland, 2007). Employment, enterprise, education and welfare rights are partly restricted as a result of policies such as the habitual residence condition, which restricts new immigrants from access to certain social welfare assistance payments and child benefits (DSFA, 2011; Nasc, 2012).

Separated children

Amongst the thousands of individuals, families and groups migrating to Ireland, many are children, accompanied or unaccompanied, seeking refuge and asylum. In 2002 there were 2,678 children applying for asylum in Ireland; by 2010 this figure had decreased to 573 of which thirty-seven (6.5 per cent) were received from separated children (ORAC, 2010). These children are considered vulnerable and depend upon a humane and compassionate response from Ireland's social care services. Their situation has prompted research to explore procedures and working relationships between Irish social care professionals and separated children of ethnic minority backgrounds. The Irish Refugee Council (IRC, 1999) and Barnardos (2011a) argue that, for separated children, immigration status should not be the state's priority, rather their wellbeing as children should take precedence. Care should also be delivered in the context of the Irish state's obligation to treat all children in its jurisdiction equally (UNCRC, 2005). The vast majority of separated children are referred to the Eastern region of the HSE and most are placed in voluntary care under the Child Care Act 1991. In 2011 there were approximately 180 separated children in the HSE's care (HSE, 2011c).

While we know little about why separated children leave their country of origin, research by Vekić (2003) and Conroy (2004) cite factors such as escaping war and discrimination, parental detention or death, and poverty. Joyce and Quinn (2009) reveal that children seek entry to Ireland to receive medical attention or education or to join family members. Their findings also show that some children are trafficked into the country to enter forced labour or prostitution. Regardless of why children arrive, the UN Convention on the Rights of the Child, in Article 22(1), states that:

> . . . parties shall take appropriate measures to ensure that a child who is seeking refugee status . . . shall, whether unaccompanied or accompanied by his or her parents or by any other person, receive appropriate protection and humanitarian assistance in the enjoyment of applicable rights set forth in the present Convention and in other international human rights or humanitarian instruments to which the said States are Parties.

The parties to this Convention also undertook, in Article 22(2), to co-operate with different organisations, not only to protect and assist refugee children but also to help trace family members in order to facilitate family reunification. Articles 19, 34, 37(a) and 37(c) of the Convention state that, if reunification with family is unsuccessful, the child shall be accorded the same protection as any other children permanently or temporarily deprived of their family environment. In Ireland, explicit provisions in the Child Care Act 1991 specify that unaccompanied minors are to be provided for. This includes an obligation under Article 3(2)(a) on the part of the HSE to identify children who are not receiving adequate care and protection. In addition, it is the duty of the HSE, under Article 4(1), to take into care any child residing or located in its area who is requiring care or protection.

Significant concerns arise in relation to social care provision for children who are members of ethnic minority groups and separated from their families. Until recently, separated children in care did not automatically benefit from the same services as Irish children in care. Older teenagers were placed in hostels rather than residential children's homes and the Social Services Inspectorate did not monitor their accommodation and subsequent services. Older children who were not reunited with their family were placed in self-catering hostels, where they received full supplementary welfare allowance (€124.80 per week) and prepared their own meals. Interim care became the responsibility of a social welfare team who worked in partnership with hostel staff to access medical and social services for minors, including appointments with the Refugee Legal Service, ORAC and Refugee Appeals Tribunal. Hostels did not have round-the-clock trained carers on site and were run by managers and security personnel. Consequently, between 2000 and 2010, 513 separated children went missing from state care and 440 of them remain unaccounted for (Barnardos, 2011b).

According to a report by McEvoy and Smith (2011) on behalf of the Department of Children and Youth Affairs, the use of residential hostels for older teenagers ceased in December 2010 and the HSE has taken steps to ensure that all unregistered hostels for separated children are closed, with children being placed for assessment towards foster care or supported lodging. Four residential units became operational in early February 2010 and all were registered with the Social Services Inspectorate and the Health Information and Quality Authority (HIQA) and are subject to inspection. The HSE also appointed a social care agency to run the units and provide a 24-hour care service. Resulting from this change of practice, the HSE progressed towards implementing equity of treatment and care for all separated children in the state to ensure equal access to care placement and education services. One possible result of these changes is that figures for 2011 indicate that no separated children have gone missing from state care; however, there are still concerns for those missing from earlier care (Barnardos, 2011b).

As the Child Care Act 1991 does not specifically refer to 'separated children', non-Irish unaccompanied minors seeking refuge or asylum are treated as homeless Irish children for welfare purposes. Care, therefore, is often inappropriate and disordered as it has not been designed for specific circumstances such as experience of recent trauma, coping with a new and unfamiliar culture, a different language, an unfamiliar educational system or the absence of family and friends. In addition, social care providers are constrained by a lack of resources such as training in language and cultural diversity. In response, the Office of the Minister for Children published *Diversity and Equality Guidelines for Childcare Providers* (OMC, 2006a). This provides relevant and practical information regarding steps towards supporting equal and inclusive treatment and encourages the development of services that are inclusive of all children and their families.

Other issues related to cultural diversity

As crucial as it is to implement practical and effective care for separated children, we must not overlook the increasing challenge that faces the profession in providing care for other service-user groups. As in the 'Irish' community, ethnic minority groups have members who are disabled, elderly, homeless or socially troubled. Many newcomers enter Ireland as family groups and will present needs to professional care services that are broader than the requirement to assist separated children. In many ways, care practitioners are already overstretched and under-resourced — how much more stretched will the profession be when caring for young and heavily pregnant women, people with disabilities or older people who have little English and unfamiliar cultural practices?

Practitioners and service users recognise that language and cultural barriers can limit the provision of effective and meaningful social care. When a service user and a worker do not speak the same language, we can expect that cultural understanding may also be absent or at least problematic. The social care profession, therefore, is faced with the challenge of informing its practice with theoretical knowledge, skill-based experience and attitudinal competencies that reflect an inclusive, multicultural Ireland. This is not a challenge that will be easily met, but it can be addressed purposefully and systematically.

O'Loingsigh (2001) maintains that although structural barriers inhibit the active or real participation by ethnic minorities in the educational system, intercultural education is an education for both the minorities and the majority community in Irish society. Fundamental instruction in communicative and cultural acquisition could be required as part of the curriculum offered to future care practitioners, a curriculum that explores and applies tolerance, human rights, democracy and respect for difference, rather than concerning itself with 'integrating' ethnic minorities into a social care system that makes service users 'more Irish'.

Many of the third-level institutions offering qualifications in social care practice integrate intercultural training into their academic programmes. Some offer full modules on cultural diversity, as well as research opportunities for undergraduate and postgraduate students. This is facilitated through regular exposure to, and experience with, diverse ethnic communities and practices throughout Irish society as well as participation in social care practice placement arrangements outside Ireland.

CURRENT CHALLENGES

As a profession, social care practice is faced with the challenge of providing adequate and appropriate care to vulnerable service users, such as minors, people with disabilities, older people and homeless people. For some service users, their national and cultural characteristics may be different from those of the dominant Irish culture. Such distinctions do not make physical and social needs less legitimate, nor do they dilute the legal responsibility or social obligations to provide a fair and humane service to all those residing in the state.

By definition, social care services reflect more than physical or material support, thus, practitioners are drawn into an ethical and philosophical sphere, where cultural uncertainties cause them to examine their beliefs and values. The following questions deserve consideration by all social care practitioners:

- Can society continue to prioritise care on the basis of dominant social and cultural practices?
- Is social care afforded only to those in society who are 'worthy' members of the dominant culture (such as Irish or EU citizens) or perhaps only to those individuals who make 'genuine' contributions through voluntary or paid work?
- Are Irish social services provided or withheld on the basis of nationality, contributions, ethnicity or need?
- Will the state develop and deliver social care services that are capable of providing effective support for all residents in Ireland who need care?
- Whose interests are being served in the present provision of social care: those of state officials, administrators or taxpayers, or those who are users of care services?
- Will the Irish social care profession progress to ensure that ethnic and cultural differences are embraced thoughtfully and sensitively, guaranteeing a truly caring service that is inclusive of all those seeking or depending on its provision?

Questions such as these are difficult to ask, but even more problematic to answer. Responses and solutions are dependent on complex systems that involve philosophies, politics and practices from a variety of perspectives. Inevitably they involve the use of concepts such as ethnicity, racism and oppression.

Ethnicity

The term 'ethnicity' derives from the Greek *ethnos*, meaning people or tribe. Simply defined, ethnicity describes characteristics that relationally connect people together in a manner that negotiates a group identity, be it political, religious, cultural or social. The underlying beliefs and values that support such a bond offer solidarity and a 'sense of belonging', collective membership and shared experiences. According to Smith (1991), ethnic groups may be defined both internally and externally, offering a way of distinguishing 'them' from 'us'. Members of an ethnic group possess cultural solidity that often extends from generation to generation, making them eligible to access the social, emotional and physical benefits of 'inclusion' within their community. Unity is reinforced when an ethnic group sustains a collective sense of continuity by adopting a specific name, sharing historical memories and/or common ancestry, associating with a specific homeland or differentiating elements of common culture, beliefs and boundaries (Glazer and Moynihan, 1975; Jenkins, 1996, 1997).

The issue of ethnicity is inevitably linked with questions of identity and difference. Although not unique, until recently Ireland has been categorised as a monocultural society with social institutions that reinforce sameness. As a result, Irish identity has exhibited specific forms of approved social practices, be they political, economic, religious, educational or familial. This 'institutionalised culture' has informed and influenced individuals and group relationships and has defined dominant values and patterns of behaviour. Similar to sociological norms in other cultures, Ireland's ethnic and other minority communities have been socially stratified, being organised in a subordinate fashion and allowed, at the very most, to be identified as Irish subcultures (see the discussion of Traveller ethnicity in Chapter 21).

Racism

Racism is a term used by sociologists to denote a belief (or an action based on belief) that one racial category is superior or inferior to another racial category. Racism defines patterns of thought or action that allow individuals or groups to be considered different, often with negative consequences. Whether or not the thought or action intends to inspire discrimination is irrelevant, as racism is seen to exist when a deliberate or unintentional attitude or behaviour disadvantages the social position of a specific racially defined group in society. Ireland has participated in the debate about racism and nationalism, seeking its own clarity as to the implications of 'Irishness' and citizenship. It has sought answers in relation to the rapid changes from traditional understandings of national identity within the economy, family structure, religion and language (Farrell and Watt, 2001; Lentin, 1998; Royal Irish Academy, 2003).

Institutional oppression

Oppression describes a complex situation that may result from many processes. It is a condition that is relatively stable and may be reflected in, for example, the education system, the legal system, the media and social customs. What separates it from other kinds of mistreatment is its systematic nature; that is, the mistreatment is part of the social system. It is a structure of inequality where one group systematically dominates the other by means of interrelated social practices

(Frye, 1983). Systematic domination is also present when hierarchical controls exist that are not consensual and that involve institutionalised inequality (Moane, 1994). Whenever there is systematic domination of the members of one group by the members of another group or by society in general, we call it oppression. The presence of ethnic or racial discrimination in society is categorised as oppressive, then, when social structures are organised and operate in a way that maintains discriminating and unequal practices. For example, the social ranking or stratification of particular ethnic groups or communities may disadvantage their access to and equal participation in social services.

Oppression is not a random affair: it is predictable (Knoppers, 1993). If we say that individuals or particular groups (such as refugees) are oppressed in Irish society, we should be able to predict the kinds of experiences they are likely to confront. These experiences will be encountered regardless of which individual member is involved. Although oppression can take the form of deliberate and premeditated abuse of vulnerable individuals or groups, it is described more often as camouflaged and operating within socially approved and authorised structures. Difficulty (or unwillingness) to discern the systematic nature of oppression facilitates its continuance and helps to maintain unequal power structures.

Knoppers (1993) claims that oppression is easily reproduced because its features become intertwined in society, where both dominants and subordinates fail to 'see' or 'feel' it in their lives. Moane (1994, 1999) maintains that although patterns of oppression are generally unrecognised, most signs that are visible are viewed as unalterable. This helps to sustain longstanding hierarchical management and social systems. It is therefore understandable that institutional oppression, as encountered in the social care system, may be viewed as impenetrable. Although social care practitioners may not consciously participate in oppressive behaviour, existing mechanisms that surround and support them facilitate the continuation of discriminating programmes and regimes.

Moane (1994) has identified psychological and social patterns associated with being dominant or subordinate in a hierarchical system. She emphasises the link between oppression and areas of psychological functioning that can be understood only by analysing the social context of individuals' lives. The central feature of this social context is that it is hierarchical, or stratified, so that a select number of people have access to power and resources, while other people are deprived of the same. Applying this framework, we now go on to explore the provision of social care services in Ireland and to draw parallels that reveal institutionalised patterns of control that legitimate the domination of dependent and vulnerable ethnic minority groups.

THE NATURE OF OPPRESSION IN SOCIAL CARE PRACTICE

Six indicators of oppression are listed below. Each demonstrates an association between existing social care practice and the institutional oppression of some ethnic minority groups in Ireland. Bear in mind that oppression is predictable, therefore experiences in any of the following categories are likely to apply to most members of discriminated groups, regardless of which individual encounters them.

1. *Physical control* is a primary mechanism of oppression and is reflected in punishment or the threat of it to ensure co-operation. It operates in a hierarchical system that depends on forms of coercion, intimidation, threats, imprisonment or beatings. Asylum seekers are physically controlled through the legal processes of immigration. The Refugee Act 1996, as amended by the Immigration Act 2003, incorporates provisions for asylum seekers under Section 9(10)(a). The legislation states that the individual must be brought before a judge of the District Court 'as soon as is practicable'. In practice, this would normally be the next sitting of the court. Individuals can be committed for ensuing periods of up to twenty-one days without charge by a judge, pending the determination of their application under Section 9(10)(b)(i). This is a recurring obligation if the judge orders the individual's continued detention. Asylum seekers are by definition then, subject to absolute physical control. They may additionally be referred to: one or more agencies under the Department of Justice and Equality (such as the Asylum Policy Commissioner or Refugee Appeals Tribunal), the UN High Commissioner for Refugees or non-statutory bodies. Non-compliance with any of these agencies may result in imprisonment.

2. *Economic control* reinforces physical control as members of the oppressed group are kept powerless by a prohibition on paid employment or by locating them in low-paid or low-status jobs. While such jobs may be a simple reflection of minimal skills, training or education, it can be argued that members of oppressed groups have a higher incidence of poverty and are less secure in their jobs than members of other groups because they regularly experience discrimination and lack of access to education and training. For refugees and asylum seekers, employment is prohibited while status decisions are pending; the HSE provides accommodation and 'direct provision' plus a personal allowance of just €19.10 per week to adults and €9.60 per week per child. Furthermore, lack of state support, language skills and information regarding their entitlements increases the risk of disadvantaged social status and economic control for refugees and asylum seekers in Ireland.

3. *Sexual exploitation* is a form of oppression, often operating through rape and prostitution. Research confirms that some minors who disappeared from the welfare system have subsequently been involved in trafficking or prostitution (Conroy, 2004; Joyce and Quinn, 2009).

4. *Exclusion* is a form of oppression that removes authority from the subordinate group by withholding power, either through restrictions or lack of representation. Exclusion can take on various forms. When members of minority ethnic groups are demeaned through physical and economic controls (such as

peripheral housing, language barriers, economic and employment restrictions), they are often excluded and marginalised socially, emotionally and politically from mainstream Irish society. They are perceived as 'different' and often 'unworthy' of meaningful participation or involvement in decision making. Under-representation by ethnic minorities in social care practice renders them less influential over decision making and service provision to service users. This may apply to input regarding policy change, care planning, cultural and religious practices, medical ethics and educational practices. It should be noted that the Office for Social Inclusion (OSI, 2007) and The Integration Centre (2011) have proposed that individuals directly affected by policies should be a part of the group(s) that are creating those policies.

5. *Psychological control* underlies most of the above forms of control. It is maintained by the dominant group controlling the definition of what is 'natural' or 'normal' for members of the oppressed group. 'Irish' ideology and culture are managed through the dominance of influential social systems such as education, the media, religion and language. As part of psychological control, there is a suppression (or erasure) of history and the propagation of stereotypes of inferiority, widely facilitated through prejudice, myths, misinformation and unawareness. As members of minority ethnic groups in Ireland, individuals are subjected to an Irish society that has, until recently, been culturally restricted and purposefully isolated. Social care services reflect this background and consequently provide support (and expect co-operation from service users) that largely operates according to the customs and routines of the dominant culture.

6. *Fragmentation and tokenism* regularly occur in a system that promotes a select few of the subordinate group, thereby creating competition and envy among the subordinates: a situation of 'divide and conquer'. Representation of most non-Irish ethnic groups is minimal in administrative departments in Irish social care. Members from minority ethnic communities may be seen in roles as interpreters or as volunteer workers and some are now visible as trained personnel, but individuals from minority ethnic backgrounds remain all but absent from decision-making authority and significant influence in the sector.

The above indicators demonstrate how members of some ethnic minority groups are oppressed and subsequently marginalised in Irish society. Whether for reasons of race or ethnic origin, physical or economic control, subjection to sexual exploitation, exclusion from meaningful participation and/or psychological dominance, many are left exposed and vulnerable. Even with the best of intentions, social care providers may fail to 'see' or 'feel' oppressive features that are systematically woven into the fabric of care services. As explained, 'systematic' implies that oppression is part of a larger social system and is marked by interrelated social practices that camouflage an inequitable structure of power differentials. Intent, therefore, is not an essential factor and an examination of social care services alone is not sufficient to determine whether social care environments are flawed or inadequate.

While most social care practitioners value self-reflective practice and operate with transparency, existing structural forms (for example, legislation and HSE regimes) reinforce the preservation of hierarchical decision making, enforced authority and management of services. Consequently, members of ethnic minorities who participate in social care services (including asylum seekers and refugees) may internalise their oppression (Ruth, 1988), believing they hold an inferior social status and are powerlessness to change things. They may comply with the status quo and so fail to confront the disadvantages and inequalities they are subjected to. As a result, many are pushed towards the margins of Irish society and are more likely to remain dependent upon inadequate social services in the future.

A MODEL FOR CHANGE

Irish society is at a crossroads and must choose whether or not to embrace diversity. The choice is between 'doing care unto them' in a patronising and oppressive manner or implementing care policies that are representative and inclusive. Even though Irish legislation, including the Refugee Act 1996 and the Child Care Act 1991, establish legal definitions and procedures for dealing with refugees and asylum seekers, the jury is still out as to whether Irish society will accept ethnic minorities as 'deserving' and 'worthy' social care service users.

An equally demanding test for Irish society will be whether or not to facilitate institutional change at all levels, including the dedicated recruitment of ethnic minority group members as social care practitioners and administrators. In other words, the Irish social care profession is faced with a dilemma: is there to be a restructuring of care participation and delivery? In order to explain how social care might renegotiate current service provision, four categories are proposed below within a new model for strategic change.

The identifier

The identifier is the individual or group with the authority or resources to ask and answer the following questions:

- Who or what determines and/or defines a given social need or problem?
- On what basis is it drawn into the public arena?
- Who or what sets the standards of what is worthy of disclosure, discussion, treatment, funding or change?

To some extent, EU membership brought Irish social services to account for the management and treatment of ethnic minority groups through relevant European directives and regulations. As a member state, Ireland is obliged to implement EU legislation at a national level for the benefit of Europe at large. A steady increase in immigrant numbers has been identified by Irish social institutions as requiring attention at a number of levels. Government departments and interest groups concerned with justice, education, employment, health, welfare and so on have provoked debate concerning the legitimacy of traditional Irish social practices and cultural beliefs based on homogeny. As *identifiers*, the EU, Irish government and special interest groups have contributed to the objectives and organisational structures of social care provision.

The identified

The identified may be a situation, problem, individual, group, agency or institution. Relevant questions that may be asked regarding the identified include:

- What role, if any, do the identified have in naming a given problem or situation?
- What power relationships exist between the identifier and the identified?
- Are there social structures that serve to advantage, disadvantage or equalise all participants?

Ethnic minorities have been *identified* as different or not 'belonging' in Ireland. Apart from a small number of token contributors, members from such communities are precluded from naming their care needs or solutions, thereby minimising their participation in social care services. Their existence is acknowledged, but little if any attention is given to ethnic members' analysis of their circumstances. Although gradually increasing through various agencies such as the Irish Refugee Council, the Centre for Criminal Justice and Human Rights and the Irish Human Rights Commission, research by or about refugees and/or asylum seekers remains insufficient. A lack of qualitative data providing first-hand accounts of the physical and social needs of ethnic minority groups will keep such groups on the fringes of meaningful social participation, leaving them in inferior positions and disadvantaged within a hierarchical social system.

The movement

Sometimes movement occurs because the identifier changes, or the identified changes or they both change. Sometimes neither changes. In order for movement to occur (or not occur), one must observe:

- Who or what changes?
- Does change occur as a result of pressure (or lack of pressure) from existing social structures and institutions?

- Does change come about as a result of public awareness, dissatisfaction, a sense of justice, or economic reality?
- How is change directed?
- What path does change take during the process of movement?
- When is change implemented and by whom or by what?

Although some movement concerning care provision for multicultural service users is occurring, most has been reactive rather than as a result of strategic social policy. Challenges include limited resources, lack of protective legislation, alarmist media coverage and indifferent public opinion regarding perceptions of 'foreigners' gaining access to 'our' social services (Christie, 2003; Lentin, 2007; Ní Chonaill, 2007).

An example of movement was evidenced through the 2004 constitutional amendment that redefined Irish citizenship. The result left multicultural Ireland socially divided, as some voters considered the new definition of 'Irish' as strengthening Irish identity, while others saw the constitutional change as intensifying racism and intolerance (see, for example, JCFJ, 2004; Lentin, 2004; Maguire and Cassidy, 2009). Citizenship prescribes equality between citizens not only in terms of rights but also in the way those rights are realised. Citizenship presumes that individuals will have an opportunity for meaningful participation in the economic and social life of their communities and guarantees, in principle, that citizens can access services without unnecessary restrictions or barriers.

To date, *movement* has been directed at providing minimal services for 'non-Irish' service users who are believed to be draining already-limited social care resources. While language, dietary, religious and other cultural distinctions have been integrated into some social care environments, they are less visible in many other settings. Care providers are largely from the dominant Irish culture and few are sufficiently trained in ethnic or cultural diversity.

The beneficiary

The beneficiary is the individual or group who receives assistance or who gains socially, economically, politically or culturally from social change. Clarification of this category requires answers to the following:

- Who or what benefits from movement or lack of movement?
- Is there an economic, social or cultural cost incurred?
- If change occurs, who or what is advantaged or disadvantaged?
- If change does not occur, who benefits from the status quo?

If change does not occur, there may be some short-term savings for the Exchequer, but there are no social *beneficiaries* and social services will probably be compromised. In order for Irish social care to benefit, a radical shift is needed in the social value of service users as well as standards of provision. All social care service users are entitled to an equality of service provision and are deserving of sensitive, respectful and non-discriminatory care. Inevitable benefits occur when changes focus on empowerment, inclusion and extended agency to minority groups as users and providers of care services. Only when multiculturalism inspires, rather than immobilises, social care services will there be the potential for meaningful reform.

CONCLUSION

A care service based on best practice must have at its core a regard for cultural diversity and a framework that incorporates the development and inclusion of 'difference'. It must unite service providers, service users, a range of communities and 'traditional Irish' society into an effective and transparent integrated whole. Integration within the social care profession will facilitate all participants to contribute fully without having to relinquish their cultural identity.

According to the then Department of Justice, Equality and Law Reform (DJELR, 2000: 9), 'the emphasis of integration policy should be on supporting initiatives which enable the preservation of ethnic, cultural and religious identity of the individual'. Accepting this assertion, it can be argued that an integration policy is not operating equitably if it requires cultural compromise or assimilation on the part of ethnic minorities. Recipients of Irish social care services are, by definition, vulnerable and dependent service users who are linked to state care, protection, support, welfare and advocacy. They are entitled, as indicated by government policy, to benefit from these 'initiatives which enable the preservation of [their] ethnic, cultural and religious identity'. They should not be required or expected to embrace a predefined form of Irishness, but should instead be provided with a service that strengthens material, social and emotional supports while respecting and valuing diversity, including cultural traditions and practices.

This chapter has shown that the rise in the numbers of immigrants entering Ireland has been paralleled by complexities associated with service provision to an ethnically diverse population. While attempting to meet its legislative obligations, the state has failed as a social institution in many of the challenges associated with models of best practice in social care (equally of service provision and anti-oppressive practice). It is time to reform routines and procedures and become a service that not only considers the practical challenges of care that face an increasing number of individuals and groups from diverse backgrounds and experiences, but also philosophically embraces a multicultural Irish society. It is time to eliminate our prejudices and insecurities and replace them with an integrated service that provides support, equal access and full participation in the identification and elimination of institutional oppression. It is our social moment to care!

References

ACYCP [Association for Child & Youth Care Practice] (2007) 'The North American Certification Project update'. <acycp.org>

Adams, R., Dominelli, L. and Payne, M. (2002) *Social Work: themes, issues and critical debates*. London: Open University Press.

Aiach, P. and Carr-Hill, R. (1992) 'Inequalities in health: the country debate', in J. Fox (ed.) *Health Inequalities in European Countries*. Aldershot: Gower.

Ainsworth, M., Blehar, M., Waters, E. and Wall, S. (1978) *Patterns of Attachment: a psychological study of the strange situation*. Hillside, NJ: Lawrence Erlbaum.

AITHS [All Ireland Traveller Health Study] (2010) *Our Geels (summary of findings)*. Dublin: All Ireland Traveller Health Study Team, School of Public Health, Physiotherapy and Population Science, University College Dublin.

AITHS (2011) *All Ireland Traveller Health Study: the birth cohort study follow up*. Dublin: University College Dublin. <www.dohc.ie/publications/aiths_ follow_ up. html>

Aldridge, M. and Evetts, J. (2003) 'Rethinking the concept of professionalism: the case of journalism', *British Journal of Sociology* 54(4), pp. 547–64.

Alimo-Metcalfe, B. and Nyfield, G. (2002) 'Leadership and organizational effectiveness', in I. Robertson, M. Callinan and D. Bartram (eds.) *Organizational Effectiveness: the role of psychology*. Chichester: Wiley.

Allen, D. and Tynan, H. (2000) 'Responding to aggressive behaviour: impact of training on staff members' knowledge and confidence', *Mental Retardation* 38, pp. 97–104.

Allen, G. and Langford, D. (2008) *Effective Interviewing in Social Work and Social Care: a practical guide*. Basingstoke: Palgrave Macmillan.

An Garda Síochána (2012) *Annual Report of the Committee Appointed to Monitor the Effectiveness of the Diversion Programme*. Dublin: An Garda Síochána. <garda.ie/Documents/User/Monitoring%20Committee%20Annual%20 Report%20English.pdf>

Anderson, I. and Christian, J. (2003) 'Causes of homelessness in the UK: a dynamic analysis', *Journal of Community and Applied Social Psychology* 13, pp. 105–18.

Anderson, I. and Tulloch, D. (2000) *Pathways through Homelessness: a review of the research evidence*. Homeless Task Force Research Series. Edinburgh: Scottish Homes.

Anderson, I., Kemp, P. and Quillars, D. (1993) *Single Homeless People*. London: HMSO.

Anderson, S. and Graham, G. (2002) 'The custodial remand system for juveniles in Ireland: the empirical evidence', in K. Lalor, F. Ryan, M. Seymour and C. Hamilton (eds.) *Young People and Crime: research, policy and practice*. Dublin: Centre for Social and Educational Research, Dublin Institute of Technology. <dit.ie/cser/media/ditcser/images/young-people-and-crime.pdf>

Anglin, J. (1992) 'How staff develop', *FICE Bulletin* 6, pp. 18–24.

Anglin, J. (2001) 'Child and youth care: a unique profession', *CYC-Net* 35, pp. 1–3.

Anglin, J. (2002) 'Staffed group homes for children and youth: constructing a theoretical framework for understanding', PhD thesis, School of Social Work, University of Leicester.

Antonovsky, A. (1984) 'The sense of coherence as a determinant of health', in J. Matarazzo (ed.) *Behavioural Health*. New York: Wiley.

APA [American Psychiatric Association] (1994) *Diagnostic and Statistical Manual of Mental Disorders, DSM-IV*. Washington, DC: American Psychiatric Association.

APA (2000) *Desk Reference to the Diagnostic Criteria from DSM-IV – TR*. Washington, DC: American Psychiatric Association.

Aviles de Bradley, A. (2011) 'Unaccompanied homeless youth: intersections of homelessness, school experiences and educational policy', *Child and Youth Services* 32(2), pp. 155–72.

Baker, J., Lynch, K., Cantillon, S. and Walsh, J. (2009) *Equality: from theory to action*. Basingstoke: Palgrave Macmillan.

Balanda, K. and Wilde, J. (2001) *Inequalities in Mortality 1989–1998: a report on all-Ireland mortality data*. Dublin: The Institute of Public Health in Ireland. <publichealth.ie/publications/inequalitiesinmortality19891998>

Balibar, E. (1991) 'Racism and crisis', in E. Balibar and I. Wallerstein (eds.) *Race, Nation, Class: ambiguous identities*. London: Verso.

Bandura, A. (1965) 'Influence of models' reinforcement contingencies on the acquisition of imitated responses', *Journal of Personality and Social Psychology* 1, pp. 589–95.

Bandura, A. (1977) *Social Learning Theory*. Englewood Cliffs, NJ: Prentice Hall.

Bandura, A., Ross, D. and Ross, S. (1961) 'Transmission of aggression through imitation of aggressive models', *Journal of Abnormal and Social Psychology* 63(3), pp. 575–82.

Bank-Mikkelsen, A. (1976) 'Misconceptions on the principle of normalisation', address to IASSMD conference, Washington, DC.

Banks, S. (2004) *Ethics, Accountability and the Social Professions*. London: Palgrave Macmillan.

Banks, S. (2007) 'Between equity and empathy: social professions and the new accountability', *Social Work and Society* 5(3), special issue: Festschrift Walter Lorenz. <socwork.net/sws/article/view/131>

Banks, S. (2012) *Ethics and Values in Social Work*. Basingstoke: Palgrave Macmillan.

Barnardos (2011a) *Missing Separated Children in Ireland*. Dublin: Barnardos. <Barnardos.ie/assets/files/Advocacy/Separated%20Children/Barnardos%20 Briefing%20Note%20on%20Missing%20Separated%20Children.pdf>

Barnardos (2011b) 'Separated children in foster care: seminar paper'. Dublin: Barnardos.   <Barnardos.ie/assets/files/Advocacy/Separated%20Children/Barn-ardos%20Seminar_Paper_on_Fostering_Separated_Children.pdf>

Barnes, C. (1991) *Disabled People in Britain and Discrimination: a case for anti-discrimination legislation*. London: British Council of Organisations of Disabled People. <www.leeds.ac.uk/disability-studies/archiveuk/Barnes/bcodp.pdf>

Barnes-Holmes, Y., Barnes-Holmes, D., McHugh, L. and Hayes, S. (2004) 'Relational frame theory: some implications for understanding and treating human psychopathology', *International Journal of Psychology and Psychological Therapy* 4, pp. 355–75.

Barrett, A., Savva, G., Timonen, V. and Kenny, R. (eds.) (2011a) *Fifty Plus in Ireland 2011: first results from the Irish Longitudinal Study on Ageing* (TILDA). Dublin: Trinity College. <epubs.rcsi.ie/psycholrep/45>

Barrett, B., Fogel, S., Garrett, J. and Young, M. (2011b) 'Assessing health care needs among street homeless and transitionally housed adults', *Journal of Social Service Research* 37(3), pp. 338–50.

Barrington, R. (2004) *Poverty is Bad for Your Health*. Discussion paper 5. Dublin: Combat Poverty Agency. <combatpoverty.ie/publications/DP5_PovertyIs BadForYourHealth_2004.pdf>

Baum, W. (2005) *Understanding Behaviorism: behavior, culture and evolution*. Oxford: Blackwell.

Beattie, A. (1997) 'Evaluation in community development for health: an opportunity for dialogue', in M. Sidell, L. Jones, J. Katz and A. Peberdy (eds.) *Debates and Dilemmas in Promoting Health*. London: Macmillan.

Beauchamp, D. (1997) 'Lifestyle, public health and paternalism', in M. Sidell, L. Jones, J. Katz and A. Peberdy (eds.) *Debates and Dilemmas in Promoting Health*. London: Macmillan.

Beech, B. and Leather, P. (2006) 'Workplace violence in the health care sector: a review of staff training and integration of training evaluation models', *Aggression and Violent Behaviour* 11, pp. 27–43.

Beker, J. (2001) 'Development of a professional identity for the childcare worker', *Child and Youth Care Forum* 30(6), pp. 345–54.

Belbin, M. (2012) *Team Roles at Work*. Oxford: Elsevier.

Bell, D. and Blanchflower, D. (2009) 'What should be done about rising unemployment in the UK?' Discussion paper 4040. Bonn: IZA (Forschungs-institut zur Zukunft der Arbeit/Institute for the Study of Labor). <ftp.iza.org/ dp4040.pdf>

Bentley, A. (1997) 'The psychological effects of homelessness and their impact on the development of a counselling relationship', *Counselling Psychology Quarterly* 10(2), pp. 195–210.

Berger, P. and Berger, B. (1976) *Sociology: a biographical approach*. Harmondsworth: Penguin.

Berube, P. (1984) 'Professionalisation of childcare: a Canadian example', *Journal of Child and Youth Care* 2(1), pp. 13–26.

Bessant, J. (2004) 'Risk technologies and youth work practice', *Youth and Policy* 83, pp. 60–77.

Bettelheim, B. (1950) *Love Is Not Enough: the treatment of emotionally disturbed children*. Glencoe, IL: Free Press.

Bibby, P. (1994) *Personal Safety for Social Workers*. Aldershot: Arena.

Blake, R. and Mouton, J. (1985) *The Managerial Grid III. The Key to Leadership Excellence*. 3rd edn. Houston, TX: Gulf.

Blome, W. and Steib, S. (2004) 'Whatever the problem, the answer is "evidence-based practice" – or is it?', *Child Welfare* 83(6), pp. 611–15.

Böhnisch, L. and Schröer, W. (2011) 'Social pedagogy of the life stages', in J. Kornbeck and N. Rosendal Jensen (eds.) *Social Pedagogy for the Entire Lifespan. Volume 1*. Bremen: Europäischer Hochschulverlag.

Bombay, A., Matheson, K. and Anisman, H. (2011) 'The impact of stressors on second generation Indian residential school survivors', *Transcultural Psychiatry* 48(4), pp. 367–91.

Bowlby, J. (1952) *Maternal Care and Mental Health*. WHO monograph 2. Geneva: World Health Organization. <whqlibdoc.who.int/monograph/WHO_MONO _2_(part1).pdf>

Bowlby, J. (1969) *Attachment and Loss. Volume 1: attachment*. New York: Basic Books.

Bowlby, J. (1973) *Attachment and Loss. Volume 2: separation*. New York: Basic Books.

Bowlby, J. (1978) 'Attachment theory and its therapeutic implications', in S. Feinstein and P. Giovacchini (eds.) *Adolescent Psychiatry: developmental and clinical studies*. Northvale, NJ: Jason Aronson.

Braun, D. (2001) 'Perspectives on parenting', in P. Foley, J. Roche and S. Tucker (eds.) *Children in Society: contemporary theory, policy and practice*. Basingstoke: Palgrave.

Braye, S. and Preston-Shoot, M. (1995) *Empowering Practice in Social Care*. Milton Keynes: Open University Press.

Brechin, A. (2000) 'Introducing critical practice', in A. Brechin, H. Brown and M. Eby (eds.) *Critical Practice in Health and Social Care*. London: Sage.

Brechin, A. and Siddell, M. (2000) 'Ways of knowing', in R. Gomm and C. Davies (eds.) *Using Research in Health and Social Care*. London: Sage.

Brennan, P. (2012) 'Importance of training the self in social care education', interview with D. Lyons, 10 August.

Brock, A. (2013) 'Building a model of early years professionalism from prac-titioners' perspectives', *Journal of Early Childhood Research* 11(1), pp. 27–44.

Bronfenbrenner, U. (1979) *The Ecology of Human Development*. Cambridge, MA: Harvard University Press.

Bronfenbrenner, U. and Evans, G. (2000) 'Developmental science in the 21st century: emerging questions, theoretical models, research designs and empirical findings', *Social Development* 8(1), pp. 115–25.

Bruner, J. (1993) *Child's Talk: learning to use language*. New York: Norton.

Bryman, A. (2012) *Social Research Methods*. Oxford: Oxford University Press.

Bubeck, D. (1995) *Care, Gender and Justice*. London: Clarendon.

Buckley, H., Skehill, C. and O'Sullivan, E. (1997) *Child Protection Practices in Ireland: a case study*. Dublin: Oak Tree Press.

Burke, D. (2008) 'A place to call home? Issues in housing provision for homeless persons', in D. Downey (ed.) *Perspectives on Irish Homelessness, Past, Present and Future*. Dublin: The Homeless Agency.

Burmeister, E. (1960) *The Professional Houseparent*. New York: Columbia University Press.

Burnard, P. (1992) *Communicate!* London: Edward Arnold.

Burns, E. (2007) 'Positioning a post-professional approach to studying professions', *New Zealand Sociology* 22(1), pp. 72–101. <www.massey.ac.nz/~cprichar/OIL/NZ%20Soc%20special%20issue%20papers/Burns.pdf>

Burns, N. and Grove, S. (1997) *The Practice of Nursing Research: conduct, critique and utilisation*. Philadelphia, PA: Saunders.

Burton, J. (1993) *The Handbook of Residential Care*. London: Routledge.

Byrne, J. (2005) 'Social care workers' and students' perspectives on issues related to professional status and representation of social care in Ireland', MA thesis, Waterford Institute of Technology.

Byrne, J. (2008) 'Personal and professional development for social care workers', *Curam* 38.

CAAB [Children Acts Advisory Board] (n.d.) 'What is special care?' <srsb.ie/Functional-Areas/Special-Care/What-is-special-Care.aspx>

Cairde (2003) *A Health and Related Needs Analysis of Minority Ethnic Communities in Ireland*. Dublin: Cairde.

Cameron, C. and Moss, P. (eds.) (2011) *Social Pedagogy and Working with Children and Young People*. London: Jessica Kingsley.

Cameron, W. (1963) *Informal Sociology: a casual introduction to sociological thinking*. New York: Random House.

Caplan, R. and Holland, J. (1990) 'Rethinking health education theory', *Health Education Journal* 49, pp. 10–12.

Carpenter, M. (2011) *The Handbook of Research on Top Management Teams*. Cheltenham: Edward Elgar.

Carr, A. (2007) *The Effectiveness of Psychotherapy: a review of research by Prof. Alan Carr*. Wexford: Irish Council for Psychotherapy.

Carr, A. and McNulty, M. (2006a) 'Cognitive behaviour therapy', in A. Carr and M. McNulty (eds.) *The Handbook of Adult Clinical Psychology: an evidence-based practice approach*. London: Routledge.

Carr, A. and McNulty, M. (2006b) *The Handbook of Adult Clinical Psychology: an evidence-based practice approach*. London: Routledge.

Carr, E., Dunlap, G., Horner, R., Koegel, R., Turnbull, A., Sailor, W., Anderson, J., Albin, R., Kern Koegel, L. and Fox, L. (2002) 'Positive behavior support: evolution of an applied science', *Journal of Positive Behavior Intervention* 4, pp. 4–16.

Carter, W. (2006) *Challenging Behaviour and Disability: a targeted response*. Report to Honorable Warren Pitt MP, Minister for Communities, Disability Services and Seniors. Brisbane: Government of Queensland.

Case, R. and Okamoto, Y. (1996) 'The role of central conceptual structures in the development of children's thought', *Monographs of the Society for Research in Child Development* 61(1–2).

Cashmore, J. (2011) 'The link between child maltreatment and adolescent offending: systems neglect of adolescents', *Family Matters* 89. <aifs.gov.au/institute/pubs/fm2011/fm89/fm89d.html>

Cavanagh, K. and Cree, V. (eds.) (1996) *Working with Men: feminism and social work*. London: Routledge.

CBI [Confederation of British Industry] (2007) *Absence and Labour Turnover Survey*. London: CBI and AXA.

Cedefop [European Centre for the Development of Vocational Training] (2010) *Quality Assurance in the Social Care Sector*. Luxembourg: Publications Office of the European Union. <cedefop.europa.eu/EN/publications/16821.aspx>

Cemlyn, S. (2008) 'Human rights and gypsies and Travellers: an exploration of the application of a human rights perspective to social work with a minority community in Britain', *British Journal of Social Work* 38(1), pp. 153–73.

Chakrabarti, M. and Hill, M. (2000) *Residential Child Care: international perspectives on links with families and peers*. London: Jessica Kingsley.

Chappell, D. and Di Martino, V. (2006) *Violence at Work*. Geneva: International Labour Organization.

Charles, G. and Gabor, P. (1988) *Issues in Child and Youth Care Practice in Alberta*. Lethbridge: Lethbridge Community College.

Charles, G. and Gabor, P. (1991) 'An historical perspective on residential services for troubled and troubling youth in Canada', in G. Charles and S. McIntyre (eds.) *The Best in Care: recommendations for the future of residential services for troubled and troubling young people in Canada*. Ottawa: Canadian Child Welfare Association.

Charles, G. and Gabor, P. (2006) 'An historical perspective on residential services for troubled and troubling youth in Canada revisited', *Relational Child and Youth Care Practice* 19(4), pp. 17–26.

Charles, G. and White, J. (2008) 'Outcome research, best practices and the limits of evidence', *Canadian Social Work Review* 25, pp. 8–15.

Charles, G., Dagnino, M., Gemmel, L. and Mayer, A. (2012) *Taking Stock: supporting Canadian child and youth agencies in economic crisis*. Ottawa: National Alliance of Children and Youth.

Charles, G., Ernst, K. and Ponzetti, J. (2003) 'Ethics and outcome measures', *Canada's Children, Canada's Future: the Journal of the Child Welfare League of Canada* 10(2), pp. 5–11.

Charleton, M. (2007) *Ethics for Social Care in Ireland*. Dublin: Gill & Macmillan.

Chomsky, N. (1968) *Aspects of the Theory of Syntax*. Cambridge, MA: MIT Press.

Chrisjohn, R. and Young, S. (1997) *The Circle Game: shadows and substance in the Indian residential school experience in Canada*. Penticton: Theytus.

Christie, A. (1998) '"Balancing gender" as men social workers', *Irish Social Worker* 16(3), pp. 4–6.

Christie, A. (ed.) (2001) *Men and Social Work*. London: Palgrave.

Christie, A. (2003) 'Unsettling the "Social" in social work: responses to asylum seeking children in Ireland', *Child and Family Social Work* 8(3), pp. 223–31.

Christophe, A. and Morton, J. (1998) 'Is Dutch native English? Linguistic analysis by 2 month olds', *Developmental Science* 1, pp. 215–19.

CIB [Citizens Information Board] (2012) 'Checklist for people with disabilities and long-term illness'. <citizensinformation.ie/en/reference/checklists/checklist_disability.html>

Clark, C. (2005) 'The deprofessionalisation thesis, accountability and professional character', *Social Work and Society* 3(2), pp. 182–90. <socwork.net/sws/article/view/193>

Clarke, M. (1998) *Lives in Care: issues for policy and practice in children's homes*. Dublin: Mercy Congregation and Children's Research Centre, Trinity College.

Clarke, M. (2003) 'Fit to practice: the education of professionals', paper to Irish Association of Social Care Educators conference, Cork.

Cleary, A., Corbett, M., Galvin, M. and Wall, J. (2004) *Young Men on the Margins*. Dublin: Katharine Howard Foundation.

Clough, R. (2000) *The Practice of Residential Work*. Basingstoke: Macmillan.

Cohen, S. (2002) *Folk Devils and Moral Panics: the creation of the mods and rockers*. London: Routledge.

Collins, B. (2001a) 'The development of services. Module 1. Introduction to disability', *Bachelor of Arts in Applied Social Studies (Disability)*. Dublin: The Open Training College.

Collins, J. (2001b) *Good to Great*. London: Random House.

Combat Poverty Agency and Equality Authority (2003) *Poverty and Inequality: applying an equality dimension to poverty proofing*. Dublin: Combat Poverty Agency and Equality Authority.

Commission of Enquiry on Mental Handicap (1965) *Report*. Dublin: Stationery Office.

Commission on the Future of Multi-Ethnic Britain (2000) *The Future of Multi-Ethnic Britain* [Parekh report]. London: Profile Books.

Commission on the Status of People with Disabilities (1996) *A Strategy for Equality. Report of the Commission on the Status of People with Disabilities*. Dublin: Stationery Office.

Commission to Inquire into Child Abuse (2009) *Report of the Commission to Inquire into Child Abuse* [Ryan report]. Dublin: Stationery Office. <childabusecommission.ie/rpt>

Condon, M. (2001) *The Health and Dental Needs of Homeless People in Dublin*. Dublin: Northern Area Health Board.

Condron, M. (1989) *The Serpent and the Goddess*. San Francisco: Harper Collins.

Conklin, J. (2006) *Dialogue Mapping: building shared understanding of wicked problems*. London: Wiley.

Connell, R. (1987) *Gender and Power*. Oxford: Blackwell.

Connell, R. (2001) *The Men and the Boys*. Los Angeles: University of California Press.

Connell, R. (2005) *Masculinities*. Cambridge: Polity.

Connolly, L. (2002) *The Irish Women's Movement*. Basingstoke: Palgrave.

Conroy, P. (2004) *Trafficking in Unaccompanied Minors in Ireland*. Dublin: International Organisation for Migration.

Considine, M. and Dukelow, F. (2009) *Irish Social Policy: a critical introduction*. Dublin: Gill & Macmillan.

Coombes, Y. (1997) 'An international perspective on primary health care', in M. Sidell, L. Jones, J. Katz and A. Peberdy (eds.) *Debates and Dilemmas in Promoting Health*. London: Macmillan.

Cooper, C., Hoel, H. and di Martino, V. (2003) *Preventing Violence and Harassment in the Workplace*. Dublin: European Foundation for the Improvement of Living and Working Conditions. <eurofound.europa.eu/pubdocs/2002/112/en/1/ef02112en.pdf>

Cooper, J., Heron, T. and Heward, W. (2007) *Applied Behavior Analysis*. Upper Saddle River, NJ: Prentice Hall.

CoRe (2011) *Competence Requirements in Early Childhood Education and Care: a study for the European Commission Directorate-General for Education and Culture*. London and Ghent: University of East London, Cass School of Education and University of Ghent, Department for Social Welfare Studies. <ec.europa.eu/education/more-information/doc/2011/core_en.pdf>

Corry, M. and Tubridy, A. (2001) *Going Mad: understanding mental illness*. Dublin: Newleaf.

Corsini, R. and Wedding, D. (2008) *Current Psychotherapies*. New York: Brooks/Cole.

CORU [Health and Social Care Professionals Council] (2012) *Criteria and Standards of Proficiency for Education and Training Programmes*. Dublin: CORU.

Costello, C. (2005) *Professional Identity Crisis: race, class, gender, and success at professional schools*. Nashville, TN: Vanderbilt University Press.

Costello, L. and Howley, D. (1999) *Under Dublin's Neon: report on street drinkers in Dublin*. Dublin: Centre Care.

Coughlan, M., Cronin, P. and Ryan, F. (2007) 'Step-by-step guide to critiquing research. Part 1: quantitative research', *British Journal of Nursing* 16(11), pp. 658–63.

Courtney, D. (2012) 'Taking stock: the development of social care education and training in Ireland', paper to Social Care Ireland conference, Kilkenny.

Craig, J. (2006) 'Production values: building shared autonomy', in J. Craig (ed.) *Production Values: futures for professionalism*. London: Demos. <demos.co.uk/publications/productionvalues>

Crane, M. and Warnes, A. (2005) 'Responding to the needs of older homeless people: the effectiveness and limitations of British services', *Innovation* 18(2), pp. 137–52.

Cree, V. (2001) 'Men and masculinities in social work education', in A. Christie (ed.) *Men and Social Work*. London: Palgrave.

Crimmens, D. (1998) 'Training for residential child care workers in Europe: comparing approaches in the Netherlands, Ireland and the United Kingdom', *Social Work Education* 17(3), pp. 309–20.

Crosscare, Doras Luimní and Nasc (2012) *Person or Number? Barriers Facing Immigrants Accessing Social Protection in Ireland*. Dublin: Crosscare, Doras Luimní and Nasc. <flac.ie/download/pdf/person_or_number.pdf>

Crowley, N. (2006) *An Ambition for Equality*. Dublin: Irish Academic Press.

Crowley, N. (2010) *Bringing the Equality Authority to Heel*. Dublin: Farmar.

Crowley, F. (2003) *Mental Illness: the neglected quarter*. Dublin: Amnesty International Ireland.

CSO [Central Statistics Office] (2007) *Ageing in Ireland*. Dublin: Stationery Office.

CSO (2010) *National Disability Survey 2006. Volume 2*. Cork: CSO.

CSO (2011a) *Census of Population 2011. Preliminary Results*. Dublin: Stationery Office. <cso.ie/en/media/csoie/census/documents/prelim%20complete.pdf>

CSO (2011b) *Population and Migration Estimates April 2011*. Dublin: Stationery Office. <cso.ie/en/media/csoie/releasespublications/documents/population/current/population%20and%20migration%20estimates%20April%202011.pdf>

CSO (2011c) *Profile 8. Our Bill of Health – health, disability and carers in Ireland*. Cork: CSO.

CSO (2011d) *Statistical Yearbook of Ireland 2011*. Dublin: Stationery Office.

CSO (2012a) *Homeless Persons in Ireland: a special census report*. Dublin: Stationery Office.

CSO (2012b) *Profile 6. Migration and Diversity*. Dublin: Stationery Office. <cso.ie/en/media/csoie/census/documents/census2011profile6/Profile,6,Migration,and,Diversity,entire,doc.pdf>

CSO (2012c) *Profile 7. Religion, Ethnicity and Irish Travellers*. Dublin: Stationery Office. <cso.ie/en/media/csoie/census/documents/census2011profile7/Profile,7,Education,Ethnicity,and,Irish,Traveller,entire,doc.pdf>

CSO (2012d) *Survey on Income and Living Conditions 2010*. Cork: CSO.

CSO (2012e) *This is Ireland, Highlights from Census 2011, Part 1*. Cork: CSO.

CSO (2012f) *Women and Men in Ireland 2011*. Dublin: Stationery Office.

CSO (2013a) 'Chapter 3. Social inclusion', in *Survey on Income and Living Conditions (SILC)*. Dublin: Stationery Office. <cso.ie/en/media/csoie/releasespublications/documents/statisticalyearbook/2012/c3socialinclusion.pdf>

CSO (2013b) 'Survey on Income and Living Conditions (SILC) 2011 and 2010 revised results'. <cso.ie/en/media/csoie/releasespublications/documents/silc/2011/silc_2011.pdf>

Cullen, E. (2006) 'Growth and the Celtic cancer: unprecedented growth but for whose benefit?', in T. O'Connor and M. Murphy (eds.) *Social Care in Ireland: theory, policy and practice*. Cork: Cork Institute of Technology Press.

Curry, D., Eckles, F., Stuart, C. and Qaqish, B. (2010) 'National child and youth care practitioner professional certification: promoting competent care for children and youth', *Child Welfare* 89(2), pp. 57–77.

CYCAA [Child and Youth Care Association of Alberta] (2000) *Certification Manual*. Edmonton: CYCAA.

CYCABC [Child and Youth Care Association of British Columbia] (2012) 'Definition of child and youth care'. Victoria: CYCABC. <cycabc.com>

Dahlgren, G. and Whitehead, M. (1992) *Policies and Strategies to Promote Social Equity and Health*. Copenhagen: World Health Organization.

Davies, H. and Nutley, S. (1999) 'The rise and rise of evidence in health care', *Public Money and Management* 19(1), pp. 9–16.

Davis, A. (2012) *Modern Motherhood: women and family in England, 1945–2000*. Manchester: Manchester University Press.

Davison, C., Frankel, S. and Davey Smith, G. (1997) 'The limits of life-style: re-assessing "fatalism" in the popular culture of illness prevention', in M. Sidell, L. Jones, J. Katz and A. Peberdy (eds.) *Debates and Dilemmas in Promoting Health*. London: Macmillan.

DCYA [Department of Children and Youth Affairs] (2011) *Children First: national guidance for the protection and welfare of children*. Dublin: Stationery Office.

DCYA (2013) *National Quality Standards for Volunteer-led Youth Groups*. Dublin: DCYA.

De Róiste, Á. (2005) 'Attachment', in P. Share and N. McElwee (eds.) *Applied Social Care: an introduction for Irish students*. Dublin: Gill & Macmillan.

De Winter, M. and Noom, M. (2003) 'Someone who treats you as an ordinary human being: homeless youth examine the quality of professional care', *British Journal of Social Work* 33(3), pp. 325–37.

DeCasper, A. and Fifer, W. (1980) 'Of human bonding: newborns prefer their mothers' voices', *Science* 28, pp. 174–6.

DECLG [Department of the Environment, Community and Local Government] (2013) *Homelessness Policy Statement*. Dublin: DECLG. <www.environ.ie/en/PublicationsDocuments/FileDownLoad,32434,en.pdf>

Degener, T. (2004) *Definition of Disability*. Europe: EU Network of Experts on Disability Discrimination.

DEHLG [Department of the Environment, Heritage and Local Government] (2008) *The Way Home: a strategy to address adult homelessness in Ireland 2008–2013*. Dublin: DEHLG.

Dennehy, T. (2006) 'Winnicott and the care worker', in T. O'Connor and M. Murphy (eds.) *Social Care in Ireland: theory, policy and practice*. Cork: Cork Institute of Technology Press.

Dent, M. and Whitehead, S. (2002) 'Introduction: configuring the "new" professional', in M. Dent and S. Whitehead (eds.) *Managing Professional Identities: knowledge, performativity and the 'new' professional*. London: Routledge.

Department of the Environment and Local Government, Department of Health and Children and Department of Education and Science (2002) *Homelessness Preventative Strategy*. Dublin: Stationery Office.

Derman-Sparks, L. and Olsen Edwards, J. (2010) *Anti-Bias Education for Young Children and Ourselves*. Washington, DC: National Association for the Education of Young Children.

DES [Department of Education and Science] (2003a) *Code of Good Practice: child protection guidelines for the youth work sector (revised)*. Dublin: Stationery Office.

DES (2003b) *National Youth Work Development Plan 2003–2007*. Dublin: Stationery Office.

DES (2003c) *Preschools for Travellers. National Evaluation Report*. Dublin: Stationery Office.

DES (2006) *Report and Recommendations for a Traveller Education Strategy*. Dublin: Stationery Office.

DES (2012) 'Minister Quinn protects frontline education services in budget 2013', press release, 5 December. <education.ie>

Dessler, G. (2007) *Human Resource Management*. 11th edn. Florida: Florida International University.

Devlin, M. (2006) *Inequality and the Stereotyping of Young People*. Dublin: Equality Authority and National Youth Council of Ireland.

Devlin, M. (2008) 'Youth work and youth policy in the Republic of Ireland 1983–2008: "Still haven't found what we're looking for?"', *Youth and Policy* 100, pp. 41–54.

Devlin, M. (2010) 'Youth work in Ireland: some historical reflections', in F. Coussée, G. Verschelden, T. Van de Walle, M. Mędlińska and H. Williamson (eds.) *The History of Youth Work in Europe and Its Relevance for Youth Policy Today. Volume 2*. Strasbourg: Council of Europe.

Devlin, M. (2013) 'Youth work, professionalism and professionalisation in Europe', in F. Coussée, G. Verschelden, T. Van de Walle, M. Mędlińska and H. Williamson (eds.) *The History of Youth Work in Europe and Its Relevance for Youth Policy Today. Volume 3*. Strasbourg: Council of Europe Publishing.

Devlin, M. and Gunning, A. (2009) *The Purpose and Outcomes of Youth Work: report to the Interagency Group*. Dublin: Irish Youth Work Press.

Devlin, M. and Healy, D. (eds.) (2007) *'Work in Progress': case studies in participatory arts with young people*. Dublin: National Youth Council of Ireland.

Dewe, B., Otto, H.-U. and Schnurr, S. (2006) 'Introduction: new professionalism in social work', *Social Work and Society* 4(1).

Dines, A. (1997) 'A case study of the ethical issues in health promotion: mammography screening: the nurse's position', in M. Sidell, L. Jones, J. Katz and A. Peberdy (eds.) *Debates and Dilemmas in Promoting Health*. London: Macmillan.

Dingwall, R. (2008) *Essays on Professions*. Aldershot: Ashgate.

DJELR [Department of Justice, Equality and Law Reform] (2000) *Integration: a two way process*. Dublin: Government Publications.

DoE [Department of Education] (1970) *Reformatory and Industrial Schools Systems Report* [Kennedy report]. Dublin: Stationery Office.

DoH [Department of Health] (1988) *The Years Ahead: a policy for the elderly*. Dublin: Stationery Office.

DoH (1994) *Shaping a Healthier Future: a strategy for effective healthcare in the 1990s*. Dublin: Stationery Office.

DoH (2012) *Value for Money and Policy Review of Disability Services in Ireland*. Dublin: Stationery Office.

DoH (2013) *Value for Money and Policy Review of Disability Services in Ireland: National Implementation Framework*. Dublin: Stationery Office.

DoHC [Department of Health and Children] (1998) *Adding Years to Life and Life to Years: a health promotion strategy for older people*. Dublin: Stationery Office.

DoHC (1999) *Children First. National Guidelines on Child Protection and Welfare*. Dublin: Stationery Office.

DoHC (2001a) *National Standards for Children's Residential Centres*. Dublin: Stationery Office.

DoHC (2001b) *Quality and Fairness: a health system for you. Primary Care Strategy*. Dublin: Stationery Office.

DoHC (2001c) *Youth Homelessness Strategy*. Dublin: Stationery Office.

DoHC (2004) *Working for Children and Families: exploring good practice*. Dublin: Stationery Office.

DoHC (2005) *Report of the Working Group on Treatment of Under-18 Years Presenting to Treatment Services with Serious Drug Problems*. Dublin: DoHC.

DoHC (2007) *National Standards for Residential Care Settings for Older People*. Dublin: Stationery Office.

DoHC (2009) *National Quality Standards for Residential Care Settings for Older People*. Dublin: Stationery Office.

DoJE [Department of Justice and Equality] (2011) *Ireland's National Traveller/ Roma Integration Strategy*. [Traveller Policy Division]. Dublin: Stationery Office. <ec.europa.eu/justice/discrimination/roma/national-strategies/index_en.htm>

DoJE (2012a) 'ASBOs'. <justice.ie/en/JELR/Pages/ASBOs>

DoJE (2012b) 'Minister Shatter publishes Inspector of Prisons Report on St Patrick's Institution, and Visiting Committee Reports for 2011 for Dóchas Centre, Midlands, Limerick, Shelton Abbey, Training Unit, Castlerea, Loughan House and Portlaoise Prisons', press release. Dublin: Department of Justice and Equality. <justice.ie/en/JELR/Pages/PR12000283>

Dominelli, L. (1997) *Sociology for Social Work*. London: Macmillan.

Dominelli, L. (2007) 'The post-modern "turn" in social work: the challenges of identity and equality', *Social Work and Society* 5(3), pp. 173–86.

Donahue, M., McVeigh, M. and Ward, M. (2007) *Misli, Crush, Misli: Irish Travellers and nomadism*. Dublin: Irish Traveller Movement and Traveller Movement (Northern Ireland). <itmtrav.ie/uploads/publication/MISLI-CRUSH-MISLI.pdf>

Donald, A. (2006) 'Facilitating community action', in D. Pencheon, C. Guest, D. Melzer, J. Muir Gray (eds.) *Oxford Handbook of Public Health Practice*. Oxford: Oxford University Press.

Dondio, P., Barrett, S., Weber, S. and Seigneur, J.-M. (2006) *Extracting Trust from Domain Analysis: a case study on Wikipedia project*. Dublin: School of Computer Science and Statistics, Distributed System Group, Trinity College. <cui.unige.ch/~seigneur/publications/ExtractingTrustfromDomainAnalysis finalcorrected.pdf>

DoT [Department of the Taoiseach] (2006) *Towards 2016: ten-year framework social partnership agreement 2006–2015*. Dublin: Stationery Office.

DoT (2012) *National Reform Programme for Ireland 2012 Update under the Europe 2020 Strategy*. Dublin: DoT. <taoiseach.gov.ie/eng/Work_Of_The_Department/Economic_and_Social_Policy/Economic_Policy/National_Reform_Programme>

Doyle, A. (2012) *Annual Report of the National Physical and Sensory Disability Database 2011*. Dublin: Health Research Board.

Doyle, J. and McGarty, P. (2012) 'Social care managers. Action or reaction?' Dublin: DIT and ITT. <arrow.dit.ie/cseroth/54>

Dozier, M., Case Stovall, K., Albus, K. and Bates, B. (2001) 'Attachment for infants in foster care: the role of caregiver state of mind', *Child Development* 72(5), pp. 1467–77.

Dryden, W. (1988) *Key Issues for Counselling in Action*. London: Sage.

Dryden, W. and Neenan, M. (2004) *The Rational Emotive Behavioural Approach to Therapeutic Change*. London: Sage.

DSFA [Department of Social and Family Affairs] (2011) *Habitual Residence Condition: guidelines for deciding officers on the determination of habitual residence*. Dublin: Stationery Office. <www.welfare.ie/EN/OperationalGuidelines/Pages/habres.aspx#5>

Dubos, R. (1991) 'Biomedical philosophies', in P. Worsley (ed.) *The New Modern Sociology Readings*. London: Penguin.

Duffy, C. and Healy, O. (2011) 'Spontaneous communication in autism spectrum disorder: a review of topographies and interventions', *Research in Autism Spectrum Disorders* 5, pp. 977–83.

Duffy, M. (2011) *Making Care Count: a century of gender, race and paid care work*. New Brunswick, NJ: Rutgers University Press.

Dunn, J. (1993) *Young Children's Close Relationships Beyond Attachment*. London: Sage.

Duyvendak, J., Knijn, T. and Kremer, M. (eds.) (2006) *Policy, People and the New Professional: de-professionalisation and re-professionalisation in care and welfare*. Amsterdam: Amsterdam University Press.

Edmond, T., Megivern, D., Williams, C., Rochman, E. and Howard, M. (2006) 'Integrating evidence-based practice and social work field education', *Journal of Social Work Education* 42(2), pp. 277–396.

Edmund, N. and Price, M. (eds.) (2012) *Integrated Working with Children and Young People: supporting development from birth to nineteen.* London: Sage.

EHB [Eastern Health Board] (1998) *Childcare and Family Support Service in 1998: review of adequacy.* Dublin: EHB.

EHB (1999) *Ten Year Action Plan for Services for Older Persons 1999–2008.* Dublin: Stationery Office.

Ehrenreich, B. and English, D. (2010) *Witches, Midwives, and Nurses: a history of women healers.* New York: Feminist Press at CUNY.

Elias, B., Mignone, J., Hall, M., Hong, S., Hart, L. and Sareen, J. (2012) 'Trauma and suicide behaviour histories among a Canadian indigenous population: an empirical exploration of the potential role of Canada's residential school system', *Social Science and Medicine* 74, pp. 1560–9.

Emerson, E. (1995) *Challenging Behaviour: analysis and intervention in people with learning disabilities.* Cambridge: Cambridge University Press.

Engel, G.L. (1977) 'The need for a new medical model: a challenge for biomedicine', *Science* 196, pp. 129–36.

Equality Authority (2006) *Annual Report 2006.* Dublin: Equality Authority. <equality.ie/Files/Annual%20Report%202006.pdf>

Equality Tribunal (2011) *Annual Report 2011.* Dublin: Equality Tribunal. <www.equalitytribunal.ie/Publications/Annual-Reports/Annual-Report-2011.pdf>

ERHA [Eastern Regional Health Authority] (2001) *Review of the Implementation of the Ten Year Action Plan for Services for Older People 1999–2008.* Dublin: Stationery Office.

Erikson, E. (1970) *Childhood and Society.* New York: Norton.

Erikson, E. (1980) *Identity and the Life Cycle.* New York: Norton.

Eriksson, L. and Markström, A. (2000) *Den Svårfångade Socialpedagogiken.* Lund: Studentlitteratur.

Esping-Andersen, G. (1990) *The Three Worlds of Welfare Capitalism.* New Jersey: Princeton University Press.

ESRI [Economic and Social Research Institute] (2011) *Annual Monitoring Report on Integration 2010.* Dublin: ESRI and The Integration Centre.

European Agency for Safety and Health at Work (2002) *Working on Stress: prevention of psychosocial risks and stress at work in practice.* Luxembourg: Office for Official Publications of the European Communities. <osha.europa.eu/en/publications/reports/104>

European Commission (2012a) *Communication from the Commission to the European Parliament, the Council, the European Economic and Social Committee and the Committee of the Regions. National Roma Integration Strategies: a first step in the implementation of the EU framework.* Brussels: European Commission. <ec.europa.eu/justice/discrimination/files/com2012_226_en.pdf>

European Commission (2012b) 'Europe 2020 in Ireland'. <ec.europa.eu/europe2020/europe-2020-in-your-country/ireland/index_en.htm>

Eurostat (2009) *The Social Situation in the European Union 2009.* Luxembourg: Publications Office of the European Union. <epp.eurostat.ec.europa.eu/cache/ITY_OFFPUB/KE-AG-10-001/EN/KE-AG-10-001-EN.PDF>

Evans, L. (2008) 'Professionalism, professionality and the development of education professionals', *British Journal of Educational Studies* 56(1), pp. 20–38.

Evetts, J. (2010) 'Organizational professionalism: changes, challenges and opportunities', paper to DPU conference, *Organizational Learning and Beyond,* Copenhagen, 20 October.

Evetts, J. (2012) 'Professionalism in turbulent times: changes, challenges and opportunities', paper to Propel international conference, Stirling, 9–11 May. <www.propel.stir.ac.uk/downloads/JuliaEvetts-FullPaper.pdf>

Fahey, T., Maître, B., Nolan, B. and Whelan, C. (2007) *A Social Portrait of Older People in Ireland.* Dublin: Economic and Social Research Institute. <socialinclusion.ie/publications/documents/Older_lowres2.pdf>

Fahlberg, V. (1994) *A Child's Journey Through Placement.* London: British Association for Adoption and Fostering.

Fanning, B. (2006) 'The new welfare economy', in B. Fanning and M. Rush (eds.) *Care and Social Change in the Irish Welfare Economy.* Dublin: University College Dublin Press.

Fanning, B. and Rush, M. (2006) *Care and Social Change in the Irish Welfare Economy.* Dublin: University College Dublin Press.

Fanning, B., Veale, A. and O'Connor, D. (2001) *Beyond the Pale: asylum seeking children and social exclusion in Ireland.* Dublin: Irish Refugee Council.

Farrell, F. and Watt, P. (eds.) (2001) *Responding to Racism in Ireland.* Dublin: Veritas.

Farrelly, T. and O'Doherty, C. (2005) 'The Health and Social Care Professionals Bill (2004) – implications and opportunities for the social professions in Ireland', *Administration* 53(1), pp. 80–92.

FEANTSA (2005) *Street Homelessness: FEANTSA's thematic report 2005.* Brussels: FEANTSA.

FEANTSA (2007) *European Typology of Homelessness and Housing Exclusion.* Brussels: FEANTSA. <feantsa.org/spip.php?article120>

Feder Kittay, E. (1999) *Love's Labour.* New York: Routledge.

Feldman, A., Gilmartin, M., Loyal, S. and Migge, B. (2008) *Getting On: from migration to integration. Chinese, Indian, Lithuanian and Nigerian migrants' experiences in Ireland.* Dublin: Immigrant Council of Ireland.

Fenson, L., Dale, P., Resnick, S., Bates, E., Thal, D. and Pethick, S. (1994) 'Variability in early communicative development', *Monographs of the Society for Research in Child Development* 59, pp. 1–73.

Ferguson, H. and Kenny, P. (1995) *On Behalf of the Child: child welfare, child protection and the Child Care Act 1991.* Dublin: A&A Farmar.

Ferguson, H. and O'Reilly, M. (2001) *Keeping Children Safe: child abuse, child protection and the promotion of welfare*. Dublin: A&A Farmar.

Ferguson, R. (1993) 'Introduction: child and youth care education: approaching a new millennium', *Child and Youth Care Forum* 22(4), pp. 251–61.

Fewster, G. (1990) 'Growing together: the personal relationship in child and youth care', in J. Anglin, C. Denholm, R. Ferguson and A. Pence (eds.) *Perspectives in Professional Child and Youth Care*. London: Haworth.

Fielder, F. (1967) *A Theory of Leadership Effectiveness*. New York: McGraw-Hill.

Fink, J. (ed.) (2004) *Care: personal lives and social policy*. Bristol: The Open University and The Policy Press.

Finnerty, K. (2012) 'Professional identity and the Irish social care worker', Doctorate in Applied Social Science thesis, University of Leicester.

Fitzpatrick, S., Bramley, G. and Johnsen, S. (2013) 'Pathways into multiple exclusion homelessness in seven UK cities', *Urban Studies* 50(1), pp. 148–68.

Fitzpatrick, S., Kemp, P. and Klinker, S. (2000) *Single Homelessness: an overview of research in Britain*. Bristol: The Policy Press.

Fivush, R. (2006) 'Scripting attachment: generalised event representations and internal working models', *Attachment and Human Development* 8(3), pp. 283–9.

Flick, U., von Kardoff, E. and Steinke, I. (2004) 'What is qualitative research? An introduction to the field', in U. Flick, E. von Kardoff and I. Steinke (eds.) *A Companion to Qualitative Research*. London: Sage.

Focus Ireland (1996) *Focus on Residential Child Care in Ireland: 25 years since the Kennedy report*. Dublin: Focus Ireland.

Focus Ireland (2000) *The Mental and Physical Health and Well-Being of Homeless Families in Dublin*. Dublin: Focus Ireland.

Fodor, J. (1992) 'A theory of the child's theory of mind', *Cognition* 44, pp. 286–93.

Fook, J. (2002) *Social Work: critical theory and practice*. London: Sage.

Fook, J. (2012) *Social Work: a critical approach to practice*. London: Sage.

Foucault, M. (1970) *The Order of Things: an archaeology of the human sciences*. London: Tavistock.

Foucault, M. (1972) *The Archaeology of Knowledge*. London: Tavistock.

Fournier, S. and Crey, E. (1997) *Stolen from Our Embrace: the abduction of First Nations children and the restoration of Aboriginal communities*. Toronto: Douglas and McIntyre.

Fraser, A., Padillia-Walker, L., Coyne, S., Nelson, L. and Stockdale, L. (2012) 'Associations between violent video gaming, empathic concern and prosocial behaviour towards strangers, friends and family members', *Journal of Youth and Adolescence* 41(5), pp. 636–49.

Frazer, H. (2010) 'Silencing dissent', blog entry, originally published in the *Irish Examiner*. <mediabite.wordpress.com/2009/07/07/silencing-dissent-by-hugh-frazer-former-director-of-combat-poverty-agency>

FRC [Family Resource Centre] National Forum (2006) *Supporting Families, Building Communities 2006–2009 Strategic Plan*. Dublin: Family Support Agency.

Friedson, E. (1970) *Profession of Medicine: a study of the sociology of applied knowledge.* New York: Dodd, Mead.

Friedson, E. (1990) 'Professionalisation, caring, and nursing', paper prepared for the Park Ridge Center, Park Ridge, Illinois. <virtualcurriculum.com/N3225/Freidson_Professionalism.html>

Friedson, E. (1994) *Professionalism Reborn: theory, prophecy and policy.* Cambridge: Polity.

Friedson, E. (2001) *Professionalism: the third logic.* Cambridge: Polity.

Fristrup, T. (2012) 'Gerontopedagogicalization: a critical approach to perform AGE in later life', in J. Kornbeck and N. Rosendal Jensen (eds.) *Social Pedagogy for the Entire Lifespan. Volume 2.* Bremen: Europäischer Hochschulverlag.

Frye, M. (1983) *The Politics of Reality.* Freedom, CA: Crossing Press.

FSA [Family Support Agency] (2007) *Family and Community Services Resources Centre Programme. SPEAK FRC National Database Trends 2004–2007.* Dublin: FSA.

FSA (2010) *The Family and Community Services Resource Centre Programme SPEAK FRC Report.* Dublin: FSA.

FSA (2012) *Strategic Plan 2010–2012.* Dublin: FSA.

Furlong, M., McGilloway, S., Bywater, T., Hutchings, J., Smith, S. and Donnelly, M. (2012) 'Behavioural and cognitive-behavioural group-based parenting programmes for early-onset conduct problems in children aged 3 to 12 years (Review)', *Cochrane Library* 2.

Fusco, D. (ed.) (2012) *Advancing Youth Work: current trends, critical questions.* London: Routledge.

Gaffney, M. and Harmon, C. (2007) 'Overview and policy conclusions', in *Evidence-based Policy Making: getting the evidence, using the evidence and evaluating the outcomes,* conference proceedings. Dublin: National Economic and Social Forum.

Gallagher, C. (2008) *The Community Life of Older People in Ireland.* Oxford: Peter Lang.

Gallagher, C. and Kennedy, K. (2003) 'The training implications of a social care approach to working with older people', *Irish Journal of Applied Social Studies* 4(1), pp. 21–35.

Gallagher, C. and O'Toole, J. (1999) 'Towards a sociological understanding of social care work in Ireland', *Irish Journal of Social Work Research* 2(1), pp. 69–86.

Gannon, B. and Nolan, B. (2007) *Dynamics of Disability and Social Inclusion in Ireland.* Dublin: Equality Authority and National Disability Authority.

Garavan, M. (2012) *Compassionate Activism: an exploration of integral social care.* Oxford: Peter Lang.

Garfat, T. (1998) 'The effective child and youth care intervention', *Journal of Child and Youth Care* 12(1–2), pp. 1–168.

Garfat, T. (2009) 'Barbarians on the horizon: reflections on the advent of evidence-based practices in child and youth care', *Relational Child and Youth Care Practice* 22(4), pp. 56–64.

Garfat, T. and Charles, G. (2012) *A Guide to Developing Effective Child and Youth Care Practice with Families*. Cape Town: Pretext.

Gaughan, P. and Gharabaghi, K. (1999) 'The prospects and dilemmas of child and youth care as a professional discipline', *Journal of Child and Youth Care* 13(1), pp. 1–18.

Gerstel, N. and Gallagher, S. (2001) 'Men's caregiving', *Gender and Society* 15(2), pp. 197–217.

Gharabaghi, K. (2012) *Being with Edgy Youth*. New York: Nova Science.

Gharabaghi, K. and Stuart, C. (2013) *Right Here, Right Now: exploring life-space interventions for children and youth*. Toronto: Pearson.

Gibbs, L. (2003) *Evidence-based Practice for the Helping Professions: a practical guide with integrated multimedia*. Pacific Grove, CA: Brooks/Cole.

Gibbs, L. and Gambrill, E. (2002) 'Evidence-based practice: counterarguments to objections', *Research on Social Work Practice* 12, pp. 452–76.

Gibson, D.E. and Schroeder, S.J. (2002) 'Grinning, frowning and emotionless: agent perceptions of power and their effect on felt and displayed emotions in influence attempts', in N. Ashkanasy, W. Zerbe and C. Härtel (eds.) *Managing Emotions in the Workplace*. New York: M.E. Sharpe.

Gilchrist, A. (2004) *The Well-Connected Community*. Bristol: The Policy Press.

Gilligan, R. (1991) *Irish Child Care Services: policy, practice and provision*. Dublin: Institute of Public Administration.

Gilligan, R. (2001) *Promoting Resilience: a resource guide on working with children in the care system*. London: British Association for Adoption and Fostering.

Glaser, R. (1984) 'Education and thinking: the role of knowledge', *American Psychologist* 39, pp. 93–104.

Glazer, N. and Moynihan, D. (1975) *Ethnicity: theory and experience*. Cambridge, MA: Harvard University Press.

Goebel, B. and Brown, D. (1981) 'Age differences in motivation related to Maslow's need hierarchy', *Developmental Psychology* 17(6), pp. 809–15.

Goffman, E. (1968) *Stigma: notes on the management of spoiled identity*. London: Penguin.

Gossett, M. and Weinman, L. (2007) 'Evidence-based practice and social work: an illustration of the steps involved', *Health and Social Work* 32(2), pp. 147–50.

Goswami, U. (2001) 'Cognitive development: no stages please – we're British', *British Journal of Psychology* 92, pp. 257–77.

Gould, T. and Williams, A. (2010) 'Family homelessness: an investigation of structural effects', *Journal of Human Behavior in the Social Environment* 20(2), pp. 170–92.

Government of Ireland (1985) *In Partnership with Youth: the national youth policy*. Dublin: Stationery Office.

Government of Ireland (1990) *Needs and Abilities: a policy for the intellectually disabled. Report of the Review Group on Mental Handicap Services*. Dublin: Stationery Office.

Government of Ireland (1993) *Report of the Second Commission on the Status of Women*. Dublin: Stationery Office.

Government of Ireland (1995) *Report of the Task Force on the Travelling Community*. Dublin: Stationery Office.

Government of Ireland (2000) *Our Children, Their Lives. The National Children's Strategy*. Dublin: Stationery Office.

Government of Ireland (2002) *Report to the United Nations on the National Plan for Women 2002 on the Implementation of the Beijing Platform for Action*. Dublin: Stationery Office. <justice.ie/en/JELR/UNReportBeijing.pdf/Files/UNReport Beijing.pdf>

Government of Ireland (2004) *National Disability Strategy*. Dublin: Stationery Office.

Government of Ireland (2006a) *A Vision for Change: report of the Expert Group on Mental Health Policy*. Dublin: Stationery Office.

Government of Ireland (2006b) *Sectoral Plans under the Disability Strategy*. Dublin: Stationery Office.

Government of Ireland (2007) *National Action Plan for Social Inclusion 2007–2016*. Dublin: Stationery Office.

Gradener, J. and Spiers, M. (2006) 'Empowerment of social services professionals: strategies for professionalisation and knowledge development', in J. Duyvendak, T. Knijn and M. Kremer (eds.) *Policy, People, and the New Professional: de-professionalisation and re-professionalisation in care and welfare*. Amsterdam: Amsterdam University Press. <oapen.org/download?type=docu ment&docid=340171>

Graham, A. (2004) 'Dignity and difference: context and theoretic framework for day service development', in *Conference Proceedings: the role and future development of day services for older people in Ireland*. Report 74. Dublin: National Council on Ageing and Older People.

Graham, G. (1995) 'The roles of the residential care worker', *Journal of the European Association of Training Centres for Socio-Educational Care Work* 1, pp. 125–53.

Graham, G. (2006a) 'Attachment theory and wellbeing for the young person in residential care: the provision of a second chance secure base for the child in crisis', *Relational Child and Youth Care Practice* 19(1), pp. 23–34.

Graham, G. (2006b) 'Social care work with families in crisis: attachment strategies and effective care-giving through life-space opportunities', in T. O'Connor and M. Murphy (eds.) *Social Care in Ireland: theory, policy and practice*. Cork: Cork Institute of Technology Press.

Greene, S. (1994) 'Growing up Irish: development in context', *Irish Journal of Psychology* 15(2–3), pp. 354–71.

Gregg, M. (2011) *Work's Intimacy*. Cambridge: Polity.

Grier, A. and Thomas, T. (2009) 'Troubled and in trouble: young people, truancy and offending', in R. Adams, L. Dominelli and M. Payne (eds.) *Practising Social Work in a Complex World*. Basingstoke: Palgrave Macmillan.

Griffin, C. (2008) *Nomads under the Westway: Irish Travellers, gypsies and other traders in west London*. Hatfield: University of Hertfordshire Press.

Gustavsson, B. (2010) 'Knowledge, *bildung* and action in social pedagogy', in L. Eriksson and T. Winman (eds.) *Learning to Fly: social pedagogy in a contemporary society*. Göteborg: Daidalos.

Habermas, J. (1984) *The Theory of Communicative Action. Volume 1: reason and the rationalization of society*. Boston: Beacon.

Hagan, J. and McCarthy, B. (1997) *Mean Streets: youth crime and homelessness*. New York: Cambridge University Press.

Haines, K. (2009) 'Youth justice and young offenders', in R. Adams, L. Dominelli and M. Payne (eds.) *Critical Practice in Social Work*. Basingstoke: Palgrave Macmillan.

Hall, S. (ed.) (1997) *Representation: cultural representations and signifying practices*. London: Sage/Open University Press.

Hallstedt, P. and Högström, H. (2005) *The Recontextualisation of Social Pedagogy: a study of three curricula in the Netherlands, Norway and Ireland*. Malmö Studies in Educational Sciences 21. Malmö: Holmberg.

Halpern, D. (2005) *Social Capital*. Cambridge: Polity.

Hämäläinen, J. (2012) 'Social pedagogic eyes in the midst of diverse understandings, conceptualisations and activities', presentation to ITSligo/Thempra/SPDN/IASCE symposium, Sligo, 24–25 May. <thempra.org.uk/SPDNmeeting6.htm>

Hamilton, C. (2012) *Irish Social Work and Social Care Law*. Dublin: Gill & Macmillan.

Hamilton, C. and Seymour, M. (2006) 'ASBOs and behaviour orders: institutional intolerance of youth', *Youth Studies Ireland* 1(1), pp. 61–76. <iywc.ie/wp-content/uploads/2010/11/YouthStudiesIreland-ASBOs-_and_Behaviour_Orders-2.pdf>

Hanley, L. (2009) 'The way we live now', *The Guardian*, 14 March.

Hanlon, N. (2007a) 'An equality perspective on residential child care', *Scottish Journal of Residential Child Care* 6(1), pp. 22–31.

Hanlon, N. (2007b) 'Positioning equality within social care education: a framework for teaching practice', *European Journal of Social Education* 12–13.

Hanlon, N. (2009) 'Valuing equality in Irish social care', *Irish Journal of Applied Social Studies* 9(1), pp. 6–14. <arrow.dit.ie/ijass/vol9/iss1/3>

Hanlon, N. (2012) *Masculinities, Care and Equality*. Basingstoke: Palgrave Macmillan.

Hanmer, J. and Statham, D. (eds.) (1999) *Women and Social Work*. London: Macmillan.

Harré, R. (1998) *The Singular Self: an introduction to the psychology of personhood*. London: Sage.

Harris, M. (2004) 'First words', in J. Oates and A. Grayson (eds.) *Cognitive and Language Development in Children*. Milton Keynes: Open University Press.

Harris, M., Barlow-Brown, F. and Chasin, J. (1995) 'The emergence of referential understanding: pointing and the comprehension of object names', *First Language* 15, pp. 19–34.

Harris, M., Jones, D. and Grant, J. (1983) 'The nonverbal context of mothers' speech to infants', *First Language* 4, pp. 21–30.

Harter, L., Berquist, C., Titsworth, B., Novak, D. and Brokaw, T. (2005) 'The structuring of invisibility among the hidden homeless: the politics of space, stigma, and identity construction', *Journal of Applied Communication Research* 33(4), pp. 305–27.

Haslett, D. (2003) *The Role and Future Development of Day Services for Older People in Ireland*. Report 74. Dublin: National Council on Ageing and Older People.

Hastings, R. and Remington, B. (1994) 'The emotional dimension of working with challenging behaviours', *Clinical Psychology Forum* 79, pp. 11–16.

Hattie, J. (1992) *Self-concept*. Mahwah, NJ: Lawrence Erlbaum.

Hawkins, P. and Shohet, R. (2007) *Supervision in the Helping Professions*. Buckingham: Open University Press.

Hayes, S., Barnes-Holmes, D. and Roche, B. (2001) *Relational Frame Theory: a post-Skinnerian account of human language and cognition*. New York: Plenum.

Health Promotion Agency (2008) *Cook It! An Evaluation of a Community Nutrition Education Programme in Northern Ireland – the summary report*. Belfast: HPA of Northern Ireland. <healthpromotionagency.org.uk/Resources/nutrition/pdfs/cookitreportfinal_04_09.pdf>

Hearn, J. (1999) 'A crisis in masculinity or new agendas for men?', in S. Walby (ed.) *New Agendas for Women*. Oxford: Polity.

Helliwell, J. and Putnam, R. (2005) 'The social context of well-being', in F. Huppert, N. Baylis and B. Keverne (eds.) *The Science of Well-being*. Oxford: Oxford University Press.

Henderson, J. and Atkinson, D. (eds.) (2003) *Managing Care in Context*. London: Routledge.

Herd, P. and Meyer, M. (2002) 'Care work: invisible civic engagement', *Gender and Society* 16(5), pp. 665–88.

HETAC [Higher Education and Training Awards Council] (2010) *Social Care Work Awards Standards*. Dublin: HETAC. <www.hetac.ie/docs/B.2.9-5.5_Awards_Standards_Social_Care_Work_2010.pdf>

Heumann, L., McCall, M. and Boldy, D. (2001) *Empowering Frail Elderly People: opportunities and impediments in housing, health, and support service delivery*. New York: Praeger.

Hilliard, B. (2003) 'The Catholic church and married women's sexuality: habitus change in late twentieth Ireland', *Irish Journal of Sociology* 12(2), pp. 28–49.

HIQA [Health Information and Quality Authority] (2009) *National Quality Standards: residential services for people with disabilities in Ireland*. Dublin: HIQA. <hiqa.ie/system/files/Standards_Residential_Services_People_with_Disabilities_1.pdf>

HIQA (2012) *National Standards for the Protection and Welfare of Children*. Dublin: HIQA. <hiqa.ie/system/files/Child-Protection-Welfare-Standards.pdf>

HIQA (2013) National Standards for Residential Services for Children and Adults with Disabilities. Cork: HIQA. <hiqa.ie/system/files/standards-disabilities-children-adults.pdf>

Hoffman, L. and Coffey, B. (2008) 'Dignity and indignation: how people experiencing homelessness view services and providers', *The Social Science Journal* 45, pp. 207–22.

Holmes, J. (1993) *John Bowlby and Attachment Theory*. London: Routledge.

Home Office (1999) *The Stephen Lawrence Inquiry: report of an inquiry by Sir William MacPherson of Cluny* [MacPherson report]. Cm 4262–1. London: Home Office.

Homeless Agency (2006) *Counted In, 2005*. Dublin: Homeless Agency.

Homeless Agency (2008) *Counted In, 2008: a report on the extent of homelessness in Dublin*. Dublin: Homeless Agency.

Honohan, I. and Rougier, N. (2012) *Tolerance and Cultural Diversity in Ireland: concepts and practices*. San Domenico di Fiesol: European University Institute. <cadmus.eui.eu/handle/1814/23258>

Hough, J. (2011) 'DNA study Travellers a distinct ethnicity', *Irish Examiner*, 31 May.

Houghton, F. (2005) 'Hiding the evidence: the state and spatial inequalities in health in Ireland', *Irish Geography* 37(2), pp. 96–106.

Houghton, F. and Houghton, S. (2013) 'Health inequalities in Ireland: an often unclear but ever present danger', in C. Lewis (ed.) *Ireland: economic, political and social issues*. Hauppauge, NY: Nova Science.

Houser, J. (2008) *Nursing Research: reading, using and creating evidence*. London: Jones & Bartlett.

Housing Agency (2011) *Housing Needs Assessment 2011*. Dublin: Housing Agency. <housing.ie/Our-Services/Research-Services/Most-Viewed-Publications/Housing-Needs-Assessment-Report_web.aspx>

Howes, C. and Hamilton, C. (1992) 'Children's relationships with child care teachers: stability and concordance with parental attachments', *Child Development* 63, pp. 867–78.

HSA [Health and Safety Authority] (2011) *Summary of Workplace Injury, Illness and Fatality Statistics 2010–2011*. Dublin: Stationery Office. <www.hsa.ie/eng/Publications_and_Forms/Publications/Corporate/Summary_of_Workplace_Injury,_Illness_and_Fatality_Statistics_2010-2011.pdf>

HSA (2012) *Health and Safety at Work in Residential Care Facilities*. Dublin: HSA.

HSE [Health Service Executive] (2011a) *Child Protection and Welfare Practice Handbook*. Dublin: HSE. <hse.ie/eng/services/Publications/services/Children/WelfarePractice.pdf>

HSE (2011b) *Review of Adequacy for HSE Children and Family Services*. Dublin: HSE. <hse.ie/eng/services/Publications/services/Children/reviewofadequacy2011.pdf>

HSE (2011c) *Services for Separated Children Seeking Asylum*. Dublin: HSE.

HSE (2011d) *Time to Move on from Congregated Settings: a strategy for community inclusion*. Dublin: HSE.

HSE (2012a) *HSE National Service Plan 2012*. Dublin: HSE. <hse.ie/eng/services/Publications/corporate/nsp2012.pdf>

HSE (2012b) *New Directions. Review of HSE Day Services and Implementation Plan 2012–2016: working group report*. Dublin: HSE.

HSE (2013) 'Nursing homes support scheme, a fair deal'. <hse.ie/eng/services/Find_a_Service/Older_People_Services/nhss>

HSE and IAYPIC [Irish Association for Young People in Care] (2009) *Guide to Living in Residential Care*. Dublin: HSE. <epiconline.ie/your-guide-to-living-in-residential-care.html>

Huesmann, L. and Taylor, L. (2006) 'The role of media violence in violent behaviour', *Annual Review of Public Health* 27, pp. 393–415.

Hug, C. (1999) *The Politics of Sexual Morality in Ireland*. London: Macmillan.

Hugman, R. (1991) *Power in Caring Professions*. London: Macmillan.

IASCE [Irish Association of Social Care Educators] (2009) *Practice Placement Manual – Bachelor of Arts in Applied Social Studies (Social Care)*. <http://staffweb.itsligo.ie/staff/pshare/iasce/Placement%20Manual%2029mar09.pdf>

IASCE (2011) *Social Care Student Practice Placement Policies*. <dit.ie/socialscienceslaw/media/ditsocialscienceslaw/iasce%20social%20care%20placement%20guidelines.pdf>

ICTU [Irish Congress of Trade Unions] (2012) *Changes in Employment and Services in the Voluntary and Community Sector in Ireland, 2008–2012*. Dublin: ICTU.

Ilan, J. (2011) 'Reclaiming respectability? The class-cultural dynamics of crime, community and governance in inner-city Dublin', *Urban Studies* 48(6), pp. 1137–55.

ILCU [Irish League of Credit Unions] (2012) 'Third Irish League of Credit Unions' "What's Left?" Tracker Survey'. <creditunion.ie/communications/news/2012/title,7005,en.php>

Illeris, K. (2007) *Lärande*. Lund: Studentlitteratur.

Illich, I. (1976) *The Limits to Medicine: medical nemesis, the expropriation of health*. Harmondsworth: Penguin.

ILO [International Labour Organization] (2003) *Decent Work and the Informal Economy*. Report 6. 90th Annual General Meeting. Geneva: ILO.

ILO, International Council of Nurses, World Health Organization and Public Services International (2002) *Framework for Addressing Workplace Violence in the Health Sector*. Geneva: International Labour Office.

Indecon (2012) *Assessment of the Economic Value of Youth Work*. Dublin: National Youth Council of Ireland.

Inglis, T. (1998a) 'Foucault, Bourdieu and the field of Irish sexuality', *Irish Journal of Sociology* 7, pp. 5–28.

Inglis, T. (1998b) *Lessons in Irish Sexuality*. Dublin: University College Dublin Press.

Inglis, T. (2008) 'The Neary case', in M. Corcoran and P. Share (eds.) *Belongings: shaping identity in modern Ireland. Irish Sociological Chronicles. Volume 6 (2005–2006)*. Dublin: Institute of Public Administration.

Inskipp, F. and Proctor, B. (1993) *Making the Most of Supervision: a professional development resource for counsellors, supervisors and trainees*. Twickenham: Cascade.

Institute for Health Research (2005) *The Impact of Person Centred Planning*. Lancaster: Lancaster University.

Inter-departmental Committee on the Care of the Aged (1968) *Care of the Aged Report*. Dublin: Stationery Office.

IPRT [Irish Penal Reform Trust] (2012) 'Facts & figures'. <iprt.ie/prison-facts-2>

IRC [Irish Refugee Council] (1999) *Separated Children Seeking Asylum in Ireland: a report on legal and social conditions*. Dublin: IRC.

Irish Traveller Movement (2011) *Cuts to Traveller Education: submission paper*. Dublin: Irish Traveller Movement.

IYJS [Irish Youth Justice Service] (2012a) 'Children detention schools'. Dublin: IYJS. <www.iyjs.ie/en/IYJS/Pages/WP08000052>

IYJS (2012b) 'Community sanctions'. Dublin: IYJS. <www.iyjs.ie/en/IYJS/Pages/WP08000063>

IYJS (2012c) *National Youth Justice Strategy 2008–2010*. Dublin: IYJS. <www.iyjs.ie/en/IYJS/Strategy%20PDF.pdf/Files/Strategy%20PDF.pdfed>

IZA and ESRI [Forschungsinstitut zur Zukunft der Arbeit and Economic and Social Research Institute] (2011) *Study on Active Inclusion of Migrants: a final report*. Bonn and Dublin: IZA and ESRI. <esri.ie/UserFiles/publications/bkmnext211/BKMNEXT212.pdf>

Jack, G. and Gill, O. (2003) *The Missing Side of the Triangle*. London: Barnardos.

Jackson, A. and O'Doherty, C. (2012) *Community Development in Ireland: theory, policy and practice*. Dublin: Gill & Macmillan.

Jay, D. (1962) *Socialism and the New Society*. London: Longman.

JCFJ [Jesuit Centre for Faith and Justice] (2004) 'Statement on the citizenship referendum'. Dublin: JCFJ. <jcfj.ie/content/view/71>

JCSCP [Joint Committee on Social Care Professionals] (2002) *Final Report of Joint Committee on Social Care Professionals*. Dublin: Health Service Executive for the Department of Social and Family Affairs. <lenus.ie/hse/bitstream/10147/46110/1/10672.pdf>

Jenkins, R. (1996) '"Us" and "them": ethnicity, racism and ideology', in R. Barot (ed.) *The Racism Problematic: contemporary sociological debates on race and ethnicity*. Lampeter: Edward Mellen.

Jenkins, R. (1997) *Rethinking Ethnicity: arguments and explorations*. London: Sage.

Jordan, B. (2007) *Social Work and Well-being*. Dorset: Russell House.

Joyce, C. and Quinn, E. (2009) *European Migration Network: policies on unaccompanied minors*. Dublin: Economic and Social Research Institute. <emn.ie/files/p_20100715105236Policies%20on%20unaccompanied%20minors%20in%20Ireland.pdf>

Jull, D. (2001) 'Is child and youth care a profession?', *Journal of Child and Youth Care* 14(3), pp. 79–88.

Juul, J. (2011) *Higher Inequality Lowers Wealth*. Brussels: Foundation for European Progressive Studies. <www.feps-europe.eu/en/news/61_high-inequality-lowers-wealth>

Kadushin, A. (1976) *Supervision in Social Work*. New York: Columbia University Press.

Kearney, N. and Skehill, C. (eds.) (2005) *Social Work in Ireland: historical perspectives*. Dublin: Institute of Public Administration.

Keating, D. (2004) 'Cognitive and language development', in R. Lerner, L. Steinberg and N. Hoboken (eds.) *Handbook of Adolescent Psychology*. Hoboken, NJ: Wiley.

Kelleher, K. and Kelleher, P. (1997) *Family Resource Centres*. Dublin: Stationery Office.

Kelleher, P., Kelleher, C. and Corbett, M. (2000) *Left Out on Their Own: young people leaving care in Ireland*. Dublin: Oak Tree Press.

Kelly, C. (2012) *Annual Report of the National Intellectual Disability Database Committee 2011*. Dublin: Health Research Board.

Kelly, C. and Houghton, F. (2009) 'Social care practitioners as agents of health promotion? An examination of attitudes, knowledge and training', *NIHS Health Bulletin* 5(1), pp. 68–9.

Kennedy, K. and Gallagher, C. (1997) 'Social pedagogy in Europe', *Irish Social Worker* 15(1), pp. 6–8.

Kennefick, P. (2006) 'Aspects of personal development', in T. O'Connor and M. Murphy (eds.) *Social Care in Ireland: theory, policy and practice*. Cork: Cork Institute of Technology Press.

Kenny, M. and McNeela, E. (2003) *Caring for Diversity: report on a research project to identify the need and potential for culturally appropriate child welfare and protection services for Travellers*. Dublin: Pavee Point. <paveepoint.ie/pdf/CaringForDiversity.pdf>

Kenny, M. and McNeela, E. (2006) *Assimilation Policies and Outcomes: Travellers' experiences*. Dublin: Pavee Point. <paveepoint.ie/pdf/AssimilationPolicies.pdf>

Keogh, F. (2011) *Report of Disability Policy Review*. Dublin: Expert Group on Disability.

Kerry Family Support Team (2012) *Annual Report*. Cork: HSE South.

Kidd, S., Miner, S., Walker, D. and Davidson, L. (2007) 'Stories of working with homeless youth: on being "mind-boggling"', *Children and Youth Services Review* 29, pp. 16–34.

Kilkelly, U. (2006) *Youth Justice in Ireland: tough lives, rough justice*. Dublin: Irish Academic Press.

Kirby, P. (2001) 'Inequality and poverty in Ireland: clarifying social objectives', in S. Cantillon, C. Corrigan, P. Kirby and J. O'Flynn (eds.) *Rich and Poor:*

perspectives on tackling inequality in Ireland. Dublin: Combat Poverty Agency and Oak Tree Press.

Kirby, P. (2006) 'The changing role of the Irish state: from welfare to competition state', in T. O'Connor and M. Murphy (eds.) *Social Care in Ireland*. Cork: Cork Institute of Technology Press.

Kissane, S. and Guerin, S. (2010) 'Paper 4: meeting the challenge of challenging behaviour'. Dublin: National Disability Authority. <www.nda.ie/Website/NDA/CntMgmtNew.nsf/0/49A078AFD1407C358025706600506DF6?OpenDocument>

Knoppers, A. (1993) 'A critical theory of gender relations', in M. Van Leeuwen (ed.) *After Eden*. Grand Rapids, MI: Eerdmans.

Knorth, E., van den Bergh, P. and Verheij, F. (eds.) (2002) *Professionalization and Participation in Child and Youth Care: challenging understandings in theory and practice*. Aldershot: Ashgate.

Kochanska, G. (2001) 'Emotional development in children with different attachment histories: the first three years', *Child Development* 72(2), pp. 474–90.

Kolb, D. (1984) *Experiential Learning: experience as the source of learning and development*. Upper Saddle River, NJ: Prentice Hall.

Kornbeck, J. and Rosendal Jensen, N. (eds.) (2011) *Social Pedagogy for the Entire Lifespan. Volume 1*. Bremen: Europäischer Hochschulverlag.

Kornbeck, J. and Rosendal Jensen, N. (eds.) (2012) *Social Pedagogy for the Entire Lifespan. Volume 2*. Bremen: Europäischer Hochschulverlag.

Kosonen, M. (1996) 'Siblings as providers of support and care during middle childhood: children's perceptions', *Children and Society* 10(4), pp. 267–79.

Krojer, T. (2001) *Comparative Research on Social Care: the state of the art*. Brussels: European Commission.

Krueger, M. (1998) *Interactive Youth Work Practice*. New York: CWLA Press.

Krueger, M. (2002) 'A further review of the development of the child and youth care profession in the United States', *Child and Youth Care Forum* 31(1), pp. 13–26.

Kuhn, D., Amsel, E. and O'Loughlin, M. (1988) *The Development of Scientific Thinking Skills*. San Diego, CA: Academic Press.

Lalor, K. (2009) 'How many social care students does Ireland need? Audit of social care student numbers and programme providers in Ireland', paper to IASCE/IASCW conference, *Social Care Education and Practice: learning lessons together*, Sligo, February. <arrow.dit.ie/aaschsslcon/8>

Lalor, K. and Share, P. (2009) 'Understanding social care', in P. Share and K. Lalor (eds.) *Applied Social Care: an introduction for Irish students*. Dublin: Gill & Macmillan.

Lalor, K., de Róiste, Á. and Devlin, M. (2007) *Young People in Contemporary Ireland*. Dublin: Gill & Macmillan.

Laming, Lord (2003) *The Victoria Climbié Inquiry: report of an inquiry by Lord Laming presented to parliament by the secretary of state for health and the secretary of state for the home department*. London: HMSO.

Lanyado, M. (2003) 'The roots of mental health: emotional development and a caring environment', in A. Ward, K. Kasinski, J. Pooley and A. Worthington (eds.) *Therapeutic Communities for Children and Young People*. London: Jessica Kingsley.

Lawless, M. and Corr, C. (2005) *Drug Use among the Homeless Population in Ireland: a report for the National Advisory Committee on Drugs*. Dublin: Stationery Office.

Layard, R. (2005) *Happiness: lessons from a new science*. London: Penguin.

Layder, D. (1993) *New Strategies in Social Research*. Cambridge: Polity.

Layte, R., McGee, H., Quail, A., Rundle, K., Cousins, G., Donnelly, C., Mulcahy, F. and Conroy, R. (2006) *The Irish Study of Sexual Health and Relationships*. Dublin: Department of Health and Children and Crisis Pregnancy Agency.

Leadbetter, C. (2006) 'Production by the masses: professionals and postindustrial public services', in J. Craig (ed.) *Production Values: futures for professionalism*. London: Demos.

Leadbetter, M. (2002) 'Empowerment and advocacy', in R. Adams, L. Dominelli and M. Payne (eds.) *Social Work: themes, issues and critical debates*. Basingstoke: Palgrave.

Leary, M. and Tangney, J. (2012) *Handbook of Self and Identity*. New York: Guilford.

Leavy, A. and Kahan, B. (1991) *The Pindown Experience and the Protection of Children: the report of the Staffordshire child care enquiry*. Stafford: Staffordshire County Council.

Lees, S. (1993) *Sugar and Spice: sexuality and adolescent girls*. London: Penguin.

Lentin, R. (1998) 'Irishness, the 1937 Constitution and citizenship: a gender and ethnicity view', *Irish Journal of Sociology* 8, pp. 5–24.

Lentin, R. (2004) 'From racial state to racist state', *Variant* 2(20), pp. 7–8.

Lentin, R. (2007) 'Illegal in Ireland, Irish illegals: diaspora nation as a racial state', *Irish Political Studies* 22(4), pp. 433–53.

Lesovitch, L. (2005) *Roma Educational Needs in Ireland: context and challenges*. Dublin: City of Dublin VEC in association with Pavee Point Travellers Support Centre and the Roma Support Group.

Lewis, J. (2001) 'What works in community care?', *Managing Community Care* 9, pp. 3–6.

Lewis, M. (2005) *Asylum: understanding public attitudes*. London: Institute for Public Policy Research.

Lewis, M., Feiring, C. and Rosenthal, S. (2000) 'Attachment over time', *Child Development* 71(3), pp. 707–20.

Likert, R. (1961) *New Patterns of Management*. New York: McGraw-Hill.

Lindsay, M. (2002) 'Building a professional identity: the challenge for residential child and youth care', in E. Knorth, P. van den Bergh and F. Verheij (eds.) *Professionalization and Participation in Child and Youth Care*. Aldershot: Ashgate.

Linehan, J. and Lynch, D. (2009) 'Clonakilty Community Hospital: a new model of care', presentation at Nursing Homes Ireland annual conference, Dublin, 22 October.

Littleton, K., Miell, D. and Faulkner, D. (2004) *Learning to Collaborate, Collaborating to Learn*. New York: Nova Science.

Lorenz, W. (1994) *Social Work in a Changing Europe*. London: Routledge.

Lorenz, W. (1998) 'Cultural diversity as a challenge for social work', *Irish Social Worker* 16(3), pp. 15–17.

Lundberg, K. (2011) 'Hamnen mäter vårt människovärde', *Sydsvenska Dagbladet*, 13 February.

Lynch, K. and Lyons, M. (2008) 'The gender order of caring', in U. Barry (ed.) *Where Are We Now? New Feminist Perspectives on Women in Contemporary Ireland*. Dublin: New Island and TASC.

Lynch, K. and McLaughlin, E. (1995) 'Caring labour and love labour', in P. Clancy, S. Drudy, K. Lynch and L. O' Dowd (eds.) *Irish Society: sociological perspectives*. Dublin: Institute of Public Administration.

Lyon, D. and Glucksman, M. (2008) 'Comparative configurations of care work across Europe', *Sociology* 42(1), pp. 101–18.

Lyons, D. (2007) 'Just bring your self: exploring the training of self in social care education', Masters thesis, Dublin Institute of Technology.

Lyons, D. (2010) *Creative Studies for the Caring Professions*. Dublin: Gill & Macmillan.

MacGabhann, C. (2011) *Voices Unheard: a study of Irish Travellers in prison*. London: The Irish Chaplaincy in Britain. <iprt.ie/contents/2138>

MacGréil, M. (2010) *Emancipation of the Travelling People: a report on the attitudes and prejudices of the Irish people towards the Travellers based on a national social survey 2007–'08*. Maynooth: National University of Ireland, Maynooth.

Macionis, J. and Plummer, K. (2012) *Sociology: a global introduction*. London: Pearson Prentice Hall.

MacKenna, P. (1994) 'Ontario Association of Child and Youth Care Counsellors: effectiveness and future directions', *Journal of Child and Youth Care* 9(4), pp. 1–10.

MacLaughlin, J. (1995) 'The evolution of anti-Traveller racism in Ireland', *Race and Class* 44(4), pp. 47–63.

Madsen, B. (2007) *Socialpedagogik: integration och inklusion i det moderna samhället*. Lund: Studentlitteratur.

Maguire, M. and Cassidy, T. (2009) 'The new Irish question: citizenship, motherhood and the politics of life itself', *Irish Journal of Anthropology* 12(3), pp. 18–28.

Main, M. (1995) 'Recent studies in attachment', in S. Goldberg, R. Muir and J. Kerr (eds.) *Attachment Theory: social, developmental, and clinical perspectives*. Hillsdale, NJ: Analytic Press.

Male, D. (2003) 'Challenging behaviour: the perceptions of teachers of children and young people with severe learning disabilities', *Journal of Research in Special Educational Needs* 3(3), pp. 162–71.

Mansell, J. (1992) *Services for People with Learning Disabilities and Challenging Behaviour or Mental Health Needs* [Mansell report]. London: HMSO.

Maroda, K. (2004) *The Power of Counter Transference Innovations in Analytic Technique*. Hillsdale, NJ: Analytic Press.

Marsh, P. and Fisher, M. (2005) *Developing the Evidence Base for Social Work and Social Care Practice*. London: Social Care Institute for Excellence.

Martin, V., Charlesworth, J. and Henderson, E. (2010) *Managing in Health and Social Care*. London: Routledge.

Maslach, C. (2003) *Burnout: the cost of caring*. Dallas, TX: Majors Books.

Maslow, A. (1970) *Motivation and Personality*. New York: Harper & Row.

Maurice, C., Green, G. and Luce, S. (1996) *Behavioural Intervention for Children with Autism: a manual for parents and professionals*. Austin, TX: Pro-Ed.

Mayock, P. (2008) 'Young people's pathways through homelessness: the offender–victimisation nexus', in D. Downey (ed.) *Perspectives on Irish Homelessness: past, present and future*. Dublin: The Homeless Agency.

Mayock, P. and Carr, N. (2008) *Not Just Homeless . . . A Study of 'Out of Home' Young People in Cork City*. Cork: Health Service Executive.

Mayock, P. and O'Sullivan, E. (2007) *Lives in Crisis: homeless young people in Dublin*. Dublin: The Liffey Press.

Mayock, P. and Sheridan, S. (2012) *Women's 'Journeys' to Homelessness: key findings from a biographical study of homeless women in Ireland*. Research paper 1. Dublin: School of Social Work and Social Policy and Children's Research Centre, Trinity College.

Mayock, P. and Vekić, K. (2006) *Understanding Youth Homelessness in Dublin City: key findings from the first phase of a longitudinal cohort study*. Dublin: Stationery Office.

McCann-James, C., de Róiste, Á. and McHugh, J. (2009) *Social Care Practice in Ireland: an integrated perspective*. Dublin: Gill & Macmillan.

McCarthy, D. and McCarthy, P. (1998) *Market Economies: trading in the Traveller economy*. Dublin: Pavee Point Publications.

McDonagh, M. and McVeigh, R. (1996) *Irish Travellers in the USA*. Belfast: Belfast Traveller Education and Development Group.

McDonnell, A. (1997) *Managing Aggressive Behaviour in Care Settings: understanding and applying low arousal approaches*. Chichester: Wiley Blackwell.

McDonnell, A., Sturmey, P., Oliver, C., Cunningham, J., Hayes, S., Galvin, M., Walshe, C. and Cunningham, C. (2008) 'The effects of staff training on staff confidence and challenging behaviour in services for people with autism spectrum disorders', *Research in Autism Spectrum Disorders* 2(2), pp. 311–19.

McDonnell, P. (2007) *Disability and Society: ideological and historical dimensions*. Dublin: Blackhall.

McEvoy, O. and Smith, M. (2011) *Listen to Our Voices! Hearing children and young people in the care of the state*. Dublin: Government Publications. <dcya.gov.ie/viewdoc.asp?DocID=1606/>

McGaughey, F. (2011) *Irish Travellers and Roma: shadow report – a response to Ireland's third and fourth report on the international Convention on the Elimination of All Forms of Racial Discrimination* (CERD). Dublin: Pavee Point. <www2.ohchr.org/english/bodies/cerd/docs/ngos/PPTC_Ireland78.pdf>

McGuinness, C. (1993) *Report of the Kilkenny Incest Investigation*. Dublin: Stationery Office.

McKay, S. (2007) *Silent People and Other Stories*. Dublin: Combat Poverty Agency.

McMahan-True, M., Pisani, L. and Oumar, F. (2001) 'Infant mother attachment among the Dogon of Mali', *Child Development* 72(5), pp. 451–66.

McMillan, M. (2004) *The Person-Centred Approach to Therapeutic Change*. London: Sage.

McVeigh, R. (2007) '"Ethnicity denial" and racism: the case of the government of Ireland against Irish Travellers', *Translocations* 2(1), pp. 90–133. <www.imrstr.dcu.ie/volume1issue2/volume1issue2-6.pdf>

Mearns, D. and Cooper, M. (2007) *Working at Relational Depth in Counselling and Psychotherapy*. London: Sage.

Mearns, D. and Thorne, B. (2007) *Person Centred Counselling in Action*. 3rd edn. London: Sage.

Meenan, D. (2002) 'The phenomenology of career and personal development as perceived by residential child care workers in the North Western Health Board', MBA (Health Services Management) thesis, University College Dublin and Royal College of Surgeons in Ireland.

Mehler, J. and Dupoux, E. (1994) *What Infants Know*. Oxford: Blackwell.

Mhic Mhathúna, M. (2012) 'Child language in the early years', in M. Mhic Mhathúna and M. Taylor (eds.) *Early Childhood Education and Care: an introduction for students in Ireland*. Dublin: Gill & Macmillan.

Miller, T. (2008) 'Implementing competencies and their impact on social education', *European Journal of Social Education* 14–15, pp. 113–20.

Moane, G. (1994) 'A psychological analysis of colonialism in an Irish context', *Irish Journal of Psychology* 15(2–3), pp. 250–65.

Moane, G. (1999) *Gender and Colonialism: a psychological analysis of oppression and liberation*. London: Macmillan.

Monk, L. (2011) 'Self-care for social workers: a precious commodity, an ethical imperative', *Perspective: Newsletter of the BC Association of Social Workers* 33(1), pp. 4–7. <bcasw.org/wp-content/uploads/2011/06/Perspectives-January-2011.pdf>

Morris, J. (2005) *Citizenship and Disabled People*. London: The Disability Rights Commission.

Morrison, T. and Horwath, J. (1999) *Effective Staff Training in Social Care: from theory to practice*. London: Routledge.

Moss, B. (2008) *Communication Skills for Health and Social Care*. London: Sage.

Moss, P. and Cameron, C. (2004) 'Does care work have a future?', *Socialvetenskaplig Tidsktif* 3–4, pp. 223–37.

MTCMI [Midlands Traveller Conflict and Mediation Initiative] (2009) *Midlands Traveller Conflict & Mediation Initiative: Laois, Offaly, Longford, Westmeath Report*. Dublin: Health Service Executive. <hse.ie/eng/services/Publications/services/SocialInclusion/InterculturalGuide/Traveller/Midlands_Traveller_Conflict_Mediation_Initiative.pdf>

Mulkeen, M. (2012a) 'Gendered processes in child protection: "mother-blaming" and the erosion of men's accountability', *Irish Journal of Applied Social Studies* 12(1), pp. 74–88. <arrow.dit.ie/ijass/vol12/iss1/7>

Mulkeen, M. (2012b) 'Professional socialization in social care: navigating a winding path', MA (Learning and Teaching) thesis, Waterford Institute of Technology.

Murgatroyd, S. (1996) *Counselling and Helping*. London: Routledge.

Murphy, C. (2012) 'Transferring knowledge and life experiences between generations: the potential of community based intergenerational projects', M.Phil. thesis, Dublin Institute of Technology. <arrow.dit.ie/appamas/37>

Murphy, C., O'Shea, E., Cooney, A., Shiel, A. and Hodgins, M. (2006) *Improving Quality of Life for Older People in Long Stay Care Settings in Ireland*. Report 93. Dublin: National Council on Ageing and Older People.

Murray, C. and Urban, M. (2012) *Equality and Diversity in Early Childhood: an Irish perspective*. Dublin: Gill & Macmillan.

Naidoo, J. and Wills, J. (2009) *Foundations for Health Promotion*. Oxford: Elsevier.

Nally, M. and Walsh, S. (2004) 'Developing social clubs/centres', in Y. McGivern (ed.) *The Role and Future Development of Day Services for Older People in Ireland: conference proceedings*. Report 79. Dublin: National Council on Ageing and Older People. <www.ncaop.ie/publications/research/reports/79_Day%20Services%20Conf%20Procs.pdf>

Nasc – The Irish Immigrant Support Centre (2012) *Person or Number? Barriers Facing Immigrants Accessing Social Protection in Ireland*. Cork: Nasc.

National Coalition for the Homeless (2009) 'Who is Homeless?'. <national-homeless.org/factsheets/Whois.pdf>

NCEA [National Council for Educational Awards] (1992) *Report of the Committee on Caring and Social Studies*. Dublin: NCEA.

NDA [National Disability Authority] (2004) *Guidelines on Person Centred Planning in the Provision of Services for People with Disabilities in Ireland*. Dublin: NDA.

NDA (2005) *How Far Towards Equality? Measuring How Equally People with Disabilities Are Included in Irish Society*. Dublin: NDA.

NDA (2006) *Mainstreaming Position Paper 2006*. Dublin: NDA.

NDA (2011) *A National Survey of Public Attitudes to Disability in Ireland*. Dublin: NDA.

Nelson-Jones, R. (2009) *Six Key Approaches to Counselling and Therapy*. London: Sage.

NESF [National Economic and Social Forum] (2005) *Care for Older People*. Report 32. Dublin: NESF.

Neville, H.J., Bavelier, D., Corina, D., Rauschecker, J., Karni, A., Lalwani, A., Braun, A., Clark, V., Jezzard, P. and Turner, R. (1998) 'Cerebral organization for language in deaf and hearing subjects: biological constraints and effects of experience', *Proceedings of the National Academy of Science* 95, pp. 922–9.

Neville, P. (2012) 'Volunteers as managers of family resource centres: the experiences of voluntary management committee members', in A. Jackson and C. O'Doherty (eds.) *Community Development in Ireland: theory, policy and practice*. Dublin: Gill & Macmillan.

Ní Chonaill, B. (2007) 'The impact of migrants on resources: a critical assessment of the views of people working/living in the Blanchardstown area', *Translocations* 2(1), pp. 70–89. <dcu.ie/imrstr/volume1issue2/volume1issue 2-5.pdf>

Ní Shúinéar, S. (2004) 'Apocrypha to Canon: inventing Irish Traveller history', *History Ireland* 12(4), pp. 15–19. <historyireland.com/volumes/volume12/ issue4/features/?id=114362>

Nilsson, R. (2004) 'Om omsorg och utbildning', in F. Magnusson and L. Plantin (eds.) *Mångfald och Förändring i Socialt Arbete*. Lund: Studentlitteratur.

Nilsson, R. (2006) 'Äldrepedagogik: socialt arbete med äldre i nytt perspektiv', *Nordisk Socialt Arbeid* 4, pp. 341–51. <idunn.no/file/ci/3043694/nsa_2006_04_ pdf.pdf>

Nirje, B. (1985) 'Setting the record straight: a critique of some frequent misconceptions of the normalization principle', *Australia and New Zealand Journal of Developmental Disabilities* 11(2), pp. 69–72.

Northouse, P. (2010) *Leadership: theory and practice*. 5th edn. London: Sage.

NYCI [National Youth Council of Ireland] (2006) *What is Youth Work?* Information leaflet. Dublin: NYCI.

NYCI (2010) *Starting Out: a national induction training programme for volunteers engaged in youth work practice*. Dublin: NYCI. <www.youth.ie/startingout>

NYCI (2012) *Access All Areas: a diversity toolkit for the youth work sector*. Dublin: NYCI.

NYHP [National Youth Health Programme] (2000) *Health Promotion in Youth Work Settings*. Dublin: National Youth Health Programme.

NYPC [National Youth Policy Committee] (1984) *Final Report*. Dublin: Stationery Office.

OACYC [Ontario Association of Child and Youth Counsellors] (n.d.) 'The field of child and youth work'. <www.oacyc.org/index.php?page=13>

Oakley, A. (1972) *Sex, Gender and Society*. London: Temple Smith.

O'Brien, E. (2011) *Psychology for Social Care: an Irish perspective*. Dublin: Gill & Macmillan.

O'Brien, G. (2003) *Coming Out: Irish gay experiences*. Dublin: Currach.

O'Brien, J. and O'Brien, L. (1989) *Framework for Accomplishment*. Georgia: Responsive Systems Associates.

Observer (2012) 'Parenting classes are a good idea. But families need so much more', 20 May.

O'Carroll, I. and Collins, E. (eds.) (1995) *Lesbian and Gay Visions of Ireland*. London: Cassells.

O'Carroll, P. (1998) 'Blood', in M. Peillon and E. Slater (eds.) *Encounters with Modern Ireland: a sociological chronicle, 1995–1996*. Dublin: Institute of Public Administration.

O'Connor, P. (1992) 'The professionalisation of childcare work in Ireland: an unlikely development', *Children and Society* 6(3), pp. 250–66.

O'Connor, P. (1998) *Emerging Voices: women in contemporary Irish society*. Dublin: Institute of Public Administration.

O'Connor, S. and Pettigrew, C. (2009) 'The barriers perceived to prevent the successful implementation of evidence-based practice by speech and language therapists', *International Journal of Language and Communication Disorders* 44(6), pp. 1018–35.

O'Connor, T. (2006) 'Social care practice: bringing structure and ideology in from the cold', in T. O'Connor and M. Murphy (eds.) *Social Care in Ireland: theory, policy and practice*. Cork: Cork Institute of Technology Press.

O'Connor, T. (2008) 'Towards a holistic model for social care', paper to Irish Association of Social Care Educators conference, Dublin, March.

O'Connor, T. and Murphy, M. (eds.) (2006) *Social Care in Ireland: theory, policy and practice*. Cork: Cork Institute of Technology Press.

O'Doherty, C. (2003) 'Shanakill Family Resource Centre: an evaluation', unpublished report for HSE South.

O'Doherty, C. (2004) 'Towards the construction of an international model for the promotion of child and family welfare practice: family support activities of the Irish health boards under the Child Care Act, 1991', PhD thesis, University College Dublin.

O'Doherty, C. (2006) 'Social care and social capital', in T. O'Connor and M. Murphy (eds.) *Social Care in Ireland: theory, policy and practice*. Cork: Cork Institute of Technology Press.

O'Doherty, C. (2007) *A New Agenda for Family Support: providing services that create social capital*. Dublin: Blackhall.

O'Doherty, C. (2008a) 'Critical social care practice', paper to Irish Association of Social Care Educators conference, Dublin, March.

O'Doherty, C. (2008b) 'Social work and social capital: re-imagining the helping relationship', in K. Burns and D. Lynch (eds.) *Child Protection and Welfare Social Work: contemporary themes and practice perspectives*. Dublin: A&A Farmar.

O'Hanlon, A., McGee, H., Barker, M., Garavan, R., Hickey, A., Conroy, R. and O'Neill, D. (2005) *Health and Social Services for Older People II (HeSSOP II)*

Changing Profiles from 2000 to 2004. Report 91. Dublin: National Council on Ageing and Older People.

O'Higgins, K. (1996) *Disruption, Displacement, Discontinuity? Children in Care and Their Families in Ireland*. Aldershot: Avebury.

Oireachtas (2012a) 'Reply to parliamentary questions by Minister of State at the Department of Health, Deputy Kathleen Lynch', 1 May. <debates.oireachtas.ie/dail/2012/05/01/00348.asp>

Oireachtas (2012b) 'Written reply by Minister for Health, Dr James Reilly, to parliamentary question by Deputy Tom Flanagan', 26 June. <debates.oireachtas.ie/dail/2012/06/28/unrevised2.pdf>

O'Leary, P. and Halton, C. (2009) 'Young persons' probation in the Republic of Ireland: an evaluation of risk and assessment', *Irish Probation Journal* 6, pp. 97–112.

Oliver, B. and Pitt, B. (eds.) (2011) *Working with Children, Young People and Families*. Exeter: Learning Matters.

O'Loingsigh, D. (2001) 'Intercultural education and the school ethos', in F. Farrell and P. Watt (eds.) *Responding to Racism in Ireland*. Dublin: Veritas.

Olson, E. (1999) 'There is no problem of the self', in S. Gallagher and J. Shear (eds.) *Models of the Self*. Exeter: Imprint Academic.

Ombudsman for Children's Office (2011) *Young People in St. Patrick's Institution. A Report by the Ombudsman for Children's Office*. Dublin: Ombudsman for Children's Office. <oco.ie/assets/files/St%20Pats%20Report.pdf>

OMC [Office of the Minister for Children] (2006a) *Diversity and Equality Guidelines for Childcare Providers*. Dublin: OMC. <dcya.gov.ie/documents/childcare/diversity_and_equality.pdf>

OMC (2006b) *State of the Nation's Children*. Dublin: Stationery Office.

OMCYA [Office of the Minister for Children and Youth Affairs] (2010) *National Quality Standards Framework for Youth Work*. Dublin: Stationery Office.

O'Neill, E. (2004) *Professional Supervision: myths, culture and structures*. Fethard: RMA Publications.

OPACYO [Office of the Provincial Advocate for Children and Youth for Ontario] (2010) *Review of Hamilton Wentworth Detention Centre*. Toronto: OPACYO. <provincialadvocate.on.ca/documents/en/HWDC%20Report%20Jan%2011%202010.pdf>

ORAC [Office of the Refugee Applications Commissioner] (2010) *Annual Report*. Dublin: Stationery Office.

O'Reilly, E. (2011) 'Health care in Ireland: an Ombudsman perspective', address by Emily O'Reilly at the Doolin Memorial Lecture 2011, Royal College of Surgeons. Dublin: Office of the Ombudsman Ireland. <ombudsman.gov.ie/en/news/speeches-articles/2011/health-care-in-ireland-an-ombudsman-perspective-.html>

Ó Riain, G. (ed.) (1997) *Travellers: nomads of Ireland*. Dublin: Pavee Point.

Orme, J. (2001) *Gender and Community Care*. London: Palgrave.

Orme, J. (2002) 'Social work: gender, care and justice', *British Journal of Social Work* 32, pp. 799–814.

Osborne, R. (2002) '"I may be homeless, but I'm not helpless": the costs and benefits of identifying with homelessness', *Self and Identity* 1, pp. 43–52.

O'Shea, E. (1997) 'Male mortality differentials by socio-economic group in Ireland', *Social Science and Medicine* 45(6), pp. 803–9.

O'Shea, E. (2006) 'Public policy for dependent older people in Ireland', in E. O'Dell (ed.) *Older People in Modern Ireland: essays on law and policy*. Dublin: First Law.

OSI [Office for Social Inclusion] (2007) *Fourth Meeting of the Social Inclusion Forum: conference report*. Dublin: Department of Social and Family Affairs.

O'Sullivan, E. (2006) 'Homelessness in rural Ireland', in P. Milbourne and P. Cloke (eds.) *International Perspectives on Rural Homelessness*. Abingdon: Routledge.

O'Sullivan, E. (2008) 'Researching homelessness in Ireland: explanations, themes and approaches', in D. Downey (ed.) *Perspectives on Irish Homelessness: past, present and future*. Dublin: The Homeless Agency.

O'Toole, F. (2008) 'Inequality now official policy', *Irish Times*, 15 January.

O'Toole, F. (2009) *Ship of Fools: how stupidity and corruption sank the Irish Celtic Tiger*. Dublin: Penguin.

O'Toole, J. (1998) 'Young women in rural Ireland', M.Soc.Sc (Sociology) thesis, University College Dublin.

Palmer, S. and Woolfe, R. (2000) *Integrative and Eclectic Counselling and Psychotherapy*. London: Sage.

Parekh, B. (2002) *Rethinking Multiculturalism: cultural diversity and political theory*. Cambridge, MA: Harvard University Press.

Parfitt, T. (2006) 'Bell tolls for Hemingway's fake', *Observer*, 12 February.

Parton, N. (2009) 'Postmodern and constructionist approaches to social work', in R. Adams, L. Dominelli and M. Payne (eds.) *Critical Practice in Social Work*. Basingstoke: Palgrave Macmillan.

Pavee Point (2011a) 'Joint statement on cuts to Traveller education'. Dublin: Pavee Point. <paveepoint.ie/2011/02/joint-statement-on-cuts-to-traveller-education>

Pavee Point (2011b) *Towards a National Traveller Roma Integration Strategy 2020*. Dublin: Pavee Point.

Pavee Point (2012) 'Are young Travellers from your groups engaging with mainstream services?'. Dublin: Pavee Point. <paveepoint.ie/tempsite/question/are-young-travellers-from-your-groups-engaging-with-mainstream-services/>

Pavlov, I. (1927) *Conditioned Reflexes: an investigation of the physiological activity of the cerebral cortex*. London: Oxford University Press.

Pawson, R. (2003) *Social Care Knowledge: seeing the wood for the trees*. Working paper 12. London: ESRC UK Centre for Evidence Based Policy and Practice.

<kcl.ac.uk/sspp/departments/politicaleconomy/research/cep/pubs/papers/assets/wp12.pdf>

Pawson, R., Boaz, A., Grayson, L., Long, A. and Barnes, C. (2003) *Types and Quality of Knowledge in Social Care*. London: Social Care Institute for Excellence.

Payne, M., Adams, R. and Dominelli, L. (2009) 'On being critical in social work', in R. Adams, L. Dominelli and M. Payne (eds.) *Critical Practice in Social Work*. Basingstoke: Palgrave Macmillan.

Pease, B. (2002) 'Rethinking empowerment: a postmodern reappraisal for emancipatory practice', *British Journal of Social Work* 32(1), pp. 135–47.

Pease, B. (2011) 'Men in social work: challenging or reproducing an unequal gender regime?' *Affilia* 26(4), pp. 406–18.

Peberdy, A. (1997) 'Communicating across cultural boundaries', in M. Sidell, L. Jones, J. Katz and A. Peberdy (eds.) *Debates and Dilemmas in Promoting Health*. London: Macmillan.

Pedler, M., Burgoyne, J. and Boydell, T. (2004) *A Manager's Guide to Leadership*. London: McGraw-Hill.

Pencheon, D., Guest, C., Melzer, M. and Muir Gray, J. (eds.) (2006) *Oxford Handbook of Public Health Practice*. Oxford: Oxford University Press.

Petrie, P., Boddy, J., Cameron, C., Heptinstall, E., McQuail, S., Simon, A. and Wigfall, V. (2005) 'Pedagogy – a holistic, personal approach to work with children and young people across services. European models for training, education and qualification'. Briefing paper. London: Thomas Coram Research Unit, Institute of Education, University of London. <k1.ioe.ac.uk/tcru/Ped_BRIEFING_PAPER.pdf>

Petrie, P., Boddy, J., Cameron, C., Wigfall, C. and Simon, A. (2006) *Working with Children in Care: European perspectives*. Maidenhead: Open University Press and McGraw-Hill.

Phelan, M. (1988) 'The certification of child and youth care workers', in G. Charles and P. Gabor (eds.) *Issues in Child and Youth Care Practice*. Lethbridge: Lethbridge Community College.

Phillips, A. (1999) *Which Equalities Matter?* Oxford: Polity.

Phillips, G. (2012) 'What is family support anyway?', in A. Jackson and C. O'Doherty (eds.) *Community Development in Ireland: theory, policy and practice*. Dublin: Gill & Macmillan.

Phillipson, C., Bernard, M., Phillips, J. and Ogg, J. (2001) *The Family and Community Life of Older People*. London: Routledge.

Piaget, J. (1959) *The Language and Thought of the Child*. London: Routledge and Kegan Paul.

Pillinger, J. (2007) *Homeless Pathways: developing effective strategies to address pathways into, through and out of homelessness*. Dublin: Focus Ireland.

Pinker, S. (1994) *The Language Instinct: the new science of language and mind*. London: Penguin.

Plath, D. (2006) 'Evidence-based practice: current issues and future directions', *Australian Social Work* 59(1), pp. 56–72.

Pollard, K., Sellman, D. and Senior, B. (2005) 'The need for interprofessional working', in G. Barrett, D. Sellman and J. Thomas (eds.) *Interprofessional Working in Health and Social Care*. London: Palgrave.

Powell, F., Geoghegan, M., Scanlon, M. and Swirak, K. (2012) *Youth Policy, Civil Society and the Modern Irish State*. Manchester: Manchester University Press.

Probation Service (2012a) 'Criminal justice process'. <probation.ie>

Probation Service (2012b) 'Family conferences'. <probation.ie/pws/websitepublishing.nsf/Content/Offenders+and+their+families~Family+Conferences>

Probation Service (2012c) 'Supervision of community sanctions involving young persons'. <probation.ie/pws/websitepublishingdec09.nsf/Content/Supervision+of+community+sanctions+involving+young+persons>

Probation Service (2012d) 'The family conference process'. <probation.ie>

Probation Service (2012e) 'The route through the probation process'. <probation.ie>

Public Health Alliance (2007) *Health Inequalities on the Island of Ireland*. Dublin: Public Health Alliance.

Punch, M. (1998) *Introduction to Social Research: qualitative and quantitative approaches*. London: Sage.

Quinn, M., Carr, A., Carroll, L. and O'Sullivan, D. (2007) 'Parents Plus Programme. Evaluation of its effectiveness for preschool children with developmental disabilities and behavioural problems', *Journal of Applied Research in Intellectual Disabilities* 22, pp. 345–59.

Quinn, P. and Eimas, P. (1997) 'A reexamination of the perceptual-to-conceptual shift in mental representations', *Review of General Psychology* 1(3), pp. 271–87.

Quinton, D. (2005) 'Themes from a UK research initiative on supporting parents', in J. Scott and H. Ward (eds.) *Safeguarding and Promoting the Well-Being of Children, Families and Communities*. London: Jessica Kingsley.

Qureshi, H. (1994) 'The size of the problem', in P. Emerson, P. McGill and J. Mansell (eds.) *Severe Learning Disabilities and Challenging Behaviour: designing high quality services*. London: Chapman & Hall.

Raftery, M. and O'Sullivan, E. (1999) *Suffer the Little Children: the inside story of Ireland's industrial schools*. Dublin: New Island.

Rappaport, J. (1984) 'Studies in empowerment', cited in C. Lupton and P. Nixon (1999) *Empowering Practice: a critical appraisal of family group conference approach*. Bristol: The Policy Press.

Residential Forum (1998) *A Golden Opportunity: a report on training and staff development for people working in residential services for children and young people*. London: National Institute for Social Work.

Ricks, F., Laliberte, P., Savicki, V. and Hare, F. (1991) 'Child and Youth Care Education Consortium: report on the consideration of accreditation for child and youth care education programmes', *Journal of Child and Youth Care* 7(1), pp. 110–17.

Ridgeway, C. (2009) 'Framed before we know it: how gender shapes social relations', *Gender and Society* 23, pp. 145–60.

Riley, J. (2008) *Low Income, Social Growth, and Good Health: a history of twelve countries*. Berkeley, CA: University of California Press.

Rittel, H. and Webber, M. (1973) 'Dilemmas in a general theory of planning', *Policy Sciences* 4, pp. 155–69.

Robbins, S. and Coulter, P. (2002) *Management*. Upper Saddle River, NJ: Prentice Hall.

Robins, J. (1986) *Fools and Mad: a history of the insane in Ireland*. Dublin: Institute of Public Administration.

Rogers, C. (1951) *Client Centred Therapy*. London: Constable & Robinson.

Rogers, S., DeGagné, M. and Dewar, J. (2012) *Speaking My Truth: reflections on reconciliation and residential school*. Ottawa: Aboriginal Healing Foundation.

Rolfe, G., Jasper, M. and Freshwater, D. (2011) *Critical Reflection in Practice: generating knowledge for care*. Basingstoke: Palgrave Macmillan.

Rosen, A. (2003) 'Evidence-based social work practice: challenges and promise', *Social Work Research* 27(4), pp. 197–208.

Royal Irish Academy (2003) *Mosaic or Melting Pot? Living with Diversity*. Dublin: European Cultural Foundation and Royal Irish Academy.

Ruch, G. (2005) 'Relationship-based practice and reflective practice: holistic approaches to contemporary child-care social work', *Child and Family Social Work* 10, pp. 111–24.

Ruddle, H., Donoghue, F. and Mulvihill, R. (1997) *The Years Ahead Report: a review of the implementation of its recommendations*. Dublin: National Council on Ageing and Older People.

Runciman, D. (2009) 'How messy it all is', *London Review of Books* 31(20), pp. 3–6.

Ruth, S. (1988) 'Understanding oppression and liberation', *Studies* (Winter), pp. 434–4.

Rutter, M. (1981) *Maternal Deprivation Reassessed*. Harmondsworth: Penguin.

Rutter, M. (1995) 'Clinical implications of attachment concepts: retrospect and prospect', *Journal of Child Psychology and Psychiatry* 36(4), pp. 549–71.

Ryan, A. (1999) *Walls of Silence*. Callan: Red Lion Press.

Ryan, D., McNamara, P. and Deasy, C. (2006) *Health Promotion in Ireland*. Dublin: Gill & Macmillan.

Sadeler, C. and Gharabaghi, K. (2007) 'What's wrong with them? Youth, the culture of fear and kids on the edge', *Child and Family Journal* 10(2), pp. 5–12.

Salhani, D. and Charles, G. (2007) 'The dynamics of an interprofessional team: the interplay of child and youth care with other professions within a residential treatment milieu', *Relational Child and Youth Care Practice* (20)4, pp. 12–20.

SAMHSA [Substance Abuse and Mental Health Services Administration] (2011) *Current Statistics on the Prevalence and Characteristics of People Experiencing Homelessness in the US*. <homeless.samhsa.gov/ResourceFiles/hrc_factsheet.pdf>

Sarantakos, S. (2005) *Social Research*. Basingstoke: Palgrave Macmillan.

SCA [Social Care Association] (2002) *Keyworking in Social Care: an introductory guide*. Surbiton: SCA Publications.

Schön, D. (1991a) *The Reflective Practitioner: how professionals think in action*. Aldershot: Arena.

Schön, D. (1991b) *The Reflective Turn: case studies in and on educational practice*. New York: Teachers' College Press.

Scott, A. (2008) 'Confronting challenge: enabling care home staff to understand and work effectively with challenging behaviours in dementia', *European Psychiatry* 23, p. 395. <em-consulte.com/en/article/150452>

Scrambler, G. (1991) 'Stigmatizing illness', in P. Worsley (ed.) *The New Modern Sociology Readings*. London: Penguin.

Seymour, M. (2006) 'Transition and reform: juvenile justice in the Republic of Ireland', prepared for the Thematic Working Group on Juvenile Justice, European Society of Criminology. <esc-eurocrim.org/files/ch05.pdf>

Seymour, M. and Costello, L. (2005) *A Study of the Number, Profile and Progression Routes of Homeless Persons before the Court and in Custody*. Dublin: Government of Ireland.

Share, P., Corcoran, M. and Conway, B. (2012) *A Sociology of Ireland*. Dublin: Gill & Macmillan.

Sheaff, R., Rogers, A., Pickard, S., Marshall, M., Campbell, S., Sibbold, B., Halliwell, S. and Roland, M. (2003) 'A subtle governance: "soft" medical leadership in English primary care', *Sociology of Health and Illness* 25(5), pp. 408–28.

Sheppard, M. (2004) *Appraising and Using Social Research in the Human Services: an introduction for social work and health professionals*. London: Jessica Kingsley.

Shore, B., Iwata, B., Vollmer, T., Lerman, D. and Zarcone, J. (1995) 'Pyramidal staff training in the extension of treatment for severe behaviour disorders', *Journal of Applied Behaviour Analysis* 28(3), pp. 323–32.

Sidell, M. (1997) 'Older people's health: applying Antonovsky's salutogenic paradigm', in M. Sidell, L. Jones, J. Katz and A. Peberdy (eds.) *Debates and Dilemmas in Promoting Health*. London: Macmillan.

Sinclair, I. and Gibbs, I. (1998) *Children's Homes: a study in diversity*. Chichester: Wiley.

Skehill, C. (1999) *The Nature of Social Work in Ireland: a historical perspective*. Lampeter: Edwin Mellen.

Skehill, C. (2003) 'Social work in the Republic of Ireland', *Journal of Social Work* 3(2), pp. 141–59.

Skehill, C. (2005) 'Child protection and welfare social work in the Republic of Ireland: continuities and discontinuities between the past and the present', in

N. Kearney and C. Skehill (eds.) *Social Work in Ireland: historical perspectives.* Dublin: Institute of Public Administration.

Skinner, A. (1994) *Another Kind of Home: a review of residential child care.* Scotland: HMSO.

Skinner, B. (1953) *Science and Human Behavior.* New York: Macmillan.

Skott-Myhre, H. (2004) 'Radical youth work: creating a politics of mutual liberation for youth and adults', *Journal of Child and Youth Care Work* 19, pp. 89–95.

Skott-Myhre, H. and Skott-Myhre, K. (2007) 'Radical youth work: love and community', *Relational Child and Youth Care Practice* 20(3), pp. 48–57.

Smith, A. (1991) *National Identity.* London: Penguin.

Smith, K. (2012a) 'Sociological perspectives on childhood', in M. Mhic Mhathúna and M. Taylor (eds.) *Early Childhood Education and Care: an introduction for students in Ireland.* Dublin: Gill & Macmillan.

Smith, M. (2001) 'David A. Kolb on experiential learning', *The Encyclopaedia of Informal Education.* <infed.org/biblio/b-explrn.htm>

Smith, M. (2005) *Surviving Fears in Health and Social Care.* London: Jessica Kingsley.

Smith, M. (2009) *Rethinking Residential Child Care: positive perspectives.* Bristol: The Policy Press.

Smith, M. (2012b) 'Social pedagogy', in *The Encyclopaedia of Informal Education.* <infed.org/biblio/b-socped.htm>

Smith, M., McGee, H. and Shannon, W. (2001) *One Hundred Homeless Women: health status and health service use of homeless women and their children in Dublin.* Dublin: Royal College of Surgeons in Ireland and Children's Research Centre, Trinity College.

SMWCDSA [South and Mid-West Community Development Support Agency] (2006) *A Profile of Community Development Projects and Family Resource Centres in the South and Mid-West Regions.* Limerick: South and Mid-West Community Development Support Agency.

Snyder, J., McEachern, A., Schrepferman, L., Zettle, R., Johnson, K., Swink, N. and McAlpine, C. (2006) 'Rule-governance, correspondence training, and discrimination learning: a developmental analysis of covert conduct problems', *The Journal of Speech and Language Pathology – Applied Behavior Analysis* 1(1), pp. 43–55.

Social Services Inspectorate (2003) *Report on the Monitoring of the Implementation of Children First National Guidelines for the Protection and Welfare of Children.* Dublin: Social Services Inspectorate.

Southwood, I. (2011) *Non-stop Inertia.* Winchester: Zero Books.

Spence, J. (2007) 'What do youth workers do? Communicating youth work', *Youth Studies Ireland* 2(2), pp. 3–18.

Stephens, P. (2013) *Social Pedagogy: heart and head.* Bremen: Europäischer Hochschulverlag.

Stevens, M., Liabo, K. and Roberts, H. (2007) 'A review of the research priorities of practitioners working with children in social care', *Child and Family Social Work* 12, pp. 295–305.

Stewart, A., Livingston, M. and Dennison, S. (2008) 'Transitions and turning points: examining the links between child maltreatment and juvenile offending', *Child Abuse and Neglect* 32, pp. 51–66.

Stirling, C. and McHugh, A. (1997) 'Natural therapeutic holding: a nonaversive alternative to the use of control and restraint in the management of violence for people with learning disabilities', *Journal of Advanced Nursing* 26(2), pp. 304–11.

Stogdill, R. (1948) 'Personal factors associated with leadership: a survey of the literature', *The Journal of Psychology* 25(1), pp. 35–71.

Storø, J. (2013) *Practical Social Pedagogy: theories, values and tools for working with children and young people*. Bristol: The Policy Press.

Stuart, C. (2001) 'Professionalising child and youth care: continuing the Canadian journey', *Journal of Child and Youth Care Work* 15–16, pp. 264–82.

Stuart, C. (2003) 'Musings on the art and science of professionalizing child and youth care', *Relational Child and Youth Care Practice* 16(1), pp. 15–20.

Stuart, C. and Sanders, L. (2008) *Child and Youth Care Practitioners' Contributions to Evidence-based Practice in Group Care*. Toronto: Ryerson University.

Stuart, C., Carty, W. and Dean, M. (2007) 'The role of competence in outcomes for children and youth: an approach for mental health', *Relational Child and Youth Care Practice* 20(1), pp. 47–56.

Suizzo, M. (2000) 'The socio-emotional and cultural contexts of cognitive development: neo-Piagetian perspectives', *Child Development* 71(4), pp. 846–9.

Sutton, C. (2001) 'Reviewing and evaluating therapeutic progress', in S. Palmer and G. McMahon (eds.) *Client Assessment*. London: Sage.

SVP [Society of St Vincent de Paul] (2011) *Older People: experiences and issues. Report of the Commission of Older People*. Dublin: SVP.

TASC (2010) *The Solidarity Factor: public responses to inequality in Ireland*. Dublin: TASC. <tascnet.ie/upload/file/Solidarity%20Factor_upload.pdf>

TASC (2011) *Winners and Losers? Equality Lessons for Budget 2012*. Dublin: TASC. <issuu.com/tascpublications/docs/winners_and_losers_141111>

Task Force on Child Care Services (1980) *Final Report to the Minister for Health*. Dublin: Stationery Office.

Tawney, R. (1952) *Equality*. London: Allen & Unwin.

Taylor, C. (2002) 'The dialogical self', in D. Hiley, J. Bohman and R. Shusterman (eds.) *The Interpretive Turn: philosophy, science and culture*. New York: Cornell University Press.

TCWG [Traveller Consanguinity Working Group] (2003) *A Community Genetics Approach to Health and Consanguineous Marriage in the Irish Traveller Community*. Dublin: Traveller Health Unit, Eastern Regional Health Authority.

Tew, J. (2006) 'Understanding power and powerlessness: towards a framework for emancipatory practice in social work', *Journal of Social Work* 6(1), pp. 33–51.

The Integration Centre (2011) *Roadmap to Integration 2011*. Dublin: The Integration Centre. <integrationcentre.ie>

Thomas, A. and Chess, S. (1977) *Temperament and Development*. New York: Brunner/Mazel.

Thompson, N. (2002) *People Skills*. New York: Palgrave Macmillan.

Thompson, N. (2011) *Promoting Equality: working with diversity and difference*. 3rd edn. Basingstoke: Palgrave Macmillan.

Thompson, N. (2012) *Anti-Discriminatory Practice, Equality Diversity and Social Justice*. Basingstoke: Palgrave Macmillan.

Thornberry, T., Ireland, T. and Smith, C. (2001) 'The importance of timing: the varying impact of childhood and adolescent maltreatment on multiple problem outcomes', *Development and Psychopathology* 13, pp. 957–79.

Thrane, L., Hoyt, D., Whitbeck, L. and Yoder, K. (2006) 'Impact of family abuse on running away, deviance, and street victimization among homeless rural and urban youth', *Child Abuse and Neglect* 30, pp. 1117–28.

Tiernan, S., Morley, M. and Foley, E. (2006) *Modern Management: theory and practice for Irish students*. 3rd edn. Dublin: Gill & Macmillan.

Timmins, E., O'Connell, M., O'Gorman, C., Quinn, G., Dolan, J., Carroll, D., Nolan, C., Felton, M., Hynes, A., Howard, B., Barry, O., Loughlin, L., O'Donnell, B., Rogers, M., Saunders, J., Gilligan, P. and O'Neill, A.-M. (2012) '"Outdated" mental capacity laws', letter to the *Irish Times*, 1 May.

Timonen, V. and Doyle, M. (2008) 'From the workhouse to the home: evolution of care policy for older people in Ireland', *International Journal of Sociology and Social Policy* 28(3–4), pp. 76–89.

Timonen, V. and O'Dwyer, C. (2009) 'Living in institutional care: residents' experiences and coping strategies', *Social Work in Health Care* 48(6), pp. 597–613.

Tolmie, A., Thomson, J., Foot, H., Whelan, K., Morrison, S. and McLaren, B. (2005) 'The effects of adult guidance and peer discussion on the development of children's representations: evidence from the training of pedestrian skills', *British Journal of Psychology* 96, pp. 181–204.

Tones, K. (1997) 'Health education as empowerment', in, M. Sidell, L. Jones, J. Katz and A. Peberdy (eds.) *Debates and Dilemmas in Promoting Health*. London: Macmillan.

Tones, K. and Green, J. (2005) *Health Promotion: planning and strategies*. London: Sage.

Toolan, D. (2003) 'An emerging rights perspective for disabled people in Ireland: an activist's perspective', in S. Quin and B. Redmond (eds.) *Disability and Social Policy in Ireland*. Dublin: University College Dublin Press.

Tremblay, R. and Downey, P. (2004) 'Identifying and evaluating research-based publications: enhancing undergraduate student critical skills', *Education* 124(4), pp. 734–40.

Tripodi, T. (1974) *Uses and Abuses of Social Research in Social Work*. New York: Columbia University Press.

Tuairim (1966) *Some of Our Children: a report on the residential care of the deprived child in Ireland*. London: Tuairim.

Tuckman, B. and Jensen, M. (1977) 'Stages of small group development revisited', *Groups and Organization Studies* 2, pp. 419–27.

Tunstill, J., Aldgate, J. and Hughes, M. (2007) *Improving Children's Services Networks: lessons from family centres*. London: Jessica Kingsley.

Tyler, K. and Johnson, K. (2006) 'Pathways in and out of substance use among homeless-emerging adults', *Journal of Adolescent Research* 21(2), pp. 133–57.

UCC [University College Cork] (n.d.) 'What is social work?', Cork: UCC. <www.ucc.ie/en/msw/whatissocialworkandwheredosocialworkerswork/>

UN [United Nations] (1994) *Guide for a National Action Programme on the International Year of the Family*. New York: United Nations.

UN (2007a) *Convention on the Protection and Promotion of the Rights and Dignity of Persons with Disabilities*. New York: United Nations.

UN (2007b) *United Nations Human Development Report 2007–2008*. Basingstoke: Palgrave Macmillan. <hdr.undp.org/en/reports/global/hdr2007-2008>

UNCRC [United Nations Committee on the Rights of the Child] (1989) *UN Convention on the Rights of the Child*. Geneva: United Nations. <unicef.org.uk/UNICEFs-Work/Our-mission/UN-Convention>

UNCRC (2005) 'General comment no. 6: treatment of unaccompanied and separated children outside their country of origin'. Geneva: United Nations. <www.unhcr.org/refworld/docid/42dd174b4.html>

Ungerson, C. (1997) 'Social politics and the commodification of care', *Social Politics* 4(3), pp. 362–82.

Van Ewijk, H. (2008) 'Social change and social professions', *European Journal of Social Education* 14–15, pp. 9–19.

Vandemark, L. (2007) 'Promoting the sense of self, place, and belonging in displaced persons: the example of homelessness', *Archives of Psychiatric Nursing* 21(5), pp. 241–8.

Vedan-Jones, S., McLean, C., Gregory, V. and Freedman, L. (2008) 'A survey of policies and practices of government agencies involved in the administration of youth justice and custodial care with respect to complaints of child sexual abuse and complaints by adults of historical child sexual abuse who were provided with government services, whether by employees of the government or by volunteers', report submitted to the Cornwall Public Inquiry, Ontario. <attorneygeneral.jus.gov.on.ca/inquiries/cornwall/en/report/index.html>

Vekić, K. (2003) *Unsettled Hope. Unaccompanied Minors in Ireland – from understanding to response*. Dublin: Marino Institute.

Vygotsky, L. (1978) *Thought and Language*. Cambridge, MA: MIT Press.

Walby, S. (1990) *Theorising Patriarchy*. Oxford: Blackwell.

Walker, M. (2008) *Suicide among the Irish Traveller Community 2000–2006*. Wicklow: Wicklow County Council.

Wall, M. (2012) 'HSE to implement home help cuts', *Irish Times*, 5 October.

Walsh, K. (2004) 'The effects of living in a nursing home on the cognitive, sensory, and sensorimotor abilities of low-dependency older adults', summary report of a Doctor of Philosophy thesis, University of Limerick.

Walsh, K. (2012) 'Rathmullan Centre – a great lunch', *The Ozanam Bulletin.* Dublin: Society of St Vincent de Paul.

Ward, A., Kasinski, K., Pooley, J. and Worthington, A. (2003) *Therapeutic Communities for Children and Young People.* London: Jessica Kingsley.

Warde, M. (2009) *The Turn of the Hand: a memoir from the Irish margins.* Transcribed and edited by Michael Hayes. Newcastle-upon-Tyne: Cambridge Scholars.

Warnes, A. and Crane, M. (2006) 'The causes of homelessness among older people in England', *Housing Studies* 21(3), pp. 401–21.

Waters, H. and Waters, E. (2006) 'The attachment working models concept: among other things, we build script-like representations of secure base experiences', *Attachment and Human Development* 8(3), pp. 185–97.

Watson, D., Lunn, P., Quinn, E. and Russell, H. (2012) *Multiple Disadvantage in Ireland: an equality analysis of census 2006.* Dublin: Economic and Social Research Institute. <esri.ie/publications/latest_publications/view/index.xml?id=3499>

Watson, J. and Rayner, R. (1920) 'Conditioned emotional reactions', *Journal of Experimental Psychology* 3(1), pp. 1–14.

WHO [World Health Organization] (1946) 'Preamble to the Constitution of the World Health Organization as adopted by the International Health Conference, New York, 19–22 June 1946; signed on 22 July 1946 by the representatives of 61 states and entered into force on 7 April 1948', *Official Records of the World Health Organization 2.* Geneva: WHO. <whqlibdoc.who.int/hist/official_records/2e.pdf>

WHO (1980) *International Classification of Impairments, Disabilities and Handicaps: a manual of classification relating to the consequences of disease.* Geneva: WHO.

WHO (1986) *The Ottawa Charter for Health Promotion.* First International Conference on Health Promotion, Ottawa, 17–21 November. Copenhagen: WHO Regional Office for Europe. <who.int/healthpromotion/conferences/previous/ottawa/en>

WHO (2002) *Toward a Common Language for Functioning, Disability and Health.* Geneva: WHO.

Wilkinson, R. and Marmot, M. (2003) *Social Determinants of Health: the solid facts.* Copenhagen: WHO.

Wilkinson, R. and Pickett, K. (2009) *The Spirit Level: why more equal societies almost always do better.* London: Allen Lane.

Williams, D. and Gilligan, R. (2011) 'Self injury and the challenges of responding to young people in care: the experiences of a sample of social care workers', *Irish Journal of Applied Social Studies* 11(1). <arrow.dit.ie/ijass/vol11/iss1/2>

Williams, D. and Lalor, K. (2001) 'Obstacles to the professionalisation of social care in Ireland', *Irish Journal of Applied Social Studies* 2(3), pp. 73–90. <arrow. dit.ie/ijass/vol2/iss3/6>

Williams, G. (2000) 'Research agenda and social care in Wales', paper to 'What works as evidence for practice? The methodological repertoire in an applied discipline' seminar, 27 April, Cardiff.

Williams, J. and Gorby, S. (2002) *Counted In 2002: the report of the assessment of homelessness in Dublin*. Dublin: The Homeless Agency and Economic and Social Research Institute.

Williams, J., Greene, S., McNally, S., Murray, A. and Quail, A. (2010) *Growing Up in Ireland: the infants and their families [Infant cohort: report 1]*. Dublin: Stationery Office. <growingup.ie/fileadmin/user_upload/Conference_2010/ Growing_Up_in_Ireland_-_The_Infants_and_their_Families.pdf>

Wilson, R. (2005) 'Wrong policies to build social capital', *Irish Times*, 6 September.

Wolfensberger, W. (1972) *The Principle of Normalization in Human Services*. Toronto: National Institute on Mental Retardation.

Wolfensberger, W. (1983) 'Social role valorization: a proposed new term for the principle of normalization', *Mental Retardation* 21(6), pp. 234–9.

Wren, M. (2003) *Unhealthy State: anatomy of a sick society*. Dublin: New Island.

Wynne, R., Clarkin, N., Cox, T. and Griffiths, A. (1997) *Guidance on the Prevention of Violence at Work*. Luxembourg: European Commission DG-V.

Young, I. (2011) *Justice and the Politics of Difference*. Princeton: Princeton University Press.

Youth Service Liaison Forum (2005) *Strategy for the Delivery of Youth Work in Northern Ireland*. Belfast: Department of Education for Northern Ireland.

Zehr, H. (2002) *The Little Book of Restorative Justice*. Intercourse, PA: Good Books.

Zemon Davies, N. (1971) 'The reasons of misrule: youth groups and charivaris in sixteenth-century France', *Past and Present* 50, pp. 41–75.

Zola, I. (1991) 'Medicine as an instrument of social control', in P. Worsley (ed.) *The New Modern Sociology Readings*. London: Penguin.

Index

Page numbers in **bold** and *italic* indicate figures and tables.